MW01555985
Desire
Variable
BINARY HEARTS BOOK ONE
HELLO
WORLD
CONVENTION

ISBN: 978-2-9592344-5-3

Publisher: Ana D'Arcy

Cover & interior art: Marta García Navarro

Design and formatting: Ana D'Arcy

Editor: Katie Ducharme

First Edition: October, 2024

https://anadarcy.com

Content Warning:

This work contains sexually explicit content and mature language and is intended for an adult audience only (18+).

This book is part of a continuous trilogy, which follows the same characters, and it ends on a cliffhanger. But because Ana isn't *that* much of a sadist, she'll be releasing the sequel as quickly as possible.

Read at your own discretion.

ANA D'ARCY

Table of Content

To those who know that the line between love and hate can be very, very thin.

Here's to passionate arguments and even more passionate makeups.

is_new_chapter = True

chapter_number = "01"

pov_name = "Andrea"

"I'M STANDING OUT LIKE A boner at a pool party, Kate," I complain into the phone.

"Well, it's too late to go home and change, so get in there."

Anxiously standing at the foot of a sleek skyscraper, I look around at the somber-looking business men and women. Amongst all these very serious, very professional people, I feel like an awkward teenager again—out of place and underdressed.

"Maybe I can find a nearby store to buy a nice sweater."

"Arriving late on your first day is even worse."

I look down at my clothes and cringe. "I'm not sure."

Even from here, I know she's rolling her eyes. "Which one are you wearing?" Kate asks with a sigh.

"The Hulk one. With the 'Hulk smash!' on it."

"Jesus Christ, Andy!"

"I know," I say with a grimace. "I couldn't find the box with the nice clothes, and this is basically the standard programmer's uniform, so I thought it would be fine. But now that I'm seeing everyone in suits …"

"I'm sure you'll be okay, babe."

"What if they fire me before I even reach my desk?"

I take a deep breath and tell myself that won't happen. Kelex is the most open-minded and inclusive company I've ever heard of, so they won't even bat an eye at my T-shirt.

"If they fire you, then you'll come back to Portland, and we'll be in the same city again. It's a win-win situation."

She's wrong. Going back home wouldn't make up for losing this job. This is everything, and I already know this is my professional peak. It's the perfect position, in the perfect company, in a perfect city. Well, maybe Seattle isn't the perfect city, but it's convenient. And it is the closest tech hub to home, even though I would have traveled the entire country for a position at Kelex.

My new employer aims to simplify the lives of people with disabilities through specialized apps, operating systems, and various software programs. Their goal is to allow everyone to experience the perks of technology equally, if not use it to improve their lifestyle. And that means everyone—people who are deaf or hard of hearing, people with low vision or blindness, wheelchair users, those who suffer from a debilitating medical condition, people diagnosed with neurodivergence … the list goes on. Kelex serves as many people as possible.

I hear someone talk to Kate on the other end of the line, and she answers something about a margin of error or something. Then, she refocuses on me. "Okay, I need to go back to work, or I'll get fired as well."

"What do you mean, '*as well*?!'"

"You know what I mean, stop being a whiny little bitch."

I should probably be offended, but this is exactly the kind of tough love I need right now. "You really think I'll be fine?" I insist.

"Yes, I promise. Now, you need to take a deep breath, tell yourself you got this, and be the badass I know you are."

Because it sounds like the best thing I can do right now, I comply. I fill my lungs, exhale, and assert, "I got this."

"That's my girl! Get in there, or you'll show up underdressed *and* late."

"Alright. Thanks, babe."

"You owe me a pep talk."

"I'm still ahead on those, you know."

"Yeah, only three left, and we're even." There's a pause while someone talks to her again, and after a few seconds of this, she returns to me. "Okay, I really have to go, and so do you—to kick asses and take names!"

I don't even have time to answer before she hangs up. A glimpse at my phone tells me I need to hurry. I pass a nervous hand through my short, curly bob and get a move on. I let myself be guided by the crowd of lawyers, traders, and other suit-wearing people walking toward the entrance.

Nervous energy buzzes inside me as I pass the massive doors, but I don't let it slow me down. I walk to the wall where the companies in the building are listed. It doesn't take long to spot Kelex, which occupies two floors. Somehow, seeing it right there worsens my anxiety, tightening my throat with it.

When I reach the elevators, I rush to the one that's the closest to this floor. I'm not the only pragmatic person here, as many people soon join me in my wait for the doors to open.

The stainless steel panels part with an elegant 'ding,' and everyone rushes into it. Since I'm on the front line, I'm unceremoniously pushed toward the few people already inside. I miraculously manage to press the button for my floor before being shoved further into the confined space.

The eager mob forces me toward someone standing in the corner, but I successfully stop before I bump into them. At least until an elbow shoves me in the back and I stumble into the stranger. My hand instinctively reaches up to secure my balance, flattening over the solid plane of a stomach—my only option. That's when I realize it's a man. A very fit man.

"I'm *so* sorry," I mumble as I remove my hand, quickly glimpsing up at him. He doesn't even bother looking down, but his face distracts me from that fact.

Holy shit.

He's hot.

Like, damn …

Before I can properly take in his features, other than the intense eyes, square jaw, dark hair, and stubble, I'm pushed into him again, probably by the same elbow.

God, that is one muscular chest.

"Will you stop shoving, please?" I frustratedly ask, twisting around the best I can. Then I mumble to myself, "People have no respect for personal space."

"They don't."

That came from the hot stranger against me. Of course, his voice is alluring as well. Low, a little husky, as though he just woke up. His eyes are on me this time, but they don't stay there for long as he quickly looks ahead again. Finally, the doors close, and we rise to the upper floors, providing little distraction from the warm body I'm pressed against.

"I'm very sorry for being all over yours, by the way," I say with a wince. "Personal space, I mean."

With a barely perceptible shrug, he mumbles, "It's fine."

The elevator keeps halting and resuming its course. At this pace, it'll take ages to get to my floor. To make matters worse, the man against me makes me grow embarrassingly hot. Great, I'll arrive late, underdressed, and sweaty …

Since he isn't paying attention to me, I peer up at him discreetly. Like my abuela always says, the least we can do when God provides eye candy is to appreciate it. He seems to be in his early to mid-thirties, tall and imposing, which is like a magnet for shorter women like me. I never really got why. Maybe some deeply-rooted need from when men had to fend off wild animals.

When I look down again, my mind is out of the gutter enough to notice his gray T-shirt, which comforts me about my outfit. Not everyone who works here wears suits. Although it isn't a tight fit, I can guess at the broadness of his chest underneath and the defined pecs.

As a sapiosexual with a mild sex drive, I'm never attracted to men at first sight. So I don't understand why my stomach flutters every time I peek at the stranger. Maybe it's the sharpness of his eyes. He *looks* smart, not just handsome. There's a pair of reading glasses tucked into his collar, and I crave to see him with those on. They must make him look like a nerdy genius.

Something jolts between us, right around his crotch area, and I freeze, my eyes going huge.

Oh my …

"Excuse me," he says before reaching for his pocket, his hand gliding over the front of my T-shirt. Good thing I'm wearing a padded bra because the girls perk up from the platonic graze.

He takes his phone out, and I realize it buzzed. That's what happened—not an impromptu boner over me. *Andy, you cretin. You look like an underdressed imp.*

Because of the lack of space, he has no choice but to settle it between us. He unlocks the screen to check the text he received and—

Holy fuck.

It's a nude.

The man instantly locks the screen again, but it's too late; I saw the steamy picture he received. The youthful platinum-blonde goddess in it was in a very suggestive pose, showing off her perfect breasts and toned stomach. I'd probably be more into sending out nudes if I had such amazing tits instead of, as per an ex's words, "mosquito bites."

Since the situation is rather comical, a laugh bubbles in my chest, but I do everything I can to suppress it.

What a way to begin a first day of work.

I'm slowly accepting my terrible fate—being pressed against a dashing guy for the rest of eternity—when the space clears a little. We aren't intimately flushed together now. Upon noticing the next stop is mine, I look up one last time to give the man an apologetic smile. His eyes lower to mine, and then he glances at my T-shirt.

His face remains remarkably neutral, and I can't tell if it's a good or bad sign.

Because humor is my best defense against embarrassment, the next thing my mouth spews is, "As fun as that was, let's never do it again."

It takes everything in me not to cringe at my own words. To my relief, a semblance of a smile stretches the man's lips, and … Fuck, he truly is devastatingly handsome.

"Let's not," he answers, his baritone voice doing something primal to my insides.

The doors finally open for me, and before I can melt into a puddle at his feet, I wiggle my way out of this tedious hell. Once out, I take a deep breath, my lungs filling with fresh air again. Using the stairs next time comes to mind, but I'm too out of shape for that. The ass that workout would give me, though.

After a quick look at my surroundings, I silently rejoice when I notice people wearing casual clothes. Behind the reception desk is a gorgeous blonde typing on a laptop. She looks intimidating, especially with her septum piercing and immaculate makeup. The closer I get to her, the more I feel like an Oompa-Loompa showing up for duty.

I stand there, smiling awkwardly, but she doesn't notice me. So, I clear my throat to make my presence known. She immediately lifts her eyes, and her gaze takes me in up and down as one of her perfectly drawn eyebrows rises slightly.

"Welcome to Kelex. How may I help you?"

"Hi," I say, my voice a little shaky. "I start today, and I'm wondering if you could give me some directions."

"Yes, of course. What's your name, and what department will you work in?"

"I'm, uh, Andrea. Andrea Walker. And I'm with the development team."

The woman frowns and looks up from her screen. "You're *Andy* Walker." I nod, surprised my name means something to her. "We weren't expecting … We thought you were a … man."

I do my best to look innocent, batting my eyes at the receptionist when I, in fact, did my best to keep the lines blurred. Anything to make sure I'd get my dream job. The receptionist apparently realizes she is staring and shakes her head to snap out of it.

"Sorry, you just really surprised me there. The nerds from dev have been talking about you a lot. I doubt they expect you to be a woman. And with this," she explains with a soft laugh, pointing at my shirt, "they will all be at your feet by the end of the day."

I smile humbly, definitely reassured now. We geeks are pretty serious about our superheroes.

"You'll probably need to drop by HR first," she explains. "They're right upstairs, fifth door on the left."

Before I can panic about getting into the elevator again, I notice a door that must lead to a staircase. "I'll do that, thank you!"

"No problem. Come back when you're done, and I'll take you to the Troll's Lair."

As I journey toward the upper floor, my mind drifts back to the attractive man in the elevator. My front is still warm, as if the ghost of his presence lingers on me. Unless he's only visiting, we might meet again on future elevator rides. One more reason to look forward to coming to work.

The HR woman is lovely, and because we've had a video call during the hiring process, she isn't surprised that I'm a woman, and I don't have to justify myself. I never lied about my actual name, but I did sign off as "Andy" everywhere since I almost exclusively go by that.

Within a few minutes, I've signed everything, so she hands me my version of each document and a copy of the company's rules and regulations.

I'm quick to return downstairs with everything sorted, and this time, the blonde at reception welcomes me back with a smile. "All good?" she asks.

I can't shake the grin from my face. "Yes, it's official. I'm a full-stack developer here."

"Congratulations! I'll introduce you to the nerds." She stands up and is much taller than I expected. She extends her hand, a kind smile on her lips. "I'm Dakota, by the way. I work with the graphic design team. Our receptionist called in sick this morning, and I drew the short straw. Come, the Troll's Lair awaits." With a wave, she invites me to follow her.

Contrary to upstairs where it's all corridors and closed offices, most of this floor is open, with only a handful of enclosed workspaces. The desks are huge, and everyone has plenty of room to move around. The whole place is very bright, with vivid hues here and there.

We get to a closed part of the floor and stop before a glass door. I smile at the various notes taped on it. **Don't tap the glass, it scares the geeks**, one reads. **Please, don't feed the trolls. They are on a special diet**, and under, someone added with a ballpoint pen, **of Cheetos and Red Bull**. Then, **Do not trespass during Counter-Strike sessions. Trespassers will be shot. Survivors**

will be shot again—then Steven will T-bag them. That last one makes me chuckle, and I already know I'll like these guys.

"Are you ready?" Dakota asks, gripping the handle. I nod, telling myself I will do just fine.

With great energy, she pushes the door open. "Listen up, you animals!" she announces as we enter. The five men sitting inside lift their heads from their computers, glancing in our direction. "This is Andrea Walker, a.k.a. 'the script whisperer,' as you brainiacs have been calling her for the past three weeks." The nickname makes me grin with pride.

Several jaws drop as they process that information. It seems that hiding the fact that I have boobs and a vagina was more of a scam than I thought.

"You virgins might not be familiar with this, but yes, Andy is a female specimen of our kind," Dakota explains with sarcasm.

The first one to get over that little gender-bender trick stands up from his chair. In a boyish kind of way, he's charming. Slender and tall, he's wearing a plaid shirt and seems to be in his late twenties, with ginger hair, light brown eyes, and freckles dusting his pale skin.

He comes to me with a few long strides and extends his hand. "Welcome to Kelex, Andy. We're thrilled to have you here with us."

I shake his hand, returning his genuine smile. "Thank you. I'm delighted to be here."

"I'll let the boss know you've arrived," he offers, returning to his desk and quickly typing something.

The next one who speaks, the only one who looks over forty, is a hefty man with an impressive beard, brown hair tied in a ponytail, and thick-rimmed glasses. "Damn, I made a bet that you'd have a beard."

"I have one, but you'll never see it," I joke.

The instant the words leave my lips, I regret them and freeze from head to toe. When heat creeps up my face, I know I'm crimson.

I need to be gagged. Right fucking now.

They all stare at me, as shocked as I am, and no one speaks for what seems to be minutes but is probably five seconds. Next to me, Dakota does her best to hold back her laughter.

A blond guy raises his hands to ask his colleagues a question in sign language—which I'm familiar with. "I didn't get that. What did she say?"

"She told him he'd never see her 'beard,'" someone signs back.

I've never wished for the ground to open up and swallow me as hard as I do at this moment. Was my awful joke really worth repeating?

Utterly shocked, the guy who asked stares at me. Dakota can't hold back anymore, and she explodes in a fit of laughter. That seems to trigger the others, and soon enough, I'm waiting for them to calm down.

When she regains control of her breathing, Dakota carefully wipes a tear from the corner of her eye. "Yeah, you'll do great. They constantly make dick jokes around each other, so it's about time someone introduced them to vagina ones."

"We weren't prepared," the ginger says with a grin. "Consider us warned from now on." The others nod, confirming his statement.

The glass door opens, distracting the room from the shitshow that is me. Everyone's focus shifts to the newcomer, so I also turn around. When I see the man standing in the doorway, my breath catches in my throat.

Holy Mother of God …

So, he works here after all.

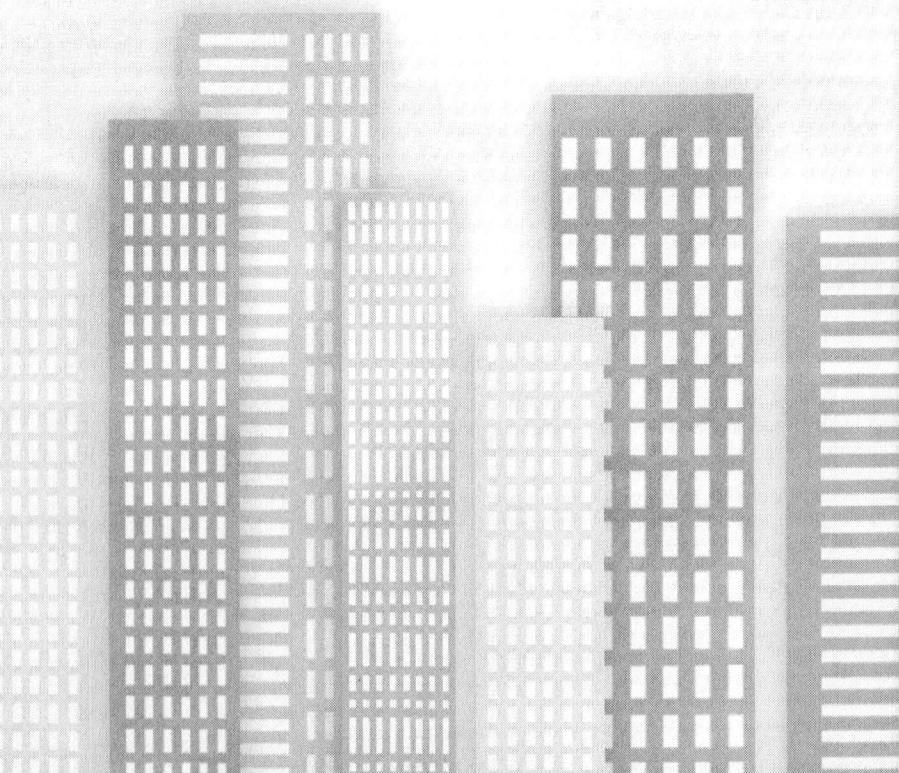

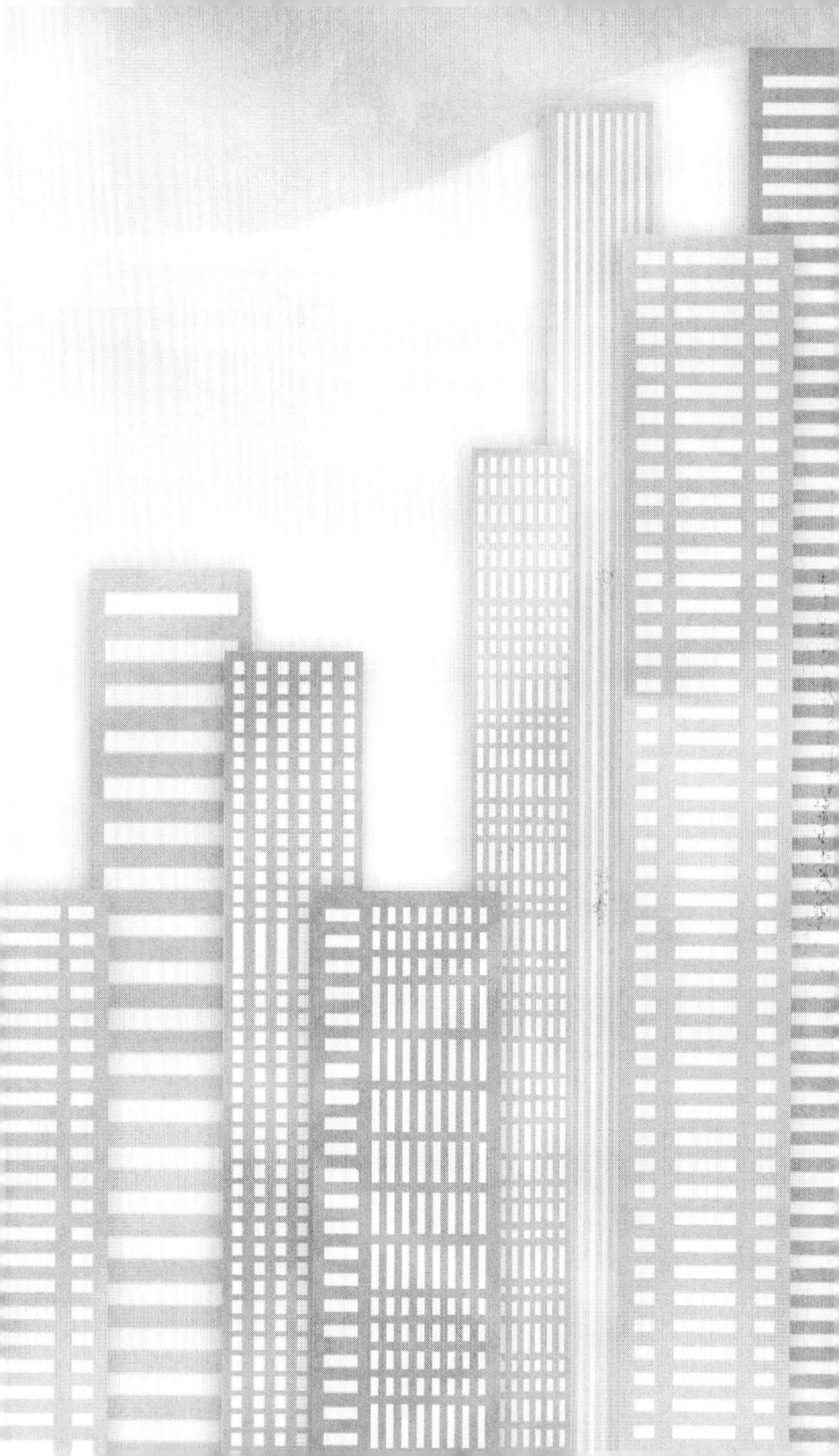

is_new_chapter = True

chapter_number = "02"

pov_name = "Andrea"

I STARE AT THE MAN standing by the door, my brain malfunctioning so hard I can't even think of closing my gaping mouth.

It's the elevator guy! He's right there, still dashing, all tall and sexy. He doesn't notice me right away, so I use this opportunity to observe his features.

His face was either engineered in a lab, or he won the genetic lottery over everyone else. He has a sharp jaw covered with three-day-old stubble. His short, dark hair is a little messy—as if he only ran his fingers through it this morning. Thick eyebrows rest under a flat forehead, and underneath them, two narrow eyes. Then, the bridge of a straight, perfectly balanced nose, and lower, a pair of lavish lips, a shade darker than his skin, with a touch of pink.

His sharp gaze quickly scans the room, and I avert mine when it reaches me, embarrassed to have been caught staring. Thank God I'm not drooling, but close call.

"Oliver, you told me Andy arrived?"

Oh, wow. Oh, shit. This is the boss. *He* is the boss. The guy I lusted after in the elevator is my new boss. That has to be the worst way to start a new job.

Dakota smiles. "Yes, *she* has."

He processes her words, and something lights up in his eyes when he understands. Next thing I know, his attention is back on me, studying me in an entirely new light. Under his authoritative stare, I regret hiding my gender from the company. But I know how hard it can be for women to get into such positions, so it's only normal that I made sure the odds would be in my favor.

Now that they know the truth, they can't fire me for not having Y chromosomes. Not without risking the mother of all lawsuits.

When he's done examining me, I embarrassingly wave with a faint, "Hi."

"You're not an Andrew," he stoically states.

I bite the inside of my cheek at his icy tone, suppressing my urge to lecture him about manners. "No, I'm an Andrea."

His jaw clenches slightly, and after an instant, he turns to the oldest of the guys. "You owe me ten bucks. She doesn't have a beard."

"Actually—"

As soon as I realize what the bearded guy is about to say, I panic and let out a loud, forced laugh, determined not to let him repeat my stupid joke. Not a third time, and not in front of *that* man. "Haha! Yeah, no!" I loudly say. "No beards here!"

The others do their best to contain their amusement while the elevator guy—our boss—stares at me as if my IQ is in the negatives.

Today is not my day. I can't catch a break.

"Well, as entertaining as this is, I have to leave you nerds," Dakota explains, freeing us from the awkward tension. "But before I go, Lex, this is Andrea Walker, your new computer engineer, vagina-bearer, and slayer of scripts. Andy, this is Alexander Coleman, head of development, co-owner of the company, killer of joy."

Since I'd researched this company before applying, the name is familiar. But while I saw pictures of his business partner, Kevin Langley, I never stumbled on a photo of *him*—not that I looked for it. The elevator guy isn't just in a high position; he co-owns the whole thing.

Once the door closes behind Dakota, the broody hunk tells me to choose one of the free desks. When I reach for the empty one just in front of me, he stops me with a harsh command.

"This one's mine. Pick another one." I nod, biting the inside of my cheek so I don't say something about his abrasive manners. Dismissing my ire, I turn to another spot between two guys and settle my bag on the seat. When I spin back to the boss, he's looking at me with an intense, disapproving stare.

His confusion about my appearance is becoming offensive. I clear my throat, hoping it'll snap him out of it. "Is everything alright?" I ask with diplomacy.

"I didn't expect you to be so …" he trails off, looking for the right word.

"Womanly?"

"Young. From your results on the test, I expected someone with at least a decade in the field. How old are you?"

"Twenty-six. But I have been coding for over sixteen years now, so I do have a decade of experience—just not in the field."

He remains unimpressed. "Having fun setting up a website for you and your friends is nothing like what we do here."

A twinge of anger rises in me, and my eyes narrow. *What the hell?!* "I can assure you I am well aware of that," I say, mustering my best amiable smile. "As you may have seen with the test I took to get here, I'm quite competent."

One of his eyebrows moves up arrogantly. "Are you sure no one helped you with it? Like a friend or your older brother?"

Oh, now he's asking to be put back in his place. I violently quench my urge to react to his provocation and stay level-headed. I'm not into letting people walk all over me, but I really want this job, so I can't possibly get into an argument with my boss on the first day.

We'll see about tomorrow.

"My brother couldn't differentiate C# from PHP." A few of the guys chuckle behind me. Ignoring them, I continue, "If you have doubts, by all means, test me again. I'm certain I can manage whatever you'll throw at me."

It only takes him three seconds to think about it before he turns to one of the guys. "Brian, what's the script you've been stuck on for the last iOS update?"

Whispers erupt among the dev team. I'm about to face a challenge harder than I imagined, right? Luckily, I have a quick brain to go with my quick mouth, so I'll teach this man a lesson.

"Are you sure you want to give her that one?" the guy to my left asks. He's wearing a bold red jacket that suits his dark complexion well. Of all of them, he's the one who looks the most put together—cleanly shaven, neat edges, and impeccable style.

"Well, you heard the lady: she can manage anything. And since you five have been stuck on this for two weeks, we might as well let her take a crack at it."

They nod and look at me, seemingly sorry for what's about to happen. Again, someone needs to gag me for my own good.

With a deep breath to summon my confidence, I sit at my chosen desk between the blond guy who used sign language and the red jacket guy. "Hi, I'm Mason," the latter greets me before pointing at my neighbor on the other side, "and that's Joseph."

"Hi, I'm Andy," I greet back with a smile, signing the words with my hands for Joseph, who grins in return.

"We have a shared server, and all our work is backed up daily," Mason explains. "You can use the script on the server. If you mess it up, we can always get it from the backups."

"Thanks, but I won't mess it up."

"Yas, girl," he approves while snapping his fingers.

The computer is on, so Mason tells me where to find the file. As it opens, a movement to my right catches my attention. It's the boss, rolling a chair next to mine before sitting on it.

"What are you doing?" I ask, sounding more aggressive than I meant to.

"I'm curious to see you in action."

What kind of fresh hell is this? "I'm more efficient when no one's breathing down my neck."

Not minding my reticence, he reaches for the glasses tucked in his collar. "Then I won't breathe on you."

There are no words to describe how much I hate this. I'm very aware of his presence, and I can't imagine my mind not drifting back to it every second. How on earth am I supposed to focus on my task? I turn to him, ready to negotiate some space, but something stops me.

Gray.

His irises are an icy, colorless shade that steals the words from my mouth. I don't think I've ever seen eyes so striking.

"What are you staring at? Get on with it," he says, pointing at the screen. "You have ninety minutes, starting now."

I have an acerbic remark ready to go, but he puts his glasses on, and my brain forgets how to compute. *Oh, fuck me* … He went from Kal-El to Clark Kent real fast, and I can't decide which version I prefer. The sporty, confident hunk or the nerdy, brainy one?

My body couldn't care less about the fact that he is an ass because I feel the urge to press my knees together. From this close, I can smell the fresh scent of his soap, the spicy aroma of his deodorant, and even feel the heat emanating from his large body.

Since it's the only way I can focus in these conditions, I ask permission to put my headphones on. He agrees, but when it takes me forever to pick the right playlist—something good enough to distract me from his proximity—he lets out an annoyed sigh. "You're wasting time, Andrea. Eighty-seven minutes."

"I'll only need sixty."

The jab is more of a grumble to myself, but his answer comes anyway. "Let's go for sixty minutes, then."

At that moment, I swear to myself I'll cut off my tongue if I survive the day.

But it's on. I am now an emissary for *all* women. This arrogant and misogynistic ass needs to be taught that we are as good and as worthy as men.

pov_name = "Alexander"

Time is the one thing that comes with limitations for all of us. Some get a hundred years' worth of it, some barely an hour, but the finality of it is true for everyone. Aside from maintaining a healthy lifestyle, one cannot do much to earn themselves more of it, and even then, nothing is ever certain. That is why time is one of the things I value most in life.

And this whole hiring process seems to have been a massive waste of it.

All the hours I poured into preparing the test, selecting applicants, reading through their résumés … If my suspicions are correct, they've all been for nothing, and I'll have to do it all over again.

The test I designed wasn't meant to be passed but to evaluate the applicant's resilience. So, when "Andy" Walker's score turned out nearly perfect, I struggled to believe it. The cover letter that came with the application piqued my interest, mentioning a deaf older brother and a genuine desire to work with us because of it. But the LinkedIn profile was incomplete, with no picture and nothing past three years at a shitty cybersecurity company in Portland. With a score like that, though, I decided to go for it, thinking I found a gemstone among the masses, someone whose programming skills might be equal to mine.

But in came a petite brunette who looks fresh out of college. And she has an attitude, which I don't appreciate—especially not from a new hire whom I believe lied to get here. She has sixty minutes to prove me wrong, but with the way she keeps stalling, I think I already have my answer.

How disappointing …

While I rationally couldn't believe she was the same Andy who passed my test, a small part of me hoped she would be. I'll have to find someone else if I fire her, and I don't look forward to that.

Finally, she settles on what she wants to listen to, and indiscernible screeches seep from her headphones. What the hell is that? Metal? She seems undisturbed by it as she leans in and gets to work. She focuses on the screen, hands hovering over the keyboard, and I come closer as well, eager to get my answer.

I discreetly observe her while she quickly scrolls down the script to familiarize herself with it. I'm seeking a crack, something that'll unveil the subterfuge. But before it comes, she begins typing, so my focus shifts to the screen instead.

Forty-seven seconds. That's all it takes for me to realize I was wrong. She won't need the rest of her sixty minutes because she proves herself in less than one. She's organized, meticulous, and very competent. The messy script is barely understandable at points, but it doesn't stop her as she makes her way through it. I meant to address this issue because the team has been stuck on it for too long. But by minute three, I already know I won't need to bother. Her sharp mind is quick to find errors and even quicker to fix them.

I try to remain focused on the screen, observing what she changes, removes, or rearranges, but I soon find myself drawn elsewhere. Down to her slim fingers and the way they move over the keyboard with dexterity, typing fast and flawlessly. Or how her short brown curls bounce as she bobs her head up and down in rhythm with her music. A verse sometimes slips past her mouth, barely a whisper, which also becomes distracting. Especially since it draws my eyes to her lips, which are plump, pink, and deprived of makeup.

While she loses herself in the script, I peer at her, rediscovering her in an entirely new light. Now that I know she didn't lie, the wall I mentally built between us is gone, and I can *see* the woman next to me.

I barely glimpsed at her back in the elevator, but enough to notice her almond eyes and the thick fringe of lashes surrounding them. And the way her slightly upturned nose is dusted with freckles, which spill onto her cheekbones. But as I look at her arms, I don't find more of those brown specks. I'm unsure what to make of the intrusive thought that makes me want to pull on her collar and see if there are any on her shoulders.

Why am I somehow even more intrigued by her now? Is it the relentless pride and assurance lying underneath her stubbornness? Is it because there's no way someone this young should be this skilled? Unless she's nearly as smart as I am, which is a very rare thing. Maybe I've found my match, and that's why I'm so confusingly interested in her.

In the elevator, I noticed her flowery scent, but it was lost among the crowd there, spoiled by overpriced perfumes and colognes. Now, though, I can make out a specific smell. I lean closer to discreetly breathe it in, and she tenses, her fingers missing a couple of keys. But she gets over it quickly, and I get my answer. Jasmine. She smells of jasmine flowers and something else, something entirely her.

As my body reacts to her scent, a familiar swell tugging in my jeans, I forcefully rip my eyes off her and stare at the screen, where she's still adamantly proving me wrong.

Switching on the chair, I adjust my uncomfortable state and frown. I'm normally good at balancing out my needs, but it's been almost three weeks since Celeste and I gave it one last fuck and parted ways. And because I haven't found anyone to replace her, the lengthy hiatus is messing with my head.

Given the picture Celeste sent me this morning, something tells me she wouldn't mind meeting up tonight. But she was already asking too much from me then, despite our original agreement, and I'm not sure it would be a good idea. I need to find someone else. Soon.

Going around lusting after employees isn't acceptable. Thankfully, it isn't a problem I've had before.

I glance at Andrea Walker with a mix of confusion and frustration, wondering what triggered this issue. When I can't find a satisfactory answer, I force myself to look away one last time and focus on her corrections. Her clever mind is just as attractive as the rest of her, though, so it doesn't exactly help.

On top of all that, time seems to have slowed, so the moment lasts longer than it should. As soon as the sixty minutes are through, though, I hastily put an end to it.

Slowly, so I don't frighten her, I pull on her headphones and say, "Time's up, Andrea."

She tenses all over, probably worried about what comes next, but there's no need for that.

I made a fool of myself by questioning her abilities, and she more than earned her spot on this team.

is_new_chapter = True

chapter_number =

"03"

pou_name =

"Andrea"

I'M ALMOST OUT OF BREATH as I remove my headphones, and System of a Down's song fades away as I sink back into reality. Time passed so much faster than I expected, and the hour flew by in what felt like ten minutes. There wasn't enough time to do a final sweep, but I don't think I missed anything. *Please,* I pray in my head, *let me have this one at least.*

Without removing his eyes from my screen, my new boss slightly tilts his head to the side.

"It won't work," he says with certainty.

Making my chair roll a few inches away, he comes closer.

When I see what he edits far up the script, I wince. I forgot a reference, and as he said, the script wouldn't have worked. Three extra minutes and I would have found it …

Behind me, the guys don't hide their disappointment, and the ginger one gives the bearded man a five-dollar bill. I don't have time to take offense because the boss returns his attention to me.

"It was still impressive, though," he concedes, removing his glasses and slipping them back into his collar. Just like that, Kal-El has returned. "You did a good job."

When he looks at me again with those mesmerizing and intense eyes, I suddenly understand why some people have a praise kink. And I think I'm one of them, because something happens in my core. I'm pretty sure it actually *throbs*, which is beyond disconcerting.

Well, someone is definitely masturbating tonight. And that someone is me.

"Welcome to the dream team, Andrea," he says, finally acknowledging that I belong here.

"Andy," I correct him.

He ignores it and stands from his chair. "Have you met your new colleagues yet?"

"Not formally."

"This is Steven," he explains, pointing at the older, bearded guy who extends his hand to shake mine. "When I'm not here, he's the one in charge, with Oliver," the boss continues, gesturing toward the red-haired one. We shake hands again as he offers me a friendly smile.

Brian is then introduced. He has Southeast Asian heritage, if I had to guess, and is also wearing a Marvel-themed T-shirt. "Your coding is so aggressive, we never thought you'd look …" he says as we shake hands, his sentence trailing off as he searches for the right word.

Our boss doesn't let him find it, moving on with the introductions. "And you've already met Mason and Joseph." His steely eyes fall on me next. "Your desk neighbors will help you settle in, and you can work with them for now. Until I find you a specific task, you'll put your sixteen years of experience to good use on whatever project they give you."

The underlying jab isn't lost on me, and my eyes narrow with displeasure.

Maybe I can just return to Portland and beg for my stupid job back after all. It sounds better than having to deal with this man. Hopefully I won't have to suffer his presence too often. It looks like his desk here is unoccupied, so I guess he has an office elsewhere. I can probably tolerate this pompous ass for an hour or so every day.

"Will do, sir," I say.

"You can call me Alexander. Or Lex, since everyone else takes that liberty."

I nod, even though I refuse to be on a nickname basis with him. "Alexander" is the best I can do, and even that's too much.

Satisfied with his work here, he gives me a dry nod and makes his way toward the exit. He turns around just before he leaves to say, "Steven, you still owe me ten bucks."

Before my bearded colleague can contest the statement, our boss is off, leaving us alone. I stare at the door, wondering what the hell is his deal.

I'm quickly distracted by the guys who gather around me.

"Girl, you ate!" Mason cheers.

"I did?"

"Absolutely," Oliver insists. "You did amazing."

Brian nods and adds, "When I started here, Lex took three weeks to welcome me into the team."

"You did it in an hour," Steven says, impressed.

"So, he's always this … intense?" I ask, signing for Joseph.

They all nod.

"He has a crazy IQ that comes with a no-nonsense brain," Oliver explains. "He's always five steps ahead and doesn't care about conventions. That's why he barely ever says hello, thanks, please, goodbye … It's like a waste of time to him."

"It's not that he's a dick, though," Mason points out. "It's just that his brain ain't working like ours."

"Don't worry," Oliver says. "You'll get used to it. Did Dakota give you a tour of the place?"

"Just some quick notes as we walked here."

"Okay, I think we can take ten minutes so I can show you around." He gallantly moves to the side and points toward the door, encouraging me to lead.

As he guides me through the floor, I quickly realize that the company is bigger than I thought. Over seventy people work on our level, and there's a little under sixty upstairs. According to Oliver's estimates, those numbers should double within a year. To my delight, everyone is warm and welcoming.

"Half of this floor is the dev team," he explains as we cross the open space. "We're in the top-dog team, meaning project leaders. The rest of the developers basically work under us. Once you're settled in, Lex might assign you a few of them to help you with whatever you need."

"Wow … I didn't realize I'd be high on the food chain."

"Yeah, we're all senior developers. Well, I guess you're a junior, but your skills got you an instant spot with us."

Eventually, he leads me to a massive break room with tables, lounge chairs, couches, and a TV. It also has a ping-pong table, foosball, an old arcade game, vending machines … This is heaven compared to the pitiful excuse of a break room I had before—a chair and a microwave in a revamped broom closet.

"This is the leisure room and the breakroom," Oliver explains. "Or at least, that's what they call it. To us, it's the Arena of Doom. This is where you settle a beef with one of the nerds. Darts, foosball, ping-pong … you name it." He comes closer, as if he wants to confide a secret. "Ping-pong would be Steven and Joseph's weakness. For Brian, it's foosball, and Mason is laughably bad at darts."

I let out a silent giggle, amused by his playfulness. "And what's *your* weakness, Oliver?"

"Call me Oli. And I don't have any weaknesses. I'm the final boss."

This time, I chuckle, shaking my head. "I've always been great with those, so be careful."

He smiles broadly, causing dimples to appear in his cheeks.

A woman comes our way, holding a cup of fresh coffee. She has a beautiful Afro, and her gleaming skin is a light shade of brown. She's pretty in a cute way and gives off a very kind, very gentle vibe. Oli waves for her to join us, so she does with curiosity.

"This is Tamika," Oliver introduces while signing fluently. "She works upstairs with R&D. Tami, this is Andy. She's with the dream team." Tami smiles at me, revealing a perfect set of pearly teeth.

We both extend our hands at the same time. "It's a pleasure to meet you, Tami," I say while signing the words.

"Let me know if you need anything," she offers with genuine kindness before leaving.

"It's awesome that you know ASL," Oliver notes as he guides me to our next destination. "It's not exactly a requirement, but almost everyone in the company does. There are eight people who are deaf or hard of hearing working here, so the company offers free ASL training to anyone interested. How did you learn it?"

"My brother was born deaf, so I know American and Mexican Sign Language."

"Mexican, too?"

"Yeah. Rafa wanted to show our mom that her side mattered as much as our father's, so he insisted we speak both languages, as any mixed family would."

"That's so cool of him. I love that."

"Me too. My brother is the reason why I'm so invested in this new job. I want to be part of the team that helps make the world more accessible for people like him."

"Well, you're part of it now."

I am. All I need to do is remain diplomatic enough to not be fired by my obnoxious boss.

My suspicions that I'll fit right in are clearer than ever when we come back from our tour. The guys are debating about who is the best Batman. I end up settling the argument when I mention my personal favorite, Kevin Conroy, from *The Animated Series*. That's one they can all agree on.

Mason and Joseph give me my tasks for the morning, and I easily breeze through them. So far, working for Kelex isn't proving as challenging as I worried it might be. Aside from my boss, of course.

Then, as if I need more proof that I've found my people, lunch break comes. That's when I accept I've landed in heaven. These nerds play first-person shooting video games in their downtime, and I decide this job is the best thing that will ever happen to me.

"We usually play *Counter-Strike*," Oliver explains to me. "You in, young Padawan?"

"I haven't played it in ages."

"Are you worried you'll lose?" Brian snickers.

"I'm sure I can still kick your ass."

I haven't prepared anything for my lunch, so I buy a few things from the vending machines to eat during the loading screens. I set my name as She-Hulk, so everyone knows it's me. After a few rounds, I'm happy to see myself in second place for my team—behind Grizzly, Steven's alias. As the game progresses, I get more comfortable and gain on him. That is, until a player named Luthor joins us. He quickly rises up to my score with his impressive skills. Because of this new player, my team gets slaughtered round after round.

When Luthor kills me for the fourth time in a row, and with a perfect headshot at that, I groan and frustratingly take a bite of my Snickers bar. "Who the hell is that?" I ask, angrily chewing as my patience runs thin.

Oliver laughs before sending me a compassionate look. "It's the boss."

Really? But why—

Lex. Lex Luthor. Oh, that's clever ...

I've been comparing him to Superman when, all along, he's been his nemesis. The man assimilates himself to an evil genius, which should be enough to quench my curiosity about him. But maybe I'm a little twisted in the head because I kinda like the idea.

We keep playing, and when the lunch break ends, I sourly stare at the final scoreboard. I'm close to Steven but still far from "Luthor."

Joseph gives me a shoulder tap, so I turn to him. "Don't worry," he signs. "You'll beat them in no time."

"Thanks. I may have a chance with Steven but not much with the boss."

"He barely ever joins us. You'll have to settle for second place when he does." His kindness brings a wide smile to my lips.

I work for about an hour before receiving an email from someone in the HR department. They forgot a document I needed to sign for my benefits, so I decide to sort it right away.

On my way to the stairs, I pull out my phone to check my messages. In our family group chat, my parents wished me luck, while Rafa told me to be normal for once and not bomb this one. Kate also texted, saying that since she didn't get any desperate texts from me, I probably wasn't fired on the spot, and she hopes it's going well. As I climb up the stairs, I respond to my family and invite Rafa to go fuck himself with a separate message, making sure I don't trip on a step and fall on my face.

When I reach the twenty-eighth floor, I push through the door, a cheerful smile on my face as I answer Kate. We've been friends for most of our lives. She's the sister I never had, and I'm hers. Since we keep no secrets from one another, I decide to tell her about my misogynistic BILF—boss I'd like to fuck.

Just as I send it, I violently bump into a firm, warm, and broad body. My phone slips from my hands and falls on the carpeted floor with a dull thump.

"I'm so sorry!" I apologize, lifting my head. I go rigid when I see who I collided with, and my lower stomach does some kind of backflip.

Of course, of all the people I can run into, it has to be *him*. Do I have the ability to summon the man with my thoughts?

I stare up into the icy gray eyes behind his glasses. When he sees it's me, he frowns and bends to grab my phone before I can. He glances at the crack on the screen—already there before the fall—and then hands it back to me.

"You should look ahead when you walk." His voice is stern and cold, but I barely notice as he adjusts his glasses, and my brain goes MIA. Damn it, since when do I have a thing for men wearing glasses?

Trying to appear unfazed, I look at the papers in his hands. He wasn't looking ahead either, or this wouldn't have happened. He seems to catch my train of thought. "I'm working. You were texting. Not the same." Well, he isn't totally wrong, so I keep my mouth shut.

"Are you looking for HR?"

"Yes, they forgot to have me sign something this morning."

"I see." That's all I get before he's back on his way. After two steps, he turns to me again, hesitant. A faint touch of appreciation veils his stoic expression. "By the way, not too bad, She-Hulk."

Not waiting for my answer, he resumes his course. I stand there like an idiot, watching him walk away. Pride swells in my chest, not because he is my boss, but because he is a fantastic player, and getting recognition from him means a lot.

As he walks away from me, I can't help but take a few seconds to admire his form. He's around 6'3", has broad shoulders, narrow hips, and is muscular. He isn't buff, but he definitely works out. There is no doubt he does squats—not with that ass.

Eventually, he disappears into a room, and losing sight of him gives me back control of my brain.

For the tenth time today, I scold myself when I glance down at my phone. My screen is still on, and the message I sent Kate is displayed.

ME

It's going great, except for my boss, who's both a sexist asshole and the hottest man I've ever seen.

Okay, if I wanted the ground to open up and swallow me earlier, it's nothing compared to now. I'm one embarrassing moment away from leaving everything and becoming a llama shepherd in the Andes mountains.

Could he have read it? He had his glasses on, so he could have, but he didn't gaze at my phone for more than two seconds, and the cracked screen could have distracted him from what lay behind it. It's very possible he didn't read it. He would have fired me or argued he isn't sexist.

My phone buzzes in my hand. Kate replied.

KATE

OMG! You have to tell me everything in detail tonight!!! Can you snap a picture of him?

I roll my eyes and type a quick answer.

ME

Calma tus tetas, blondie, I'm not taking a picture of him. I'll spill the tea tonight, tho. Gtg, love you.

With a sigh, I shove my phone into my pocket and head to HR to sign those last papers.

Once I return to the Lair, I spend the rest of the afternoon working with Mason, slowly getting accustomed to how things are run here. When we reach five-thirty, everyone packs up, ready to go home. It's nice to have regular hours for once. I'm particularly exhausted after this intense first day. Once all my things are ready to go, I hook my headphones around my neck and walk out at the same time as Oliver.

"Is it creepy if I say I'm thrilled you turned out to be a woman?" he asks as we walk to the elevators.

"Maybe a little," I laugh, half-amused, half-flattered.

"Yeah, I figured … I'm not sure how to explain it. I feel like you'll add some delicateness to the Lair."

"I wouldn't bet on that." I wince.

He laughs and pushes the elevator button. "Well, I'll say you're nicer to look at than another bearded nerd, then. Steven is enough."

Unfamiliar with this kind of situation, I don't know how to reply to his compliment, so I plaster an awkward smile on my face. Oliver is cute and charming in his own way, and he has the confidence that comes with it. Discreetly looking at him, I take in his profile. He's a good seven inches taller than me, and his auburn hair makes him stand out. His build is slender but not to a fault, and his face is a little angular, but it gives him an undeniable charm.

We chat the whole way down, and I love hearing more about his experience with the company and the team. Honestly, I'll love working here, despite some unforeseen circumstances.

"Are you taking the bus?" Oliver asks once we're out of the building. We're two blocks from Pike Street, where I have a direct bus line to my neighborhood.

"Yes, to Ballard."

"Ah, I'm heading south. I get off at Lincoln Park. At least we get to walk to the station together."

Okay, now he has to be flirting, just a bit. It isn't so far-fetched that someone would be interested in me like this, but it isn't common. I'm agreeable to look at, from what I've been told—and not only by my mother. But I'm not breaking necks when I pass people in the streets, either.

I'm taken out of my thoughts when Oliver clears his throat, still waiting for my answer. "Yes! Sorry, of course. We'll walk together to the stop."

As we walk, we talk about anything and everything. Turns out we have many of the same interests, from video games to movies, and a passion for old science fiction shows. We stop at a crossing, and it's already time to part. His body leans forward for a fraction of a second before he eventually extends his hand. I shake it, and we part with friendly grins.

I reach my platform and see him step on his at the same time. Our eyes meet, and we smile at each other one last time.

is_scene_break = True

My excellent mood hasn't faded by the time I arrive home. A little out of breath, I get to my door on the third floor. I wrestle with it, only to be greeted by my very unfamiliar living room, which also serves as a bedroom and a kitchen, with a single window overlooking the building's pitiful courtyard.

The piles of boxes have me sighing, and I wonder if I'll have the strength and courage to take care of them tonight. I haven't unpacked anything yet and only opened boxes to take what I need as I go. Today has been tiring enough, though, so I'm not starting the unpacking now.

I drop my bag, pop open the button of my jeans, pull my shirt out of it, and unhook my bra before removing it with practiced ease. When the cumbersome accessory is taken care of, I throw it on a chair where clothes are already piling up. I drop on the couch, which unpleasantly reminds me of the presence of my phone in my back pocket. There's a message from Kate when I pull it out.

KATE

I'm waiting!

With a smile, I open our conversation and tap the camera icon to call her. It rings twice before she picks up. My smile widens when her familiar face appears on the screen. "Oh, hello, Jabba the Hutt," she greets me.

My face in the upper corner of the screen easily explains the insult. "You nasty bitch! You know I'm not to be teased about my double chin."

"You don't have a double chin."

"I do."

"You don't."

"I do when I do that," I insist, shoving my head into my shoulders.

"Everyone has a double chin when they do that, you idiot."

"Not everyone."

"Yeah, you're right. Chris Hemsworth probably doesn't." No need to even try arguing about this one. "You're back at your studio, I see?"

"Yeah, just got here."

"So, how was your first day, babe?"

"It went great. It's like I was born for this job and this team. The guys are total nerds like me, so it's been awesome so far." I tell her about everything—the company, the office, the "dream team," even about Dakota and Tami. When I'm done, I stop talking, searching for what else to tell her, staring at the ceiling. A few seconds pass before I notice that the paint is peeling. This apartment is truly horrible, but it's the only one I could find on such short notice.

"Now that you've told me all about the uninteresting things," Kate eventually says, "on to the good stuff. How about that sexy boss of yours?"

I wince and look away from the screen, not knowing how to explain it to Kate without her getting any weird ideas. "He's strange," I eventually say. "Apparently, he is some sort of asocial genius, so he's super rude."

"But he's hot."

"It doesn't make up for being an asshole. He thought I cheated to get in. He couldn't believe I did it without the help of a *male* friend."

"That dick!" she protests with an appalled face, finally getting my vibe. "I hope you proved that idiot wrong."

"You know I did. I made him regret it."

"That's my girl!" There is a short silence, and I look away from my phone to my messy room. "Did you finish unpacking?"

"No. I still need to find the courage to even start."

"You've been there for three days. Stop procrastinating and get your lazy ass to work."

"I can't tonight. I have plans," I pretend.

"What plans?"

"I'm gonna Netflix and chill."

"I know you mean Netflix and actually chill," she answers, not duped. "Since you haven't unpacked, you most definitely haven't found Idris yet."

Idris, named after one of the sexiest men to have ever lived, Idris Elba, is my clitoral massager, my most trusted companion in the darkest hours of the night. I'm a little offended, even though she has every reason to assume I'm not talking about an actual human.

"Maybe I meant with a real man."

"No, you didn't. You never do."

"Hm, that's fair."

"Since you don't actually have an excuse, chop chop, bitch. Get those boxes done."

"But I can't right now … I'm exhausted."

"Well then, tonight you rest, but tomorrow you unpack, and I want a picture to prove you did it."

"I swear I will," I promise. My phone buzzes in my hand, and on the top of my screen, I see it's my mother. "Mom's calling, I have to go. Love you!"

She barely has time to reply before I hang up and take my mother's call, eager to hear her comforting and familiar voice. With a broad smile, I hold the phone to my ear. "*¡Hola, mamá! ¿Cómo estás?*"

"I'm great, *mija*. And you, how are you?" she continues in Spanish.

"I'm great too. Except I miss you guys."

"We miss you too," she says with palpable emotion. I hear my father's voice close to the phone. "Your dad says hi."

"Hi, Dad!" I yell, hoping he can hear me.

"Hey, peanut!" He definitely has his ear pressed against my mom's phone. "We're very proud of you, you know?"

A twinge of melancholy tightens my heart. My parents and I are close, especially since I only moved out of the family house three years ago when I got my first proper job. It was still in Portland, though, so I've never lived so far from them.

I tell them about my day and how great things will be. I, of course, don't tell them about my frustrating boss and the confusing thoughts he triggers in me, but I do tell them about the few people I met.

Despite a rocky start, today was great.

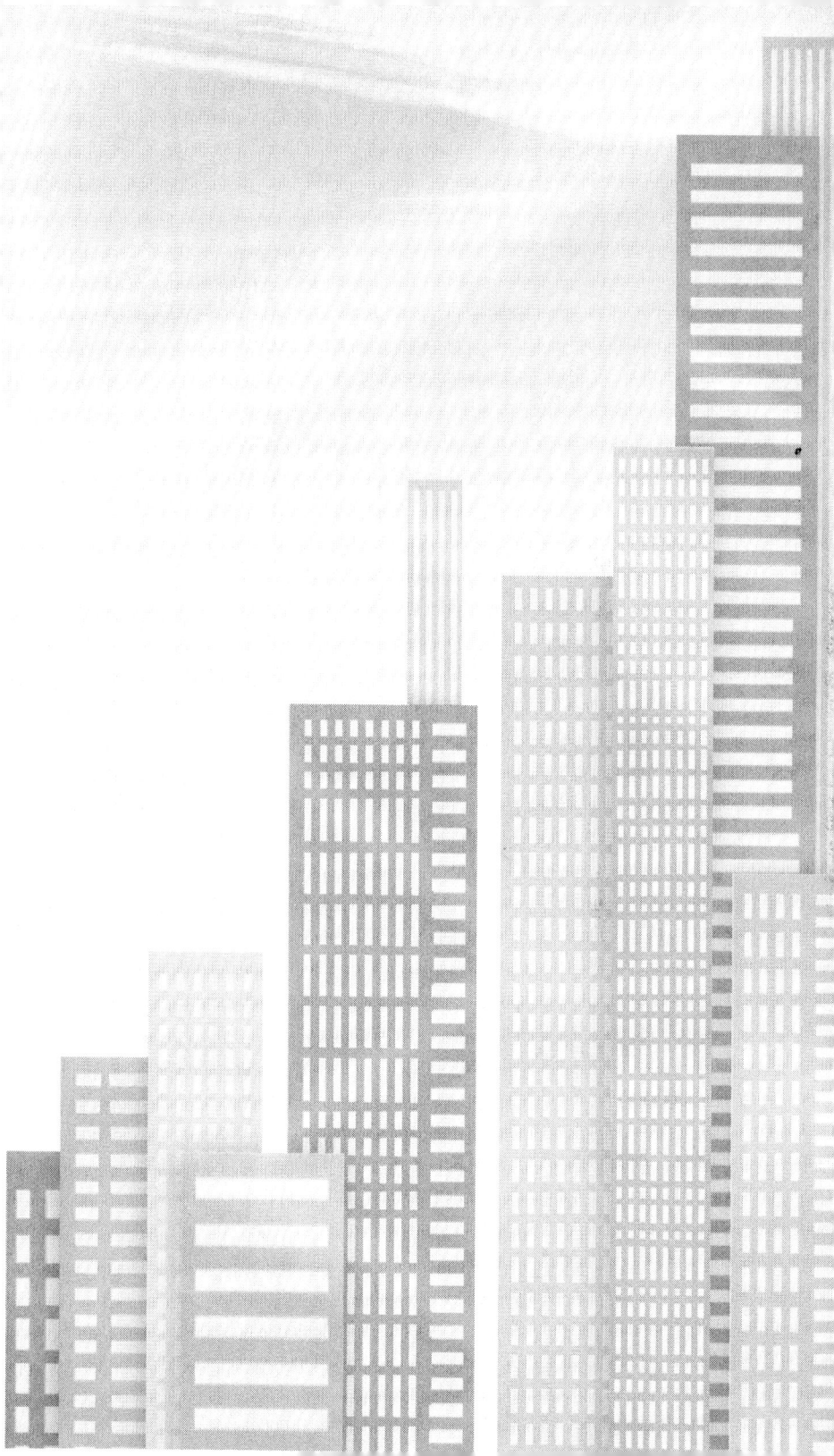

is_new_chapter = True

chapter_number = "04"

pov_name = "Andrea"

I'M STILL NOT USED TO the abnormally loud AC unit that rattles all night, so I don't have the most restful sleep. My studio is horrible, but I'm nothing if not adaptable. Once I'm settled in and know this city better, I'll start looking for another place.

But the direct line to Pike is handy, and I arrive a solid ten minutes early for my second day. On my way to the Troll's Lair, I stop by the break room to make myself a cup of coffee, which speaks volumes about my tired state. I despise the taste of it.

I'm adding a fifth spoonful of sugar when a masculine voice says, "Would you like some more coffee with that sugar?" It's Oliver, looking at me with a teasing smile. Now that I have slept on it, he's rather attractive. Not in the classical way, but there's something kind about him that's reassuring and enticing.

I grimace, scrunching my nose. "Don't tell anyone, but I *hate* coffee," I confess.

"My lips are sealed." I can't help but smile when he mimics the gesture. "It seems we had the same idea," he adds, lifting his empty mug in front of him. His cup is in the shape of Darth Vader's helmet. The detail makes my appreciation of him even greater.

"So, now that you've slept on it, what did you think of your first day here?"

"It was … surreal. I still can't believe I got the job."

"I get that," he says with compassion as he pours himself some coffee. "When I started here, I felt the same."

"How long have you been here?"

"Almost since the beginning, seven years ago. We were nine, including Steven, Kev, and Lex."

"Kev?"

"Kevin Langley, the co-owner."

"Oh, right."

"He and Lex are childhood friends. Kev is the face of the company, the social one, and Lex is the engineer, the brain behind it all."

"Ke-Lex," I say, understanding where the company's name comes from.

"Yup." Oliver glances at the sugar that I'm still holding. "Can I have a spoonful before you finish it?"

I smile at his teasing. There is at least a pound of sugar in there. I pour him a dose, and before he can react, I add a second one.

"Oh no, you lunatic!" he protests with a laugh, covering his mug. "I will know who to blame when my arteries clog up."

We both chuckle at his antics before heading to the Lair. Steven and Brian are already here, and the latter looks up to give us a suspicious look. "Why are you two arriving at the same time?" he asks.

I turn to Oliver, whose eyes are throwing daggers at our coworker. "I slept at his place. Best night of my life. Nothing will ever be the same," I pretend with a broad smile. This isn't even me trying to sound convincing, but Brian's jaw falls open.

"We met in the break room, you moron," Oliver explains, slightly blushing. Brian lets out a disappointed sigh and returns his attention to his screen.

As my computer boots, I take a sip of my coffee, inevitably grimacing at the awful taste. My eyes cross Oliver's, who witnessed my disgust, and he gives me a falsely judgmental head shake. I shrug and take another sip, not breaking eye contact. I try not to show my revulsion but fail, making him laugh softly.

The morning goes smoothly as I work on more tasks Mason and Joseph give me, and before I know it, the lunch break arrives. This time, the guys and I have lunch in the break room. It turns out they only play on Mondays and Thursdays, so we're all seated around a table, and I think I even prefer this to the game lunches.

I bought the most appetizing sandwich I could find in the vending machine, ham and cheese, and I envy their meals. Aside from Brian, they all have something home-cooked, and I haven't eaten anything prepared on a stove in days.

Once I'm done with my sandwich, I rest my chin in my palm, my elbow on the table, distractedly listening to them. My short night becomes an oppressive reality, and I feel myself dozing off.

"Hi, boss," Brian suddenly says, shaking me out of my tired state. I straighten up, gathering that one of our bosses is standing behind me. *Please, tell me I'm about to meet Kevin …*

The low voice is all too familiar, alas. True to himself, Alexander doesn't greet anyone and goes straight to business. "Mason, I'll need you to finish the script for the eye-controlled keyboard. Brian, I'm still waiting for your edits on the braille app. Andrea," he starts, and I hold my breath, anxious even though I haven't done anything wrong. "I can't control your life outside of this office, but when you come in, I expect you to be well-rested and efficient. We don't pay you to nap."

Outrage fills me as I turn around to face him. I quickly forget what I want to say, though, as I'm reminded that this man is ridiculously attractive. I almost forgot the way his gray eyes seem to pierce right through mine, straight into my soul.

But I can't let that get the best of me. Not when he's being ridiculous. My voice isn't as strong as I wish when I speak. "You aren't paying me at all right now since it's my lunch break. So, if I want to spend it napping, I will," I explain in a matter-of-fact tone.

While he chews on my words, as stoic as ever, I take in the sight of him. His navy blue T-shirt is tighter than the one he wore yesterday, and the shade highlights his tan. The stubble is still there, and his hair is still a little messy. He isn't wearing his glasses, but I can totally envision him ripping his shirt open in the middle to reveal a red and yellow 'S' plastered on his chest.

It's wicked to want him that much, and I scold myself internally. Especially since he's Lex Luthor, not Superman.

Apparently, I'm not worth debating with because he doesn't even answer; he just turns around and leaves. The guys are watching me with wide eyes when I face them again. "What?" I wonder, suddenly worried.

"Andy, do you have a death wish?" Mason asks.

"I—No. Why?"

"I don't think I have ever seen someone talk to Lex like that and get off so easily."

"Was I rude?"

"Not really … But he doesn't like people talking back since he's right ninety-nine percent of the time. And being second-guessed by your employees must be a pain in the ass," Steven explains.

"I'm so sorry. I didn't realize my attitude was problematic."

"It's okay, Andy," Oli reassures me. "Just be careful. You don't want to poke the bear. Alexander Coleman has a limited stock of patience, and you don't want to see what happens when he runs out of it."

Brian nods. "Last time, the walls trembled."

"What happened?" I ask, curiosity getting the best of me.

Steven is the one who fills me in. "Someone leaked essential pieces of information before a patent was fully negotiated. The company probably lost a few million because of it."

Well, that seems like a good reason to get mad. I'd get mad for a hundred dollars. And growing up with two Mexican women, I know how to yell at people—with the *chancla* and everything.

All things considered, I'd yell for twenty dollars.

Shortly after lunch, Mason, Joseph, and I find a bug we can't solve. This means our boss comes to the Lair to help us deal with it. The entire time he sets up his laptop at his desk, I keep track of him from the corner of my eye. I'm about to focus back on work when he slips on his glasses.

Alexander Coleman wears his intelligence very accurately. With one glimpse at him, it's abundantly clear that his intellect is off the charts. Maybe it's the way he holds himself, the assurance he lets off, or the sharpness of his eyes. When his glasses are added to the mix, it pushes that reality even further, bringing him closer to the evil genius he channels.

Yeah, I'm in deep shit.

Of course, I forget to pretend I'm working, and straight-up stare. His lush lips are tempting despite the stiff line they form, and I wonder what it would feel like to have them against mine. Surely, they wouldn't remain so rigid.

"Earth to Andy," Mason calls next to me.

I spin around to face him, mortified he caught me staring at our boss. Oh God, how long have I been out of it?

"Sorry, I got distracted," I apologize in a low voice.

"You and me both, sis," he says with a knowing smile, glancing at our very focused boss. Oh, so not only do we play for the same team, but we also have the same type?

"Anyways," he continues. "Have you had the time to work on the script I gave you?"

"Yes! I need ten more minutes to clean it up, and we're good."

is_scene_break = True

GROOVING TO THE BEE GEES' "Stayin' Alive", I moonwalk into my building's entrance hall. I'm nailing it as much as I can—meaning not at all—until I bump into someone behind me.

Startled and embarrassed beyond words, I turn around with a squeal, only to find my landlady glaring at me, unamused.

"Mrs. Godfrey!" I say, putting my hand over my racing heart and pushing back my headphones.

She's one of the few people I don't have to look up to, yet she's somehow still intimidating. In her late sixties or early seventies, she has a large upper body and skinny legs. It's my third time seeing her, and she's always in a variation of the same outfit: an oversized T-shirt, leggings, crocs, round glasses with thick lenses, and a bandanna protecting her hair.

"I'm so sorry!" I blurt out.

"You Gen Z, with your savage music. Never minding where you walk."

I nod docilely, pretending I wasn't this enthusiastic over a song decades older than me. "Yes, so sorry. It won't happen again."

"You've been here for almost a week and still haven't signed your lease."

I'm not sure what to say to that. I arrived on Saturday, so it's been four days instead of a week. And we both know she's the problem here. I've texted her several times to let her know I was available to sign whenever she wanted. "We can handle it now if you want," I diplomatically offer.

She hesitates, assessing me from head to toe for a few moments. Eventually, she gives me a dry nod and waves for me to follow her. She leads me to a small office by the stairs and makes me sit at the desk. After she's shuffled inside a drawer, she takes out some papers and hands them to me, showing me where to sign. I don't trust her enough to do it blindly, so I go through it rapidly.

"Excuse me, Mrs. Godfrey, there seems to be a problem here," I say with a frown, pointing at the wrong number. "We agreed on eleven hundred."

"Miss Walker, Ballard is one of Seattle's trendiest neighborhoods. I have to adapt to the market."

"I'm pretty sure it didn't become this trendy between a week ago, when we agreed on the price, and now, Mrs. Godfrey."

"I decide what it's worth, Miss Walker."

"Have you seen the room you're renting? It really isn't worth nearly two grand," I try to reason.

"Your generation doesn't know any better. I can rent it for that price with a snap of my fingers."

I'm about to protest when something in her cunning expression stops me. She's trying to scam me. And I don't think it's her first time doing it. She might even account for some bargaining in that price, and I might get it lowered by a few hundred, but it would still be too high.

"Is this your schtick?" I ask, suspicious. "You lure people in with acceptable prices, give them time to settle in, and then change the deal?"

"Watch your tongue, young lady."

I let out an incredulous laugh. Her scam won't work on me because I've been a lazy slob, so most of my boxes are untouched and ready to go. Moving out wouldn't be nearly as tedious as she expects.

"I'm not paying that much for an awful studio that violates several safety standards," I protest. "Who the hell puts an electric plug so close to the showerhead?"

Everything in me dislikes the way I'm talking to an elderly woman, but she deserves all of it and more. Mrs. Godfrey looks beyond pissed, her face reddened, and her lips squeezed into a thin line. I expect her to blow up at me, but after a moment of silent reflection, she leans forward to snatch the papers from my hands. "You paid for a week, so I want you out by Friday evening," she states.

For a second, I consider agreeing with her price. The prospect of having to find a new place in three days isn't great. Especially since I have a new job and an annoying new boss to worry about.

But I have my pride, and I won't let her get away with this. "Alright, I'll be gone," I confidently reply. I stand, straighten up, and stare down at her. "You should be ashamed of yourself."

With that, I turn around and leave the small office, back to the hall, then up to the studio. The piles of boxes have me sighing, but for once, it's from relief rather than because I need to find the courage to start unpacking. Who knew being a lazy fucker could have its advantages?

At least I have an excellent excuse to break my promise to Kate and not unpack …

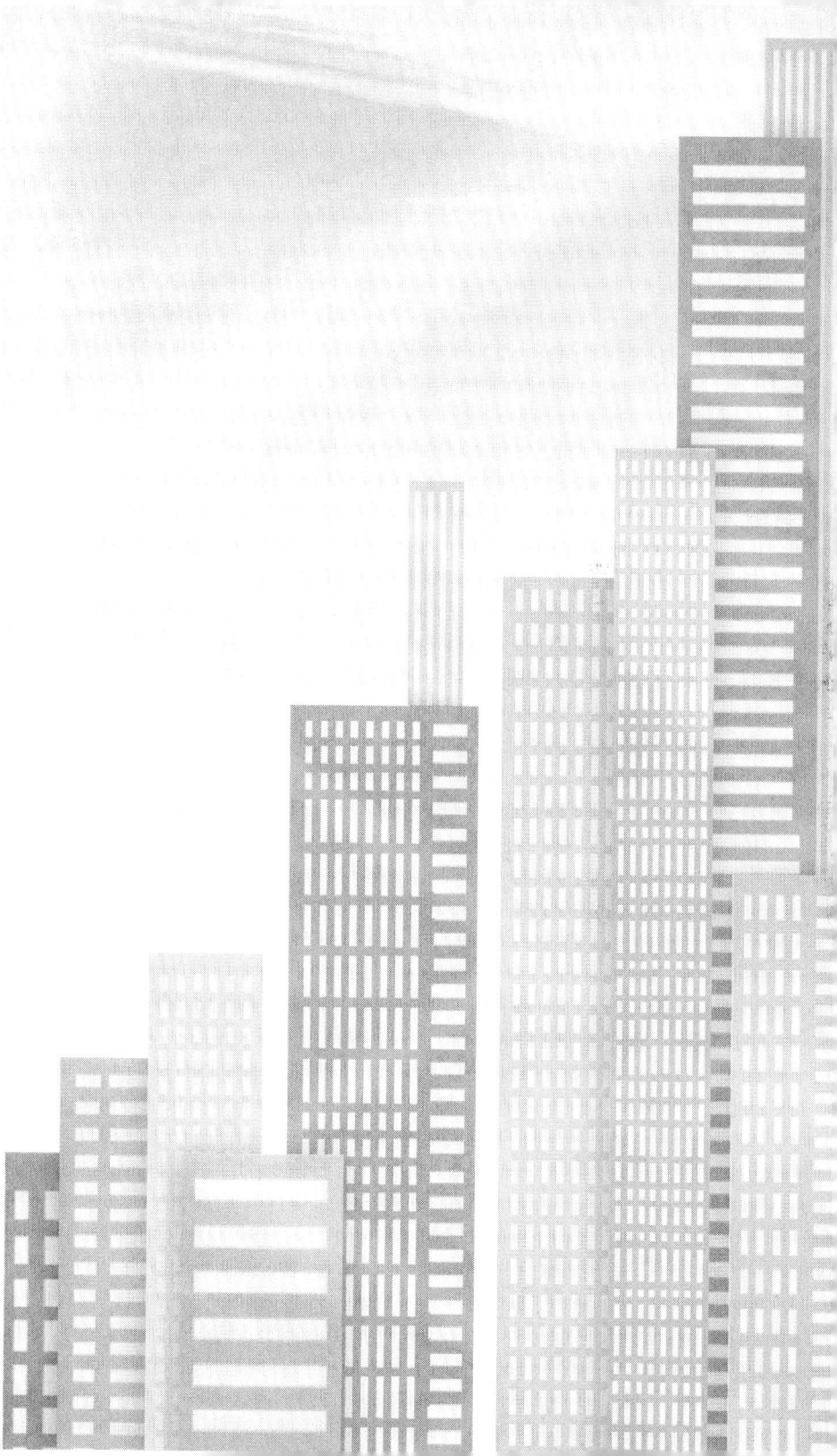

is_new_chapter = True

chapter_number =

"05"

pov_name =

"Andrea"

My trip to Kelex the following morning is spent looking for a new place and sending emails. I sent a bunch yesterday and have received four unfavorable responses so far. And by the time I arrive at work, I have three more replies telling me the time frame won't work for them. It's technically possible, but I can't see how I'll find a new place so quickly.

Once more, I pour myself a cup of coffee with way too much sugar before I head to my desk. I'm just settling in when my phone buzzes. When I glance at the screen, I see it's another email. What shows on the notification already tells me this is another no, and I sigh.

I'm not as focused as I'd like, but I still manage to get some work done. It takes everything not to spend my morning looking for a solution to my precarious living situation, but I tell myself I'll have the lunch break to do that.

That's why, as soon as half past noon hits, I'm on my feet and walking to the breakroom. I buy another sandwich, find an empty table, and sit down with my phone in hand, ready to find something. I can even rent a storage unit for my stuff and find a cheap hotel to buy some time until I find a new place.

I've barely started my search when a plate of steamy Bolognese pasta is set in front of me.

Startled and confused, I look to my left and notice Oliver holding a similar plate.

"I suspected you'd be having another one of those horrible sandwiches, so I cooked for two," he explains as he sits beside me.

Shocked, I stare at him, then at the well-filled plate. I should refuse, but it's too late for that. And if I'm being honest, it smells *really* good, so I'm dying to try it.

"You cooked this?" I ask, still surprised.

"I did, so you have to accept the offering, or I'll be offended."

With a small smile and a shake of my head, I pick up the fork planted in the spaghetti. I practically moan at the first bite of pasta. Ugh, he's a great cook, which I add to the mental list I have in his favor. It seems this man is all assets and has no flaws.

"Thanks, Oli. I'll pay you back as soon as I have a decent kitchen."

"No worries. I love cooking."

We're eating and talking about the app he's working on when a familiar voice makes us turn around. It's Brian at the arcade machine, arguing with Steven. "Is that *Donkey Kong*?" I ask Oli.

"Yup, an original from the '80s and all. It must have cost a fortune, but I bet it's worth even more now."

"What do you mean?"

He leans forward, coming closer to me as if he has a secret to share. "Do you know who Nammota is?"

Anyone who dabbles in coding knows Nammota. He's our modern-day Robin Hood, the hacker we all aspire to become. For his first hit, he exposed embezzlements in several Fortune 500 companies. Not only that, but he also stole the embezzled money and redistributed it to charities and people in need. The affair was shushed pretty hard by the rich and influential people in charge, but the internet forever knows.

Nammota is a national treasure.

Or at least he was, until maybe four years ago when his activities abruptly came to an end. A lot of people speculated he was arrested or that he died. The one sure thing is that now, no one will ever know the identity of the legendary hacker.

"Everyone knows Nammota," I tell Oli.

"Come see," he says with a mysterious grin, getting up from his chair. I follow him, and he takes us to the old *Donkey Kong* machine. Brian's playing again. "Brian, can you lose?"

"What? No way, man. I'm feeling it. This game will be a good one."

"I want to show the Nammota thing to Andy," Oliver insists.

Brian reluctantly complies, so Mario dies, the "Game Over" screen comes, and then I get it. I see what Oliver meant. Right there, the three highest-ranking scores are 'NAM,' 'MOT' and 'AAA,' forming an unmistakable NAMMOTAAA.

Without looking away from the game, I ask Oliver, "Is it legit?"

"We can't know for sure, but we like to think it is," Oliver confirms, somewhat smug about it.

"So what? Nammota works here? Or did the machine arrive like this?"

"The scoreboard was blank when it was delivered after we moved into this building. But I've never seen someone play with a score so high, so this happened after hours. We all have our little theories."

"Who do you think it is?"

"Well, there are people in and out all the time, so it might not even be someone who works here," Steven explains. "But we had another developer around that time who fits the profile perfectly. Gregory stopped working here shortly after the leaderboard's final input. And he had a kid around the same time Nammota stopped being active."

"That's why we think it's Greg," Oliver says, nodding.

I stare at the high scores, almost starstruck. Could Nammota really have worked here? That's crazy. The NSA, FBI, IRS, Homeland … everyone's looking for him. The man is a fucking legend.

"I think you broke her," Brian whispers to Oli.

"Come on, the food will be cold," Oliver insists.

That's enough for me to rip my eyes off the scoreboard and follow Oli back to our chairs. We eat the rest of our meal in silence, and the whole time, I'm ruminating slowly, still not over the fact that I'm—possibly—working in the same place as the legendary Nammota.

It's only when my phone buzzes with another rejection email that I remember I had a mission. I barely have five minutes left on my break, so I doubt I'll get anything done.

Disappointed in myself, I let out a sigh and turn my phone face down.

"Everything good?" Oli asks.

I consider saying yes because I'm not the type to lay my problems on a stranger. But he's from around here, so maybe he'll be able to help somehow.

"I'm getting evicted in three days, and I can't find anywhere else to live," I impulsively blurt out.

His shock is almost amusing, but I hold back from smiling. "What happened?"

I explain everything to him and end with, "If you know someone who's got an apartment or house for rent, let me know."

Like the kind person he is, he genuinely thinks about it for a moment.

"You know …" he starts, "I think Tamika is looking for a roommate."

"Really?"

"Yeah, her last one ditched her, and I remember she complained about having to find a new one."

A spark of hope flickers in my chest, and I turn around to look at where Tamika was having her lunch just a moment ago. It looks like she already went back upstairs to work, so I sigh again. "I'll have to ask her next time I see her," I decide.

"I think this is urgent enough to pay her a visit now. Come, I'll take you to her office."

We get rid of our lunch stuff, and he determinedly leads me upstairs. We walk up to a door, he knocks on it, and a feminine voice invites us in. We enter the office where several people are working, including Tamika in the far left corner.

We walk up to her, and when she notices us, Tami smiles with a wave of her hand.

"Hey, I was wondering if you're still looking for a roommate?" Oliver signs when we reach her. She nods, and my heart begins to beat a little faster.

"Great! Andy is looking for a new place, kind of urgently, but I'll let you two sort it out."

With one of his friendly and warm smiles, he leaves.

I turn to Tami. "Would you seriously have me as a roommate?" I sign, so relieved that my hands are shaking.

"Are you allergic to peanuts?" Taken aback by the question, I shake my head. "Good. Peanut butter is the one thing I can't exist without, so I can't live in a peanut-free household."

I giggle and then catch myself so I don't disturb her coworkers.

For the following ten minutes, Tami and I have a silent but thorough conversation to ensure neither of us is making a mistake—though beggars can't be choosers, so I'm in no matter what. She promises to send me a few pictures, gives me the address, tells me about the neighborhood … We agree on a three-month trial period, and if it works out, then I can stay for good. After we exchange numbers, I leave the office, ecstatic.

Oliver is leaning against the wall, and when he notices I'm out, he puts his phone away.

"So?"

"Well, my ulcer will now slowly heal thanks to you."

"So it's good? She's taking you in?"

"Yes! We'll work out a few things before Friday, but I have a roof for at least three months." I wriggle with excitement and happiness. "Thank you so much for this."

"Anything for a friend in need."

A friend … Not even a week in, and I already have a friend here. And it feels as amazing as the relief of having a home again.

Since I don't know how else to express my elation, I get closer and wrap my arms around him. I hug him tightly, grateful for what he did.

He freezes for a moment, unsure how to react, and then his arms slowly close around my shoulders.

"Thank you, Oli. Really," I say, my voice half-muffled by his plaid shirt. He smells good, clean, and earthy—something comfortable and cozy.

"To tell you the truth, it was purely selfish. Now you'll have to take the same bus as me, and I'll get more nerdy debates."

My chuckle is cut short when a door opens next to us. We separate instantly and turn to see who interrupted us.

Of course, it's *him*.

Alexander Coleman, in all his mightiness, stares at us with a judging glare, his eyebrow cocked up. Somehow, I feel ashamed he caught us like this, even though we did nothing wrong.

He's dashing, as usual, and I feel my skin warm up under his stare. How can this man reduce me to mush with his eyes alone? What kind of sorcery is this?

He's holding his laptop between his thumb and fingers as if it's a weightless piece of cardboard, not a heavy Alienware of nearly twelve pounds. My eyes linger on the flexed muscles of his forearm under a veil of thin, dark hair. His hands are massive, the hard lines of the tendons and veins enhanced by the neon lights above us.

"Weren't you two supposed to be in front of your computers ten minutes ago?" he coldly asks.

"Yes, sorry. We came to see Tami for a personal matter," Oli explains with diplomacy.

"Was the matter resolved?"

"Yes, it was."

Our boss does nothing for a few seconds, staring at me specifically. I have a great excuse for being here, but something tells me it won't fly with him. Only my untimely death would.

Maybe.

Possibly.

When he rips his eyes from mine, it's to check the silver watch around his wrist. "Correct me if I'm wrong," he starts, looking at me again, "but we're past your lunch break, aren't we?"

"Yes, but—"

"And somehow," he rudely cuts me off, "you've decided to corrupt one of your colleagues so you two can frolic around rather than work."

Okay, now I can't contain my anger anymore. He's right about the fact that we should be working, but he doesn't have to be an ass about it.

"We weren't frolicking around," I begin. "Human warmth might be a mysterious notion to y—"

"We're heading back downstairs right now," Oli says hurriedly, cutting my rant short. With that, he grabs my arm, just above my elbow, and pulls me to the stairs.

As we walk, I look behind to send an enraged glare at the pompous idiot, earning myself a defying stare. Oli is the only reason why I don't say anything.

"That man needs to chill the fuck out," I mumble as we get further.

"Seriously, Andy, let it go."

"I can't! He is so strict and frigid! How have you been tolerating him for *seven* years?"

"He isn't normally like this. I guess he's in a mood."

"It doesn't give him the right to lash out at his employees," I mumble under my breath.

"Andy. I promise he's a nice guy. He's just ... a little off today."

Unable to hold back, I twist around to glare at our boss one last time. He's still standing there, perfectly still as he watches us leave. Something about him riles me up, and if I don't get better at containing myself, I won't keep this job for much longer.

I want to trust Oliver's judgment, so if he thinks our boss is worth the effort, maybe I should listen. I turn away from Alexander and promise myself I'll try harder to be amiable.

I need this job too much to let some stupid feud with my boss ruin my chances here.

pov_name =

"Alexander"

AS I STARE AT MY newest employee walking away, I wonder why she rattles me so much. I've never been good with people, but I can safely say that with her, I'm the worst I've ever been.

That is becoming clearer with every interaction we have. I'd decided to avoid her today, even though I'm needed in the Lair. But since that just happened, I might as well head downstairs and help.

My eyes lower of their own will, locking on the generous roundness of her behind. Her jeans aren't a tight fit, except there, and the blue fabric leaves very little to the imagination. There's something utterly feminine in her shape, but not in the stereotypical hourglass way. Her waist is narrow, like her shoulders, but her hips are wide and round. I envision them bare, with my hands firmly gripping them to pull her in as I—

She twists around to look back at me, and her nasty scowl is enough to kill the vivid fantasy.

This is what's going on. My biological needs are catching up with me, and she's alluring enough to trigger them. That's why my brain turns useless any time she's around. Before interacting more with her, I need to take care of that.

I shouldn't have said anything just now. I should have let them go without a word. But the anger I felt upon finding them there, holding each other in a tight embrace, compelled me to say something.

This is a company, not a fun little retreat to meet new people and make friends. And her audacity, lecturing me on break times one day, and then returning to work ten minutes late the next …

I don't like dealing with attitude, and she needs to remember who's in charge here.

They disappear into the staircase, and I shake myself out of my thoughts to head to my office. There, I pick up my phone and the hard drive I'll need, and head downstairs. The fact that I'll have to work closely with her displeases me, but I can limit my interactions to Joseph and Mason instead. She might already have a good grasp on the project they're working on, but they remain the leads on it.

As soon as I enter the Lair, to which the door was left open, my eyes glide toward her. She's seated in front of her computer, but her attention is on her phone.

Again, her lack of work ethic bothers me. She'll have to do better if she's to be a part of this team. I'd rather not have her around otherwise. She's too … distracting.

Using the fact that she has no idea I'm here, I silently walk toward her. Once I'm close enough to see her phone, I understand she's scrolling through pictures of an apartment.

"You seem determined not to work today, Andrea."

She tenses all over, and I can almost see the thin hairs on her forearms rise. Slowly, she puts her phone down and twists her chair to face me. She at least has the decency to look sheepish about her behavior.

I'm expecting another one of her defying comebacks because of her temper. I'll give her three more of those outbursts before I fire her. It's more generous than most.

But instead of getting heated again, she remains contained and calmly says, "You're right, I'm sorry. I'm done now, so I'll get on with it."

Did something happen between five minutes ago and now? Where is the fiery Andrea who was ready to gouge my eyes out?

Something in me feels compelled to test her, so I look down at my watch. "You'll stay for an extra twenty minutes to compensate for the time you wasted."

She nods, which I'm not expecting again. Am I disappointed, proud, or impressed?

Maybe some of each.

Once I'm settled with my laptop on my desk, I can't help but take quick and discreet glimpses at her. Although she's focused on her screen, I catch her peering at me a couple of times.

I work with Brian for a while, then I have to sit by Mason's side to help him solve the few issues he's having. Seated right next to Andrea, I do my best to ignore her. But I use the fact that she's lost in her script to gaze at what she inputs. She's brilliant at this, and I have no doubt that once she's up to speed with our current apps in development, she'll be able to replace me and assist her colleagues when they're stuck.

I won't have to come down here as much and can keep to my office instead. In peaceful silence, without any jasmine-scented distractions.

Five-thirty arrives, and aside from her, the team slowly filters out after turning their computers off. Oliver is the last one to leave, and before he does, he stops by Andrea's desk.

Because there aren't as many machines running, the room is silent enough for me to hear their brief conversation.

"I would stay, but I have an appointment," he reluctantly explains.

"Don't worry, I think I can find the bus stop without your wise guidance," she quips in return.

They exchange some goodbyes, and then it's just us. She takes out her headphones and slips them on, then the barely perceptible sound of whatever she's listening to reaches me.

Ignoring her becomes nearly impossible, so I consider heading back upstairs. Especially since she sometimes gets carried away and sings along with her music. Something tells me she doesn't even realize she's doing it, absorbed by her work on the screen.

She's so engrossed by it, actually, that she doesn't pay attention to the time. I'm the one who notices she's done with her penance, so I stand and walk up to her.

When she notices me standing by her side, she removes her headphones, slightly startled.

"Your twenty minutes are over," I explain.

"Already?" She checks the time on her screen. "Crap, I'm almost done. I hate leaving something halfway. It takes forever to get back into it."

"I know the feeling." She gives me a dubious look, but I ignore it. "What do you have left to do?"

"It doesn't work, but I can't find why. I'm doing the final sweep now."

The sooner she's done, the sooner I'm alone again and can work in peace, so I grab Joseph's chair and roll it closer to hers. She looks discontent, so I sit down and say, "What? Four eyes are better than two, no?"

I'm close enough to hear her mumble, "I think you mean six eyes," and the amusement it brings lifts the corners of my lips just a little.

There she is. The snappy woman I hired.

Slowly enough so we can read it, she scrolls down the script. About two-thirds into it, we jolt in our chairs simultaneously, having found the issue. Surprised that we reacted in unison, we briefly side-eye one another. With the keyboard in front of her, she starts the corrections. There's nothing I would have done differently, so I let her handle it, observing her in silence.

"I like your work," I say when she's done, removing my glasses. "It's clear and concise, so it's easy to follow your chain of thought."

She nods and gives me a smile that I can tell is forced. Did I do it wrong? Was that not an acceptable compliment?

Before I can let it go to my head, I roll my chair back and stand. "Time to head home, Andrea."

"Sorry for earlier. I'm not usually this scattered. I promise it won't happen again," she says as I return to my laptop.

I'm the one answering with a simple nod this time.

She turns her computer off, and once the cooling fans stop spinning, I become keenly aware of the silence surrounding us. She must feel the same way because she grabs her stuff and walks to the door.

"See you tomorrow," she offers, fleeing into the nearly empty office space.

That was … almost courteous. Maybe we can work together after all.

is_new_chapter = True

chapter_number = "06"

pov_name = "Andrea"

I'M NOT REALLY SURE WHAT to make of those ten minutes working with Alexander. He was oddly pleasant and even gave me something that resembled a compliment. And I didn't, at any point, imagine myself slapping his handsome face.

It was … weird.

But despite that, the tension that always fills the air between us was there, as strong as ever. It is strange how Oliver's presence makes me feel calm and comfortable, but I'm tense and jumpy with Alexander. The physical reaction I have to the man frustrates me. Up to this point, I never felt that sort of undesired and unrequited attraction to anyone. Wanting someone I don't actually want is exhausting.

"Is that everything?" Oliver asks, ripping me from my thoughts.

"Uh, I think so, yes," I say, looking at the boxes filling my old car from floor to roof.

Oli is becoming a great friend, which is crazy since we have known each other for less than a week. When he offered to help with my move, I initially refused, not wanting to impose. But he insisted, arguing he didn't mind, so I caved in. Moving nearly got the best of me the first time, even though Kate and my dad helped. Doing it all over again alone would have surely killed me.

We're just done getting everything down from my apartment, and after a quick check to make sure I didn't forget anything, I'll head to Mrs. Godfrey's office to give her back her key.

"I need ten minutes," I explain. "Then we'll drive to Tami's, and after that, you're free."

"Take your time, Hulkette. I'm not in a rush."

The nickname, which he came up with after seeing me carry three boxes at once, makes me chuckle.

"Be right back," I insist.

As I climb up to my studio, I scold myself for not caring for my body like the temple it is. I'm twenty-six, in the prime of my youth, and my fat ass can't even handle the few rounds up and down those stairs we did today.

I look everywhere in the studio, making sure there's nothing left. I cleaned up the best I could, and honestly, it's better than when I moved in, so I decide it's good enough, even though my abuela would disagree.

Mrs. Godfrey is her usual sunshine self when I knock on her door once I'm back downstairs. "Miss Walker, I hope you left the studio in the same state you found it," she bitterly mumbles.

"Wait, do you mean I have to put back those two dead roaches and the three flies?" I ask with sarcasm. She gives me a very unamused glare, and I come closer to hand her the keys. "I'd say it was a pleasure to have met you, but it really wasn't."

She raises one of her poorly drawn eyebrows, not used to being addressed like this. But I have nothing to lose, so I keep going. "I got this for you," I explain, pulling out a tall prayer candle with Jesus plastered on it. I set it on her desk and give her a fake smile. "You should light it and pray for your soul. And next time you try to scam someone, remember that his sky daddy is always watching," I say, pointing at Jesus.

With that, I put my hand forward, still holding the keys, and drop them into her awaiting hand. "Andy out."

I feel light and unburdened as I leave the dreaded building, especially since I finally managed to get rid of that haunting candle my *tia* gave me before I left Portland.

Oli is waiting for me by my car, leaning on it. "All good?" he asks.

"Yep, I'm ready for my new home."

"Let's go, then. I texted Tami to let her know we were on our way."

"Perfect! All aboard!"

As we enter my car, I internally hope it doesn't die on us. It's at least a hundred years old in car years, with peeling paint that I've always known as this pinkish shade even though it's supposed to be bright red, and the doors always creak no matter how much I oil them.

Only when Oli joins me am I reminded of the smell etched into the seats. Three "Hawaiian Dreams" air fresheners are hanging from the rearview mirror, but it's not enough. The resulting scent is tropical cocktails and butts. But no matter how many asses have sat in this car, it's mine, and I love it. I struggled a whole summer at McDonald's to pay for it.

"Sorry for the smell," I say with a wince.

"Believe it or not, I've been in worse cars."

"That, I don't believe," I chuckle.

Half an hour later, we're at my new place. I parallel park miserably the first time and much better when I try again. Oli, thankfully, says nothing. Tami's already here, ready to help me with the boxes.

"Hey, roomie!" I sign with a broad smile.

"Hi, Andy!"

We share a quick hug, and then she does the same with Oli.

"I'm sorry, guys, the elevator malfunctioned during the night, so we'll have to carry everything up the stairs," she explains with a wince.

Oh, God, no! Not this!

After a few seconds, she lets out a small, breathy laugh, and so does Oli. "Sorry, I'm joking," she signs. "He texted me to do it."

I let out a reassured sigh and give Oli's arm a feeble punch. "Ouch! Gentle there, Rocky." He rubs the spot, pleased with his joke.

In barely ten minutes, the car is empty, and we're on the elevator up, pressed against one another.

Between the boxes and the three of us, there isn't much room for comfort. Stuck between Oli and Tami, with my entire front pressed against his, I feel strange. Although there's a pleasant, friendly warmth, there isn't any spark there. Nothing compared to the last time I was plastered against a man in an elevator.

I know for a fact that if it was Alexander Coleman instead of Oli, my entire body would be on fire.

It really isn't fair. Why can't we choose who we desire or love? Everything would be so much easier if I could want Oliver as much as I crave Alexander. I can see it working. We click very well, and the connection of our minds is a rare thing.

I'm almost sure that Oli likes me. His offer to help me out today is proof of it. Why else would anyone endure the nightmare that is moving out? Especially if it's for an acquaintance of five days. Kate—my relationship expert—seems confident that Oli likes me that way. I, however, am not ready yet for more than platonic interactions.

I'm taken out of my thoughts as we reach Tami's floor and the doors part, revealing a corridor with beige walls and blue carpet. We take everything out of the elevator to free it, and she guides us down the hallway.

The main door opens to a small entrance hallway with closets on the walls and a shoe organizer. At the end of that hallway, we enter the living area by two windows, with a cushioned couch, an armchair, and a coffee table made of wooden crates. There's also a sixty-inch flat screen on a low console. Three doors are in front of us, and a kitchen to the left. It looks well-equipped, and although I'm not fond of cooking, I'm glad making meals won't be too much of a chore.

Tami goes for one of the three doors, the one on the right, and opens it before going inside. We follow her, and I discover my new bedroom. It's as warm as the rest of the apartment, with a sash window that leads to the fire exit. My selective brain decides to ignore the fact that it's an easy way in for robbers and only think of the fresh air I can get from there, like in movies. Or maybe to escape a psycho killer. Hopefully, I won't need to.

It takes us another five minutes to get all my boxes in there, and then Tami offers us a cold drink to satiate our thirst. As we sit down to drink it, I pull my phone out and order pizzas and beers for everyone. I need to thank Oli for helping me out and Tami for taking me in.

They're delighted by my offering and insist on helping me unpack as we eat. Oli's in charge of setting up my computer, and Tami gets my kitchen box because she'll know better than me what's redundant.

"That's a nice setup you have here," Oli appreciatively says as he looks through the clear computer case.

"Thanks. I need a new graphics board, but it works well for now."

Instead of answering, he frowns and points to his mouth. "You have …"

"What?"

"You've got—Wait, let me get it for you."

Displaying a boldness I haven't seen from him yet, he reaches for my face and swipes the pad of his thumb under my bottom lip. The pleasant sensation of his gentle fingertip reminds me how desperately touch-deprived I am. A nine-month dry spell will do that.

He shows me his thumb, where there's some tomato sauce. I don't even have time to be embarrassed about it and all but gape when he engulfs it in his mouth. Stunned by how flirty the gesture is, I stand there like an idiot with my mouth open while he returns to the computer to plug the screen in.

Maybe chemistry *can* be fabricated because I'm feeling almost lightheaded now. *Damn …*

It's nearly nine when I escort Oli out. He probably would have stayed longer, but I feel bad about taking even more of his time.

"Thanks again, Oli. I don't know what I would have done without you," I say as we step outside.

"You're welcome, Hulkette. Oh! Almost forgot." He reaches for something in his leather messenger bag, and hands me a small box wrapped in craft paper.

"Are you kidding? You're the one who helped, and *I* get the present?"

"Well, it's a housewarming gift."

I don't even know what to say, staring at him with my jaw hanging open. "Open it before you complain, woman. It's nothing. A trinket," he defends himself.

Since I don't know how to handle his generosity, I say nothing for once. After a brief hesitation, I take the package and carefully rip the paper open. It's a blank cardboard box. The lid opens easily, and a mug reveals itself. I take it out, and a laugh escapes me as I see what's on it. It has to be the ugliest, most kitsch mug I've ever seen, with a sunset, pearly glaze all over, and a dolphin as the handle.

"I know you wanted your own mug at work, and I found this masterpiece at Goodwill, so I had to get it for you."

I gaze up at him with a chuckle. "Thanks, Oli, it's perfect," I say before getting on my tiptoes to kiss him on the cheek. He tenses for a second before a blush slowly creeps up his face. Ah, that's adorable …

"Are you sure you don't want me to pay for an Uber?" I offer, knowing he'll refuse as he did the first four times.

"Yeah, there's a bus going right to my street. We're practically neighbors now," he explains with a wink as he walks backward and away from me. "I'll see you on Monday, Andy! Have fun with the rest of your unpacking!"

"Thanks! And thank you again for everything!"

With one of his trademark friendly smiles, he gives me one last wave and walks away.

I'm still grinning when I return to my new apartment. Tami is in the living room, eyes on the TV where an episode of *Friends* unfolds.

I give her a broad smile when she notices me and head into my new room. I video call Kate to proudly show her I *finally* unboxed my stuff. She's delighted about my improved situation and asks me loads of questions about the neighborhood and Tami. Once we hang up, I have the same call with my parents.

It takes me a couple of hours until I'm completely done unboxing everything, but I finally feel like Seattle can become my home. As I lie in my new bed, showered and ready for the night, I no longer feel like a stranger in a new city.

As I replay the week in my head, my mind inevitably drifts to Alexander Coleman. There's something about him that I can't shake off. Is it because he's terribly intelligent? Or because he seems so unattainable? Oh, it could be that jawline and the stubble that accentuates it. Maybe it's because of how hard his chest was when a bunch of wild lawyers and traders shoved me into it.

My covers become unbearable, so I push a leg out in the colder air of the room. The man really has an effect on me. Especially when I recall how nice he smells, how bewitching his eyes are, his deep voice …

Okay, I need to do something about this horniness because it's getting out of hand. Without a second thought, I pull down my pajama bottoms and underwear and reach for Idris in my nightstand. I finally found it in one of the boxes, where Kate hid it as "motivation to unpack."

With it in hand, I open an incognito tab on my phone, type in my trusted ethical porn site's domain, and start scrolling through the options. I'm picky, so I only find something suitable on page three.

My eyes are glued to the couple on my phone fucking each other to oblivion as my hand travels south to press the vibrating little hole right over my clit. For ten entire minutes, I play my clit like a maestro, but it's not enough. The sensation is enjoyable, but nothing is building up. I'll need ages to come like this.

I'm either not in the mood after all, or the three videos I've tried aren't good enough.

Time to change strategies. I dismiss the phone and close my eyes instead. Pleasure happens in the brain, so it may work if I can focus on it.

I conjure a mental image of a dashing man worshiping me. The dark-haired hunk in my mind slowly moves down my stomach, laying kisses and bites on my skin until he reaches between my thighs. My breathing quickens, and I press Idris a little harder. A shiver runs through my body as I imagine gray eyes gazing up at me, intense and domineering.

Yes! I'm rapidly getting there.

In the fantasy I'm fabricating, the man darts out his pink tongue and slowly samples me. My legs tremble, and I whimper. Fuck, this is working so well. Changing the pressure, I imagine his tongue licking me, teasing my most sensitive spot, his hands holding my thighs apart so that I have no choice but to endure the sweet torture. I can feel my orgasm right around the corner. A few more seconds, and I'll reach it.

I look down in my fantasy, and my whole body goes tense when I see *him*. Alexander fucking Coleman. It's not a vaguely-faced stranger anymore. It's my very real, very alive boss.

My first instinct is to stop everything and remove Idris from my clit, but I'm so, *so* close … With a trembling breath, I close my eyes harder and keep the fantasy alive, imagining my boss devouring me. He isn't so obnoxious now, lowered between my legs, eating me out.

A moan escapes me, and my left leg begins to tremble. In my fantasy, Alexander travels up, laying more kisses on me, and meets my eyes as he whispers, "You taste so fucking good, Andrea." Then, this perfect, not-so-frustrating version of him reaches between us and aligns himself with my soaked opening.

The instant fantasy-Lex thrusts inside me, I tilt into a bone-melting orgasm. I can't contain the small cry that escapes me, but I guess it's okay. If there's one perk to having a deaf roommate, it's that she can't hear what goes on in my room.

I keep Idris pressed right where I need him, drawing out my orgasm until it becomes uncomfortable, and I turn it off. Then, panting and disoriented, what I just did sinks in as I stare up at the white ceiling of my new room.

Fuck. I just gave myself one of the best orgasms of my life thinking of my boss.

What the hell, Andy?!

How am I supposed to face him on Monday? How can I look him in the eye and not think of the fact that I imagined him eating me out?

With a groan, I roll until my face is in my pillow, and let out a frustrated scream.

I'm such a fucking idiot …

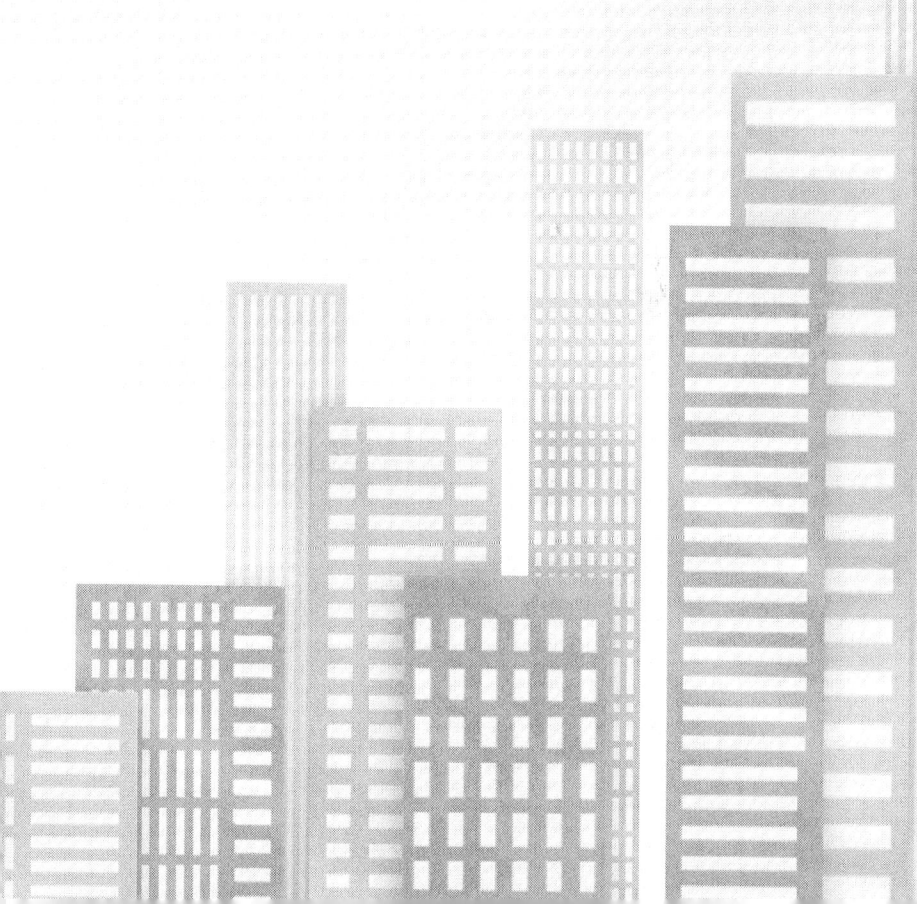

is_new_chapter = True

chapter_number = "07"

pov_name = "Andrea"

AFTER THIS FIRST WEEKEND, I know Tami and I will get along very well. We discovered a mutual fondness for romantic comedies from the early 2000s, as well as a deep appreciation for Mexican telenovelas. To my surprise, she asked that I display some of my figurines and collectibles in the living room, insisting it is also my place now, so my personality is allowed to shine through. She also expressed how much she enjoys that I know ASL, which is a nice change from her past roommates. On Sunday morning, she offered me to join her for her weekly Pilates session in the living room, but I politely declined, arguing my legs were still sore from the move. In all truth, I really don't like exercising. Maybe I'll come around, though. We'll see.

So, instead of Pilates, I sat on the couch and read Kelex's rulebook. Everything's pretty standard, and I was glad to see that relationships between colleagues aren't forbidden, even though they're strongly discouraged. Oliver is exactly the kind of man I need—kind, gentle, attentive, and who knows where that'll lead.

I dedicated the rest of my Sunday to a personal project, which I haven't worked on for a couple of weeks with everything going on. It's something I've been developing for over two years now, and I'm getting closer and closer to finishing it.

And now, it's Monday, and I'll probably have to face my boss again, knowing I climaxed thinking of him. Which isn't great. At all.

Boss problems aside, having someone to sit with on the morning bus rides is nice. Tami and I head to work together, and we get to chat the whole ride.

Maybe I'm not as cursed as I thought because the first thing I see upon turning my computer on is a message from Alexander in our group chat on the company's messaging software.

ALEXANDER COLEMAN: I'm out of town for a personal matter. You all know what you need to work on. Email me if you have questions that can't wait.

That's all we get, per usual. No hello, no goodbye, no nothing. But I'm not really surprised by it, so I guess I'm getting used to our boss being so curt.

Whatever is keeping Alexander out of Seattle lasts almost the entire week. But the dream team is a well-oiled machine, and his absence doesn't prevent us from doing our job and getting things done. He emails us daily instructions in the mornings, and with every day that passes, I grow a little more curious about what's going on. The guys are also intrigued. According to them, Alexander Coleman is a workaholic with barely any personal life, so him being away for an entire week doesn't feel right to them.

As the week goes by, we all accept that we won't see our boss until next week, and I'm okay with that. I'm much more relaxed, and my second week at Kelex is a delight. I even bring my own food to work, as Tami and I take turns preparing two lunches every day. Slowly but surely, I'm getting used to this new life and loving it.

During lunch break on Friday, I start a game of *Donkey Kong* to pass the time until the microwave line is gone. But to my surprise, and to the guys' astonishment, I'm killing it. And the longer I last, the less willing I am to stop.

The whole break flies by, and Mario is still alive and well on the screen. Shit, I'm actually getting closer and closer to the high scores. By my estimate, I need an extra twenty minutes to get in the third position, twenty-five for the second one, and thirty to end up first.

Doing extra time to make up for it is a very mild price to pay for such an exploit. That's why I'm still here, playing and winning when everyone returns to work. The guys have returned to the Lair, and they know that as soon as I die or get a high score, I'll join them.

Because I'm so absorbed by the game, I barely notice when someone comes near me after a while. "How are you still alive?" Oliver asks, impressed.

I shrug my shoulders, knowing it is due mainly to luck. In such games, skills aren't the only parameter. One wrong succession of barrels and tricks can ruin everything. So far, I haven't had one of those. Oli isn't the only one interested in seeing me beat the high scores, because the guys join us in the break room one by one. Mason even comes with a tall glass of water and a straw, which he guides into my mouth so I can hydrate without stopping. This is like the Olympics for nerds.

Only two minutes left until I beat Nammota's lowest score. I can do this—especially with the gang cheerleading around me. They're all rooting for me, and I can't let them down.

"So, this is what happens when I'm away?" a familiarly intimidating voice asks behind us.

Fuck! No! Not now!

An entire week of being God knows where, and he decides to return right now, of all times?!

The guys spin around at once to face our audibly annoyed boss. I somehow find the strength to not look away, hoping they can explain the situation.

Mason is the first to respond with, "Andy is being a baddie."

"She's about to beat Nammota's score!" Brian chimes in.

There's a moment of silence, and I wish I could see Alexander's face. I have no idea if he's impressed, angry, unfazed, or about to fire my ass.

"Does she have to do it during work hours?" he eventually asks, and from his tone, he is definitely angry. *Shit.*

"She started early during the lunch break," Oliver intervenes. "She hasn't died since. But she said she'll make up for the lost time."

"What about all of you? Will you stay as well?" our boss asks. "What about everyone in the open space being disturbed by all your ruckus? You're supposed to work during work hours and relax during your breaks. This machine is here to entertain you, not distract you. If you can't see the difference, it will be removed."

Fuck, I can't stop. I'm so close! Three thousand more points, and I'll move up to third place. Hoping that the guys can negotiate a few extra seconds, I keep playing.

The hairs on my arms go vertical, and I feel Alexander's closeness before I even see him next to me. "You have three seconds to let go of the commands before I fire you," he orders, his tone sinister.

It doesn't even take half a second to make my decision. I release the game instantly and move two steps back, still looking at the screen. With a broken heart, I watch as Mario dies. One thousand more points, and I would have made it.

My score blinks for a moment, and the following screen arrives. Because there's no input for a few seconds, the game registers my score under **AAA**. Now, the leaderboard is **NAM-MOT-AAA-AAA**.

The resentment in my eyes can't be contained when I look at Alexander. But as I gaze at him for the first time in a week, that dreaded fantasy I allowed myself to have surges into my mind vividly. This face that I imagined between my legs is as dashing as ever. And although that mouth that I pictured eating me out is pinched in an angry line, I'd still give my left ovary to feel it on my clit.

Fuck, I never should have masturbated with him on my mind. And I definitely shouldn't have done it again on Wednesday. It's getting in the way of my good sense.

I still glower at him, refusing to let his attractiveness overtake his rudeness.

Alexander gives me one of his warning glares, daring me to say something, to fight his authority. When I don't, he turns to the guys, his eyes dark with anger. "Everyone, back to work. Except you," he adds, pointing at me.

They hesitantly comply, but Oliver stays, ready to defend me. "Lex, she really planned on staying late to compensate."

"I don't care," our boss answers, still glaring at me. I hold his gaze fiercely, fueled by anger. Not breaking eye contact, he adds, "If it will reassure you, I won't fire her." But Oli is still reluctant to go, so Alexander says to me, "Tell your lover boy to go."

My eyes narrow as I resist the urge to slap his obnoxious face. For the sake of Oliver, I hold back and turn to my friend. "It's okay, Oli. I can handle it," I promise. He hesitates, his eyes going from me to our boss, and when I nod, he finally complies and returns to the Lair.

Once we're alone, I muster the courage to face Alexander again. His gray irises are dark like a stormy sky, and I worry about the hurricane coming my way.

"This will be your first and last warning, Andrea. You're here to work, not to mingle, to make friends, to play games … From now on, no more flirting, no more playing, and no more social calls during work hours."

I frown, scandalized by the injustice of this. During my two weeks here, I've seen many employees waste company time more often than I have. Yes, I might not pass as the most assiduous of workers, but I'm far from being the worst. I've been here ten minutes early every day, so those thirty minutes on *Donkey Kong* are already paid for several times over.

"I can see many thoughts running through that pretty head of yours, so let me remind you, I can replace you like this," he explains, lifting his hand and snapping his fingers. That works on me, and I bite my tongue to prevent whatever I want to tell him from spilling out. "Now that things are clear, get back to work and stop distracting your coworkers with your frivolity."

My hands clench on their own on each side of me. This is a fit of anger like I never experienced before. He's right, and I shouldn't have kept playing. But anyone with some compassion would understand where I was coming from.

And I've read the rules; I know they aren't this strict about our hours. We get to pick what's best for us as long as we do the work and get the job done well and on time. It's clear this is targeted at me specifically. He's being a sexist prick, and I can't stand it.

As I look into his murderous eyes, I want to rip his spine out and strangle him with it. Ever since meeting him that first day in the elevator, I've grown accustomed to this man making me feel ungodly things. But this anger is something entirely new to me. I've never felt so dangerously hateful toward anyone before.

But I can't lose this job, so I bottle it all up. After one last loaded glare toward him, I turn around like a well-trained bitch to head back to the Lair. When I enter, the guys send me worried looks. They wait for me to sit down, anxious to know what happened.

"So, what did he say?" Brian asks.

"Apparently, I'm too frivolous and need to stop distracting you guys," I explain, trying to stay calm despite my voice trembling with contained rage.

"I've never seen him so angry," Steven points out. "I get that you probably shouldn't have been playing during work hours, but that was disproportionate."

"Yeah, I don't know what his problem is lately," Mason agrees.

"From my perspective, women are his problem," I say dryly.

"No, Lex isn't like that. Ask any woman here; he's never been out of line."

"Then I guess it's me. I'm his fucking problem."

Without a word, Oliver gets up and comes over to me. He turns my chair, makes me stand, and wraps his arms around me in a reassuring embrace. As his familiar scent fills my lungs, my anger slowly melts away. Behind me, someone else joins in on the hug–Mason. Soon enough, all five of them are hugging me, and their support helps calm me down.

After a while, they let go to get back to work, except Oli, who bends to level his face with mine. "Are you feeling better?" he asks. Forcing a smile, I nod. "Do you want some tea or something?"

I shake my head. "I'm good, thanks. I've wasted enough of your time as it is."

"You're never a waste of time."

My boss might be an asshole, but I have the best coworkers in the world.

Even though I'm brooding the whole afternoon, I do my job and I do it well. By five-thirty, I'm fucking glad to leave this place. I consider staying, as I originally intended, but decide against it. My boss scolding the shit out of me is enough punishment. Just as I'm about to turn off my computer, I receive a message from the internal messaging software.

It's from Alexander.

ALEXANDER COLEMAN: Come up to my office.

Has he changed his mind? After giving it some thought, did he decide to fire me? I stare at the five words as if they might give me cholera. If I don't go up right now and delay it until Monday, maybe he'll change his mind again and not fire me. My pulse quickens. The possibility of losing my job two weeks in is frankly shameful.

I'm still hesitating on what to do when a sixth word makes its way into the conversation.

ALEXANDER COLEMAN: Please.

In my—albeit little—time here, I've never heard him say please. Until this point, I even doubted the word was in his vocabulary. But there they are. Six letters that change everything. He can't possibly want to fire me if he's being this abnormally nice.

My expectations for this man are so fucking low.

"Are you coming?" Oliver wonders, all packed up.

I do a quick Alt+Tab to open my last window and hide the message before turning to my friend. "No, I have one last thing to take care of before I can leave. But go, I'm good."

He exits the Lair after a warm smile and a nod.

Alone in the office, I open the conversation with Alexander and send him a dry:

ANDREA WALKER: Ok.

pov_name =

"Alexander"

NOT EVEN FIVE MINUTES. I didn't even last five minutes back at work before blowing up at Andrea.

With a sigh, I remove my glasses and throw them on my desk. I close my eyes and pinch the bridge of my nose, trying to appease the headache hammering in the back of my skull. I shouldn't have come straight here from the airport. After missing the whole week, I might as well have gone home. But I've been anxious to return after all that time away.

There's too much going on with Kelex to waste four and a half days in Dallas. Especially since I was never close to my paternal grandmother, so I didn't feel the need to attend the unplugging of her life support and then the funeral. But my sisters insisted, so I had to put everything on hold and get on a plane—which I hate—to join the extended Coleman family.

That's why I wanted to ensure everything was alright as soon as I returned and that the team didn't need my help. I didn't expect to find the Lair empty upon arriving. With all the noise they were making in the break room, it wasn't hard to find where my developers had gathered. Part of me knew *she* was the cause of this mess before I even saw her on the arcade machine.

Andrea Walker isn't the exemplary employee I expected. She talks back, sidetracks her colleagues, makes her own rules … But she's also fucking brilliant at her job. She's the most impressively skilled coder I've worked with, and I can't dismiss that. Having her with us is an asset, and it makes up for her being challenging to work with. In all truth, she could work only three hours per day and still be more efficient than any of her colleagues.

That's why I need her to come up here. We must clear the air and restart this whole thing on better terms. I need to lower my expectations regarding her work ethic.

With another tired sigh, I pick up my glasses and slip them on to return to my emails. I handled the important ones while I was away, but I still need to catch up on the rest of them.

My body instinctively tenses when I hear two hesitant knocks on the door.

"Come in."

Slowly, the handle twists and the door opens. Then she appears with her Ghostbusters T-shirt and high-waisted jeans, as well as her bag and a pair of headphones around her neck. She doesn't look at me right away but studies my office with curiosity instead.

The first thing that catches her eye is the floor-to-ceiling windows behind me and the unobstructed view over the city. Then she studies the sleek designer furniture, with gray tones and light woods, and the two anthracite armchairs with a matching sofa by the entrance. Her doe eyes don't give anything away, but maybe she'll finally understand that my rigidity isn't just because I'm the boss. It's a way of life. It's who I am at my core.

When she eventually focuses her attention on me, I look away and to my screen instead. I need a moment to gather myself and make sure this goes well.

"Please, sit, Andrea. I'm almost done," I say, gesturing at the couch.

She docilely complies, and I see her slip her hands under her thighs, visibly nervous. We wait in unbearable silence, which is only interrupted by my efficient typing. Eventually, I roll my chair back and stand up. Her eyes are on me the whole time I approach, which isn't helping the tension within me.

To give myself some time, I remove my glasses, put them on the table as I sit in one of the armchairs facing her. I give myself another few beats to think about what I'll say. She looks worried, probably thinking I'm about to fire her.

"I'm not good at this," I bluntly start. "Kevin is the people person. I'm the brain person. But it's not his job to fix my mistakes."

Already, I see her relax a little.

"About earlier, I'm sorry I lashed out at you. I shouldn't have, and I apologize for it. It doesn't excuse my behavior, but I'm in a poor mood because of a headache that will not go away." I pause, unsure why I feel the need to explain myself like this. "After I returned to my office, I received individual messages from each of your coworkers. They made it abundantly clear that you're a dedicated employee who often works overtime and has an exceptional talent for the job."

She smiles at that, a genuine, touched smile.

"I know I haven't given you any reason to believe this, but although I'm blunt and direct, I'm not a prick, nor a 'sexist asshole,'" I add, air quoting the last part.

She looks confused by that, and it takes her a few seconds to remember what I'm referring to. I should have known upon accidentally reading that text on her first day that she'd be trouble. Keeping an employee who thinks of me as a sexist asshole—but an attractive one—can't be a good idea.

Blood drains from her face as she remembers the text, and I have to refrain from smiling at her shock.

"Don't worry, I've been called much worse," I say to lessen her embarrassment. "And you're allowed your own opinion and to send whatever messages you want to your friends."

"Messages you shouldn't read, by the way," she boldly states, having found her spine.

"I was curious to see what was so important that you'd throw yourself at me."

"You were as into it as I was," she protests, her tongue quicker than her mind, as it often is. "A part of it, I mean."

"Anyhow," I continue after a short silence, "I think we should start anew. You're a valuable asset to the company, and I would hate for our strained rapport to ruin your employment here."

She hesitates, but only for a moment. If I, her superior, want to bury the hatchet, why would she refuse? She has a lot more to lose than me, and she knows it. That's why she eventually nods.

I offer her my hand to shake. "Good evening, I'm Alexander Coleman. I'm a workaholic who rarely—despite appearances—lashes out at my employees."

She barely grins, but I see it. As eager as I am to improve our future interactions, she nods and says, "Hi, I'm Andrea Walker. I might get distracted sometimes, but I always get the job done."

Her soft fingers slip over my palm, and I'm shocked by the intensity of the simple contact. A shiver, so intense it feels like electricity, runs up my arms all the way to my chest. It almost makes me recoil, but I overcome it and keep my composure. Could she feel that too?

Her hand looks small in mine, so my hold isn't as tight as usual.

"It's a pleasure to re-meet you, Andrea," I say. She doesn't return the words as I release her. "Well then, I won't hold you in here any longer," I conclude, grabbing my glasses. "I'm sure you have better things to do on a Friday evening."

"Wait," she says before looking for something in her bag. I'm not sure what I expect, but it's not the bottle of pills she takes out. She pops one out and extends it over the table. "A peace offering."

I don't immediately take it, so she insists with an encouraging nod. "These always work for me, even on the nastiest headaches."

Understanding what it's for, I bring my hand under hers, and she lets the pill fall into my palm. "Thank you, Andrea."

"You can call me Andy since everyone else takes that liberty," she says humorously—a clever callback to her first day here.

I don't have time to respond before she stands from the couch. "See you Monday, then."

Ah, yes. Formalities. "Have a good weekend," I respond.

Still seated, I watch as she nods and leaves. For the first time in a while, our interaction didn't go entirely wrong. Looking down at the pill in my palm, I feel somehow relieved.

We fixed things.

is_new_chapter = True

chapter_number = "08"

pov_name = "Andrea"

SATURDAY NIGHT, I HAVE THE most vivid sex dream of my life. Turns out my talk with Alexander didn't decrease my ridiculous attraction to him but exacerbated it instead. There was something about that man apologizing and trying so hard to earn my forgiveness that just did it for me.

After waking up with a startle because of it, I toss and turn in bed for about an hour before deciding to take Idris out. With my eyes closed, I relive the intense fuckery my subconscious came up with during my sleep. I can still hear his low, enraptured voice saying, "Look at how wet you are for me, Andrea. Such a messy girl …" Understandably, I bring myself to orgasm in less than three minutes.

I really have to stop thinking about him when I masturbate, but the relief is too good, even if it's short-lived. And it knocks me right into sleep every single time.

When I wake up again, I can hear Tami in the kitchen. After twenty minutes of doom scrolling on my phone, I kick my covers off and get up. Following the breakfast she cooked, we head out to the farmers' market a few blocks away, which is there every Sunday. The fresh air and sun have an excellent effect on me, and the distraction is much needed.

I might have made peace with my frustrating boss, but I still want to fuck his brains out. And that's not a very healthy mindset.

Once we return home, with our shopping bags full of fresh veggies, fruits, and a rotisserie chicken, Tami settles in the living room to video call some relatives, and I go to my room to work on my project.

My body isn't cooperating, and my mind is constantly drifting. It's particularly hard to focus, with too many thoughts occupying my brain. I had the best sex of my life with my boss. In a dream, yes, but still.

Who even does that?!

After three hours of fastidious and unsatisfying work, I need a new series of tests to move forward. I head out with everything I need and find Tami watching an episode of *Friends*.

The show is slowly growing on me, but Ross always gets on my nerves. Because of that, I can never watch a whole episode. Living with Tamika, who watches it on a loop, I'm learning that Chandler makes up for Ross's annoying and whiny personality, though.

"Could you give me a hand on my project?" I sign when she looks my way. She nods, pressing pause on the remote. "Great! I need to do your nails before we start, though."

"Yay! Girl time," she signs before rushing to the bathroom.

I only meant nail polish, but she insists on a full manicure. We watch two episodes as we do our hands, and I rather like it. Tami can't read all the closed captions, but she basically knows the episodes by heart and always looks up to see the important bits. Once we're done extermina-ting cuticles and filing our nails, we choose which nail polish we want. I need vivid colors for my app, so Tami decides on a carrot orange while I opt for the lapis lazuli. Her nails are a nice length and look great, which makes me feel bad about my short ones. I should grow them, but I hate the clicky sound of long nails on a keyboard.

"So, I got the idea for this app from Rafael—my brother—who complained about how hard dating is for people who are deaf or hard of hearing," I explain to her as the second coat dries, making sure I don't damage them as I sign. "The goal is that when you go on a date, you have the app on two phones, and you settle them like this," I conti-nue, sitting on the floor on the other side of the table to face Tami. I brought two phones with me earlier, and I set them down vertically, one facing me, one facing her, on a small support I built for this.

"The camera on mine will analyze the movements of your hands and translate what you're signing into written sentences on my screen as you go. Your phone will listen to what I say, analyze my lips to make sure it isn't taking someone else's words, and then put it into written sentences."

Tami's eyebrows shoot up, impressed. "You did this on your own?"

"I did the programming, yes, and my family helped. I needed a data-base for the software to analyze signing movements and compare them. My mom, dad, abuela, Rafael, and even Kate spent hours in front of a camera, signing hundreds of words five times each, so I could compile them into the data analysis algorithm. Then, it uses an AI system to build the most likely sentence. There's also a whole part I'm still poli-shing where you can pick a voice uniquely created to fit you, and it speaks what you sign. But I don't need to test that right now."

"Why the nail polish?"

"The server I'm using for the algorithm isn't powerful enough to analyze the complete hand. For now, it mostly tracks the tips of the fingers, and the bright colors help."

Once I'm sure everything's ready, I give her an encouraging nod. "You can go ahead and sign whatever you want," I say without signing this time. She smiles when my words appear on the screen facing her. Enthusiastically, she signs something in return.

American Sign Language isn't like the spoken language, as one might imagine. The hardest part of my project was working out the artificial intelligence in charge of rearranging the sentences. It has to differentiate the words and their roles in the sentence.

ASL structures sentences based on their functions, which are often divided into categories like time, subject, verb, and object. The app then has to put them back in the proper order and add in the small words that are not typically signed, like articles and some conjunctions. Facial expressions also come into play, as they can alter the meaning of a sentence and add nuance. The whole thing was a nightmare to work through, but I'm almost done perfecting it.

Tamika literally signs, "T-A-M-I-K-A I am. Happy meet you," which is what the screen writes at first. However, ASL being quite complicated, she could also have signed, "I who? T-A-M-I-K-A. I happy meet you." Once she's done signing, the app rearranges the words to translate them into, **I'm Tamika. I'm happy to meet you.**

A wide smile stretches my lips, and she jumps from the couch to see the results. An incredulous expression appears on her face. "That's awesome!" she signs.

We exchange like this for about an hour, as I write every adjustment I need to make on a notepad. When my brain is about to explode, I suggest a break and review my notes.

"You should show this to Lex or Kev. They'll lose their minds," Tamika signs with enthusiasm.

"It's not quite ready yet. I need more data to compare signs and form sentences."

"It's impressive, Andy. What do you need to make it work?"

"I've been downloading hours and hours of TV programs with a sign language interpreter in the bottom corner. I need to transcribe the spoken speech into text and then use that to turn the interpreter's gestures into usable data."

"Aren't there other existing databases you can use?"

"A good start would be to have access to the national ASL data, but when I asked for it they refused," I sourly recall.

"What if I knew someone who could hack into it?"

"You do?"

"Last year, my Facebook account was hacked, so I went to the nerds to see if one of them could help me out. Oliver volunteered, and he not only got my account back, but also found the asshole responsible for the hack and filled his computer with viruses."

I let out an incredulous laugh. Oli has some mad moves. I'm touched that he rescued a damsel in distress, but it doesn't surprise me. Oliver is the real MVP.

The rest of the day is spent considering Tamika's suggestion. She's right—my app is precisely the type of work Kelex would love to be a part of.

But for that to be possible, I need to ask for Oli's help. If he can get me that data, then maybe I'll show my app to Alexander. The man who so rudely invades my dreams.

Fun times ahead.

is_scene_break = True

SLEEPING OFTEN HELPS WITH THE decision-making process. And that's precisely what happens. When I wake up on Monday, I know exactly what I need to do.

Like Tami said, Kelex has the means to carry this project to the finish line with better servers and manpower. That's why the first thing I do when I arrive at work is head to Oli's desk.

"Hello, son of Paul," I greet him.

He turns around, already grinning. "I'm sorry to break it to you, but while my surname *is* Paulson, my dad's name is actually Jared."

I let out a false, shocked gasp. "Is everything a lie?!"

He chuckles. "It gets worse. My mom's also named Paulson, but she's the son of no one. She's a daughter."

Another gasp, with my hand on my chest this time. "When will the lies stop?!"

He laughs frankly this time, and I break character to grin with him.

"What can I do for you on this fine morning?" he asks.

With a low voice, I explain, "I need you to … hack into something."

Surprise has his eyebrows raising and his eyes widening. "Say what now?"

"Well, Tamika told me you have a very particular set of skills, skills you have acquired over a very long career. Skills that I really, really need right now."

The movie quote seems to work on him, and his smile returns as he shakes his head with amusement. "Okay, I guess the secret is out. What do you need from me?"

Making sure the others can't hear, I explain everything to him. It's not a big hack, but I've always been too scared of my mom to do anything remotely illegal like this, so I lack the knowledge to do it myself. "I'd do it myself, but I have a Tamagotchi to take care of," I pretend with humor once he's up to speed.

"I have an actual living cat that needs to be fed twice a day."

"Oh, right! I actually saw it on your Facebook profile."

"You stalked my Facebook?"

Shit. I did, yes. To see if he had a girlfriend. He doesn't.

"What's the cat's name?" I ask, not-so-subtly changing the subject.

"Her name is Princess Twilight Sparkle," he answers. I offer him a dubious look, thinking he's messing with me again. "She's my little sister's, who's off to college. I still have two years with Princess Twilight Sparkle."

"I see ..."

Silence settles between us, but he's quick to fill it again. "What do I get in exchange for the favor?"

"Well, I don't know. Do you have something in mind?"

He thinks about it for a moment. "I like to eat, and I'm free Friday evening."

"Then I'll treat you to dinner. I still don't know the good spots in Seattle, so you'll have to help me pick a place."

"I thought I'd invite you, actually," he corrects me.

"But I'm the one thanking you, not the other way around."

"I don't want our first date to be about repaying a debt."

His confidence surprises me, making my cheeks flush as my heartbeat hastens. The white knight in shining armor, the funny, smart, gentle Oli, wants a date with me. Here I am, having wet dreams about our boss, and he's planning our first date.

For once, I'll listen to good sense. Oliver is perfect for me in many ways, and there's no reason things wouldn't work out. We'll go on a date, things will be great, he'll be perfect, and eventually, I'll end up falling in love with someone for the first time in my life.

"Alright, Friday, then," I agree. "We'll find another way for me to repay you."

As I turn back to my desk, I see the guys quickly resuming their tasks, proving they were following my exchange with Oliver rather than working. Hmm, maybe we should have been a little more discreet about this.

Only Brian isn't pretending to not care, opening his mouth to say something. "Shut up, Brian," I say with a teasing smile, silencing him before he can speak.

is_scene_break = True

THANKS TO OLI'S HELP, I make momentous progress on my app in the following days. By Thursday, I feel confident enough to show it to him during our lunch break. He's more than impressed by what I created, and just like Tami, he insists that I must show it to our boss.

"We tried and failed to do what you did a few years back," Oli explains. "Lex will lose his mind when he sees how well you've done alone. You can be sure he'll never treat you like a newbie again."

The idea of showing my arrogant boss what I'm capable of is tempting. I'm not one to brag or show off, but proving to the pretentious genius that I'm as good as him, if not maybe better for this project in particular, would definitely feel great.

I know we've agreed to some kind of truce, and wanting to put him back in his place is wrong, but I can't help it. Weeks later, I'm still not over the fact that he thought I was a fraud on my first day here. Even though he apologized, I'm still pretty confident he's an asshole.

I've been avoiding him like the plague because every time I see him, I'm reminded of those fantasies I conjure whenever I take Idris out. This silent treatment is bad for our boss-employee relationship, but strategically, it makes sense. I can't help but think about his dreamed dick inside me, his voice whispering sensuous things to me, his warm mouth pleasing me … I daydream about it sometimes, absentmindedly staring at him when he's downstairs with us. He caught me doing it once, and the shame that invaded me turned my face crimson. Being constantly reminded that I find my boss attractive is frankly unfair.

"I'll give myself one more evening to work on it," I tell Oli. "Then it should be good enough."

"Trust me, he'll be impressed. You might even get a compliment out of him. Last time, three of us were working on it for about four months, full time, and we didn't even reach a quarter of what you've accomplished."

Alright, then … My app may be enough as it is. Tomorrow, Alexander Coleman will learn a lesson.

I work late into the evening to polish the app, which isn't optimal. I have my first date with Oli tomorrow, and I'll look like shit for it. But I'm proud of the improvements I made, even though I'm slowly reaching the limits of my means. Hopefully, showing it to Alexander will change that.

The first thing I do when I arrive at work the next day is send a message to our boss using the internal messaging app. My fingers tremble the whole time I type it, my heart drumming against my ribs.

ANDREA WALKER: Good morning. If you have a moment today, I'd love to show you something I've been working on.

He answers a few minutes later with his usual dryness.

ALEXANDER COLEMAN: I'll see if I can find the time.

I spend my morning anxiously waiting for a message offering me to come up. The longer it takes to arrive, the more stressed I am about it.

When I'm not thinking about Alexander, I'm obsessing over tonight. I'm excited about my date with Oli, I think? But also a little worried. I haven't had a first date in ages. I *hate* first dates. The weirdness of them, the awkward tension …

That's why I'm more silent than usual as I eat lunch with Tami and Dakota. Of course, my roommate brings up my date with Oli, so it becomes the topic of discussion. She's glad to see I'm taking the leap. I suspect she may have a little crush on Oli, which is why she's so adamant that I don't miss my shot with him.

And because I had the brilliant idea to tell Kate, my best friend is also invested in this. From what I told her about Oli, she's convinced he's perfect for me, but as much as I want to think of her as a reliable source where relationships are concerned, I can't. Katherine Knox has famously terrible taste in men despite being such a clever and accomplished woman. She's as stunning as a Victoria's Secret model—face *and* body—and could have anyone she wants. Alas, her type seems to be self-absorbed idiots who think they're God's gift to humanity.

"Don't have sex with him on the first night. Dry hump him to give him just a taste," Dakota casually suggests, making me choke on my Coke.

I'm most definitely not doing *that.*

As the afternoon progresses, I accept that Alexander won't find time for me today, and I decide it's okay. It'll give me the weekend to work on it, which will make the app even better when he's ready to see it.

The closer it gets to five-thirty, the more my eyes drift to the corner of my screen to check the time. I'm filled with both apprehension and excitement. I'm not entirely sure I want this date, but I know for certain I need it. For so many reasons, it's the right thing to do.

Literally five minutes before it's time to go, I get a notification from Alexander.

ALEXANDER COLEMAN: I have a moment now.

Now?! Seriously? Minutes before the weekend? *Son of a—*

"Everything good?" Oli asks, standing next to me.

With a dramatic sigh, I slump back into my chair, pointing at the screen. "I swear, I hate this man."

Oli looks at the message and then winces. "Oh …"

"I'll politely tell him to go fuck himself."

"No, you should go see him. It's important."

Showing Lex the app is important, but so is our date. "I'll give him the fastest presentation ever and then rush home to get ready," I suggest.

"Don't botch it for me, Andy. If you run late, it's okay. We can have our date another time."

Somehow, Oli being so sweet and understanding doesn't help. On the contrary, it makes me feel like even more of an asshole. "I promise I'll make up for it."

"Yeah, yeah … Go get 'em, tiger," he replies with a wink.

I have all my things with me when I reach our boss's door, in case I can still get home in time. As I raise my hand to knock, I'm reminded that I'm about to spend some time with Alexander. Alone. In his office. I haven't actually interacted with him in a week, and I will be alone with him while everyone else has either left or is in the process of doing so.

What could go wrong with that?

After mustering the entirety of my courage, I give the door three firm knocks.

"Come in, Andrea."

Hearing him say my name brings back the dreaded memory of my vivid sex dream. My skin tingles, the tiny hairs on my arms rising. *Look at how wet you are for me, Andrea …*

Oh, how I want to punch myself.

is_new_chapter = True

chapter_number =

"09"

pov_name =

"Alexander"

ALTHOUGH I DIDN'T DO IT on purpose–Kev and I spent the afternoon on a video call with a tech manufacturer in Korea–I was hoping that by messaging Andrea so late in the day, she'd give up and reconvene on Monday. But that was stupid of me. That woman is too relentless for that.

So now, we'll have to spend some alone time in my office on a Friday evening—again.

I thought we were okay now, considering our talk last week. But it isn't lost on me that she has avoided me every day since. I'm unsure why she wants to see me now, but I expect the encounter to be tense, like always.

Making a poor first impression is the norm for me. I'm not good at meeting new people and don't particularly enjoy it. My world is small and predictable, and I like it that way. I have a handful of old friends, and that's good enough for me—quality over quantity.

But it's been a while since someone has had such a guttural reaction to me, and although it never bothered me in the past, I dislike it this time around. It's not like I want Andrea Walker to like me, but I'd rather she didn't hate me. It seems that I fucked it up, though, and changing her opinion of me would take much more effort than I'm willing to make.

Ultimately, she doesn't have to like me as long as she respects my authority and keeps working for us.

She walks in with all her things, as well as a laptop bag. She doesn't wait for instructions and marches up to my desk. "'Evening," she greets me.

My desk is neatly organized, with my computer on one side and nearly nothing on the other, so someone could sit in front of me, and we wouldn't be blocked by anything. That's where she sits down to take her laptop out. My eyes remain on her as she prepares everything with efficient moves, and then she looks up at me for the first time since she came in.

Today, she's wearing a T-shirt with the logo of the Hello World Convention on it, which piques my interest. "Have you ever attended?" I ask, pointing at the graphic.

She looks down and understands what I mean. "Oh, no. This is some merch I got from their website. I've always wanted to go, but it's for professionals only, and the small company I worked for didn't have the budget for the trip."

"I see."

We have been attending the prestigious convention every year since Kev and I created Kelex, and this year, he even wants us to have our own presentation there. I don't say that, though, because I fear it'll sidetrack whatever she's here for.

She hesitates on how to start, her eyes tracing over my shirt for a moment, halting around my collar. I'm reminded that I opened a couple of buttons right after the video call because it was smothering me. The pressure she's putting on herself to show me whatever she's here for has her tense and flushed.

When she meets my eyes again, she almost seems flustered by it.

"You have something you want to show me?" I ask, using my most amiable voice.

"Yes, sorry. Um … I have been working on an app to help my brother because dating is hard for him. Oh, he's deaf, by the way," she adds, even though I remember that detail from her cover letter. "So, I thought I would create an app to help him. It turned out to be a little more arduous than I thought. It was supposed to take me a couple of months, and I'm over two years in now, with a lot of things still to improve."

Rambling isn't something I'm used to from her. She's usually so determined and confident that I wonder what she's about to show me. It must be something close to her heart since it has her twisting her hands before her, fingers picking at her chipped blue nail polish.

"The idea was to turn any phone into an ASL Rosetta Stone," she explains, turning her laptop around so it faces me.

The screen is divided into three parts: the webcam filming her in the top left corner, an empty text box in the lower left, and lines of code taking the whole right side.

Dismissing her anxiousness, she signs something for the camera.

Perplexed, I see the code get into action, and in the empty box, text appears. At first, it's the literal translation of the signs she just did, but it then turns into a proper sentence.

Hi, I'm Andrea. It's Friday evening, and I want to go home.

The shock of it has me freezing all over. There's no way. She can't have done it.

"Sign something else," I command, bending forward to see better as I adjust my glasses.

I'm focused on the code, so I don't see what she signs. But another sentence appears, perfectly translated. **Polite people say please.**

I gaze at her from over my glasses. "Sorry."

She did it. She actually did it. She cracked sign language recognition, which is something I've been trying to do for years.

Dazzled, I lean back in my chair and remove my glasses to pinch the bridge of my nose with closed eyes. All that information is hard to process at once. After a few seconds like this, I return to my original position.

"Andrea, this is incredible."

The utter delight on her face reminds me that I don't compliment people enough. She should know just how amazing what she did is. She shouldn't be this surprised that I'd find it extraordinary.

"Thank you," she says, flustered once more. "And I did it all on my own. My brother didn't even help me," she adds, reminding me of the misunderstanding when she started here. I probably shouldn't have implied she had help for the test, but my rational mind refused to accept the truth.

"Can I see some of the code you came up with?" I ask, pointing at her computer.

"Sure."

She joins me behind the desk and opens a script. It has to be her most impressive one, with thousands of lines of code. I'm so enthralled by it that I barely pay attention to her presence so close to me, or her flowery scent filling my lungs. This is eons ahead of everything we did when we tried to accomplish the same thing a few years ago.

I've known for a while that she was a sensational coder. But this goes so much further than my expectations. She single-handedly created one of the most impressive applications I've ever seen.

Humbled and overwhelmed, I turn to her instead. She swiftly looks away, but I gather she was staring at me, probably curious to guess my reaction from my facial expressions.

As she reads the code on the screen, I quickly take her in. It's as though she's getting prettier every time I see her. Her profile is gorgeous, and I've grown to appreciate her slightly messy curls. Her plump mouth has been invading my thoughts, even though I've barely seen her in these past two weeks. The cushiony swells of her lips beckon sin, and

I'm ashamed at how much I've been thinking of them on me—even in my sleep.

Between my grandmother's passing and everything else, I haven't gotten around to finding a new bed partner. Celeste isn't an option unless I'm willing to endure more of her demands for something serious between us. As I look at Andrea, I realize I don't want to find some random woman for some mindless release. She would pale in comparison, and I would still end up frustrated and lusting after my new employee.

No, what I crave deep down isn't just sex. It's *her.* I want to fuck her brilliant brains out. Anything other than that wouldn't be enough. Not anymore.

The thought of it has my cock swelling under my desk. The way it presses against my slacks is enough to bring me back to the moment, and I tear my gaze away and back to the screen.

"How much?" I bluntly ask.

"Um, I'm not sure. I spent well over one thousand hours on it, I'd say."

"I meant how much do you want for it?"

"Oh ..."

For some reason, this seems to be the last thing she expected me to say. But why would she show me her app if not for that?

Taken by surprise, she opens and closes her mouth several times, trying and failing to speak. When she does, she stumbles on her words.

"Uh, at a rate of fifty-five dollars per hour, which is my current salary, it would mean something along the lines of sixty thousand dollars, which seems both too much and too little. I don't want to pass for an underachieving idiot or a greedy imbecile, so how much would *you* pay for it?"

I gaze at the door, knowing I'll get an earful if Kevin hears of this. He's a ruthless business shark, but it's not my style.

"What I'm going to tell you doesn't leave this room. Is that clear?" I gravely ask. Perplexed, she nods. "For a tool like this one, finished and operational, we could be willing to spend around two million for its exclusive usage."

Her eyes widen and her lips part with shock as she understands that her life is about to change drastically.

And the first thought that comes to my mind is that, even though she's about to be rich enough to quit and stay home all day, I hope she doesn't.

pov_name =
"Andrea"

UPON HEARING LEX'S ESTIMATION, MY first thought is, Goodbye precooked meals, hello deliveries!

And the first sentence I formulate is, "Two million … dollars?"

He looks wholly unimpressed by that and answers, "No, rupees." His sarcasm takes me by surprise, and I can't even take offense to his tone. Yep, I deserved that one.

"Although yours is well-advanced, it still isn't finished, so the value decreases. Furthermore, you're a single individual, not a company, so once more, the price lessens."

Still hung up on the cold two mil he dropped on me, I'm not registering much of what he says. He notices and snaps his fingers in front of my face. "Focus, Andrea, I will only tell you this once. I have to check the extent of your work, but given what I've seen, the price you ask for should range between four to six hundred."

"Four to six hundred … thousand?" Okay, I need to shut the fuck up until my brain works again.

He doesn't even bother to answer me this time. "I can help you determine the exact value of your work if you want. I'll be the one assessing it anyway if you want to sell it to us."

"Why?"

"Why what?"

"Why are you being so honest? I mean, you can tell me pretty much any number—I don't know any better. Why are you not trying to scam me?" Or maybe he is, but he's great at hiding it.

He leans back in his chair, crossing his arms over his chest. I try to ignore how his bulging muscles stretch the fabric of his shirt, making his impressive physique even more stunning, but I'm a lost cause.

He's wearing a light blue button-down today, and the sleeves are rolled up, revealing his powerful forearms and the sparse dark hair on them. To add to his state of looseness, a few buttons are undone at his throat. I try to stop myself, but my eyes lower to the skin exposed. This is like a Bermuda Triangle, and something mystical keeps pulling me to it. His chest is tanned, like the rest of him, and I can see dark hair peeking out from the opened shirt.

"I'm not opposed to negotiating harsh prices with other companies," he explains, commanding my eyes to look up. "They have the backbone to sustain it, and it's the law of the market. But dealing with individuals, especially one of our employees, is different. Also, you're a smart woman. You can find out the truth and sell it elsewhere."

His justification makes sense, but the only thing I can think of is that he thinks I'm smart. I didn't expect him to be this honorable.

"I already told you I wasn't an asshole," he reminds me. I flinch, disconcerted to see I'm so transparent. Kate always tells me my expressive face is terrible at hiding my feelings, and this might be proof of it. "So, do you want to do an initial assessment of what your work is worth?"

I nod energetically. Hell yeah, I do!

He goes around his desk and grabs the visitor's chair—where I sat earlier—to settle it next to his in front of my computer. It isn't a small, light chair, but some kind of heavy designer armchair, and he moves it easily, veins bulging in his forearms.

It isn't helping my case to know that this man has enough strength to lift me up against a wall, keep me there for a while, and barely break a sweat. A mental image of Alexander fucking me with passion against one of the walls of his office, his perfect naked body shining with perspiration as he ravages me with deep, hard, and powerful thrusts, makes its way into my brain.

His lovely packaging has me forgetting all about the unpleasant interior.

The dry sound the chair makes when he settles it down takes me out of my naughty thoughts. Ugh, Idris is obviously not enough to contain my libido.

He literally just moved a chair, and that's enough to make me feral.

We explore my work together while I avoid glancing at him as much as possible. I'm not very good at it.

He has a gorgeous profile, with a straight nose perfectly balanced with the rest of his features. In my fantasies, when he slowly kisses my heated skin, his mouth is always tantalizingly soft and gentle. Would it be the same in real life?

Lord, it's ridiculous how much I'm drawn to him. I'm close enough to smell his cologne, something deep and heady, but he isn't wearing too much of it, so it isn't unpleasant. I observe the sharp line of his jaw, the grain of his skin and scruff …

Even when I force myself to stop peering at him, his smart brain is enough for my body to maintain a constant flush. I'm continually impressed by how quickly he catches up with my intentions, and how fast he comes up with ways to correct or improve problematic elements.

Forty-five minutes into our talk, I send a text to Oli. It's clear that I can't make it, as we've barely scratched the surface. Oli's reply comes quickly, and my heart twinges as I read it. He insists it's fine and expresses how proud he is of me.

I feel extremely guilty because a small part of me is relieved we won't have our date tonight. And I hate myself for it.

But I'm distracted away from that as we go back to work. We spend another hour on everything, and I can't get enough of Lex's appreciation for my work. He's aware of the immensity of what I programmed and voices it a few times throughout.

Eventually, when we reach the end of his appraisal, he leans back in his chair and silence fills the air. I slip my hands under my thighs, not sure what comes next. When it becomes awkward, I glance at him sideways. He's holding his folded glasses, and his eyes are on me. There's something unfamiliar in his gaze, almost as if he is enthralled. It's strange, coming from the brooding man he is, but I guess this app could really be game-changing for the company.

For several seconds, he keeps looking at me strangely, until I clear my throat to break the awkward tension. That snaps him out of it, and he returns his attention to the complex script displayed on my laptop.

"Do you want to sell it to us, or would you rather explore your options?" he asks, very businesslike.

I don't need to think much about it before saying, "I like Kelex's values, and I know that a tool like this would be made accessible for all, unlike so many other companies. I'd rather know it's in good hands than make more money. And I'd also love to be part of the team that brings it to the finish line. So, yes, I'd like to sell it to you."

"Good," he agrees with a nod. "We're supposed to wait for the sale to come through before we can start working on it," he says. "However, I would like it if we could start as soon as Monday. The app could be released in six months to a year, and I don't want to waste a day."

Wow, that's even faster than I imagined. "I don't see why we couldn't. But I need some kind of contract stating that Kelex will make me a fair offer for the app so I'm sure I won't get scammed."

"I'll have it prepared."

"Oliver is already involved in the project, so I thought maybe I could work with him on it," I suggest.

"No," he counters dryly. *No?* What does he mean, *no*? "Mason and Steven are more qualified to work on it. They are far better when it comes to movement recognition, deep learning algorithms, and artificial intelligence. I'll assign you a few people from the sub-dev team to help with smaller details. We'll also get two or three people from the graphic department so they can start sketching and find a concept."

Mace and Steven? Well, I have no problem with them. But I do feel sorry for Oli. He would love to work on this with me. It isn't rare for us in the Troll's Lair to help each other, so maybe we'll get to work together, anyway. I'm honored that I'll have my own little team to manage so soon after starting here.

"Alright, I'll work closely with Mace and Steven, then."

"No," he counters with the same authority as before. "I'll have your computer set up here. You'll work with me."

Naturally, I'm confused as fuck and think he's messing with me. But his serious expression proves he isn't, in fact, joking. My amusement dies instantly, and blood drains from my face.

What the hell just happened?!

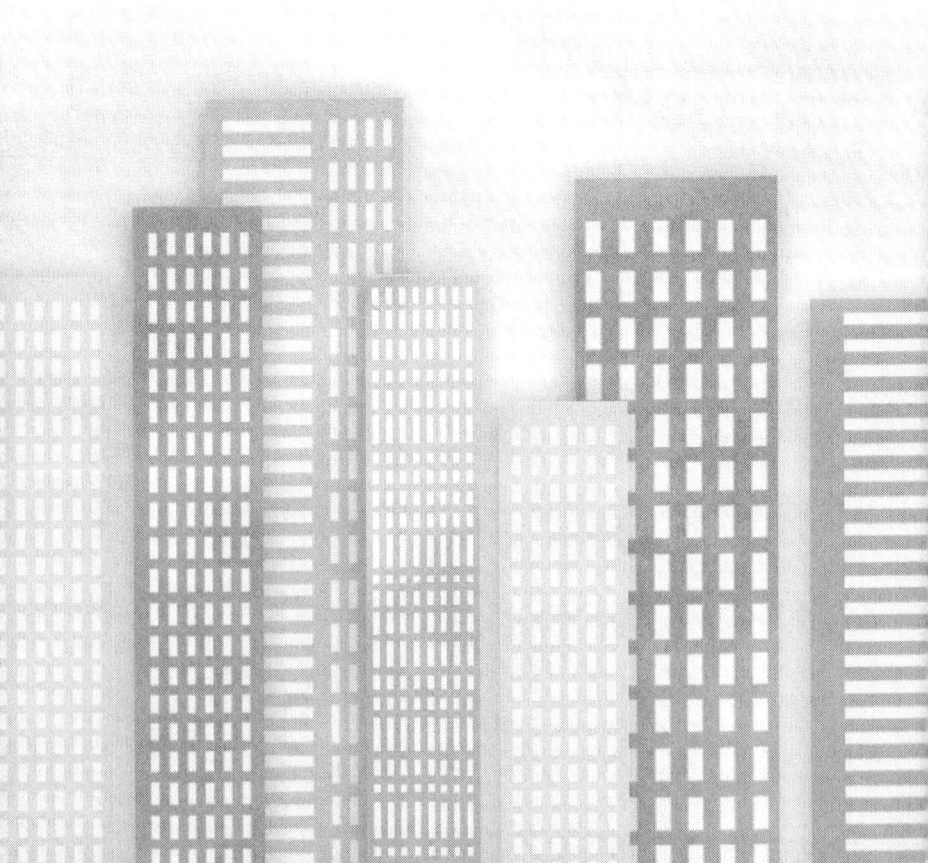

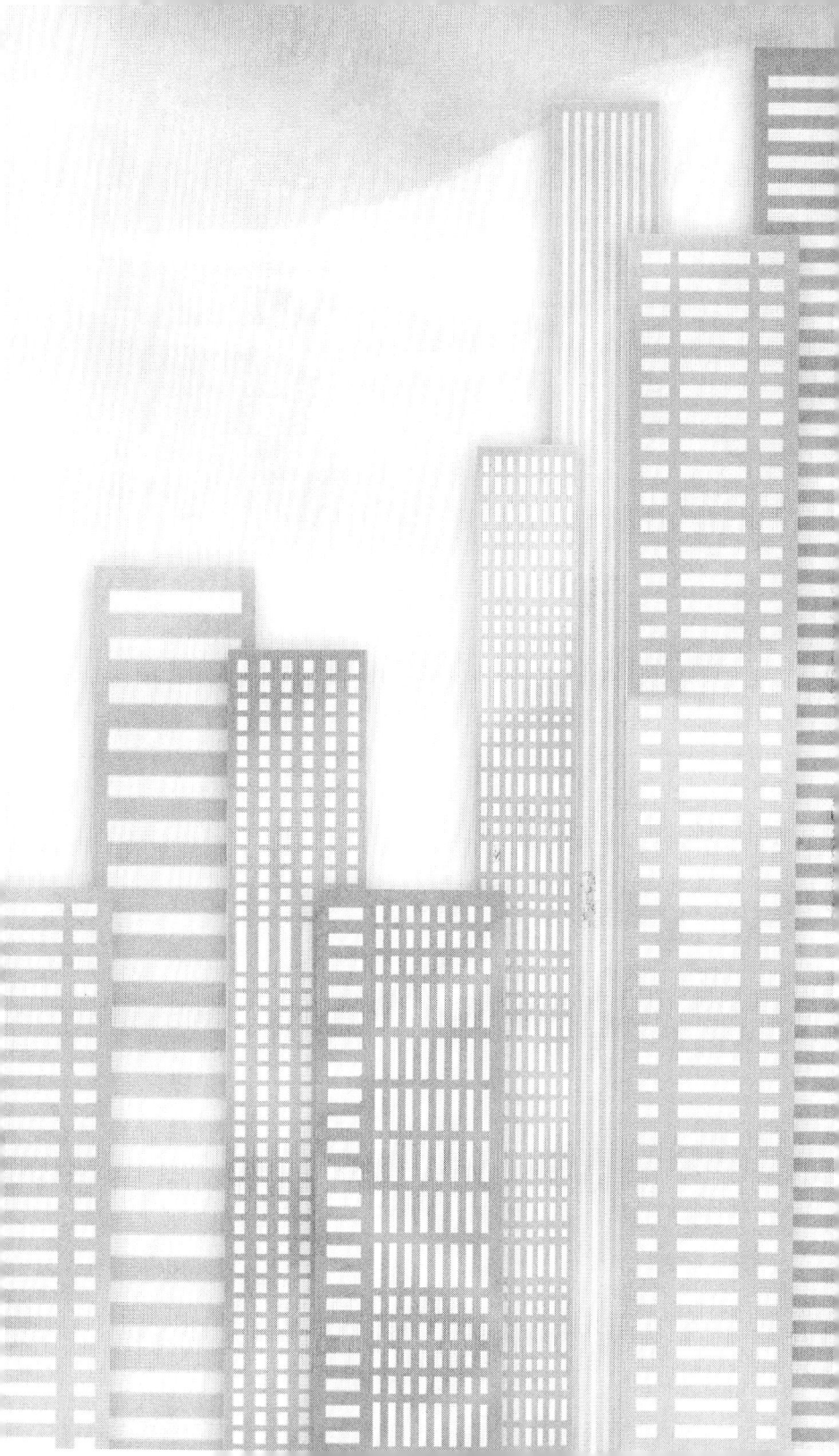

is_new_chapter = True

chapter_number = "10"

pov_name = "Andrea"

We're the only ones on the elevator ride down, which makes sense because it's really late. I'm tense everywhere, doing my best to ignore how isolated we are. He hasn't bothered putting on his jacket, so it rests over his forearm. I'm still reeling from the fact that I'll have a temporary desk in his office. Frankly, I still think it's some kind of long-winded joke he's pulling on me. No way he means it.

"I'm sorry for keeping you here so late," he says, breaking the silence in the small space. "I hope you didn't have any plans."

There's no point in guilt-tripping him for a decision I made myself, so I reply, "Nothing that couldn't be rescheduled." Then, I impulsively ask, "Are you *sure* you want me to work in your office?"

"It'll only be for a month. Two at best. Just enough time for us to get the ball rolling."

I face the stainless steel door again with a, "Hmm …"

He leans to the side toward me, and when I gaze up, he's holding back a smirk. "I swear I'll try not to insult you too often."

The self-deprecation in his voice makes a giggle bubble in my chest. Maybe he isn't as conceited as I thought.

Moments later, we reach the lobby. "Are you okay getting home?" he asks.

"Yes, I'm pretty sure the buses do their routes until midnight."

"I can drop you off if you want."

Although the offer is both generous and tempting, there's no way I'll sit with him in his car for twenty minutes. "I'm good, thanks." Before he can insist, I step out. "I'll see you on Monday," I say, forcing a smile. "Enjoy your weekend."

"You too. Thank you again for your time."

Seriously, I'm not getting used to this man being polite and pleasant.

A sense of relief fills me when the panels close behind me. Phew … I did it! I survived an entire evening by his side without spontaneous combustion or a heated argument. I need an underwear change, though.

My satisfaction goes to shit when I reach the revolving doors. It's raining cats and dogs. Fuck. Since it's not like I have a choice, I step out and walk at a quick pace, desperate to reach the bus stop before I'm soaked to the bone. Thankfully, my computer bag is waterproof, so I'm not risking much more than a cold. The street is eerily empty, without a car or person in sight. I'm reaching the corner of the building when a sleek gray car, a Mercedes halfway between a sedan and a sports car, slows down next to me. Just as I'm about to pick up the pace, the passenger window opens.

"Get in, Andrea. I'll drop you off at your bus stop."

Oh, fuck … It's *him.*

"I'm good," I answer. I don't like commanding tones, which is another reason why our dynamic is complicated.

"Stop being so stubborn for half a second and get in."

When I halt my steps, he hits the brakes. As we determinedly stare at each other, I try to remember why I shouldn't get into his car. Maybe I'm overreacting a little bit.

I know I'm just being stubborn again, like he said, so I bite my tongue and obey for once. My face is a mask of discontent as I walk to his car, and it remains that way as I enter the luxurious vehicle.

"You take your bus on Pike Street?" he asks. I nod, my eyes on the windshield wipers, rhythmically chasing raindrops.

He switches to Drive, and we're off. I know nothing about cars, but this one's high-end for sure. Even the blinker sound is lush. Alexander's driving is pleasant and experienced, and I sometimes glance at his hands smoothly gliding over the steering wheel. I can't help but wonder how those strong fingers and palms would feel on my skin, grazing it like that.

What stage of craziness is it when you wish you were a steering wheel?

I'm somehow disappointed when we reach my bus stop. As I'm about to get out, he stops me, putting his hand over my forearm. The simple contact sends shivers all the way to my chest, and I look toward where he's pointing.

The electronic sign where the bus times are usually displayed only reads three fateful words. **STRIKE! SERVICE INTERRUPTED.**

Defeated, I blow out my cheeks before throwing my head back. "I can drive you home," he kindly offers.

For the umpteenth time this evening, he's unusually amiable, and I want to grab his shoulders and shake him out of it. It's so much simpler when he's a one-dimensional jerk. If my body acts the way it does when he's rude and arrogant, how will it behave if he turns out to be a nice guy?

"I'll get myself an Uber," I suggest. But that solution quickly falls flat. With the bus strike, everyone's using such alternatives. I'd have to wait for forty-five minutes to get a ride home.

"I really don't mind," Lex insists, seemingly amused by my misfortune.

"I don't want you to make a detour for me."

"Where do you live?"

"Genesee." *Please, let him live on the other side of town.*

"That works for me."

Well, fuck … This is awkward, tense, and not how I expected tonight to go.

My boss is driving me home on a late Friday evening with my address on his GPS and my wet ass sitting on the fine leather of his seat. Wet because of the rain, of course. Not because of the way his hands move every time he takes a turn or because the surrounding air smells of him.

Okay, maybe a bit of that, too.

There's a play button on the electronic screen between us, and because the silence is so uncomfortable, I boldly press it.

"Resuming the current playlist," the feminine electronic voice answers.

Fuck, I expected it to turn on the radio or something. But I can now see that it's connected to his phone. I'm about to know even more about the man, which can't be a good thing.

When I turn to him, I notice his discreet wince. "I don't mind. But you might regret your decision. I've been told I have terrible taste in music," he confesses, never ripping his eyes from the road.

Oh, this should be interesting …

My curiosity is properly piqued, and all my attention is now on the intro that fills the silence. I'm almost ashamed of how quickly I recognize it. But it's so unexpected that I doubt myself for several seconds. This can't be it. No fucking way.

But there's no denying it. It's "Rasputin", by Boney M. The giggle that rolls in my throat turns into a graceless snort when I try to muffle it. I press my hand over my lips in a failed attempt to hide my wide smile.

"Are you making fun of me?" he asks.

"I'm sorry, it'll pass. I just really wasn't expecting that."

"What were you expecting?"

The genuine curiosity in his tone makes me consider the question. Probably something boring, like classical music or jazz, but I can't tell him that. "I didn't expect Boney M," I diplomatically say.

With a broad smile still on my face, I look out my window, listening to the catchy tunes. The words dance on my lips, but I don't allow them to be voiced.

He still notices. "You made fun of me, yet you know the words."

"Of course I know them—everybody does. I just really didn't think *you* listened to it."

"Maybe we should stop before another song starts," he suggests.

And that only triggers my need to know what comes next. I press the button to skip "Rasputin", and, to my amazement and hilarity, "Build Me Up Buttercup" resonates in the car. A new series of chuckles escapes me.

"If you're going to mock me the entire way, I'd rather we go with silence," he argues as we're stopped at a red light.

His hand flies to the screen to stop the music. Instinctively—clearly without thinking—I grab his wrist to prevent him from pressing the button. "No! I swear, I'm not making fun of you. I love those songs. It's just unexpected."

My fingers are wrapped around his wrist, and my other hand rests over the back of his. I can't help but notice that his wrist is as thick as my ankles. If there is a correlation between the size of a man's hand and the proportions of his appendage, then Lex is *seriously* hung.

And it's suddenly all I can think of.

How big, girthy, and long his—

A car honks somewhere, making me jump and release him. My cheeks are burning, and I hope to God he blames my redness on the traffic light. I swiftly slide my hands under my thighs in an attempt to keep them away from temptation.

I can feel his stare on my profile, but I keep mine up front. The light turns green, but he doesn't do anything about it, so I force myself to look his way. His expression is unreadable, as usual, his gaze locked onto mine. The exchange doesn't last long, but it feels as if his gray irises can see past my brown ones straight into my soul, reading my thoughts and desires.

Despite my best efforts, I can't look away from his entrancing eyes. This man has a magnetic pull on me that I cannot comprehend.

He gets over whatever's happening first, refocusing on the road and putting us back on our way to my place. The rest of the ride occurs without another word between us. Music is still playing, joyful and catchy, but it isn't enough to appease the tension.

As soon as we reach my building, I grab the handle. "Thank you for the ride," I say, hating how shaken I sound. "Sorry for the detour."

He keeps looking forward before turning to me. "It's fine. Don't worry about it."

With one last forced smile, I pull on the handle to exit the car. It's still pouring outside, so I run to my entrance and urge myself not to look back and enter the lobby.

Shit … That was weird, and tense, and strangely sexy. I'm feeling electric, and I don't know what to make of it.

Unless he changes his mind, I'll have to spend my working days in the same room as that man.

If that's not a recipe for disaster, I don't know what is.

is_scene_break = True

MY WEEKEND ISN'T VERY RESTFUL. Which is to be expected, given how many things are plaguing my mind. First, I missed my date with Oli, which earns me some scolding from Tami. Second, my obsession with my boss has grown substantially, which is terrible. Third, I'm expected to spend even more time around said boss. Fourth, I had another vividly realistic wet dream about the man.

The future's looking really bright.

Somehow, when I get to work on Monday, there's another parameter that I forgot to account for. "So," Steven tells me, spinning his chair to face me when I arrive, "not even here for a month, and you're already working upstairs with the boss?"

It's a joke. I know it is, but it still makes my insides churn. From their point of view, it must look so suspicious. Especially knowing how Alexander is. I didn't realize the news would spread so quickly. But my computer isn't on my desk anymore, so it makes sense they had questions.

"I explained the situation," Oliver says. "They can't wait to see the app you've created."

"Trust me," I say to Steven, eager to clarify things, "I'd rather be here with you guys than upstairs with him."

"Well, that's nice to hear," says a deep voice behind me.

Ah, shit …

I slowly spin around, worriedly glancing at Lex, but he doesn't give me any attention and turns to the guys instead. "When the rest of your colleagues arrive, I want all six of you in the conference room. We'll rearrange a few things for the weeks to come." Without another word, he leaves us.

About five minutes later, when Brian and Joseph arrive, we all head to the conference room, as instructed. It's nearly full already, with more people still filtering in. Lex is talking with a man I have seen before but never met—Kevin Langley, Kelex's co-owner. He's slightly shorter than Lex, his body is leaner, and his blond hair is neatly combed back while his face is closely shaven. The man is devilishly handsome, but not in the same way as his business partner. Alexander is dark and mysterious, while the other man is luminous and refined. The other big difference is that he's wearing a three-piece suit, while Alexander is back in his usual T-shirt and jeans. The contrast between the two men is striking, which makes the apparent familiarity between them somehow surprising.

The nerds greet our bosses before sitting or standing around the large table. Alexander waves for me to come closer, so I comply.

"Kev, this is Andrea Walker," he says. "Andrea, this is Kevin Langley."

"I can't believe we haven't met sooner. It's great to finally put a face to the name, Andrea."

"Andy, please. And yes, ditto. I've heard a lot about you," I greet back, shaking his hand.

"Lex tells me you're quite the genius with a keyboard," he continues. The compliment boosts my ego, and the utter pride I feel warms me all over. I glance at the object of the discussion, who's already busy talking to Steven and Brian.

"Well, he never used the word genius in front of me," I retort.

"Ah, you'll have to excuse my old friend. While he might be the smartest man I know, he is most certainly not the sharpest one when it comes to people. He's a good guy deep down, though, I promise."

He gives me an impish wink and then guides me to a couple of empty chairs.

The room rapidly falls silent as we sit, all because of Alexander's commanding authority. He doesn't even have to speak to make the room shut up, and it's honestly impressive.

"We're about to acquire a new project, which will now become our number one priority," he says to the gathered crowd with a clear voice. "Starting today, a few of you will be assigned to it. I want the alpha version of this app up and running by Thanksgiving, so I expect all the involved parties to do their best to respect that deadline. Andrea, if you would," he adds, moving to the side.

What? I'm supposed to improvise a speech out of the blue? Everyone's eyes are on me, so I force myself to stand up and join him. It feels like drama club all over again.

"This is Andrea Walker, who joined the dev team three weeks ago. It's her app we're looking to purchase, so I'll let her introduce it," Lex explains, stepping to the side once he's done.

God, I hate this. Unsure what to say, I scowl at the man who just threw me under the bus. All I get in return is a firm nod, spurring me on.

"Hi," I say with a weird hand wave, my voice shaky. "So, I've created the equivalent of a voice recognition software but for sign language. The app is meant to be convenient and educational, as people will pick up a few tricks when interacting with deaf and hard of hearing interlocutors. I've also been working on implementing AI voices into the mix, and the idea is that each user can have a voice that is uniquely theirs."

I could speak about this project for three hours straight, but I doubt everyone wants to listen to technicalities. So, I keep it as short and concise as I can, focusing on the few people I know to keep my social anxiety at bay.

As soon as I'm done, Alexander takes the lead again. "I want this developed and expanded to its maximum potential. By next year, I want this app in every administrative building, museum, school, college … This will set the standard; we'll make it mandatory, a basic requirement for state-run facilities, and a necessary tool for private sectors as well."

The more he talks, the stupider I feel. I worked on this so my brother could get laid—not that he needs any help with that. And Alexander fucking Coleman is already fifty steps ahead of me, seeing the big picture I was too dumb to fathom.

The government is always trying to include disabled minorities, or at least they pretend to. It isn't so far-fetched that they would invest in such a tool so deaf and hard of hearing kids can blend in more easily in their schools, patients can communicate in hospitals, as well as visitors in administrative buildings … And the same applies to the private sector.

Even if the app doesn't sell well with civilians, which I doubt, all those facilities would still make Kelex's investment very lucrative.

I watch as Lex shares his objectives and prognostics. As always when his brain is in action, I feel myself slowly slip into naughty thoughts. But as soon as I realize it, I return my attention to the crowd. There's no way I'll be caught drooling over him by all those people.

With mild amusement, I note that most women are drinking in his words with way too much enthusiasm. The man is a snack and a half, and I'm definitely not the only one to have noticed. In the corner of my eye, I see him pass a hand through his hair, and two women bite their bottom lips.

As someone who gets wet whenever he uses a polysyllabic word or puts on his glasses, I can't even blame them.

When the meeting ends ten minutes later, Lex dismisses everyone but a few so he can explain what's expected from us with this change of plans. Consumer trials, marketing, early design, and programming are distributed among us. Kevin is also present, supervising everything and weighing in on the decisions being made. Everyone has until the end of the week to finish what they're working on or pass it to someone else. On the other end, Lex and I will start working on it immediately.

Brainstorming takes us the entire morning, and lunch break with the nerds leads to more talking about my app. Then, I begrudgingly head upstairs to my temporary shared office.

Lex is already working, which I anticipated. What I didn't expect, though, is the setup. There isn't a desk in a corner with my stuff. My computer is on the formerly empty half of his desk, facing the other way from his. I'm meant to sit diagonally to him, barely four feet away from his distracting presence.

My productivity will be shit. Utter and complete shit.

I drag my feet toward my new chair, thinking this looks like some reality TV show from hell. Lex doesn't look up from his screen yet, and I don't know if I like that or not. As I get closer, I notice documents lying across my keyboard.

"This is the contract you requested," he says when I pick it up, still focused on his screen, his glasses reflecting its light.

"Oh, right."

"Optimally, you need to sign all three copies before the day ends. Take your time reading it and tell me if you need changes to be made. I ensured your interests were protected as much as ours."

"I appreciate that, thanks."

Because it's further from him and feels like a beacon of tranquility, I grab the documents and sit on the sofa to read them. I regret that a little when I sit. Crap, I forgot how rigid it is—as rigid as its owner.

As suspected, it's all very boring to read. By the time I flip to the second page, the uncomfortable couch is becoming a problem. From there, I regularly twist and wriggle, trying to find a better position. I find it as I start the fifth page. If my abuela found me like this, she'd definitely tell me to sit straight and stop being sprawled like some sea animal washed ashore.

Reading the whole thing drains me, but I'm glad I do. A couple of clauses are a little confusing, but it's nothing important. The contract really protects me as much as them.

"Was everything clear?" Alexander asks when I come back.

"Yes, I suppose. Just a couple of sentences I didn't really get."

"If you want me to clarify things, don't hesitate to ask."

"Have you read it?"

"I was the one sending memos to the lawyers all weekend," he explains after typing something on his keyboard. "I read it several times, and I assure you nothing could harm you."

I'm under the impression that Alexander Coleman isn't a liar. He may be chauvinistic, haughty, cold, and arrogant, but I'm almost sure he wouldn't lie.

So, with confidence, I sign everywhere I'm meant to. Once done, I tilt to the side and hand the papers to Lex.

For the first time since I came in, our eyes meet as he takes the documents. I stare at my booting screen, listening to him write on the papers. The scratchy noise of his ballpoint pen is abnormally loud in the quiet room. There's only silence for several seconds, then the clicking of his pen. The deed is done. Too late to back out.

"This one's for you," he says, slipping one of the copies under my screen. I take it and put it safely in my bag. It feels very official, and the reality of the upcoming sale sinks in.

"Is there something I should do first?" I ask, not bothering to look over my screen.

"Since several people will soon work on your scripts, you can clean them up and make everything as clear as possible," he recommends. Yes, of course, that makes sense. "I've dug up the ones we came up with a few years ago, and I'm trying to see if any of them can be added to your work."

I nod, which is useless because he can't see me. Motivated to find a distraction, I open a script and start working on it. For the entirety of the afternoon, I'm hyperaware of his presence, so close to me. Every time he types, moves, or stretches, my mind leaves whatever I'm doing to focus on him. Several times, he pauses his work to methodically crack his knuckles, one after the other, and I find myself counting each joint that pops.

Whenever he needs me to check something, I do my best not to come in physical contact with him, bending weirdly to read whatever is on his screen. I'll most definitely have back issues by the end of the month. And not because it got blown out by him.

Yes, my mind now lives in the gutter.

As soon as we reach five-thirty, I stand up, ready to bolt out. He doesn't seem ready to leave anytime soon, but there's no way I'm staying. "Good evening," I tell him, hoisting my bag onto my shoulder.

"Good evening, Andrea," he responds. I'm about to turn to the door when he adds, "Kevin wants to sign the official sale before the weekend. Friday afternoon will be devoted to the negotiations and reaching an agreement."

"Do you think it might take some of the evening, too?"

"No, it normally shouldn't." Okay, phew … I have my rescheduled date with Oli that evening. "I advise you to have a legal counselor accompanying you for your comfort and ours," Lex continues.

"Alright, will do."

On my bus ride home with Tami and Oli, I explain how things are going and take a moment to text my blonde best friend. I don't know any lawyers in Seattle, but she might, even though she specializes in intellectual property and not corporate law. Since I don't really have a choice, I tell her I might be selling my app before the week ends.

The minute we get home, she calls back. "Hi, blondie," I greet her.

"Oh, my God! You're so sneaky. I can't believe you're selling your app! I didn't even know you were showing it to people."

"I'm sorry, K. It all happened very fast, and I didn't want to jinx it, so I didn't tell anyone. The sale isn't effective yet, but we signed a binding agreement."

"It's pretty much the same, then. When are you signing?"

"We're negotiating Friday afternoon and signing then if we settle on a price."

"And you want me to recommend a lawyer to you?"

"Yes, Le—Alexander advised me to get one."

"Well, I have someone in mind, but they aren't exactly corporate law," she explains, a little hesitant.

"At this point, I'll take anything."

"Okay, then! Just a fair warning, you'll have to sleep with them as a payment."

The way my jaw drops is almost comical, even to me. "Kate, what the—"

"Don't worry, she's hot as hell. Blonde, 5'10", amazing tits …"

Then, it all makes sense. "Oh my God, are you serious?! You really want to come to help me out?" I ask with enthusiasm.

"Yes, if you'll have me! I'll take Friday off and spend the whole weekend with you before heading back to Portland."

"Of course I'll have you, you moron! Wait, fuck."

"What?"

"I'm seeing Oli on Friday evening."

"Eh, it's fine. I'll meet up with some old law school friends."

"You have friends other than me?!" I ask, feigning shock.

"A few, but you're my main hoe, babe. Forever."

"You better remember that," I say, my seriousness cracking.

Our voices are high-pitched as we carry on, both very excited by the prospect of seeing each other so soon. She's thrilled she'll get the chance to meet Oliver, but also that she'll spend a few hours in the presence of Alexander, as she's never one to shy away from a gorgeous sight.

The fact that my partner in crime is coming to town will most certainly distract me from him.

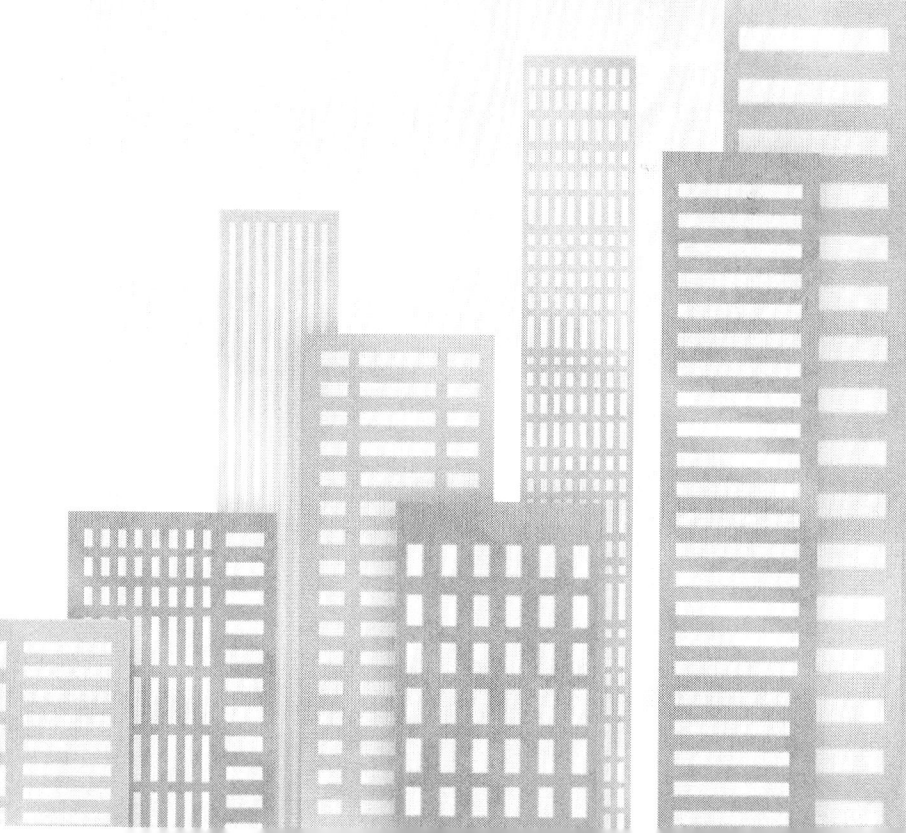

is_new_chapter = True

chapter_number = "11"

pov_name = "Andrea"

MY BORING LITTLE LIFE HAS become anything but.

I spend my days with my BILF, have a new date scheduled with the sweetest guy ever, and will have my bestie around for the weekend. Things are looking good, aside from the boss situation.

Lex and I rarely interact, but it's still hard to ignore his presence, so close I can touch him if I want. Thank God the desk is large enough that we aren't overlapping each other's spaces, and our legs have no chance of accidentally touching.

One thing I really appreciate about him, though, is how much he respects my abilities. He clearly has a natural inclination toward taking charge and being in control, but he is remarkably respectful of my aptitudes and wisdom regarding this project. I'm the lead on this, and while he supervises and weighs in on decisions, he never hesitates to give me some responsibilities. It makes sense since it's my app, but I'm still a junior employee, so this is quite gratifying.

I'm positively jittery all morning on Friday. Kate's arriving soon, I might sell my app, and to celebrate it all, I have a date tonight. What a day.

The whole thing is so exciting that, for the first time since we've started sharing an office, I almost forget about my boss's existence, right there on the other side of our wall of flat monitors.

That is, until he bluntly utters, "Will you stop?" out of the blue. It's clear that I'm getting used to his manners because I barely flinch. He catches himself, though, and adds, "Please."

"Stop what?" I ask, confused.

"The leg thing. It's distracting."

Only then do I realize I'm anxiously bouncing my knee, making the sole of my shoe repeatedly tap on the floor. "Sorry," I say with a wince, instantly ending it.

I check my phone for the tenth time in so many minutes, expecting to see an update from Kate. Nothing. It's been radio silence since her text to let me know she was in the car on her way here. I'm struggling to focus on my script when Alexander's desk phone rings. He picks it up with a frustrated sigh, and I can't quite make out what the person is saying.

Lex lets out a vague, "Hm" and hangs up. "There's someone for you at reception."

My baby!

Excitedly, I roll my chair back and jump to my feet. "I'll be right back!"

I practically sprint downstairs and immediately locate Kate standing by the reception desk. My hasty journey only stops when I harshly crash into her to hold her in a tight embrace. "I can't believe you're really here!" I squeal.

"I know. I've missed you so much!" We let go after a moment, and she takes in the sight of me, smiling. "Well, it's nice to see Seattle hasn't changed your sense of fashion."

I look down at my purposefully awful "Team Edward" T-shirt and give her a smile. It's hard to believe she owns an equally bad "Team Jacob" tee, given her attire. She's wearing a very professional pantsuit with stilettos, her wheat blonde hair neatly styled in supple and natural-looking waves, and she has on two simple pearl earrings. Her discreet makeup is as perfect as ever.

My girl is here for business, and I love to see it.

"You're early!" I say with enthusiasm.

"I wanted to surprise you so we could have lunch together," she explains. "When do you get off?"

"My break is in ten minutes, but we might as well go now. I just have to get my things."

"Lead the way."

She tells me about her trip on our way upstairs, and we come across Tami in the corridor. I quickly introduce them, and we chat for a couple of minutes. Because she was so close to my family growing up, Kate is familiar enough with ASL to carry out a solid conversation.

Then, the two of us continue our journey to my temporary office.

"Wait here," I urge Kate. "Do not move," I insist before going in. Lex is still working, forever focused. "Hey, is it okay if I leave for lunch now?" I ask him, gathering my things. "I'll come back earlier."

"That's fine. The meeting starts at two. Just be on time for it."

This means an extra half hour of break. *Awesome.*

"This office is amazing," Kate says from behind me. I whip around, only to find her standing in the middle of the room. I send her a threatening look, which she purposefully ignores.

Lex looks up from his screen, stands from his chair, and walks up to us. Using her business voice, she introduces herself, "Hello, I'm Katherine Knox, Andy's best friend and counselor."

Lex shakes the hand she extends. "I'm Alexander Coleman. Andrea's boss."

"Oh, I know. I've heard about you." Once more, she ignores my warning glare.

Lex gazes at me with curious eyes. "Have you, now? I hope it wasn't all bad."

"Not all of it, no." Her tone is way too suggestive for my taste. Elbowing her would only draw more attention to me, but if she doesn't stop, I'll commit Kathricide.

"If you'll excuse us," I say, eager to leave the room. "We're going out for lunch." I take Kate's wrist and pull her behind me. "I can't believe this! Five seconds in, and you do this to me!" I protest as soon as we're out.

"Oh, will you calm down … He already knows you find him hot."

"Doesn't mean you should bring it up."

"Well, trust me, the man is used to women swooning. My God, that jawline … And those eyes! Too bad he has to wear glasses—they hide his smoldering gaze."

"I like the glasses," I mumble.

"What was that?"

"He doesn't always wear them. How about Italian for lunch? There's a nice place around the corner."

"Fine by me. I'm craving pizza."

The place is crowded but they still find a table for us. Despite being in the heart of Seattle's business area, it has a cozy and authentic vibe I love. Ninety percent of the clients are wearing suits, but the furniture, decoration, and smells make it feel like a traditional family-owned pizzeria. There's a large window allowing the clients to see the pizzaiolos in action, and every time we come with the guys, we watch them spin and throw the dough around to flatten it, hoping to see one of them fail and let it fall. It's never happened, but none of us are giving up hope.

As we eat our cheesy dishes, Kate and I talk about her stupid ex, whom she dumped about six weeks ago after finding him cheating. Stefano was a cocky and pompous corporate lawyer I always hated, so it's great that they're through. I'll never understand why she wasted eight months of her life with that imbecile.

I have to hold back from rolling my eyes when she explains she's ready to find a new man. I love her with all my heart, but her constant need to be in a relationship prevents her from finding a genuinely good guy. She always jumps into the arms of the first hot idiot she encounters.

"Maybe you could wait a bit longer," I suggest. "You need to recenter yourself a little. When was the last time you had something genuinely good going on with a man?" I ask, already knowing the answer—Clarence, over five years ago.

"I guess it was with Clar."

"There you go. It's been prick after prick since him. If I were you, I'd wait and see. Maybe something will happen without you even looking for it."

She shrugs her shoulders, apparently skeptical about my perception of things. "If I were you, I'd try to fuck that sexy boss of yours," she says nonchalantly.

"That's because you're drawn to assholes like a moth to a flame."

She doesn't even deny it. On the contrary, she smiles with amusement, ripping a piece of bread from the basket and slipping it between her lips. "I am. Can I try to fuck him, then?"

"No." I answer that one too fast and too seriously, which she immediately notices. That was clearly a test, and I failed miserably.

"You like him!"

"No. I just don't want to end up in the middle of some shit between my best friend and my boss," I pretend. I can tell she isn't convinced by my half-lie, so I switch topics. "Now, if we're done with the men ruining our lives, how about we talk about the sale of my app?"

pov_name =
"Alexander"

WE'RE ALMOST READY FOR THE negotiations to start, but I need a moment alone with Andrea before that. That's why I leave Kevin with the lawyers and head to my office, hoping she'll be there. I meant to talk to her before, but her early departure for lunch and late return got in the way.

I swiftly enter what used to be my oasis of tranquility, and my eyes immediately land on the object of my search. The relief of finding her is instantly dismissed as I realize she's in the midst of changing out of her ugly T-shirt, which had a collage of some pale, sickly man apparently named Edward on it.

Instead of it, she's halfway slipping on an off-white blouse, her white bralette exposed underneath. Just as shocked as I am by this unexpected encounter, she stays immobile for about a second before she tugs at her shirt to shield herself from my gaze. She's quick but not quick enough, and I turn around—also too late. I had enough time to notice the brownish circles of her areolas, visible through the thin cloth of her bra.

I internally curse. Fucking hell, the image is now seared into my brain. I didn't need that. Not when I'm already obsessing over what her body would look like under mine, how her small breasts would bounce with every intense thrust into her tight little—

"Maybe you could knock?!" she scolds with a shaky voice. I can hear the ruffling of silk, her fingers probably fastening the buttons of her blouse.

"To enter *my* office?" I muse, sardonic.

"We share it."

"It's an office, Andrea. Not a locker room."

The moment stretches, and the absurdity of it has me sighing. I'm getting a semi, which is ridiculous because I barely gazed at her, and she was almost entirely dressed.

"Are you done?" I ask, irritated. "I have better things to do than this."

"Only two buttons left. No, three. Fuck, I put them wrong. Stay like that."

I huff disapprovingly. "What made you think this was a good idea?"

"I meant to change in the restroom, but you weren't here when I came back, so I thought you were busy somewhere else."

"I was."

"Clearly not busy enough," she mumbles.

The next thing I hear is the zipper of her jeans being pulled down, and I almost want to curse. This woman will drive me mad. In a vain effort to generate blood flow that isn't in my dick, I clench my fists and flex my arms all the way. It doesn't have time to work before she pulls the zipper up again and says, "All good."

Very slowly, I spin around, my expression closed off so she can't guess the turmoil she just unleashed on me. My gaze drops for the briefest instant to her now-covered chest and then back to her face.

"We need to talk," I say after an awkwardly tense moment.

Dread fills her eyes, and she hurries to say, "I'm sorry. I promise it won't happen again."

"No, not that. I mean—Yes, don't undress in here again. But I wanted to talk with you about the sale."

"Oh? Is everything okay?"

I come closer to speak with a lowered voice.

"As I told you before, I'm the one who determined the worth of your work. I estimated five hundred thousand dollars, which is still too little, in my opinion. They will start the offer much lower, probably under one hundred thousand. No matter the first offer, do not go for any less than four hundred. It's their job to make us save money, but they have been instructed to accept four hundred. Alright?"

She nods, vaguely confused. "Can't you just decide the price and be done with it?"

"Kevin is in charge of finances and investments. I can advise him, but he's the one who makes the final decisions. And he wouldn't understand."

"Understand what?"

Understand why I'm helping you out so much. Why I need to do this for you. Why you're so special.

"Kev isn't into computers," I say instead. "Coding might as well be Chinese to him. He wouldn't understand the extent of your work and what it's worth."

She takes a few steps back, setting some distance between us. "This isn't some weirdly elaborate way to scam me, right?"

"No. I wouldn't do that, Andrea."

Silence settles, and I'm tempted to take two steps forward to get rid of that distance she set between us. "Is it all clear to you?" I ask. She nods again. "Good." I'm about to head off when I'm abruptly reminded of something. "Don't speak of this."

"Yeah, no, for sure," she promises.

After one last hesitant glance toward her, I disappear into the hallway. Kevin won't like this, but I don't really care.

Andrea deserves to be rewarded for her incredible work. And unlike what my business partner would think, it has nothing to do with the fact that helping her means that maybe she'll dislike me a little less.

pov_name =

"Andrea"

I STAY THERE FOR A couple of minutes after Lex's departure, processing the information. Four hundred thousand dollars is so much money. Almost half a million in my bank account.

Someone knocks on the door, startling me. When I open, I find Kate's petulant self. "There you are! They just told me they're ready to start if we are." Then she notices I'm a little shaken. "Are you alright?"

"Yes, sorry. I was just thinking." I join her in the hallway, closing the door behind me. We silently walk to the meeting room until I feel compelled to warn her. "Kate?"

"Hmm?"

"I can't really explain why, but you have to trust me for the negotiations, ok?"

She nods, intrigued, but doesn't argue.

I could explain. I could tell her Lex is looking out for me. But I promised him I wouldn't tell anyone, and I don't want her to read into things. It isn't like that. He isn't doing it for me in particular but because of his personal code of conduct.

When we enter the conference room, Alexander and Kevin are already there with two old-ish men. Their suits and serious demeanor make it all dawn on me. This is a real, important transaction. I've never done anything like that, but I need to nail it.

We all take our seats and start right away. They pull out a bunch of documents, explain how the afternoon will unfold, and the fastidious talking starts. After barely ten minutes, I thank the gods Kate is here. It's my first time seeing her practicing, and I'm impressed by her seriousness and professionalism. This side of her is a novelty to me.

Then, when the time comes to talk about numbers, nearly an hour after we sat, I feel much better than I expected. I know exactly what to do. The oldest-looking attorney clears his throat. "Miss Walker, after considering your offer, my clients are willing to propose seventy-five thousand dollars for the sole ownership of your work."

A small smile stretches my lips, but I bite it down. "This app is the fruit of hundreds upon hundreds of hours of work. All in all, I'd say it's worth … five hundred thousand dollars," I state with audacity. Kate turns to me with round eyes, and the lawyer flinches a little.

"Miss Walker, the application you've developed certainly is convenient for my clients, but the price you're asking for is very high. We'd be willing to consider increasing our original offer by twenty-five thousand dollars, to one hundred thousand dollars."

"There are companies out there willing to pay what it's worth," I say truthfully. "Google, Meta, or Avoss will certainly have better offers for me, given their immense capital. I love Kelex's values, so I would rather sell here. But I won't settle for less than I deserve either."

I feel like I'm in *The Wolf Of Wall Street*. Thanks to Lex, this is unexpectedly fun.

The lawyers speak among themselves, and then one bends toward Kevin. My eyes meet Lex's on the other side of the table, and I can swear there's an amused sparkle in his eyes. The man is done speaking to Kev, who nods and turns back to me.

"My client will agree to an extra fifty thousand dollars. If I were you, Miss Walker, I would take the offer now and leave this room one hundred and fifty thousand dollars richer before my client removes himself from the equation."

"Four hundred and fifty, or I walk," I say gravely. Okay, now it's definitely a smile slightly stretching Lex's lips.

Once more, the other side of the table breaks into intense whispers, trying to get the last word. Kate pulls my arm before getting closer to my ear. "What are you doing?!" she mutters.

"Trust me, blondie. They'll go for four hundred." After a quick scan of my eyes, she warily nods and releases me.

They are still actively talking in front of us, and I decide to voice an idea that's been growing in my mind for the past hour. "I will also accept three hundred now and one hundred in Kelex stock. Also, regardless of the price we agree on, I want twenty-five percent royalties on the revenues my app will generate."

I have no idea where I found the guts to ask for that, but I'm glad I did. Given Lex's plans for my app, twenty-five percent will turn into much more than four hundred thousand dollars. My app is currently focused on American Sign Language, but the coding only needs small adjustments to work with sign languages from around the world. My app is a gold mine, and I'll be damned if I let them profit off of it without me.

As for the stocks, I hope I'm making the right decision here. Kelex has been steadily climbing since going public two years ago. The stock is now worth over twelve times what it was then. If the company keeps performing like this, I'll be set for the rest of my life between the stock, the royalties, and the payment.

"Seventy-five percent of the profit is better than a hundred percent of nothing," I hear Lex say to Kevin. "I think we should take it before someone else swoops in and beats us to it."

It takes a while, and they almost make me believe I won't succeed. But eventually, they accept my demands and offer me two hundred and seventy-five thousand fucking dollars, one hundred thousand in stock, and twenty percent in royalties. To my right, Kate is hyperventilating, and the lawyers before me seem displeased by the turn of events.

I got the last word and won. Lex nods humbly when I give him a discrete smile, and the slight grin on his lips makes something flutter low in my stomach.

"Well," Kevin says once everything is signed and the lawyers are gone. "I hope you're as good a programmer as you are a negotiator. That is one expensive app we just bought."

"She is," Lex intervenes, joining us. The compliment makes me blush, but I focus on Kevin.

"In the end, we both got what we wanted, so it's a good day," I point out.

"Very true. How about we celebrate it properly? Maybe in some overly expensive restaurant?"

"Tonight?" Even though I ask, I already know the answer.

"Yes, tonight. Lex, are you in?"

Fuck, no. My date with Oli …

Alexander shrugs, impartial. "Only if we don't go to that horrible molecular restaurant you liked so much. The textures were …" He doesn't finish his sentence, but his repulsed expression is enough.

Kevin lets out a laugh. "I'll tell you what, you choose the restaurant, and I'll make the reservation. Andy, is that good for you?"

My eyes helplessly travel between the two men. I just got an obscene amount of money out of them. I can't refuse, can I? If they weren't my bosses, then maybe, yeah. But asking for a rain check would make things weird.

Hoping Oliver will understand, I nod. Kevin then turns to Kate. "Miss Knox, will you be joining us?"

"I would love to, but I have plans," she answers, shaking her head.

What?! My head whips to her, my eyes pleading for her to change her mind. "Ah, what a shame," Kev says.

"Maybe another time," she replies with a polite smile.

What the fuck? Am I seriously having dinner with my two bosses? Including the one I constantly drool over? How do I keep getting into these situations?

On our way out, I cross Oli's path. To say I'm ashamed when I tell him about the change of plans is an understatement. But, as supportive as ever, he tells me to go, stating we have plenty of time to have our first date.

By the time Kate drives Tami and me home, she has lost most of her best friend privileges. She's letting me go alone to that dinner, and nothing can change her mind. I still feel like shit about Oli as I shuffle through my dresses to find something for tonight. This should be for him, not for my bosses.

Kate gasps behind me. Shoving her hand into my wardrobe, she takes out a hanger with a dress on it. "I can't believe you still have this one!"

Upon getting my first paycheck, Kate dragged me on a shopping spree, and I impulsively bought it. The lower half is an A-line skirt that reaches three inches above my knees, and the top has to be tied behind the neck. The entire back is exposed all the way to the waist.

Kate looks at the dress, then me, then the dress, and a mischievous smile claims her lips. Oh, no. She isn't winning this one. "Forget it, I'm not wearing this," I say, returning to my closet's inspection.

"Are you sure? You would look so hot in it."

"I want to look professional. Not hot."

Kate shrugs her shoulders with a pout. "You're right. And anyway, Alexander will eye-fuck you no matter what you're wearing."

I almost choke on air at her words. "What the hell! Don't say things like that," I scold her with shock.

"Like what? True things?"

"There isn't an ounce of truth in what you just said, so shut up." I take the dress from her and put it back on the rack. With angry gestures, I keep scanning through my clothes.

"You really are that blind, aren't you?" I don't need to look to know she's analyzing me with her intense blue eyes.

"What do you mean?"

"I mean your boss wants to fuck you, and you're too clueless to realize it."

My entire body stills, and then it warms up.

She's being ridiculous. Lex doesn't want me. On good days, he ignores me, and on bad days, I annoy him with my antics, like when he caught me changing. Nothing sexual about that. "I honestly don't know where you get these crazy ideas from."

"Well, I got it because I have something you don't."

I roll my eyes, unimpressed. "And what is that?"

"The ability to see him whenever you're not looking at him. And do you know what he does whenever you look away?"

I shouldn't ask. I really shouldn't. But now I need to know. "What?" I say so low it's almost a whisper.

"He devours you with his eyes. I-want-to-fuck-her eyes," she explains, her tone confident.

I try my best to remain calm and unaffected, but her words are wrenching my guts. It isn't so much the fact that Lex might want me but rather how far from the truth she is. "You misinterpreted," I counter.

"I did not. The man wants you, Deedee."

"Will you stop already? He's so out of my league we might as well be on different planets."

That's when I recall the nude he received on our first encounter. Maybe it's a girlfriend, a fiancée, an ex … The answer doesn't matter. I'm not his type. Not even close.

Kate grabs me firmly and forces me to face her. "Andy, look me in the eye and tell me this. How did you know you could ask for so much money and get away with it?"

The answer would only reinforce her ludicrous ideas, so I say nothing and avert my eyes to look at the wall with a frown.

"I know you. I know you won't accept what I'm saying until his tongue is shoved down your throat. And even then, you might argue he slipped," she says as she releases me, visibly annoyed.

"I'm not *that* dense."

"Mind putting my theory to the test, then?" I squint my eyes at her, trying to guess where she's going with this. Not waiting for my answer, she fishes out the black dress and hands it to me. "Put this on and see how he stares at you."

"I won't."

"Why? Are you scared I'm right?"

"It isn't appropriate."

"Oh, come on! Celebrities on red carpets wear so much worse than this," she argues, rolling her eyes.

I look at the dress like it's poisonous. It isn't vulgar since it shows no cleavage and isn't too short. It's just the back that's exposed, but it isn't indecent.

I don't want to prove Kate right. What if her ridiculous claims turn out to be true? What am I supposed to do then? Keep going to work, and act like I don't know my boss wants to fuck me as badly as I want to fuck him?

Kate notices my hesitation, and it's over for me. With a victorious smile, she pushes me to the door. "Go shower," she orders. "I'll find what you need to accessorize this baby."

Clearly, she's determined to win this one, so I clench my teeth and obey.

is_new_chapter = True

chapter_number = "12"

pov_name = "Andrea"

THE RESTAURANT IS PART OF a fancy hotel, and I regret not following Kate's instructions regarding my shoes. I'm not used to wearing heels, so I dismissed the ones she took out in favor of ballet flats. Now, I look like a misplaced child.

Nevertheless, I find my way to the dining room. It's magnificent, with high ceilings, cream-colored walls, several massive crystal chandeliers … The furniture looks high-end, and the whole place feels very European—not that I've ever been there. People are dressed either smart or formal, and I feel like I stain the elegant ambiance.

Trying to ignore the intense beating of my heart, I walk up to the maître d'.

"Good evening, miss. How may I help you?" he politely asks.

"Hi, I don't know if my party has arrived yet. The reservation should be under … Give me a second, I just have to make sure," I excuse myself, stepping to the side. Did Kevin tell me which name they used in the text he sent?

"I'm here for the Langley reservation," says a low, familiar voice beside me. My heart skips a beat, and the tiny hairs on my arms rise. Slowly, I look up to face the owner of the voice.

Alexander is looking at the maître d' with his eternally stern expression. His petrol-blue suit hugs him to perfection. His dress shirt is the same shade but lighter, and the first three buttons are undone. He's magnificent.

I'm not ready when he looks down at me, and he isn't either. Slight shock twists his features. Thanks to Tami's makeup skills and Kate's outfit styling, I look nothing like I usually do. Even my hair's different, held up by pins in a purposefully loose way.

I tense under his stare as he rapidly analyzes me, dismissing my discomfort. There, he's seeing me in my dress, and I'm ready to prove my point. I observe him back, waiting to see his reaction. There's no way he ever eye-fucks me, as Kate so crudely put it.

Under his insistent stare, my nipples harden under the thin fabric of my dress, and I hope he won't notice my body's absurd reaction to him.

His gaze lingers on my silhouette, appraising me, and then his eyes meet mine. Unlike what my best friend predicted, Lex isn't horny for me, but a somber expression shadows his face instead. His square jaw is clenched, and his eyes are two slits under his frowning eyebrows.

Ha! In your face, Kate! Lex isn't eating me up. I knew it!

Weirdly enough, the realization doesn't please me as much as it should.

Part of me wanted my best friend to be right. Just a little bit.

pov_name = "Alexander"

I SHOULD HAVE MENTALLY PREPARED myself for Andrea to come looking differently than she does at work. Maybe then I wouldn't stand there like a moron, taking it all in.

She discarded her usual nerdy T-shirt and jeans, replacing them with a pretty little black dress. There's more makeup on her face than usual, and I'm seeing her hair up for the first time. It allows me to discover that she has more than one earring per ear, with golden rings along their delicate arches.

Objectively, she's prettier than I've ever seen her before. So much so, actually, that I feel like an idiot for not noticing her beauty when I saw her in the elevator on our very first encounter. But I think I prefer the everyday version of her, comfortable in her clothes and not looking so stiff, almost anxious. Still, she's a sight to behold.

As I admire every last detail of her, I get the answer to a question I've been asking myself from day one. No, she doesn't have more freckles dusting her shoulders. Only her nose and cheeks are adorned by them.

When my inspection lowers, I notice that her nipples, which have been haunting me all afternoon, are like two pearls poking against the thin fabric of her dress. I got a glimpse at their size earlier, but now I wonder just how small they can get, all pebbled and hard like they are now.

"Sir?" the maître d' calls. I nearly glare at him for forcing me to look away from her. "As I was saying, your party is already seated. If you will come with me."

Reminding myself of common courtesy, I step aside and invite Andrea to go first. She diligently complies, and the maître d' leads us into the chic restaurant.

Fucking hell, the back of her dress isn't as modest as the front, and I get a plunging view of her naked back. I already noticed she wasn't wearing a bra, but knowing I could effortlessly reach her breasts from the side has my palms tingling. I distract myself with the beauty marks she has there and count all thirteen of them.

Fuck Kevin for suggesting this dinner. The asshole knew what he was doing.

I thought I was being clever with the way I handled things, but my old friend saw right through me. He drilled me with questions as soon as Andrea and her lawyer friend left. *How did she know how much she could ask for, Lex? You could have just told me you liked her. I'm not that much of a dick when it comes to money.*

But he was wrong. I don't like her. I admire her intelligence and want to fuck her senseless, but I don't *like* her.

The maître d' guides us to a table in the corner, where Kev and his wife are already seated. After a quick look at Andrea, Michelle gives me a broad, knowing smile, her light green eyes sparkling with mischief. Fuck, of course her husband told her everything. He can't keep secrets from her. They both stand to greet us as we arrive, with some difficulty for her, as she's heavily pregnant.

"Andrea, this is my wife, Michelle," Kevin introduces.

Everyone shakes hands, and I go around the table to give Shelly a brief, one-armed hug. "Behave," I whisper into her ear before I let go.

Anticipating that the maître d' will do it, I pull out a heavy chair for Andrea and then push it in as she sits. Kev asks for a bottle of champagne for the table. "To celebrate," he tells me with a wink.

I wasn't very enthusiastic about this dinner to start with, but this is ridiculous. With his wife here, it looks like a double date, making this even more uncomfortable.

"Isn't it nice we were able to do this?" Kevin says with genuineness, opening the wine menu. Andrea and I nod, our eyes skimming through the beverages listed on our own menus.

In the corner of my eye, I see her peeking at mine, and when I inquisitively turn to her, she whispers, "Does yours have prices on it?"

"Yes."

"Can I see them?"

"No."

She frowns at my rebuttal. "Why?"

"The prices don't matter."

"What if it's too expensive?"

"Nothing's too expensive. Just pick whatever you want."

I can tell she disapproves, but she doesn't argue anymore and returns to her exploration of the menu's items with a pout.

"So, Andrea, I heard you cost my husband and his partner a lot of money today," Michelle says with a smile.

"Uh, I guess I did."

"She was unyielding. Never had such a hard bargain before," Kevin notes.

"Oh, so she has the trifecta. Brains, personality, and beauty."

Because she somehow doesn't realize it's true, Andrea mumbles, "Yeah, I'm not so sure about the latter."

"Oh, but you should be. Isn't she lovely, Lex?" Michelle asks with feigned innocence.

That earns her a dark glare over my menu. "She is," I mumble.

Andrea wriggles on her chair, apparently as uncomfortable as I am.

As dinner unfolds, Michelle includes Andrea in the conversation, making this evening a little smoother than it would have been without her. Maybe Kevin was right to bring her. She's a therapist, after all, so she's good at making people comfortable.

"So, when you're not creating groundbreaking apps, what do you do in your free time?" she asks Andrea.

The freckled beauty swallows her mouthful of dessert before taking a sip of wine to help it pass. "It depends. I have many interests, like movies, TV shows, music … Before moving here, I used to teach programming for an online school. I've been thinking about doing it again, so there's that. I'm also learning Korean. Or trying to learn would be more accurate."

"Why Korean?" Kevin wonders.

"I always loved their culture and intend to go there at some point."

"That's amazing. Lex and I have a trip to Seoul planned for later this year. We're partnering up with a tech manufacturer there."

Andrea smiles politely, and before silence can fall on us, Shelly keeps the conversation rolling. "You said you loved music? I do, too, and I'm always looking to broaden my horizons. Anything you'd recommend?"

"Hm … The last playlist I really loved was one I didn't see coming," Andrea says with unmasked amusement. When she turns toward me, I realize where she's going with this. "Mind telling them about your whacky playlist?"

Fuck. That'll bring questions I'm not ready to answer.

"Lex has a playlist?" Kevin wonders. He's understandably confused since I never listen to music.

"He drove me home one evening," she explains. "The playlist was … interesting."

Kevin's eyes are inquisitive when they meet mine. "You drove Andy home, Lex?"

"There was a bus strike. It was the evening she showed me her application. I kept her late, so it was the least I could do," I explain, not shying away from his gaze.

Michelle distracts Andrea with a question about her teaching experience, but Kev and I wage some kind of silent battle.

"Shut the fuck up," I mouth, already knowing he's about to stir shit. That's thankfully enough to stop him.

A liqueur trolley is brought to us once we're done with the desserts, and Andrea and Kev are the only ones picking something from it. Then the bill arrives, and Andrea insists on paying her share. "Kelex's treat," Kev counters.

I stand first, and when Andrea does, she stumbles and loses her balance. I'm quick to help her regain it, grabbing her arm while my other hand reaches for her back. The skin-to-skin contact immediately warms my palm and fingers, and it feels almost forbidden.

"Are you alright?" I worriedly ask.

She nods, and I understand she's tipsy when I meet her glassy eyes. Petite like she is, I'd imagine it doesn't take much alcohol for it. And with servers who constantly top up glasses, it's hard to keep track.

We all walk out of the restaurant, and my hand remains on her back, just above the waistline of her skirt. I tell myself it's in case she loses her balance again, but I know it's because I don't want to let go.

"How did you get here?" I ask as I remove my hand and clench it to chase away the prickling sensation.

"I drove."

"You can't drive now."

"Where do you live?" Kevin questions as he reaches us, his arm wrapped around Shelly's shoulders.

"South," I answer before her.

"Oh, we can drop you off then."

"I'll take care of her," I insist.

My friend frowns. "But you—"

"Honey," Michelle interrupts, elbowing him slightly, "let him. I want to go home. I'm tired, and these shoes are killing me."

I understand what she's doing before he does, and I clench my teeth. "Right, of course," Kevin agrees once it clicks. "Well, Andy, it was a pleasure getting better acquainted with you. I hope our work together will last for many, many years."

He shakes her hand, then mine. I let him pull me in for a quick hug, and he whispers, "South is quite the detour for someone you don't even like."

Then, after an irritating wink, he wraps an arm around Michelle again, and they walk off to their car.

"Alright, let's get this over with," I say, pulling out my keys and unlocking my car.

"Wait," Andrea protests, pointing at a rusty pile of peeling red paint under a flickering streetlamp. "What about my car?"

I raise a judging eyebrow at it. "You'll come back tomorrow to get it," I explain, opening the door for her.

"I have a busy weekend," she insists. "I don't know when I'll be able to get it back."

Why must she be so difficult all the time? "Give me your keys."

She obeys, and I walk up to the valet at the hotel's entrance. "When does your shift end?" I ask him.

"In three hours, sir."

I pull out my wallet, grab three hundred in cash, and extend it to the man. "Can you take that car over there back to Genesee when you're done?"

"Uh, sure, sir."

"Perfect."

He uses the valet ticket pad to write down the address, and I hand him the key and the cash as I give him more instructions.

"What was that about?" Andrea asks when I return.

"He'll bring your car back to your place when his shift ends."

"What about the key?"

"In your mailbox."

"What if he steals my car?"

"Have you seen the state of it, Andrea? It's not worth losing a job over. Hell, it's barely worth the three hundred I gave him. Now, get in."

She pouts but says nothing as she sits down in the passenger seat. With a few taps on the screen between us, I set the GPS to her address, and we're off.

The drive to her place is silent, and she doesn't try to turn the radio on this time. It's so tense and awkward that I realize I should have let Kev and Shelly take her home. They live ten minutes away from her place, and they wouldn't have been tempted to gaze at her alluring profile every few seconds. And maybe she wouldn't have looked so eager to get out of the car, as if being stuck in here with me is torture.

But when I stop in front of her building, she doesn't rush outside like last time. So, I turn off the ignition and wait. We stay there for a few seconds, unsure how to break the silence.

She's the one who does. "Thank you for the ride—*again*," she says, keeping her eyes up front. "And thank you for making sure my car gets home. I'll pay you back on Mond—"

"Don't worry about it."

For once, she doesn't insist. "Sorry for drinking too much. I'm not used to servers topping up glasses all the time."

"It's fine."

Still, she doesn't exit the car, twisting her fingers on her lap, hesitating. I should tell her to go. I should tell her it's late, I'm tired, and she needs to go. Staying here with her so close is harder than it should be. There's no one in sight, and the utter silence makes me feel like we're the only two people in the world. And she's wearing a pretty dress, and I've been dying to do something about it all evening.

Again, her soft voice breaks through the stillness in the car. "I know you don't like me because I annoy you and all. But I really appreciate what you did for me and how you made sure I wasn't getting scammed. I would have made mistakes otherwise," she says, audibly nervous. "So, thank you, Alexander, for helping me out regardless of our differences."

It doesn't feel right to let her think that I dislike her. And not just because it's false, but because I can't bear the idea.

For the first time since we stopped, I turn and look down at her. "You don't annoy me," I assert after several seconds have passed. "You frustrate me."

"Because I'm annoying," she insists.

I should let her think that. It's so much simpler that way. But I can't stop myself from saying, "No."

is_new_chapter = True

chapter_number = "13"

pov_name = "Andrea"

I SHOULD HAVE EXITED THE car as soon as we arrived. But I didn't want to be rude, and I also didn't want the moment to end. This tension within me every time he's around is draining, but it's also addictive.

So, I stayed, and now, all I can see is Lex and his fiery gaze. My heart beats harder and faster with every second that passes. I'm so overwhelmed by my own feelings that it takes me a while to register what I'm actually seeing.

Need.

Want.

Desire.

No, that's the wine talking. There's no way the Alexander Colemans of this world want the Andrea Walkers. He's a god among us, and my closest celebrity doppelgänger is Dora the Explorer.

But then, why did he save my address in his car's GPS? I've been trying to make sense of that since I noticed it earlier, and I can't figure out what it means.

I need to go before I do or say something stupid. My lips part to utter a goodbye, and that catches his gaze. Right there, I get my answer. His pupils dilate until only a thin ring of dark gray surrounds them. If actions or words can be hard to interpret, biology isn't.

Kate was right. She saw something I was too blind and clueless to notice. This whole thing isn't as one-sided as I thought. Alexander *wants* me.

Alcohol seems to have knocked down the voice of reason that's supposed to counterbalance my irrational thoughts because nothing comes up to contradict them.

That's probably why the rest unfolds the way it does.

I tilt toward him hastily, only to be painfully reminded of the seatbelt, which I unbuckle with a curse. This time, he's already halfway there when I reach for his nape.

With a brutality that shows our impatience, our mouths collide.

The moment our lips touch, everything else fades. It's as though I've waited months for this, years, instead of mere weeks. The shiver that runs through my entire body and ends between my legs is indescribable. With my hand still on his neck, I pull him harder, tilting my head to the side to adjust the angle of our kiss.

I vaguely hear the clicking of his seatbelt being undone, and then he turns to face me better. His hands reach for me soon after, one on my waist and one on the back of my head, and he eagerly draws me closer despite the console separating us.

The warm, silky touch of his tongue grazes over my lips, and it sends another one of those mind-blowing shivers all the way to my core. A moan escapes my mouth as I unlock my jaw to give him the access he demands. Soon, he's invading me, demanding and voracious. My fervor equals his, and in an instant, we're battling to sample each other.

One month of unsatisfied needs and built-up frustration is unleashing at once.

This is far beyond any expectation I might have had, so much more than all the fantasies I had of him. It's all so overwhelming, and I'm burning inside out, but I still need so much more. A helpless moan travels from my mouth to his as I try to get closer to him, to feel more of him, but the wide middle console prevents it. I want his body pressed against mine, and I want it now.

As if I actually expressed my needs out loud, his hand reaches for my thigh, under the hem of my dress, and with impressive strength, he pulls me over the separation and onto him. I focus on keeping our kiss going as he maneuvers me on his lap until I'm straddling him. Hoisted up like this, our faces are perfectly aligned, and I can enjoy him more thoroughly.

His hands are now moving up and down my body, caressing my naked back, apparently as greedy as I am to feel more. I get lost in our kiss, feverish and dizzy. Starved for more, I eagerly press my throbbing core against him to find some relief. With only a thin layer of lace shielding me, my pussy might as well be directly on him.

Oh, my … Someone is as aroused as I am, and that someone *has* to be hiding a baseball bat in there.

Framing his handsome face, I devour him, giving him the boldest kiss I've ever given anyone. I'm shamelessly licking, exploring the convoluted warmth of his mouth, greedily taking everything. I could kiss him like this for hours, bending to the will of his lips, melting every time his expert tongue grazes mine in lascivious touches.

Even with my sparse knowledge and little experience, I know Alexander Coleman is particularly divine at this. He's as restless as I am to feel more, to taste more, to get more, but he isn't taking control, nor is he passive under me. We share the moment.

How many women has he kissed to become this good? How many hours of it for me to be so entranced?

Somehow, I refuse to be just one more of these women. I'm far from being the first and most certainly won't be the last. But I can leave a mark. I'm unsure how to upgrade my kissing game, but I must try.

With his wet lower lip between my teeth, I gently pull on it, biting just hard enough to make him groan without actually hurting him. When I release him, he looks at me through heavy eyelids, his cheekbones reddened by our passionate embrace. My face is probably even more flushed, my skin burning from the madness of it all.

I'm bolder than I've ever been when I bend forward to follow the outline of his lush lips with the pointed tip of my tongue. Whenever he tries to kiss me, to end the taunting, I refuse him, anchoring my resistance on the backrest behind him. His hand reaches for my nape, and he pulls me down to him, but I counter his will once more. I want to make him beg for it.

But when he fists a handful of my hair and pulls on it harshly, I'm the one about to beg. I'm drenched already, and the electric pain it unleashes only makes it worse.

"Aah, fuck," I moan, shivering from head to toe and pressing myself harder onto him.

"Andrea," he growls threateningly.

That's begging, isn't it? I decide it is.

My proud smirk when I retake his lips quickly fades. My little teasing did its trick a little too well. There's no more holding back on his part. But it's okay because I want more. I need all of it.

A primal need, the most basic of instincts, takes over my brain. Shamelessly, I slowly undulate on his lap, pressing myself at a lascivious pace over the rigid shape there. That part of me is begging for satisfaction, and I'm too inebriated to deny myself this. I can feel with incredible intensity each ripple, each fold of the thick fabric of his slacks, and it's driving me insane.

My audacity rips another groan from him, and a sudden burst of pride encourages me to keep going. His hands move up my bare outer thighs, beneath the dress, before settling firmly on my ass. Because I'm wearing a thong, they rest directly on my skin, igniting yet another lustful shiver in me.

Fuck … How is kissing this man even better than I imagined?

pou_name =

"Alexander"

I'M DROWNING IN A MISTY haze of lust, and nothing can break through it.

My nose is filled with sweet jasmine, my tongue is high on the taste of hers, and my hands are full of her ass, the flesh soft and malleable under my audacious fingers. I'm still not sure what's going on or how it happened, but it feels as though four weeks of contained lust are unleashing with voracious intensity.

Andrea fucking Walker, the petite, freckled Latina who's been driving me mad since she stepped into my life is undulating on top of me, that heated spot between her legs eagerly rubbing against mine. We're fucking completely dressed, and neither of us seems to care that we're in a car out in the street, or that she's my employee and I'm her boss. She doesn't even remember that she can't stand me.

I'm so hard it hurts, my cock rock solid under her, desperate to plunge into her soft and warm wetness. Rapturous, I tug her closer, squeezing her ass as I assist her undulations.

She wants this as much as I do. I feel blindsided by it because I never would have thought the untamable lust I've been feeling for her was reciprocated. I missed the signals, per usual. I thought I was getting better at understanding body language and nonverbal cues, but I missed them all with her.

Her lips tear away from mine with a sensuous sigh, but I'm not done with her taste yet. I lick and nibble at the delicate column of her throat, hungrily sampling her, hands still pressing her onto me in rhythm.

She's so damned wet that I can feel it seeping through the thick fabric of my slacks. My fingers slide against her drenched underwear, so damp it's slick. The light touch makes her tremble on top of me.

I pull away enough to gaze at her while I trace a firm line along her lace-clad slit. "You're fucking soaked."

She nods, and when I press on her clit, she buckles and curses. "Shit, Lex … I need you."

I should probably put an end to this, but the only thing I can think of is how easy it would be to actually fuck her. My zipper down, her thong tugged to the side, and then a long, deep, and maddening thrust.

The mere thought of it has precum leaking out of me, my hips bucking up with need. This moment could last for eternity, but it still wouldn't be enough. With a hand still on her ass, I use the other one to fondle her breast. It fits perfectly in my palm, small and perky, and I hold back from ripping the top half of her dress to free them. The nipple hardens like a diamond under my touch, and I pinch it between two fingers, just roughly enough to make her release a soft plea—half-cry, half-moan.

It seems I'm not the only one who craves more because she reaches for my belt between us. Understanding what she wants, I freeze. "I have an IUD," she breathes against my lips. "And I'm clean. Are you?"

I give her a single nod, hands clutching her ass. We shouldn't do this. For so many reasons, we shouldn't.

Her fumbling hands get the best of my belt, and she slides it out of the buckle before moving on to the button.

"Are you sure about this?" My voice is altered by passion, just like hers.

She lets out a moan, resuming her undulations. "No … But I *need* it."

Her tongue is in my mouth again before I can answer, robbing me of my ability to think.

It turns out I'm not as strong as I believe myself to be because I cave in and assist her with unfastening my slacks. This maddening need won't be satisfied until I'm deeply planted inside her.

I lift myself to lower my pants, which lifts her with me, so she clings to my neck. Just as I'm about to push the slacks down, the unexpected sound of someone hitting the car's roof startles us both.

"Woo-hoo! Yeah, man! Hit that pussy!" a man shouts outside.

It stops me more efficiently than a bucket of icy water would have, and Andrea jolts away from me. In her haste to set some distance between us, she accidentally hits the steering wheel behind her, honking. A small cluster of drunk people is passing next to the Mercedes, and the sound attracts their attention. The man who yelled is already done with us, but a few others peek inside the car.

I glare at them, cursing their horrible sense of timing.

When I turn back to her, I understand that the sensuous mood has turned into embarrassment and awkwardness. She's temptation incarnate, with her lips swollen, her eyes ravenous, her cheeks flushed …

The night doesn't have to be over yet. I can take her to my place, and we can resume in a more private setting. I'm not ready to let her go. Not now that I know she wants me as much as I want her.

"Andrea, I—"

"Don't," she stops me, reaching for the door.

She extracts herself from my lap, avoiding my aching cock as she does, and exits the car. As soon as she's out, she takes a few wobbly steps away from me, rearranging her dress and passing a hand over her face. I hastily refasten my slacks, ignoring the wetness she left there.

I join her outside, adamant to soothe the situation. We're adults who are into one another. It happens.

"Andrea," I try again, grazing her bare shoulder.

She shrugs away from my touch and turns around to face me. "No. Don't say anything. This never happened. We're drunk and tired, and it got the best of us."

Ah. So this is how she wants to play it? Like it never happened? "Right. The wine did it," I respond with sarcasm.

Like the obstinate, insufferable woman she is, she says, "Yes, of course."

Alright then. If she wants to act like none of it was real, we will. Exasperated, I pass a hand through my hair. Without another word, I return to my car, bend inside to grab her clutch, and return with it. With a dry gesture, I hand it to her.

"There you go. I'm sorry the wine made you assault me."

She angrily frowns at me, like this isn't precisely what she's implying. Halfway back to my car, I feel the need to make things clear on my side, so I spin around again. "I'm not intoxicated, Andrea, or I wouldn't have driven you home." Then, after a few seconds of hesitation, I'm gone for good, slamming the door behind me. The tires screech on the asphalt as I take off.

The entire car smells of her, so I open the windows. But I can't do anything about the scent of her arousal etched on my fingers. Not until I get home. Once that is gone as well, there will be nothing left of the heated minutes we just shared.

Nothing but the fucking memory of it, forever engraved in my mind.

pov_name =

"Andrea"

LONG AFTER HIS CAR DISAPPEARED into the night, I'm still here, holding my bag in front of me. I don't know how to fucking cope with what happened, but mostly, I don't know what to make of his admission.

It's all a drunken mistake for me, but for him … it isn't?

I'll have to share an office with the man, knowing we were ten seconds away from fucking each other's brains out. I'll have to sit next to him, aware that he almost filled me with his dick—raw at that—and he was in full control of his capacities. He wanted it.

And as much as I deny it, I wanted it too—alcohol or not.

What is wrong with me?!

With a desperate whimper, I eventually move to my building and go up to my apartment in a sour mood. Once in my room, I see Kate's sleepy form on my bed, tucked under the covers. Like a fucking idiot, I accidentally slam my shin on the corner of my bed, waking her up.

"Deedee, is that you? What time is it?" her sleepy voice asks as she reaches for the lamp on her nightstand.

"Shh … It's late, go back to sleep."

Light floods the bedroom regardless, and fuck my life. I know exactly what she'll think because I saw myself in the elevator's mirror. I look like I just had sex.

"Shut up," I order in anticipation. "Don't say it. Don't even think about it. Just go back to sleep."

"Well, at least I know you didn't get laid, or you'd be more relaxed."

As I gather what I need for my shower, she sleepily adds, "Did he trip and his tongue slipped down your throat?"

"You aren't nearly as funny as you think you are, Katherine."

"I'm hilarious. You're just too frustrated to appreciate it. Take Idris with you. I don't want you to hump me during the night."

"Fuck you," I say as I head to the door with my stuff.

"I love you too."

In the bathroom, I avoid my reflection in the mirror. I strip, throw the dress in the laundry basket, and wince at how sticky my thong is. Lex definitely left with some of me smeared on the front of his pants.

I hop in the shower, eager to erase all traces of him from my body. My moves are practical and efficient, soaping and scrubbing. They become more delicate when I reach the space between my legs. The simple motion of my hand wiping away the wetness gathered there sends jolts of pleasure through my spine. Fuck, taking Idris with me wasn't such a bad idea after all.

Feeling like a hypocrite, I roll a couple of fingers over my aching clit and close my eyes to think of *him*.

We're back in his car, and I relive the moment we were interrupted. Except this time, the drunk group never passes by, so no one stops us from continuing.

In my fantasy, he opens his pants and wiggles them down just enough to free his cock, which juts out with enthusiasm. Imaginary Andrea seizes it, tugs her panties to the side, and then slowly comes down on him, impaling herself on his sinfully hard flesh. I shiver against the cold tiles of the shower, imagining myself bouncing up and down his dick, bracing my arm against the roof of the car to take all of him, gazing into his darkened irises.

With my eyes still closed, I bite my lip and intensify the rhythm of my fingers, feeling the tension build up inside me. Back in my fantasy, he undoes the tie at my neck to pull down the upper part of my dress while I keep fucking him with increasing momentum. I can still remember with accuracy the sensation of his hand on my breast, the way he gently pinched its taut tip. In my fantasy, though, he bends down to take my nipple in his warm mouth.

My climax takes me by surprise, exploding before I can envision the imaginary couple reaching theirs. I tremble and jolt, holding back my moans as I find my release.

It's good. It's exquisite, even.

But the sweet ache of it isn't enough. Not even close. When I open my eyes, the cold light of the bathroom harshly throws me back into reality, and all the pleasure goes down the drain with the water washing over me.

I shouldn't keep doing this, but I can't seem to stop myself. Alexander Coleman has a direct line to my libido, and I've never come so easily in my life than when I think of him. I'm so pathetic.

On Monday, I'll be back with him. But not in the way I crave because I love this job too much to risk it over sex.

Not even sex with him.

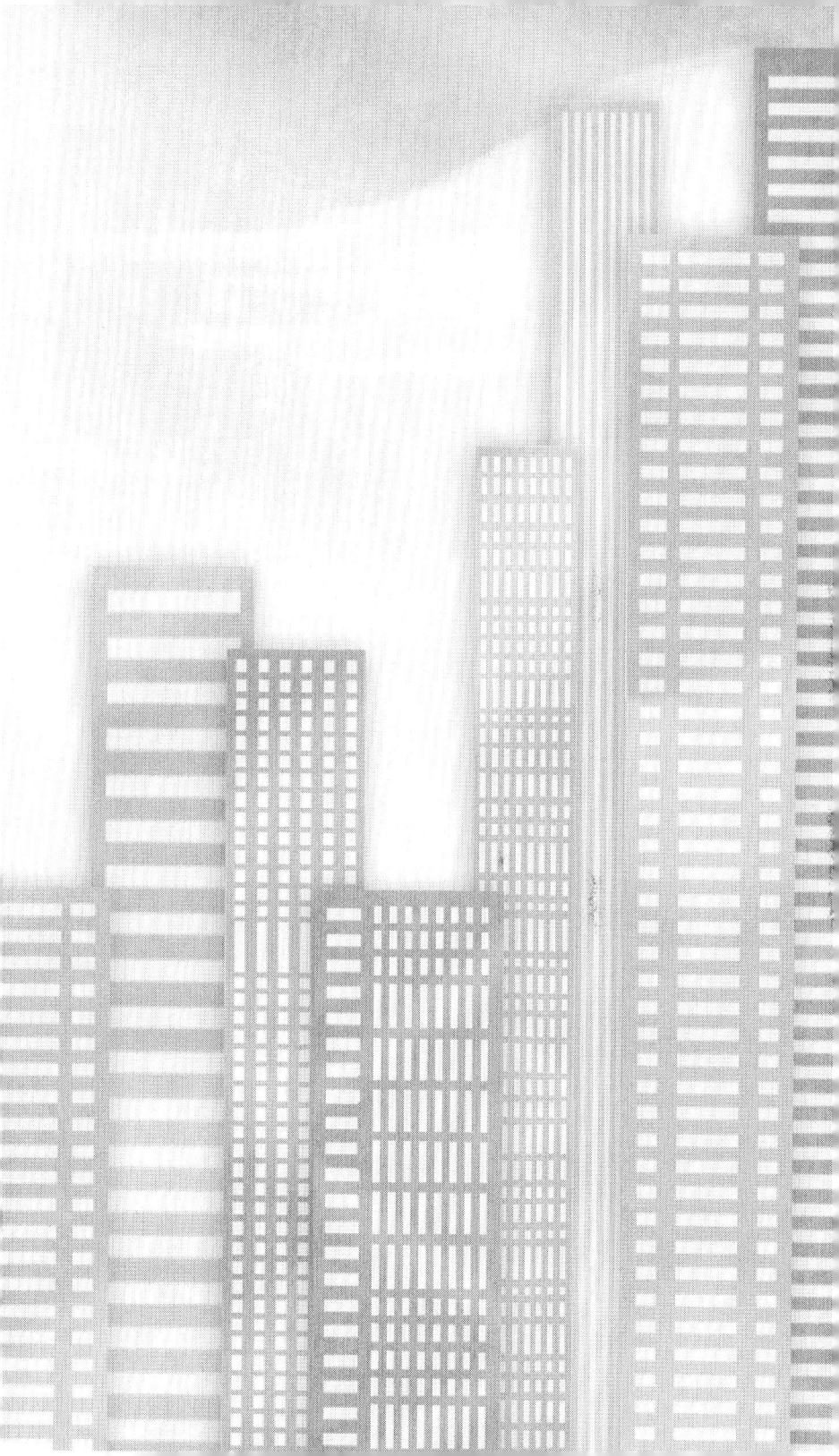

is_new_chapter = True

chapter_number = "14"

pov_name = "Andrea"

PRETENDING EVERYTHING IS OKAY WHEN my life is falling apart is unexpectedly easy. But maybe it's because Kate and Tami get along well, and we spend the weekend focusing on ourselves with self-care. They even drag me to a proper salon where I get a bikini wax because shaving isn't apparently enough.

The girls insist that it's "just in case" my date with Oli goes well. I know nothing will happen, but they refuse to hear it.

I forgot how much that shit hurt, and as I'm holding my knees against my chest so the technician can work her magic *way* down there, I wonder why the fuck we do this to ourselves.

My blonde friend hasn't peeped a word about Friday evening's events, but I know she's dying to hear some details. Kate is too smart not to have figured out what happened, but she understands the matter isn't funny or up for debate.

Sunday night provides little rest, even though I have the bed to myself again. I keep tossing and turning, wondering how things will be in the morning. There's a reason bosses and employees don't mingle, and I'm living it.

By the time my alarm rings in the morning, I slept for three hours at best, and I'm in no shape to face whatever the day will throw at me. I consider calling in sick, but it's too cowardly.

So, I get ready and go to work, bottling everything up.

To my relief, Lex isn't in his office yet. The strong facade I built deflates at once, relieved to see the confrontation won't happen right away. I sit on my chair, and as my computer boots, I stare at my keyboard, holding my head between my hands, elbows on the glass desk.

Today, Steven and Mason start their work on the app. I already devised a schedule and prepared the scripts they'll work on first, but Lex hasn't gone through it yet.

It won't do any harm to debrief them, so I head downstairs. A mini heart attack strikes me as soon as I enter the Troll's Lair.

He's there. Lex is at his desk with the guys.

Is he avoiding me, or is he needed down here?

"Hi, guys," I say, hoping I sound natural. They lift their heads and greet me back, except for Lex, who imperceptibly tenses.

Oliver gives me a wink and a grin when our eyes meet on my way to Steven, and I smile back, a little awkwardly.

I spend a solid hour there, talking to Steven then Mace. They don't seem to take the fact that I'm the project leader poorly, even though I'm the most recent hire. Selling my app to Kelex, which was such a huge personal accomplishment, is now tainted by the fact that Lex has been wanting me for God knows how long.

Surrounded by my colleagues, I wonder what they'd think if they knew. Would they imagine that I seduced our boss? Would they think I slept with him in exchange for all this?

I feel dizzy when I realize I'm not even sure of Lex's motives anymore. Yes, my app is amazing and perfect for Kelex. But did he push for the sale to get in my panties? Was this why he helped me get the best deal?

Before that dreaded kiss, I felt like a boss-ass bitch, a programmer extraordinaire. But now, I feel like a fraud, a naive imbecile.

Even when I return to Lex's empty office, I can't fully relax. Despite trying to focus, I'm constantly distracted by the fact that he might come in at any second. Every time I hear someone's footsteps, I tense, and every single time someone knocks on a door in the hallway, my heart drops—even though Lex doesn't knock, a fact I'm well aware of.

After lunch with Tami, Dakota, and more colleagues, I go upstairs again.

The office isn't empty.

Lex is on his computer, working on something. Our eyes meet over his screens, and I hold his gaze for as long as I can—not very long—before looking away and moving for my seat.

"Don't worry. I just need a few things, and I'll get back downstairs," he coldly explains.

Does this mean he's working downstairs to avoid me? We're grown adults. It's ridiculous to go to these lengths. Even if it was the most incredible kiss of my life, and I almost got his dick inside me in the process.

"Don't feel obliged to do so on my account," I say, trying to be professional. "It was just a kiss."

His gray eyes instantly seek mine, dark and angry behind his glasses.

Although many thoughts seem to cross his mind, he doesn't say anything and returns to his screen. I sit down to get back to work, tired of feeling like shit all the time. We remain in utter silence for a while, and my attention span becomes that of a four-year-old. I end up breaking the ongoing cold war out of necessity.

"Would you mind checking the shared calendar and telling me if everything seems alright?" I try to give my voice an assertiveness I'm definitely not feeling.

"I've gone through it already. I didn't see anything wrong." From him, it's almost a compliment.

About half an hour later, I'm alone again. I let out a long sigh, the tension leaving my body slowly. I hope things settle down soon because this isn't a sustainable work environment.

And I have more important things to care about.

Like my date with Oli.

is_scene_break = True

WITH EVERY DAY THAT PASSES, this tension between Lex and me becomes a little worse. We both pretend the kiss never happened and ignore each other's existence.

On the other end, Oli grows on me more and more with his gentleness, humor, and attentiveness. There's something about him that soothes me, something that I crave lately.

Hopefully, our date will finally get some sparks going, and I'll develop sensuous feelings for him—something I'm pretty sure would have happened without our infuriating boss in the picture.

Tamika is sitting on my bed as I browse through my things for our date in less than an hour. When she snaps her fingers to get my attention, I twist around, holding a white dress.

"I know you wore it recently, but the black dress you had for the sale's dinner looks amazing on you. And Oli hasn't seen it yet, so he won't mind."

I shake my head, determined not to wear that dress ever again. It can be thrown into an incinerator for all I care. By the twelfth outfit that gets discarded, I'm starting to understand why some girls take hours to get ready. This is draining. Especially since I need three approvals: mine, Tami's, and Kate's—via a video call.

The final choice is a black bell skirt with a lace overlay and a white, off-the-shoulder boho crop top. The ensemble is cute and in good taste, perfect for a first date. This time, I wear modest heels, and Tami helps me again with my makeup.

She's rooting so hard for this date to succeed that she even lends me a pair of large gold hoops and a matching necklace that highlights my neck and collarbones.

After a massive hug and the promise of my abuela's chilaquiles to thank her, I leave. On my way out, I utter a silent prayer to whatever gods might be listening—Hindu, Norse, Muslim, Greek, Jewish … any of them, I'm not picky.

Please make it so everything goes perfectly. Make it so my unwanted obsession with my boss transfers to Oli.

Lex is a matter of the flesh, and Oli is a matter of the mind. And I'm pretty strong-minded.

I learned my lesson, so I take a cab this time. The driver drops me at the corner, fifty yards from where Oliver is waiting for me, pacing anxiously. With an amused smile, I approach my date on foot, unnoticed. He's wearing an elegant outfit—camel pants, a white T-shirt, a navy blue jacket, and, on his feet, immaculate white Vans.

When I come closer, he notices my presence and turns to me. Tami's great work makes his jaw drop slightly.

"Hi," I greet once I'm before him.

He remains flabbergasted for a short moment before shaking himself out of it. "Sorry, I'm— Wow … Andy, you look—" Short of words, he shakes his head again.

"I take it Tamika did a good job, then," I say coyly, spinning to show off the extent of her miracle.

"You're always pretty, but now, I'm really wondering how a guy like me could get a date with a girl like you."

"You look pretty good yourself, Oliver Paulson. And don't worry, I'll get back to my Chucks and superhero tees in no time," I joke, sliding my arm through his. "So, where are you taking me?"

"The best Korean restaurant in the city, according to Yelp," he explains with pride, cleverly disclosing he did his homework to woo me.

"Really?!"

"Yeah, you told me you've always wanted to go there. This is the next best thing I could think of."

Our arms remain interlocked the whole walk there, about a block away, and he only lets go to open the door for me.

"Good evening," a middle-aged woman welcomes us as we enter. She's even shorter than me and has a thick Korean accent. The quaint little place is sleek and tasteful, with minimal decor and elegant furniture.

"Good evening," Oli greets her. "I have a reservation under Paulson."

"Ah! Yes! You're finally here. This is the girl?" she asks, looking at me with curiosity. Oli nods, and she smirks. "She's very pretty. Worth the wait."

I let that sink in as we follow her to our table.

"Have you eaten here before?" I ask Oli once we're alone with our menus.

"No, it's my first time here."

"Oh, she seemed very friendly."

"I guess she got more invested in this date with every call I made to postpone the reservation."

Fuck, right … "Sorry about that."

"Don't be. You were doing big, big things. Which, by the way, we need to talk about because I'm not sure I'm up to date."

I have no doubt that Oli and I are highly compatible, but the evening more than confirms it. Our brain chemistry matches, and there isn't one moment of silence throughout our entire dinner. We essentially have the same humor, and the anecdotes we share never fail to work on the other one. Our similarities were never as evident as tonight, and I often find myself thinking of what a great couple we'd make. It seems impossible we'd even argue, and I already know our matching taste in movies and hobbies would provide us with endless discussions and activities.

The restaurant is a bullseye, perfect in so many aspects. The food is so stellar that I can cross Korea off my bucket list. Ain't no way it gets any better than this.

At some point, long after the dessert plates are gone, he admits to having never seen *Jaws*, and it properly shocks me. "What! How is that even possible?"

"I don't know, I just never got to watch it," he defends himself with a laugh.

"We have to fix this right now! Okay. You get the check, I get an Uber, and we go to my place to watch it after we pay. I'm not letting you live another day without having seen *Jaws*."

He tenses for a split second, but I barely pay attention to it, already whipping out my phone from my tiny purse to get us a car. Eventually, he complies. By the time he's back, I have secured our ride to my apartment.

"Do they take credit cards?" I ask.

"It's all paid for, don't worry."

"What? Oli, we should have split."

"Call me old school, but I like to pay on a first date."

I open my mouth to insist but close it abruptly. Somehow, it momentarily slipped my mind that we were on a date. And now we're heading back to my place after a lovely dinner. We ate, drank, talked, laughed … And we're now going where my bed is. Is Oli thinking about that, too?

There's nothing about the way he is acting that indicates any expectation. He doesn't strike me as pushy, so when he agrees to come home for a movie, I'm sure that's okay with him and it's all he expects. But … still …

Maybe it's my realization, maybe it's the unspoken possibility of what comes next, but for the first time tonight, we're out of things to say. That silence lingers as we walk to the corner where the Uber will pick us up, and I have no idea what to do to lighten the mood. Now that the sun is down, it's much colder out here. Maybe I can mention that to get us back on track.

I must have shivered because as I'm observing the street, watching out for our car, Oli's warm jacket slips over my shoulders.

"How is it that women never take a jacket or something when they go out?" he humorously asks.

"Well, I don't know about other women, but I can't wear one with this top. It would ruin the fit."

He chuckles, shaking his head. "You'd look lovely in anything. I'll always remember the day you arrived in that Hulk T-shirt, surprising everyone. I'd never seen a geek that pretty. And then you worked on that script and showed me I had never seen one that smart either."

When I turn to him, slightly shocked by his bold declaration, his eyes stare into mine. I can read many things in them, including a few I'm not ready for yet.

Some strong emotion causes my chest to tighten. As much as I wish it were desire or love, it's mostly guilt. I want his compliments to make something flutter in my stomach, like when Lex gives me the tiniest bit of attention. I want Oli to awaken something in me I didn't know existed—like Lex did. I want to *want* Oli because he's what I need, what's best for me. By a whole fucking mile.

A car stops next to us, breaking the moment, and the driver rolls his window down. "Are you Andrea?"

"Yes, that's me."

Oli, who can do no wrong, opens the door for me. I climb into the sleek black Honda, then slide to the other seat to allow him inside. The car takes off, and I get lost in my thoughts again.

But they aren't about Oliver.

Why do I crave Alexander so much? Why do I harbor so many fantasies about him? Why can't I get over the passionate kiss we exchanged last week?

I don't even like the man. The little I know isn't to my taste. It makes no sense why I'd be so absurdly into him when I can barely stand him. What kind of fucked-up primitive impulse is that? Fuck the smart and athletic man, have his babies, and ensure the longevity and success of your lineage? I'm not a brainless animal living on instinct. I have a fully developed frontal lobe and free will. I don't *have* to feel like that for Lex.

I shouldn't wish so hard that the drunk group never stopped us, that we fucked in his car right there, that we spent the rest of the night in my bed, trying out every position we could come up with. I shouldn't wish I knew what it's like to have him ramming inside me, to know the sensation of his hammering dick as he makes me come hard.

"I'm thrilled we finally got to do this," Oli lets out beside me, ripping me away from my thoughts.

Shame. An enormous amount of shame takes over me. I'm right here next to Oli, out on a date with him, and my thoughts are of Alexander fucking Coleman. Not only that, but I'm growing wet at the idea of him fucking me.

I try to stop myself, but I can't. My head is filled with images of Friday night, flashing in my brain, awaking lustful needs—needs I'd give anything to feel for the man sitting beside me.

Maybe it's time to take the matter into my own hands. Time to make it happen.

So, I do just that, grabbing Oli's face to force him down onto mine, crashing our lips together.

Immediately, I know this is nothing like the unstoppable kiss I had with Lex. This is me desperately attempting to make those sparks ignite. This is me doing whatever I must to get my body to cooperate. This is me listening to reason instead of lust.

After a moment of shock, Oli eventually reacts and tilts his head to the side before raising a hand to rest it on the side of my throat, handling me delicately. I wait, unmoving, for something to happen. *Anything.*

Pressing my mouth harder on his, I intensify our kiss, trying to drag out the sensations I felt with Lex. When it still isn't enough, I open my mouth to get more. Oli follows, and soon enough, our tongues are meeting. This is pleasant but not as shattering as I'd hoped for.

His lips are soft, pliant under mine. He lets me lead and only takes control when I allow it. It's nice, enjoyable, but it still isn't enough. Undoing my seatbelt to get closer to him, I raise the intensity again. With my head further to the side, I grab his jaw with both my hands, shoving my mouth harder against his.

In my eagerness to get closer to him, to draw out those feelings, I end up half-straddling Oli, one leg hooked over his, my skirt rising on my thighs. Oli's hands are on me, but in a sweet, gentle way, like he's cradling me. But all I want is for him to need me like Lex did.

It doesn't matter how much I try … The jolts of pleasure, the desire, and the need to have him aren't coming. I want Oli to crawl into my mind like Lex did and take up all the room. I need this kiss to chase away the memory of the other one.

My experiences with my exes were less pleasurable than this. It *should* be enough. It was always enough. And he wants me; I can feel it in the hard bulge in his pants and the lascivious touches of his tongue. He wants me, so we're halfway there, aren't we?

But it isn't enough, nor okay. Now that I have tasted the immeasurable heights I can reach, it's all I crave. The raw desire, the lust, the need, the passion … I want Oli to grab me, to pull me, to devour me, to want to fuck me right here, to kiss me like he'll never kiss again.

Tears of frustration well up behind my closed eyelids.

In an attempt to get all those things, I do what I did to Lex. I lick Oli's lips, bite them, undulate … When his hands don't move, I grab them and set them on my ass, like Lex did, to show him what I need from him. But they barely stay there, quickly moving back up to my waist.

When, finally, they do something, it's to gently push me away. "Andy," he calls into our kiss. "Andy, we're here."

My blood freezes, making an icy chill run up my back. What the fuck am I doing?! Stunned, I push myself away from him and sit on my side of the car, avoiding his amber eyes. I've never, *ever,* acted like this before. Never used someone like I just did. Lex has fucked up my brain so badly that I've turned into a careless asshole.

Nauseous, I look at anything but Oli. As if to add to my shame, I meet the driver's eyes in the rearview mirror. My stomach churns with disgust at the concupiscent look the stranger gives me. I reach for the handle, ready to get out, but Oliver rests his hand on my arm, holding me back.

"Andy, I …" He struggles to find what to say, his mind still blurry. I glance at the driver, who isn't missing an ounce of this. "I really want to come up with you, but I want to do this the right way because I really like you," Oli continues. "I want this to work out, so I don't want us to rush into things."

My heart is in my bowels now, and I'm really going to be sick. I need to get away from this situation, the car, Oli …

"Yes, you-you're right," I stammer, struggling to contain myself. I just gave Oliver the impression I'm into him when, in all truth, I'm as clueless as when the whole date started.

During my moment of insanity, Oli's jacket fell from my shoulders. I pick it up from the floor and hand it to him before pulling the handle. "Thank you for everything, Oli," I say as I exit the vehicle.

The door is barely closed when I hear the driver shout at Oli, "Are you crazy, man?!"

As I make my way to the apartment, I somehow feel even worse than I did on Friday evening after Lex brought me home. And deep down, I know exactly why. Had I not kissed my boss, this just now would have been the best kiss of my life. Better than with any of my boyfriends or flings.

But I know better now. I know too much.

Tami's in the living room when I get there, and the smudged red lipstick betrays me despite how much I tried to clean it up in the elevator. When she asks me how it went, I give her two thumbs up and the best fake smile I can muster. I'm alone in my room when my phone rings. *Please, let it not be Oli …*

On the screen, I see the face of the only person I might agree to talk to right now. My voice of reason. Kate. "So!" comes her familiar voice when I pick up. "Tamika texted me that the date went great! Tell me everything!"

"I literally got home five seconds ago."

"We've been texting all evening. We're rooting for you guys." Okay, those two are getting a little too close. Since I say nothing for a while, Kate worries. "Babe, is everything alright?"

"I-I kissed him on the way home."

"And …?"

"It wasn't—it wasn't like when I kissed …" I stop, letting her fill in the blanks. Admitting it out loud is too much.

After a long moment of reflection, she asks, "Andy. Do you like Oli?"

"Yes, a lot."

"And, do you like you-know-who?"

"He isn't Voldemort, you can say his name. And no, I don't. I just want to fuck him *and* fuck him up."

"Okay, then it's just a sex thing."

"A what?"

"The man is sex on a stick. Of course he'd make your hormones squirm with want. You like Oli, but you want to bang Alexander. There's a pretty simple remedy to this."

"What?"

"You need to fuck Alexander out of your system." Her matter-of-fact tone isn't enough to sell it.

"Yeah, right. I have to fuck my boss to get over him. I don't see how that could backfire," I sarcastically say. "Brilliant plan, blondie. Call me again when another one of those moronic brain farts comes to you."

"I'm the one experienced in wanting assholes, remember? You need to fuck them to get over them. If you're lucky, he'll be amazing at it, and you'll have to do it a couple of times. Or he'll suck, and all the sex appeal will fade away."

There's a moment of silence where I try to figure out if she's pulling my leg. I might be inexperienced in these matters, but this sounds like a terrible plan. "Are you seriously suggesting that I should fuck my boss?"

"Yes, I am."

"Aren't you a lawyer or something? Don't you see how terribly this could end?"

"Babe, this is the twenty-first century. I don't see why two consenting adults who want to bang each other can't indulge. Make sure he's on the same wavelength, and just fuck him. Or let him fuck you. Regardless of who's fucking who, have his dick in you."

"How long has it been since you last got laid?"

"It's been almost two months."

"Ah, makes sense ... You're the one who needs a good dicking. Not me."

"Yeah, I know. I'm working on that. But that doesn't mean I'm wrong, Dee. I've had flings like that, and I swear, physical attraction always wears off. It always has for me, at least."

I can't believe I'm still entertaining her idea, but I ask, "What are the chances it'll actually work?"

"Since it's just sex, it will work. Just might take a few tries."

I whimper, hating that I'm genuinely considering her advice. What if that's all it takes? A few naked cardio sessions with Lex, and then he's out from under my skin so Oli can take his place.

"Well, I can hear you're calculating every possibility, so I'll leave you to it," Kate says. "If you need to talk some more, call me in the morning, babe."

"Hmm ... You know I hate you for putting this idea in my head, right?"

"Yep, I figured you would. You know me, though. I tell it like it is."

"And I love you for that. Sweet dreams, blondie."

"Sweet dreams, Deedee."

As I lie down in my bed, still wearing my date clothes, I wonder if I reached it yet—the point where I regret moving here, taking that new job, meeting those new people ...

My life was boring before, yes. But it was also so much simpler.

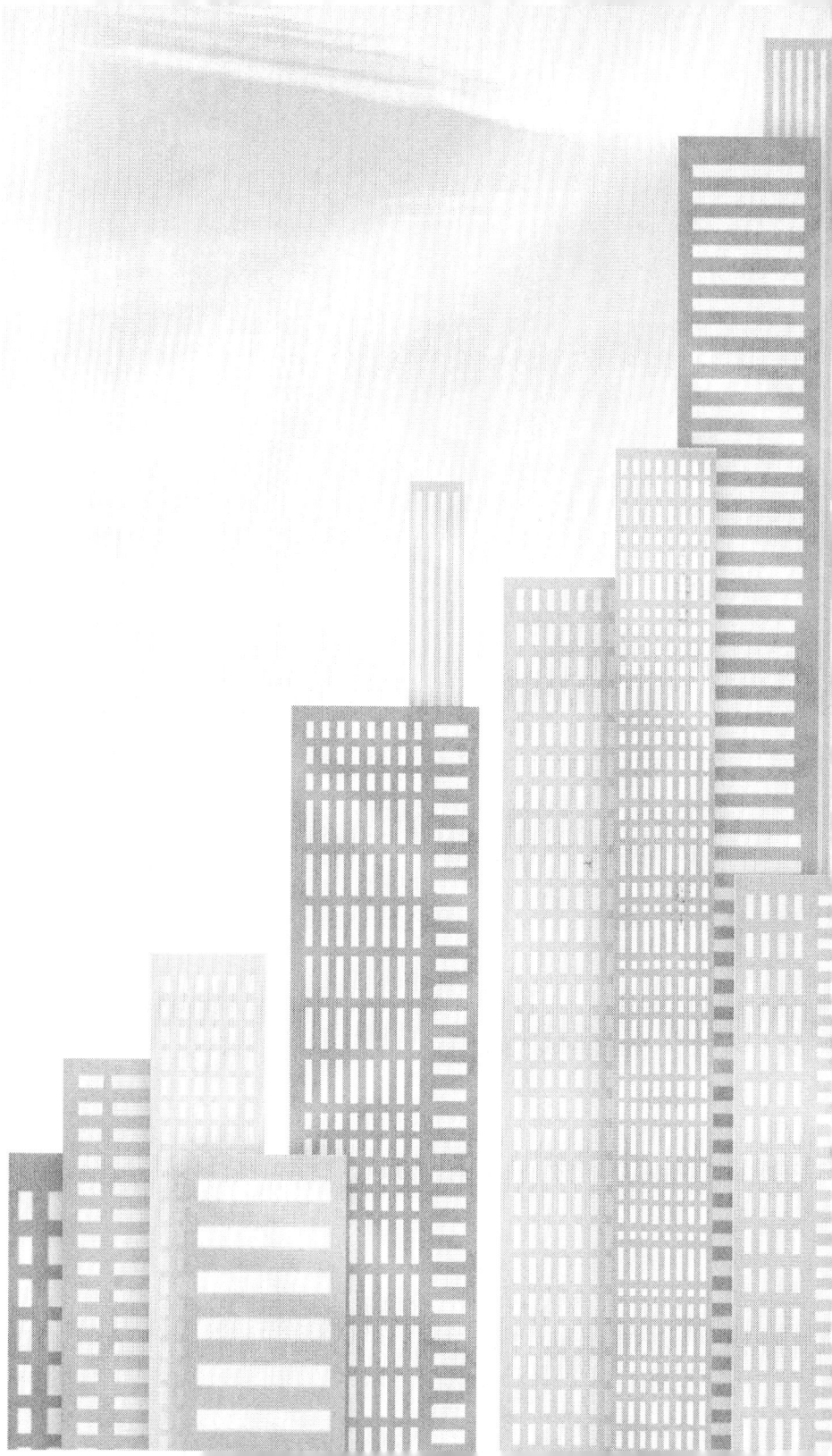

is_new_chapter = True

chapter_number = "15"

pov_name = "Andrea"

GOD HAS A TERRIBLE SENSE of humor and obviously has it out for me. There's no denying both those statements when I enter the elevator the next morning and see Lex in it. He gives me one of those icy looks before deciding I ought to be ignored again.

But then Oli gets in, and I nearly snort at the improbability of the situation. *It fucking figures* …

I'm not ready to deal with this mess, especially since I barely got any sleep.

Oblivious to my state of mind—because how could he know?—Oli makes his way to me among the many others trying to fit in here. "Hi, stranger," he greets me joyfully.

I force a smile on my lips. "Hi, Oli."

Tami's here too, next to me, pretending to pay us no mind. But I'm familiar enough with her to know she'll sneakily lipread. Which still isn't as embarrassing as Lex being right next to us and hearing *everything*.

"So," Oliver starts once the doors are shut. "Last night didn't go exactly as I'd planned, but I preferred your approach. The driver pestered me the entire way to my place."

Can I pretend to lose consciousness to get out of this?

No, that's the cowardly way, and Ibanez women don't cower. Except in the presence of poultry, because hens and geese are nasty peckers—a lesson I learned the hard way when visiting relatives in Mexico.

So, I smile and meet his honey irises. "I really enjoyed the restaurant. I'll definitely add it to my list."

"Oh, great. We parted abruptly, and I didn't get to ask if you liked it."

Because I can't help it, I glance at Lex. He's too close for me to pretend he can't hear. But his face is impassive, and if he's listening, it doesn't show.

"I really did. I've had Korean barbecue before, but never that good," I say, hoping the conversation will remain on food rather than more intimate allusions.

"Yes, you were in a great mood afterward."

Is it acceptable to faint now?

Like always, the elevator stops on every other floor, people get out, others get in … It's insufferable, and I very much want to step out of here. On floor fourteen, a shitload of people join us, as usual, and everyone's forced to shift around. I'm separated from Oli and Tami. In an attempt to make more room for the newcomers, I'm pushed against a hard body near me.

Ah, fuck … This feels like déjà vu.

Looking up, I peer at Lex. He has his brow arrogantly cocked up, his jaw tightly clenched.

Clearly, I'm not the only one aware of the similarities, as Lex bends discreetly to mutter, "I thought we agreed to never do this again?" His tone is petty, his voice between a grunt and a whisper. That, combined with his proximity, makes my knees turn to mush. This ignites me a hundred times more than full-on making out and grinding with Oli.

It's not fucking fair.

Maybe it's because of the weak legs, or maybe it's the person who elbows my back, but I stumble even closer to him, unable to keep my balance.

His large hand reaches for my hip to level me, burning my skin despite the layers of my jeans and light jacket. Instead of pushing me away, he presses me against him for an entire second before setting a more reasonable distance between us. When I look up this time, it isn't anger veiling his eyes, but something much more primitive and dangerous.

Something painfully tempting.

I know Kate's plan is bullshit, but I wish it weren't.

Angry at him as much as myself, I push against his chest, needing to set some distance before I do something stupid. It's hard to ignore the firmness of his muscles beneath my palms, and even harder not to notice the flame that dances in his eyes at my bold touch.

I make enough room for myself to twist around, but that's a terrible idea. My ass is now pressed against the front of his pants, and I could swear he hisses at the contact, taking in a sharp breath. But floor sixteen is here, and all the lazy fuckers who can't be bothered to climb two flights of stairs get out.

Within seconds, I'm back with Oli and Tami. Half a minute felt like an eternity.

"I may already have found our next destination," Oliver says enthusiastically after a moment, resuming our conversation as if nothing happened.

"Ah, you're quite the planner."

"Only when it's important. And like I told you yesterday—"

"Oh! Look!" I abruptly cut him off before he can add another word. "It's your floor. I'll walk you to the Lair."

As we step out, I peer at Lex. He looks pissed, his jaw ticking. *Fuck* …

On our way to the Lair, I rack my brain to find the words and figure out what I can tell Oli. But my silence is uncharacteristic, so he guesses something is off. "Is it something I did?" he carefully asks. The anguish in his voice nearly wrecks me.

I can't even begin to process the guilt gnawing at my insides. In need of privacy, I grab his arm and pull him to an isolated corner.

"You were perfect," I say genuinely. "You *are* perfect. Yesterday was great, but I lost control a little. A lot. I'm not usually that bold. It's just that I-I have too much going on right now. With the sale, the new job, the new city … I've been overwhelmed lately."

He takes in my words, processing them for a while. The last thing I want is for Oli to doubt himself. He's done nothing wrong, on the contrary. The man even stopped me from making a bigger mistake in my attempt to drive Lex out of my mind.

"Do you want to slow things down or stop them altogether?" he ends up asking.

"I—"

I don't know. Slowing things down isn't enough right now. I can't date Oli and give him any hope for as long as Alexander is on my mind. He deserves better than this. But I also don't want to put an end to everything. I'm too smart to let my vagina dictate my life and decisions.

"Right now, I don't really know where I'm at, and I don't want to ruin things because we had a false start," I explain. "I really like you, Oli, but I can't expect you to put everything else on hold for me. Maybe it's simpler if we're just friends for now, and when I get my shit together, we can give it another try if you're still interested?"

"I would never want to force you to do anything. I should have realized you weren't ready." Not only is he the most understanding person ever, but he's also the sweetest, most considerate one.

"How could you? I didn't even know it myself. But I swear to you, Oliver Paulson. As soon as I'm ready, I'll come and get you," I promise, hiding my doubts.

He squints his eyes, and I see a glimpse of amusement in them. "Why did that sound like a threat?"

The tension is slowly wearing off, and the relief compels me to let out a soft giggle. "Well, it's because it was. You better be ready for me."

"I will be, Hulkette. However long it takes for you to figure things out, I will still be interested."

For some reason, his statement feels both wrong and right, and I don't know what to make of it. I don't want him to wait for me, but I hope he will. We're too good together not to become a thing.

All I need is to sort out that messed up situation with my infuriating boss. Which won't be easy since we're hell-bent on ignoring the shit out of each other.

That's what we do the entire day. I barely grant him a glimpse when I get in, and then I pretend I'm alone, forcing my brain to ignore his closeness. I'm so absorbed by work that I don't notice the time. He's the one who does, his head popping over the screen that shields us from seeing each other.

Ugh, these fucking glasses …

Lex gestures to his ears, inviting me to remove my headphones. "Time's up. Go home," he says when I do, keeping it to a minimum.

Confused, I check the time on my screen, and my eyes open wide. Oh, damn. I should have left twenty minutes ago. "Oh, right, thanks."

Once everything's off and I have all my things, I throw a vague, "Bye" on my way out, not expecting or getting one in return.

Tomorrow's Friday. If it goes as smoothly as today, then I'm out of the woods until Monday. By then, I might have a better idea of how to fix this than Kate's.

Yeah, that's totally doable.

Totally.

pov_name = "Alexander"

THIS COLD WAR WE'RE WAGING is getting ridiculous. We only exchange words when we need to for the app and nothing else. She clearly has no interest in interacting with me, and I'm too proud to beg for scraps of her attention. She needs to come to me.

Admittedly, I shouldn't have allowed things to derail the way they did because she did drink that night. But she'd sobered up by the time we got to her place, and I'm not good at resisting her. And we both know that kiss wasn't due to the wine she drank.

A week has passed since that evening, and none of the tension has faded. I haven't been able to chase the memory out of my head, and because of my high capacity to retain information, I remember it all with vivid accuracy.

I've been thinking of it much more than I care to admit. On several occasions since, I've fucked my fist thinking of her in that pretty dress, of her drenched pussy, of her soft, desperate moans …

I never in my life thought I'd be lusting after an employee like this. I'm too hell-bent on following the rules and doing what's right. Kev always told me to let loose and live a little. That clearly wasn't good advice. Letting go brought nothing but frustration and a strained relationship with one of our most valuable employees.

Releasing a sigh, I lean back into my chair. Neither of us has spoken in nearly four hours, and the day is almost over, so she'll head out and disappear from my life for the weekend. It's supposed to be a good thing, but it doesn't feel like it.

Does she also think of our kiss as she lies alone in bed at night? Or is she even alone in her bed? It's my understanding that she and Oliver had a date, and it went well. The utter rage that I felt upon hearing that worried me. It shouldn't matter what she does, but the fact that she kissed me and went out on a date with him within a week is insulting. Did it really mean nothing to her?

I'm ruminating on my thoughts when she hastily gathers her things. Every day, she's out at five-thirty sharp, eager to escape my office and my presence.

She stands with her bag and, without sparing me a glance, she mumbles, "Enjoy your weekend."

"Andrea, wait a moment." She freezes, and I remember to add, "Please." That word works surprisingly well on her.

I'm walking up to her when she turns, and something about her demeanor sends my brain into a frenzy. She's trying so hard to seem unfazed, but I notice the flush of her cheeks and the way she avoids my gaze so fiercely.

"I meant to apologize for my behavior last week," I explain. It isn't a lie, but it isn't entirely true either. I don't regret the kiss, but I regret the ending and its aftermath.

She nods, still looking away. "Me too. I'm sorry. I don't know what got into me."

"I thought you said it was alcohol." That compels her to look at me. I take a step forward, and she takes one back.

"Yes, of course. The wine."

"I should have noticed you weren't yourself." Another step forward, another one back. I'm not sure what I'm doing yet, but it's happening.

She isn't good at hiding how flustered I make her. I used to think it was because she disliked me, but I know better now. Three steps later, she bumps into the armchair behind her, stopping her retreat. I halt close enough to sense the heat emanating from her body.

"Are you tired?" I ask. She shakes her head. "Have you been drinking today, Andrea?"

Confused, she silently denies again, breathing out a faint, "No."

"Perhaps you're cold?"

Her overheated face already gives me the answer I seek, but she shakes her head once more. Victorious, I slowly lift a hand between us, grazing the front of her nerdy T-shirt, my knuckles brushing the modest swell of her breast. In its path, it teases a nipple, which is hard and begging for attention. She shivers from head to toe, and her eyes unmistakably darken.

I bend forward until my lips are by her ear. "This is all me then," I rasp. Firmer this time, I run the back of my fingers against the taut tip, clearing any doubt there might have been.

She's speechless, a trembling breath flowing out of her lush lips. As I straighten up, I lower my hand to her waist, resting it on its perfect curve. It's like it was meant to be there, affirming my power over her.

Her eyes glide over my mouth, and her lips instinctively part. The cat's out of the bag. She can't keep pretending that the kiss meant nothing or was an inebriated accident. She wants me. Tipsy or not.

But just in case she thinks she can keep denying it, I slowly bend forward as if to kiss her. She has every opportunity to stop me, but she doesn't. She accepts that we're about to kiss in the middle of this office, in broad daylight, with nothing that can justify why she's allowing it.

Her head tilts to the side, and her eyes flutter closed, ready to welcome my lips over hers. Every bone in my body wants to indulge. Tasting her again is all I want. I need it with everything I have.

But like I said, she must come to me this time. And I've proven my point, whether I kiss her or not.

When the kiss she expects doesn't come, she confusedly opens her eyes again. That's when I cunningly murmur, "That's what I thought," before pulling away.

She looks as shocked and offended as if I slapped her across the face. But I ignore her and return to my computer instead. I did what I had to to prove it wasn't the wine. Now, she'll have the weekend to think about her actions and lies.

It doesn't matter if I've just brought more frustration upon myself. The victory is sweet.

But not as sweet as the intoxicating taste of her lips.

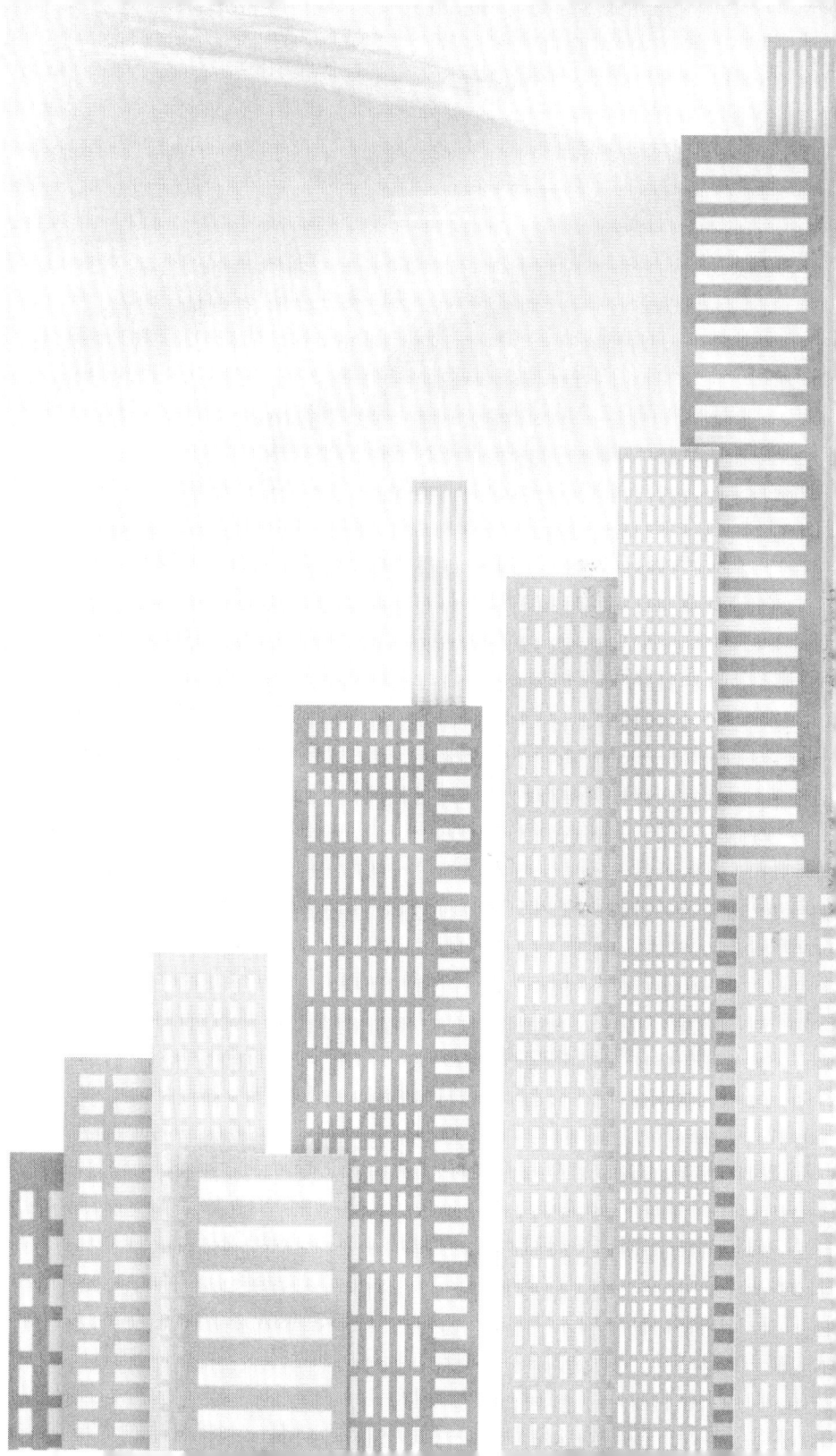

is_new_chapter = True

chapter_number = "16"

pov_name = "Andrea"

I FEEL … BAMBOOZLED. What almost happened in Lex's office haunts me the whole weekend. I've been betrayed by my rebellious nipples, and he knows it wasn't the alcohol, but pure, unaltered desire. Does it mean he knows *everything*?

That the thought of him consumes me? That I can barely think straight when he's in the room? That the idea of fucking him sometimes wakes me in the middle of the night, sweaty and horny, on the verge of orgasm? That I've been masturbating with him in my mind?

Or does he know I'd give my left kidney to kiss him again?

I guess he does because I practically offered myself to him. But he easily rejected me, like it was all a game.

It makes everything so much worse than before, which is saying a lot. I don't know what to do other than ignore him. But it works, so it's not that bad a technique. Eventually, I might even grow indifferent to him.

I'm being a coward, and I know it. Avoiding my issues and pretending they don't exist is wrong, and it isn't something I usually do. But in this particular case, I have too much to lose.

I've never dreaded a Monday as much as I did this one. But maybe I was overthinking, as usual, because nothing has happened so far. Nothing but the heavy and charged silence that has become our routine, our implicit agreement that not interacting is for the best. Someone knocks on the door about half an hour before the day ends. It's the first sound I hear in at least three hours. Lex and I are uncannily good at not talking to each other.

"Come in," he commands, not looking away from his work. Since I'm not a cold machine like him, I turn around to see who it is. I smile at the sight of Oliver as he grins back.

"Hi, guys," he says, coming toward the desk. "Lex, I passed Beatrix in the hallway, and she asked me to give you this." He hands Lex a thin folder of papers. "She said it's for the Hello World Con."

The topic makes me drop everything to listen. The Hello World Convention is halfway between a congress and a convention, and it's held in Silicon Valley, where companies, firms, and corporations from all over the country gather for three days of intense nerding. It's centered around programming, demonstrations of tools and software, as well as lectures and conferences. It's one of the nerdiest, most tech-oriented conventions in the US. So, understandably, going to the HWC is a dream of mine.

From what I've heard, Lex and Kev go there every year with two people from the dev team. I'm too much of a junior employee to get that honor, but there's always next year and the ones after.

Alexander skims over the folder's pages, his eyes focused behind his glasses. "When you get back downstairs, you can tell your colleagues everyone is going this year," Lex tells Oli, putting the papers aside.

Wait ... What? Everyone's going?!

As confused as I am, Oliver gives me a surprised look before turning to our boss. "Seriously? Everyone?"

"Yes. I'm tired of the never-ending complaints and whining of those who can't go."

"Everyone, including me?" I ask, standing up so I can see the man.

"Yes. All seven of us and Kevin are going this year. We have also scheduled an hour-long slot in one of the lecture halls to present some of our work and advances."

I can't believe I will spend a few days in the heart of the high-tech world learning about groundbreaking advances. It sounds like a fun little vacation among colleagues, and I'm here for it. Oli is grinning as well, also very pleased with the news.

"Thanks, Lex," he says. "Everyone will be ecstatic."

"The company has been doing well enough to afford a spot for everyone, so I thought we'd change things up a little."

"That's very cool of you. Thanks," Oliver insists. "Anyway, I'm here to see Andy. I'm having some issues with a script she worked on a couple of weeks ago. Mind if I borrow her?"

Lex's eyes seek mine, giving me a cold glare before looking back at Oli. "Borrow away."

Well, at least I'm not the only one acting salty and childish.

Oli and I work together for the remainder of the day, and I realize how much I miss working with people. Being here with Lex is nothing like what it used to be downstairs. When we fix the bug—much too early for my taste, even though we're ten minutes past five-thirty—Oli takes his leave, so I accompany him to the door. As soon as it closes behind him, I find Lex standing ten feet away from me.

His eyes are on me, inquisitive, as I walk to my chair. "What happened between you two?"

I stop dead in my tracks, whipping my head to glare at him. "Excuse me?"

"Why was he looking at you with those sad puppy eyes? Did you break up with him?"

Lex's intrusive attitude is enough to enrage me, and I let out an exasperated sigh. "Oh, no. You don't get to ask this. Not when this is all your fau—" I stop mid-sentence, realizing what I'm about to say.

"I'm in your head, right?" he arrogantly asks. "That's why you've been trying to ignore me since that kiss."

"I honestly don't know what you mean," I say, wanting to hurt him. "I've been doing my best to ignore you since I started working here."

"You're failing."

"It's not my fault you're keeping me hostage up here!" The volume of our voices is slowly increasing, but I don't have the presence of mind to worry about whoever might be doing overtime out there. "Admit it. I'm the one in your head."

A dark shadow passes over his face. Good, I'm not the only one getting pissed. "Why are you acting like I'm the only one at fault here? Weren't you on my lap ten days ago, begging for my cock?"

My eyes open wide, shocked by his crudeness. Oh, this is getting vicious. Maybe Kate is wrong after all. Maybe what I need is to loathe the man until he disgusts me.

"Fuck you!" I hiss, holding back the slap I desperately want to inflict on his cheek. "You're an arrogant asshole, and I can't fucking stand you."

"I don't think your body got the memo." He's being pretentious and venomous, and it's getting harder and harder not to get physical.

"Beats me why. I'm normally not into narcissistic dickheads."

His glare becomes even darker, his pupils dilating drastically. "That's the problem, right? You're so into me, you want to fuck me so badly, you can't even date Oliver."

I take a step back as if he physically hurt me. It isn't so much the brutality of his words or the harsh tone that gets me, but the accuracy of what he said. Yes, that's precisely my problem.

How pathetic …

All the insults I want to throw at him are jammed in my throat, my mind running too fast to formulate sentences. I feel helpless, more than I ever have, betrayed by my tongue, which refuses to cooperate.

Desperate not to let him win, I shove his chest with my flattened hands, wanting to hurt him. He barely moves, and it only adds to my humiliation. Even angrier, I push again, harder, and the impact makes him take a step back this time. "Fuck you," I utter along with the shove.

I do it once more, passing all my exasperation onto him, wanting to make him pay for the psychological torture he's imposing on me.

Fuck him. Fuck Alexander Coleman and his perfect face. Fuck his arrogant attitude. Fuck his hypnotizing eyes. Fuck his ego.

Why does it have to be him? Of all the men out there, why him?

To my great dissatisfaction, I never get the chance to push him a fourth time as his hands swiftly catch my wrists. I try to get free, but his hold on me is as firm as iron. When I glare up at him, he has his stern mask on.

I want to hurt him, to slap the shit out of that handsome face, to yell at him, to bite, to kick …

But as he's standing so close to me, his heat radiating across my front, his intensity making my insides melt, it becomes clear that hatred isn't the only feeling making my blood run so hot. To my greatest despair, I also want to kiss him.

Even more than I want to hurt him.

And I hate him all the more for it. For wanting him more than I loathe him.

He has to stop invading my dreams, stop occupying my mind, stop ruining my chances at a happy relationship …

Maybe it's time for me to stop blaming Lex for the things he makes me feel. This whole mess is my fault. I'm the fucking imbecile ruining her own life. I need to grow up and take responsibility for my problems instead of making excuses.

This time, he lets go of me when I writhe my wrists. As alert as he might be at that moment, the way his eyes widen when I grab his face proves he isn't expecting my next move. Hell, I'm not expecting it, either.

But here I am, pulling him down so I can bring my mouth to his.

Just like the first time, an intense wave crashes through my whole body. I barely have time to register the sensation before his arm circles my waist, while his other hand tangles in my hair on the back of my head. Two seconds into the kiss, we're already getting greedy, clinging to each other with desperate need.

It feels so … right.

Our mouths impatiently open, craving more, and I let out a soft moan at the first brush of our tongues. The very candid reaction affects him, his hand on my hip clutching the flesh harshly. With my head tilted to the side, I take and grant, devouring as much as I'm being devoured.

Our moves are feverish, our eagerness rendering our attempts clumsy. I'm on my tiptoes, one arm hooked behind his neck, trying to anchor myself while he struggles to keep our balance, his hand on the back of my head to keep me exactly where he wants me. The hand at my hip travels to my ass, his fingers squeezing the soft mound impatiently, pulling me closer to him.

"Aah, yes …" I whimper in his mouth, the rigid shape of his desire for me digging into my lower stomach.

Somehow, I end up with my back against the door while he presses me onto it with a groan. I was never into tall guys, but something about his overbearing presence reaches something deep inside of me. His massive body dominates mine in every way, making some feminine part of me swoon.

His hand in my hair mirrors the other one, lowering to fondle and squeeze my ass, which sends maddening jolts into my lower belly. The space between my legs is throbbing, my insides clenching around emptiness, dying to be filled. I arch toward him, pressing my aching core on him, grinding my lower belly against his erection. Oh, how I long to have this part of him inside me.

He growls into our kiss, and it dawns on me that we're reaching a point of no return. We're about to fuck in his office. I know I should stop it but can't bring myself to.

I need it to happen, even if he's my boss, even if it might make everything even more complicated. This thing between us isn't rational, and I'm done trying to contain it.

pov_name =

"Alexander"

WITH MY HANDS FULL OF her ass, I lift Andrea up. Her legs part instantly and wrap around my waist as I press her onto me, right where I need her so fucking much it hurts. The thickness of our jeans isn't even enough to contain the heat that seeps and transfers between us.

I press her harder onto the door, letting her feel what she's doing to me, and she moans into our kiss. There's something primal in the desperate way we cling to one another. I need this woman like I've never needed anyone before. And if the way she kisses me is any indication, she feels the same.

She kisses like she lives—with passionate impulsivity. It's not something I'm familiar with, but even though it's only the second time it's happened, I already feel myself in danger of becoming addicted to it.

She gives and demands everything, and I return every bold graze of her tongue with mine.

When she sends her hands down between us to tremblingly open my jeans, I grab her wrist and pull it away.

"Not here," I say, my voice throatier than expected. "I'm not doing it like this, where anyone can interrupt."

"They're all gone by now," she counters, boldly reaching for my belt again.

With a soft growl, I let her down and take a few steps back. The ravenous look on her face slowly fades away, replaced by a frown. It seems that the veil of lust is lifting, and she's returning to her senses. Shit, maybe I should have listened and taken her against the door.

"I can't believe I'm *begging for your cock* again," she mutters after a moment of silent pondering.

The remorse I feel upon being reminded of my bitter words makes a ball of discomfort swell in my throat. "I'm sorry, Andrea. I went too far. I shouldn't have said those things."

She looks away, still upset. "I hate this situation," she explains, avoiding my gaze. "I'm missing my chance with Oli, I'm jeopardizing my career, I'm confused all the time … At this point, I should just quit because this isn't sustainable."

Something churns in my stomach at the thought. "That's not an option."

"Why?"

"We need you here. I know I don't compliment people enough, but you're a solid addition to the team. You can't quit because of something so … trivial."

There's a long break where I curse myself for breaking the spell. How the fuck did we get from almost fucking to her thinking of quitting?

She lets out a frustrated sigh and says, "Well, I don't see another solution. Aside from fucking you out of my system."

That is something I'm definitely on board with. She can't quit, but we can fuck. This novelty, this need … it's bound to go away if we indulge, isn't it?

"Alright," I decide.

Finally, she peers at me, surprised by what I just accepted, stunned that I'm on board with fucking each other's brains out.

In the end, it's very simple. Yes, she's my employee, but she's also the smartest, prettiest, and most fascinating person I've ever met. I lasted almost six weeks. It's enough to prove my attempt at resisting the irresistible.

She wants this. I want this.

We're grown adults, and it's time to act like such.

Her voice has some determination when she asks, "How do we do this?"

"We're going to my place. We'll improvise from there."

Despite her acceptance of what we're about to do, I can sense that part of her is still unsure about it. So, I give in to my need to touch her, and slowly, as if she's a wild animal that I might scare, I frame her face with my hands. I lower my lips to hers with the same unhurried pace and give her a soft, measured kiss.

There's a chemistry between us that I've never known before. The sparks are undeniable, and the little we've done exceeds most of my experiences.

Just how maddeningly intense will the sex be if this is how I react to a kiss?

To my relief, we don't run into anyone on our way to the elevator. It's later than I thought, and everyone's gone. The ride down is overwhelmingly silent—but it's welcome, for once. It allows me to think about what we're about to do. And how much of a shit show it could turn into.

HR will have my fucking head if they hear about this. But they won't, right? No one ever has to know about what happens tonight. Just Andrea and me.

She gets into the car before I can open the door for her, and as I sit behind the wheel, she turns to me and says, "I'm not risking everything over mediocre sex, so it better be good."

Were I not so tense, I probably would have laughed at her words. I don't answer, but the look I give her should clear up her doubts.

I'll make it so good that she'll remember tonight for years to come.

I drive us out of the underground parking lot, and after I've taken a few turns, she frowns and confusedly says, "You don't live near my neighborhood."

"No, I don't."

"You lied to me when you insisted on driving me home. *Twice.*"

"I never told you where I lived, just that I was good to drive you to your place," I point out, not looking away from the road.

She doesn't seem convinced, so I continue with, "I kept you late the first time, so it was the least I could do. The second time, I wasn't leaving you to fend for yourself, drunk."

"I wasn't drunk," she defensively argues.

"You need to make up your mind, Andrea. Were you drunk or not when you kissed me?"

"I was tipsy," she mumbles after a few seconds.

It seems she's getting tenser by the minute, which is less than ideal for what we have planned. "You know you can change your mind anytime, right?" I ask, using the fact that we're stopped at a red light to focus on her.

That must have been precisely what she needed to hear because something releases in her, and her shoulders sink with relief. What she does next surprises me as she reaches for my nape and pulls me down, planting her lips on mine. After a short but intense kiss, she moves back. But I'm not done yet.

Before she's too far, I pull her in again and take her lips like she's the oxygen I need to breathe, demanding more, and she yields to my will, allowing me to sample her thoroughly. I could never get used to kissing this woman. She's pliant yet demanding, knowing when to give and when to take. The thrill of it is never-ending. I could kiss her for hours.

The car behind us honks, but I don't give a shit. They can wait. This can't. She either doesn't hear or doesn't care because she stays right there, right where I want her. The car honks again, more insistent this time, and I accept this will have to do for now. After one last hungry peck, I rip myself away from her and drive.

About five minutes later, I pull up in front of my building's underground parking lot. The wide door automatically lifts, and I drive us in. I park in my spot, and we're soon walking up to the elevator.

"Are you alright?" I ask while we wait for it to arrive.

"Yes. I just—I never do this. It feels strange."

"Never do what? Have sex?"

"*Casual* sex," she corrects me, missing the fact that I was teasing her.

The doors open before us, and I rest a hand on her lower back to gently invite her in. I have to remove it once we're in to press my floor's button, but it swiftly returns there. I'm not sure how I'll manage to keep my distance from her after tonight. This won't go away with just one night. But that's a problem for another day. A problem for tomorrow.

Silence weighs the air around us as we walk through the hallway that leads to my apartment, and with every step closer to my door, I grow more anxious about what we're about to do. What if it makes everything worse? What if I don't get enough of her and forever crave more?

Again. That's a problem for another day.

pov_name = "Andrea"

LEX LETS ME STEP IN first and follows closely behind. I'm so damn nervous that I barely register when he calls out with a clear voice, "Iris, I'm home!"

I whip around, my eyes round with shock.

Who the fuck is Iris?! Does Lex have a girlfriend? Is he expecting a threesome or something? Does he have a secret daughter I don't know about?

Before I can ask anything and humiliate myself with a chain of accusations, a feminine but undoubtedly electronic voice resonates in the apartment. "Welcome home, Alexander."

At the same time, the lights increase gradually, and the window shutters roll up without a sound, lighting up the space with the last rays of the sun.

The entire room is vast but not absurdly so, furnished, decorated, and laid out in tones of grays, from light to anthracite, with touches of light woods on the floor and a few pieces of furniture. We're in the living suite, with a large lounge room, a dining area, and an open kitchen.

The programmer in me is curious to know more about his live-in AI. "I've never heard of a home AI named Iris. Where does she come from?"

"She's my very own Intelligent Residential Interface System."

"I-R-I-S … That's clever. You programmed her?"

He nods as if it's the simplest thing. "I don't trust the other AIs. You never know how much they are recording, and I like to keep my life private."

"So you went and built one from scratch?"

"What else was I supposed to do?"

"I don't know. Open your windows manually and use the switches for the lights?" I propose with humor. He lets out a loud breath, the closest thing to a laugh I have ever heard from him.

"But where's the challenge in that?"

I genuinely laugh, amused by the way he thinks. In his genius mind, building a whole AI system isn't that far-fetched. Searching for personal clues as to who he is, I look around the place. The room looks impersonal, like a magazine home. There isn't even a picture anywhere, just generic-looking art. That's disappointing.

The place is particularly masculine, and the lack of a woman's touch reminds me of something. "Do you have a woman in your life?"

His answer takes slightly too long to come. "I don't."

"What about the one from the nude when we first met in the elevator?"

"She was a convenient arrangement, nothing more. And she wasn't one anymore at the time she sent that picture."

"Really?"

"Relationships demand too much maintenance. That's why I don't get entangled with anyone."

Message received loud and clear. We're not getting entangled. This is just a convenient arrangement—one where he hopefully rearranges my insides.

A pout is on my lips as I approach a painting. It's Pollock-inspired, with drops and splashes of paint. I'm not into modern art, but there's something fascinating about it. I don't know if it's the contrast of the colors, the slight relief of the drops, or the sheer size of the piece—as big as a door—but I adore it for some reason.

I can feel his eyes following my stroll around his place, and it warms me from the inside out. The apartment is remarkably silent, giving me a sense of isolation. We're in Downtown Seattle, close to rush hour, and I can't hear a single car. All this silence isn't helping with my nervousness. Some music would go a long way.

Feeling bold, I take a deep breath, not moving my eyes from the painting. "Iris, could you put on some music?"

I hear what almost sounds like a chuckle behind me. "Sorry, she only answers to my voice, Andrea. And I'm afraid I never programmed her for music."

He's close to me now, but I keep my back to him, resisting the urge to turn around and look at him.

"Are you telling me you don't listen to your funky playlist here?" I tease, remembering his unexpected tastes.

"I only listen to the 'funky' playlist to prevent me from falling asleep while I drive for long hours."

Confused and disappointed, I spin around to face him. "So you don't actually like disco music?"

"I don't like music in general."

That's probably a red flag, but I couldn't care less when he's so close to me. I fight the urge to press my palms on his broad chest.

"Why would you let me believe it was your playlist then?"

"You were having a blast. I didn't want to ruin your fun." Bending closer to me, he brings his mouth right next to my ear, his hand grazing my side from my hip to my ribs. "You have the most enticing laugh, Andrea."

His closeness, baritone voice, and touch are too much for me to handle. A wave of pure lust travels through my entire frame to end straight between my legs, where my clit pulsates with need. Right then and there, I cream my panties.

How does he keep doing that? Make me so weak and needy?

Perfectly aware of what he just did to me, he retreats with a smirk. "Would you like something to drink?"

Once more, the reality of what's about to happen dawns on me. I'm here to seal the deal, to have sex with Lex. Should I call it … *slex*? Okay, now my nervousness is derailing my brain.

"I'd like that, but could I use your bathroom first?" I ask, trying to seem nonchalant. I need to clean up because I'm not letting him near my chocha so long after my last shower.

He points to a hallway behind me. "Second door on the right."

Once there, I stay with my back pressed on the door for a moment, still unsure if all of this is a good idea. The setting is far from romantic, but I don't want romance, anyway. I'm here to have sex with him, then leave.

I'll go all the way because I can, but more importantly, because I want to.

is_new_chapter = True

chapter_number = "17"

pov_name = "Andrea"

LEX IS IN HIS KITCHEN when I return, and I take a second to enjoy his strong silhouette before joining him there. He's sipping on a glass of amber liquor, with the bottle on the counter before him. Yes, good idea, liquid courage.

I drop my bag on the couch as I pass it and join Lex. His eyes scan me from head to toe as I approach, making my heart slam against my ribs. I take the glass he's holding, my eyes locked on his, and bring it to my lips before drinking what is left in it with two gulps.

Whatever this is, it isn't meant to be swallowed in one go but rather sipped, so an intense burning sensation spreads in my throat. The need to cough becomes almost irrepressible, but I fight it, swiftly turning around so he doesn't notice my watery eyes. *Idiot.*

I pour another glass and twist toward him again. Lex is much closer now, trapping me between the kitchen counter and his broad body. This is very intimate, and the boldness of it suggests we're done with the pleasantries.

Shit, I need more amber courage for this. More reasonable this time, I only take a small sip before moving the beverage away from my mouth, lost in his steel grays the whole time. With a slow gesture, he takes the glass from my hand, brings it up, and twists it to lay his bottom lip where mine was. Gazing at me intensely, he drinks it up and bends to put the empty glass on the counter behind me. I move back as he leans forward, our faces only a few inches apart.

I'm caged in by his domineering position, his hands resting flat on the marble top on each side of me. I'm hypnotized by him, captivated by his intense gaze that can probably see into my soul. My entire body is tingling, my heart is drumming, and it has nothing to do with the alcohol and everything to do with Lex.

I'm so close I can see spots of dark gray in his cold irises. It isn't fair that a man would be gifted with such lush and long eyelashes, but it isn't wasted on him. His cheekbones are chiseled to perfection, giving his face an undeniable charisma. And his mouth … It's so full and tempting. Unexpectedly, his tongue darts out to lick his bottom lip, leaving it temptingly wet.

The message is loud and clear, even though he makes no move toward kissing me. He isn't pushing me to do anything. He's giving me control.

To test how much he's willing to let me be in charge, I push myself up on my toes, bringing my lips half an inch away from his. His warm breath mixes with mine, and I smell whiffs of the alcohol we drank. His pupils dilate, but he doesn't move. Aroused and playful, I move even closer until our mouths are almost touching, but not quite. I can sense the warmth of his lips but resist their tempting call. The tension, the desire, and the intensity of the moment almost make my head spin. My entire body is alert and ready.

At this very instant, I decide I'm not moving forward to get over the man or for Oliver's sake. I'm doing it for myself. I'm doing it because I might implode if I don't.

I finally press my lips against his, shivering from head to toe. His reaction is immediate, one of his hands wrapping around my waist, pulling me closer to him. I initiated the kickoff, and now the race for pleasure begins.

Our mouths open in unison, and our tongues dart out, greedy to get more. We share the flavor of whiskey and the taste of us. I'm almost vibrating with need, my body demanding what it yearns for. With my hands up and my fingers tangled in his dark hair, I pull him closer, wanting all of him.

When I move my foot to the side, he understands my intentions and obliges, slightly bending his knee so I have better access to his thigh and can straddle it. I shamelessly arch into the massive swell of his erection, and he pushes back, grabbing my ass to bring me even closer. The edge of the counter harshly digs into my skin, but I barely feel it, the entirety of my nerves focused on my front—on him.

To my great dissatisfaction, the intensity of our embrace becomes too much, so I rip my mouth away from him to take deep breaths, desperate for air. Lex's mouth drops to my neck to lay a fiery line of kisses, tasting my heated skin with his tongue and turning the blood flowing in my veins into searing lava.

The collar of my top gets in the way of his exploration, prompting his hands to remove it. In seconds, I'm in my bralette. Luckily, it isn't one of my boring cotton bras, but a pretty little garment made of blue lace. My nipples are visible through the sheer fabric, catching Lex's attention.

There isn't much there, a large A cup at best, but the way Lex looks at them, so full of desire, makes me forget about my insecurities. There's a hint of wonderment in his expression—as if he craved to see me like this.

And that inflates my ego like never before. I'm not an awkward, nerdy girl anymore. I'm a woman good enough to tempt Alexander Coleman. Feeling bold, I pull my bralette up, pass it over my head, and throw it to the side.

Before it even reaches the floor, Lex has one of my mounds in his hand while hungrily lowering his head to the other. I moan when his mouth closes around my raised nipple. He bites, sucks, and pulls on my hard tip, sending jolts of pleasure straight to my clit. His hand mirrors the same torture on the other one, pinching and tugging. It's like he knows exactly which pressure to apply and how hard he can bite before pain overtakes pleasure. My walls throb spasmodically, and I realize he can probably make me come like this, teasing my tits.

This is insane …

The only reason he stops is to lift me with baffling ease and sit me on the counter so I'm easier to access. Then, he steps in the cradle of my parted thighs to inflict the same treatment on my other nipple, his erection right against my throbbing pussy. And because I'm so fucking greedy, I writhe and arch into it.

Before I can climb closer to the orgasm building inside me, he stops his teasing and moves back, robbing me of all stimulation. He ignores my protest to press his hand over my sternum instead, silently commanding me to lie back.

The coldness of the marble bites into my heated skin as his hand grabs my ankle. With efficient moves, he loosens the ties of my black Chuck before pulling on it.

Oh, no …

If my bra was a lucky coincidence, my socks aren't. Mild amusement paints his features when he reveals my Pacman sock and sends me a questioning look. Mortified, I gnaw on my lower lip and shrug my shoulders. Still smiling, he shakes his head as his fingers slide under my jeans to grab my sock. My other shoe knows the same fate, and then he moves to the button of my jeans.

My clit throbs at his hands fidgeting so close to it. I need his fingers there. *Now.* I do my best to help him, and he manages to remove the few clothing items I have left.

Sprawled out for him to see, absolutely naked in the unforgiving light of his kitchen, I remain unmoving as he takes in the sight of my body. It feels kinky to be buck-naked when he's still wearing the entirety of his clothes.

Even if nothing in his heated gaze leads me to believe the view doesn't please him, I begin doubting myself. My arm wraps around my breasts while my hand shields the triangle of curls at the apex of my thighs from his hawk-like stare.

He doesn't like that and firmly pushes them away before he gently spreads my legs. "Andrea … You're so fucking wet for me," he says, his voice so rough it's almost a growl. He boldly slides two fingers along my folds, making me shiver when they graze my clit, and moves his hand up. "Look," he orders. His index and middle fingers are glistening with my arousal.

I blush but don't look away when we lock gazes. He's much bolder than I expected. The rigid and cerebral man I know is long gone, replaced by a lustful, enterprising, and absurdly sexual Lex.

As if to prove me right, he brings his fingers to his mouth to run his pink tongue over them, eagerly sampling my wetness. An approving "Mmm" rolls in his throat while his eyes never leave mine. The sight is so hot that I whimper and attempt to press my knees together, my core throbbing with impatience yet again.

Before I have time to recover from the incredible vision, he hooks his hands under my knees and spreads me wide, only to look at my pussy with earnestness.

"You want me so fucking much that you're dripping," he groans. That makes my walls clench, and he notices, eyes narrowing on my slit.

"Lex," I protest, attempting to bring my knees together and pushing myself up on my elbows. My gaze compels his. With audacity, I ask, "Are you going to do something about it, or will you just stare all night?"

His smile and chuckle would be panty-dropping if I weren't already pantiless. Then he lowers his face, and I brace myself. I'm about to see if his oral skills are as good as my dreams and fantasies imagined.

First, he plants a kiss on my inner thigh, and then another, closer to where I so desperately want him, then another … Finally, when he's out of thigh to explore, his eyes lock with mine. I wait, so motionless I'm not even breathing.

His tongue darts out before he settles it lower, where the slickness is gathered. I moan at the sight, as erotic as the sensations themselves, and when he moves a little higher, the muscles of my inner thighs tense, my tendons straining against his grip.

He's purposefully ignoring my clit, but the burning fervor, the softness, the way he lazily explores me … It's already too much for me. Lex takes his time, cleaning me off of all the wetness he conjured. But it's a

Sisyphean task because every time his tongue grazes me, more of it seeps out.

I'm about to beg him when the tip of his tongue pushes past my slit. *Fuck … This man is wicked …* He thrusts it in and out, and it feels good—amazing even—yet I can't help but want more. I want him to fill me, to stretch me, to ruin me.

Losing my patience, I lie back down to free my arms and weave my fingers into his thick hair to guide him. His hands release my legs to grab my wrists so he can pin them down on each side of my hips instead. I'm about to scold him when his mouth finally moves up and locks on my swollen nub. With all the built-up anticipation, intense shivers make my body jolt at the first flick.

My back arches, my legs spread further, and a whimpering cry escapes me. Relentlessly, he teases, sucks, and licks my clit, making me tremble and moan. My hips buckle and roll, my reactions uncontrollable. He immobilizes them between his forearms, his hands still firmly holding my wrists. With each lick, I'm growing closer to climax, and his pace is mercilessly fast.

"Aah, Lex! Don't stop! Don't—Oh, *fuck …*"

As I suspected, he's divine at this. I reach my orgasm crying and panting, the sensations so intense that I writhe on his kitchen island, my whole body consumed by a pleasure too extreme to handle. My legs clench of their own will, imprisoning Lex's head. Wave after wave of euphoria travels through my shaking frame as I endure my release.

He gives me no sympathy, his tongue sweeping intensely, trying to drag out the pleasure for as long as I can sustain it. One of his hands releases mine, and I quickly use my freedom to try to push him away with a whimper, confident I can't survive this for much longer. He resists my attempt and grazes my entrance with his finger instead.

"Fuck … Lex! I need—Aah!"

I'm cut short when it pushes inside of me. My walls are still throbbing hectically, swollen and sensitive, and the simple intrusion is enough to render me mad. With his tongue still working its tireless magic, he fingers me expertly. My unyielding orgasm changes into something else, and soon enough, I'm bracing myself for another mind-blowing climax. Another finger slips in, gently stretching me, and as he pumps them in and out, a new series of spasms starts.

Between my moans and soft whimpers, I can hear the rhythmic and wet sound of his ministrations on me. I can sense with accuracy everything he is doing to me, feel the stubble on his jaw against my delicate folds and thighs, the silkiness of his hair between my fingers … Everything that's happening is engraving itself into my mind, and I know for certain I'll remember all of this perfectly for decades to come.

His touch becomes lighter but faster, and it's all I need to reach bliss again. Just like before, my whole body shakes with involuntary contractions as I come, crying out his name.

Shit, I hope the apartment is soundproof both ways.

This time, he doesn't push me further, and the momentum of his tongue and fingers slows. I'm about ready to thank him for showing me mercy when he slowly pulls away.

While I gradually regain control of my mind and flesh, he lays small kisses up my limp, heaving, and satiated body. He takes his time on each of my nipples and then comes to my mouth for the grand finale.

Gladly, I welcome his lips, where I can taste myself. There's also his own flavor there, which I can't get enough of, so I hungrily seize his face between my hands to keep him in place. By the time he moves away, my breathing is almost normal again, and my heartbeat, even if it's still too fast, isn't as wild as before.

He straightens up and uses his viewpoint to look at me like a predator observing his prey—his eyes piercing and hungry. There's a thin layer of perspiration now veiling my skin, and I know my face and chest are flushed.

"Shall we begin?" he asks with a pinch of amusement.

As much as I want to do this and really begin, I'm tempted to ask for a break first. My mind changes swiftly when Lex grabs the collar of his shirt behind his head and takes it off.

Is there a consensus among men to remove their T-shirts like this? Do they know how hot it looks? Do they train in front of a mirror to master the technique?

My mind goes blank, and my mouth waters at the sight of his impressive torso, my questions fading at once. This man was always temptation incarnate in my eyes, but right now, he looks goddamn edible.

The muscles of his torso are defined and chiseled. I can see the outline of his abs, the deep V at his hips, his firm pecs … His shoulders are broad, and his arms are strong and well-balanced with the rest of him. I also like the thin veil of body hair covering his chest and descending in a narrow path to his pants. It's like every single thing about him is perfectly engineered to make me swoon.

I sit up to rest my palms on his muscular pecs, enjoying the firmness of his warm skin. When I tilt my head upward to demand his lips, he gives me an ardent kiss. Shameless, I press myself against his naked torso, my erect nipples teased by the soft hair there.

Then, I pull away to work on his belt. He waits, hands resting high on my outer thighs, his thumbs mechanically grazing my skin, as I unhook the button and pull down his zipper. Passing my thumbs under the coarse fabric, I push the jeans away, along with his boxer briefs.

His dick jerks out, and my eyes widen at the incredible sight.

This is the ultimate proof that God is a woman. Only my gender could have been this meticulous. Clearly, she took her sweet time when creating this particular man, paying keen attention to every last detail.

Taking root in a patch of trimmed dark hair, Lex's dick is thick from root to tip, with veins snaking under the smooth skin. He's cut, and his pink and plump head sits there temptingly as if daring me to kneel and welcome it into my mouth, to taste it, to run my tongue around it. It has this slight upward curve Kate once called the G-spot seeker. Even the heavy weights underneath are the ideal size and shape, hanging tightly under his lengthy girth.

Already, I know Lex's dick will be the best of my life—even though he might split me in half. I'm almost sure my hand isn't big enough to circle it completely.

Remembering I can actually try, I run my fingers over his length and marvel at its warmth, softness, and hardness. Fuck, this is going to be out of this world.

As suspected, I can barely circle it with my fingers, but almost. Invigorated by the challenge, I tighten my hold on him until the tip of my thumb meets that of my middle finger. The pressure of my grip makes him grunt something that sounds deliciously obscene, his gaze never leaving my hand massaging him. When he lets out another low moan, my proud smile grows wider. And even more when a stream of precum leaks out, revealing how much he enjoys my touch. Using my thumb, I spread the translucent liquid over his swollen head, making it shiny and tempting.

Time to get down on my knees and gag on that perfect dick.

But Lex has other plans. "I need to be inside you," he grunts, pulling away from me.

He removes the rest of his clothes, pushes the pile to the side with his foot, and grabs the base of his cock to align it with my entrance.

I jump at the contact as if struck by electricity, and it only gets more intense when he runs his hardness up and down my slit, taunting my demanding flesh in the most wicked way, coating himself with the remnants of my orgasms. Then, the pressure of his cock increases on my opening, about to enter me.

Because I have to witness it with my own eyes, I look down, mesmerized by the perfection that is his dick. Its plump tip is docked among my folds, glistening with my arousal. With more pressure from him, it slips into me, disappearing from my sight. Miraculously, some good sense makes its way into my foggy thoughts.

"Wait!" I protest with a push on his chest, dislodging him from within me.

"What?"

"Condom."

"I thought you were clean and on birth control."

"I am, but I don't know if you are," I argue. "Clean, I mean. Not on birth control."

"I'm telling you then. I'm clean."

"I don't know you enough to trust you on that, Lex."

His eyes turn dark with offense and irritation. "Well, I trust you."

"That's *your* prerogative, not mine."

He gives me a somber look but doesn't argue more. In under thirty seconds, he retrieves a condom from his wallet, opens it, sheathes himself with it, and then returns to me, retaking his place between my spread legs.

"May I enter you, now?" His formality has me giggling despite the pettiness I discern in his tone.

"Yes, you may."

His dark mood quickly vanishes as I take possession of his lips. I'm lost in it when he pushes two inches in with a firm thrust, breaching my tight opening. I let out a whimper in his mouth, the stretch almost painful.

"Slow," I beg. "It's … It's been a while."

"You better take all of me, Andrea. Down to the last inch. I've wanted this for too fucking long."

Despite his words, he takes my request seriously, and his hips roll in small, continuous nudges, slowly conquering my uncooperative flesh. Gentle, he proceeds with care and caution, and although I feel uncomfortably stretched, it doesn't hurt. To distract me, he kisses my lips, his hands play with my tits, his teeth gently nibble at my throat …

Every time he pushes a little further, jolts of pleasure spread, and every time he moves out, my walls clench to hold him there. Inch by delicious inch, his whole length enters, and when the head of it reaches the end of me—a sensation I've never experienced before—I let out a loud moan against the humid skin of his shoulder.

I watch as he slowly moves in and out with the slightest nudges, the condom shiny from how drenched I am. It's crazy that I can take it all, especially given his girth, but here we are.

Carefully, he attempts a few harder thrusts, bringing more pleasure, and lets out a moan. The fucking begins, and even though he remains gentle, I'm embarrassed by how fast I'm climbing. But I haven't had a dick inside me in ten months, so I guess it's normal to be so receptive, right?

"You're so tight …" he moans right into my ear. "The pressure of you is driving me insane," he rasps. "I could fuck you the whole night, Andrea."

His crude words, his careful thrusts, and the erotic sight when I look down again send me over the edge and trigger my third orgasm of the night. I muffle my screams against his torso, my walls spasming around his dick. I tightly clutch his shoulders to keep myself from ascending to the blissful heaven he sends me to. He holds me as I quiver, his hands firmly planted on my ass.

Shit, I've never orgasmed this hard in my life. The intensity of it wrecks me. I didn't know it was possible to feel so many things at once. Thankfully, Lex is merciful enough to stop thrusting, waiting for my climax to end.

Once the last shiver passes, he kisses the top of my head and makes me lay back on the counter, his eyes devouring me shamelessly. I wrap my legs around his waist for balance, and his hands travel the length of my thick thighs to rest on my hips.

The shadow of a smile brushes his lips. "Now, we can start."

Maybe I was in control earlier, but not anymore. Not as he vigorously slips in and out of me with powerful thrusts. The sight of his abs contracting with every move forward is insanely hot, but I can barely focus on anything other than his overwhelming ramming into my most sensitive part.

I'm being thoroughly fucked by a half-god genius.

After three mind-blowing orgasms almost back-to-back, it's too much, too soon. The intensity scares me. Each time his cock bottoms out, the sensations shatter me. I push against the solid plane of his lower abdomen with a whimper, unsure if I can survive that much pleasure. But his momentum is unyielding.

"Come on, Andrea … You can take it."

Fuck … What did I get myself into?

I cry out in his mouth when he retakes my lips, tears gathering in the corners of my eyes. How can I feel so much and not burst into a million pieces? The limits of pleasure are being bent and pushed, and Lex knows exactly how to do it.

He's tireless, and soon enough, I'm yearning for the next climax. My legs pull him harder on me with each thrust, my heels digging into his lower back.

"Ah, fuck …" he moans, giving me a more brutal shove.

Despite his intense pace, his thrusts are measured. I can feel it. He's holding back so he won't hurt me, but I want all of it. All of him.

"Fuck me hard, Alexander," I beg, my hands firmly planted on his ass, encouraging him to give me everything he has. "Fuck me like you mean it."

His groan resonates in my ears, his movements harder, faster, and deeper. *Shit, I won't be able to walk straight tomorrow.*

I can't tell for how long he keeps pounding into me like this, the noises of our intense fuckery filling the room. Everything at this moment is the most carnal experience I could have ever imagined. The fleshy slaps of his hips meeting mine, the wet sounds between us every time he rams inside, the grunts, the moans, the panting …

As I listen to them all, ravaged by his thrusts, the reality of what's happening strikes me. After weeks of holding back, weeks of resisting, weeks of temptation … I'm finally having sex with the man haunting my dreams. That very man I fantasize about daily is vigorously fucking me on his kitchen island.

Overwhelmed by those thoughts and sensations, I spiral into another mind-blowing orgasm, clinging onto him as I shatter yet again. I scream my pleasure, my limbs wrapped around him with all my strength. My entire body contracts and jolts with bliss as he keeps plowing into me. He doesn't halt his momentum or slow down, and my orgasm stretches to unimaginable heights. Fuck, I might actually pass out from how good it feels.

When he lets out a loud groan, I know he's coming too. He breaks our kiss and rests his forehead in the crook of my neck, his sweaty skin meeting mine as his hips jerk in uncontrollable jolts. His grunts as he comes make me ridiculously proud, and I hold him close while our climaxes slowly recede.

We stay like this for several minutes, his weight on my chest somehow comforting. With my hands, I graze his back softly, drawing mindless patterns with the tips of my fingers, following the shapes of his hard-earned muscles. We wait for our breathing to calm down in the silent kitchen. Both our bodies are covered in sweat now, and his breath is warm on my chest. He's slowly softening inside of me, but not entirely.

He eventually pushes up on his arms so his eyes can find mine, and we stare at each other for a moment. Then he gives me a short but intense kiss and straightens up. When he moves away, I sit up on the counter's edge, my legs dangling over the floor. I always suspected it would be good, but there isn't a word strong enough to express the magnitude of what I just experienced.

I unabashedly ogle him as he disposes of the condom. My, my … The sight of him from behind is as incredible as the front. I can almost count the different muscles on his back, and his ass is amazing.

This gorgeous man, this Greek god, just gave me four earth-shattering orgasms.

My eyes shy away from his when he turns around. Now that the deed is done, it's time for me to leave.

Before I can make my move, Lex passes a hand under my knees, the other behind my back, and gathers me against his torso.

"Lex! What are you doing!?"

"I'm taking you to my bed."

Oh … As tempting as it sounds, I'm pretty sure I've reached my limit.

is_new_chapter = True

chapter_number = "18"

pov_name = "Alexander"

I NEVER UNDERSTOOD THE CONCEPT of Pandora's box. We aren't animals driven by instincts and needs. Putting the lid back on should never be so hard it becomes impossible. But as I carry Andrea to my room, I think I finally grasp it.

For the first time in my life, I do feel like I've opened Pandora's box. And I'm not sure how I'll put the lid back on.

Sex lost its appeal a while ago for me. I indulge because I have needs, and not satisfying them leads to mood swings and a bad temper. Outside of the short-lived pleasure it brings, though, sex stopped being interesting a couple of years in and became something redundant and repetitive—but not in a good way.

What we just did, however … That was a reinvention of sex, a revelation, a thrilling twist to a mundane act. There's something about Andrea that made the experience uniquely new. Maybe it was the way she begged, how she writhed, her hiccups of pure abandon … The stubborn woman I knew was gone entirely, replaced by a greedy creature desperate for more pleasure. I doubt I could ever get tired of sex like *that.*

For fuck's sake, I came like a maniac minutes ago, and I'm already craving to start over.

Against me, Andrea wriggles with unease. "Oh, we don't need to do that," she protests. "I'm pretty confident the mission was a success, so there's no need to—"

She stops as I kick the door of my room open, eyes curiously exploring the space instead. This room is like all the others, neatly organized with neutral grays everywhere.

I don't waste a second before taking her to the bed, and barely bending, I drop her on the soft mattress. "I'm telling you," she insists while

I get another condom from my nightstand. "We effectively fucked you out of my system."

"Great." She looks so fucking good in my bed like this, naked and flushed, that my cock swells at the sight. It only takes a few strokes of my fist to get painfully hard again. Her fascinated gaze observes it all, including when I roll the new condom down my length.

As soon as I'm ready to go again, I join her on the bed, and she lets me flip her around and lift her up to her hands and knees.

I can barely hold back a groan as I look down. How many times have I imagined bending her over my desk and fucking her? I've conjured extensive fantasies of it, and yet, none of them are as glorious as reality. She has the best ass I've ever seen, round, generous, soft … And there's a little surprise I couldn't foresee right there on her left cheek: a brown birthmark about an inch wide.

After I graze it, my hands avidly fill themselves with her ass, kneading the flesh with eagerness. When I spread her open, my focus narrows on the puckered hole above her slit, and my cock twitches. The area between her legs is darker than the rest of her, and it only highlights the glistening pinkness of her folds. Her pussy is all swollen, and when I spread it with my thumbs, the tight slit that I just fucked opens up.

Shit, I need to get on with this. I let go of her ass and press the thick head of my dick where she wants me.

"Lex, it's too soo—"

Her complaints die in her throat as I push in with a slow but implacable thrust. She moans from both pleasure and protest but doesn't try to stop me. Once I'm all in, I bend over to lick the hollow path of her spine all the way to her neck. Then, right against her ear, I utter, "Now, we're fucking *you* out of *my* system."

"Oh, God …"

Because she's probably overly sensitive, I go slow, measuring my pace. It allows me to enjoy the warm tightness of her wet cunt. She feels so fucking good, and that view … The broadness of her hips against her narrow waist is enchanting, and my condom-clad cock is shiny with her arousal every time I pull out. And when she lowers to her elbows, I see how she's stretched around me.

"Your ass is fucking glorious," I say between two thrusts. "I wish you could see how well you take me. My cock disappears all the way in your tight cunt, and it comes out drenched. You're so. Fucking. Wet."

She lets out a desperate moan, and I feel the way she clenches around me. Slowly and deeply, I take my time, punctuating the moment with kisses on her back and shoulders, paying careful attention to the way her body reacts.

Every time I whisper something dirty into her ear, she shivers and pushes back harder against me. So, I keep talking. I tell her how I've imagined bending her over my desk to do this to her. How I've never had a pussy this good. How I could fuck her the entire night. How she's so fucking wet I can hear it …

She comes apart again, spasming and shivering below me, her mouth releasing the most enticing moans and soft cries. I keep thrusting through her climax, laying a stream of open-mouth kisses and small bites over her shoulders and neck. She tastes a little salty now, and I adore this new flavor.

With one last clench around my dick, she collapses on the bed, spent. The only thing holding her ass up is the firm grip I have on her hips. I knew I could make it good for her, but I had no idea it would be so easy to make her come. She's exceptionally receptive, and it only pushes me to give her more.

"My turn," I say.

This time, I'm not so gentle with her. I don't allow her a moment to recover from her orgasm before I pick up the pace. A sound that's more animal than human rumbles in her throat, and her small hands fist the sheets as she takes it. My hips slap against her ass every time, echoing into the room as the shock sends a ripple through the mounds.

With each brutal thrust, I pull her back onto me—even though she eagerly does it on her own. When she tries to muffle her cries in the duvet, I let go of her hip to grab a handful of her hair instead and tug on it. She's mine for tonight only, so I'll have *all* of her.

Again, I feel how much she enjoys the crude gesture. Who knew this defiant little woman would turn so submissive in my bed?

Just as I'm starting to worry this might all be too much for her, she whimpers with a trembling voice, "Harder."

I don't know what she wants harder, so I tighten my hold on her hair and increase the intensity of my thrusts. The smacking of my skin on hers, the throaty moans that roll past my lips, her cries and whimpers… They all create an auditory masterpiece I'll never forget.

Time loses its meaning, and everything outside of this bed disappears. There's only us left, only this overwhelmingly carnal moment.

After several minutes of this, she seems to reach her limit. "Lex, I can't take it … It's too much."

Buried deep inside her, I immediately pause and release her hair. Her head falls to the side, and I worriedly brush her messy curls away with a careful hand to see her profile. Tears are gathered in the corner of her eye, and her face is flushed.

"Are you alright?" I ask, swiping my thumb over the tear on her cheek.

She nods and sinuously rolls her hips into mine. "Just come already."

I pull out and let her fall to the side. Her eyes are on me as I rearrange myself to straddle her leg. "You will come once more, and I'll be coming with you."

"I'm not sure I can," she argues, exhausted.

"Of course you can." I push back into her, sideways.

Hooking her knee in my elbow to lift it, I resume the fucking. I enjoyed seeing her ass before, but I think I prefer seeing the rapturous expression on her face and the way her small tits move with every hard shove. Unable to resist their call, I take one in my mouth. At the first pull of her brown nipple with my teeth, I feel her walls clamp around me.

"I can feel you clench around me," I say, releasing the perky bud. "Tell me, Andrea … Tell me how much your tight little pussy wanted my cock."

"Aah, shit! Don't stop …"

"Tell me you wanted this." When she doesn't answer again, I slow my momentum, robbing her of her incoming orgasm. "Say it, Andrea. I want you to say it. I *need* you to say it."

"Lex …" she protests, trying to writhe her hips against me. But I firmly hold her in place, unmoving inside her. She gives in quickly, whispering, "I wanted this."

My cock twitches at her confession, and I pull out and in again. "Have you been thinking about this? About us having sex?"

"Yes …"

"Have you touched yourself, imagining me doing all this to you?"

A reddish blush covers every inch of her face now. "Yes."

"Say it," I command. When she looks away, I grab her jaw and force her eyes back on mine. "Say the words, Andrea."

"I—Fuck, Lex …" she sobs when I subtly change the angle of my thrusts to hit right where I know it feels the best. "I touched myself thinking about you."

"Did you come thinking about me?"

"Yes!"

The way her insides pulsate around me is all I need to resume the hard and fast rhythm. The teasing is over. She's earned her grand finale.

I lower to kiss her, spreading her more. Our breathing turns erratic, just like my thrusts. Both our climaxes are pending. My balls are drawing tight. Only a few more shoves, and we'll shatter together.

"Come now," I order against her lips.

As if she needed exactly that, she lets out a helpless cry as her insides quiver, her body jolting with pleasure once more. I keep her right there, my cock buried as far as it can go while I fill the condom with cum. The most intense and mind-blowing ripples of satisfaction roam through me. Sex was never this fantastic. Not even when I first discovered it.

I release her leg and collapse onto her once I'm done, and we stay unmoving for several moments, limbs tangled, our sweaty skin flush together. When I meet her eyes, she's already looking at me.

Fuck, she looks prettier than I've ever seen her, eyes glimmering with satisfaction, hair wild, lips swollen … I reach for her face to graze her damp hair away. Since this is just a one-night thing, I'll never see her this beautiful again, so full of me and so entirely satisfied.

With the tip of my thumb, I follow the outlines of her face, up the dorsum of her nose, through the arch of an eyebrow, across a cheekbone, over the plump curve of her upper lip, then the lower one, and a final caress on her jaw.

This is the most intimate we've been tonight, the closest I've felt to her. Overwhelmed by the thought that this will soon come to an end, I move to kiss her in a soft, almost tender way. What starts as a chaste kiss soon transforms into something needier, and we adjust our positions to be able to devour each other more thoroughly.

I feel my dick harden inside her, already eager to turn this into more sex. She must sense it as well because she gasps and pulls away from me, far enough for my cock to slip out of her.

"I'm sorry, I can't," she says, rolling to her side to face me. "I reached my limit three orgasms ago." To soften the refusal, she lays a kiss on my jaw. I return it with one on the side of her throat.

"Sorry if I've pushed you too far."

"You did, but it's okay."

As willing as I am to give her some rest, I still haven't had my fill of her, so I lay a series of pecks down her neck and shoulder before finishing with one on her nipple. Then, adamant to recharge, I sit up with enthusiasm.

"I'm starving."

I hop out of the bed, strangely energized, and walk to the en suite bathroom. There, I throw the condom away, get two hand towels, and pour warm water on them. I use one on my semi-hard dick, throw it in the hamper, and return to the bed with the second one.

She gathered a corner of the duvet over her, as if we haven't been enjoying each other's bodies for the past couple of hours.

"Can I get you something?" I ask, handing her the second towel. I'm in my dressing room when I offer, "I think I have some leftover Chinese and maybe some Italian."

"I'm just parched," she answers after a few seconds. "Go ahead. I'll join you."

With a pair of basketball shorts on and nothing else, I return to the bedroom, and after one last look at her, I head to the kitchen. There, I scavenge the fridge for anything we can eat. We need to regain some strength before the third round. I'll let her ride me this time like I've imagined more often than I care to admit. I want to lie back, trapped under her thick thighs while she bounces up and down on my dick, taking every inch of me like the greedy girl she is.

While a few boxes of leftovers heat up in the microwave, I gather our things, fold them, and make a pile of her clothes on the dinner table. By the time everything's ready, she still hasn't come out of the room.

Because she said she was thirsty, I fill a tall glass with water and rejoin her in the bedroom. I pause in the doorway when I find her sleeping on top of the covers, wrapped in my bathrobe. Quietly, I get closer and set the glass on the nightstand beside her. She looks so serene asleep like this that it's hard to imagine she's such a relentless and tenacious little thing when awake.

It looks like she needs rest more than she needs food, so I decide to let her have it. I'll eat, join her in bed, and maybe at some point in the night or tomorrow morning, we'll give the incredible sex another go.

One very last time before we have to return to reality.

Fuck, that won't be enough. Not at all.

pov_name =

"Andrea"

DISORIENTED, THIRSTY, AND HOT, I regain consciousness with a startle. These aren't my sheets, this isn't my room, and the massive body pressed against me is confusing as fuck.

All at once, the memory of the evening hits me. I'm in Lex's apartment, in his bed, we had sex the whole evening, and … Shit, I fell asleep.

Still foggy, I do a quick assessment of the situation. Dawn's faint glow is the only thing lighting up the room, so it's still early. My whole body needs about two showers to clean off all of this stickiness. I'm half-turned on my stomach, and he's pressed on my back, part of his weight resting on me. I discarded the robe during the night—the belt was uncomfortable—so I'm naked. Despite the shorts he slipped on last night, Lex is also in the nude. Did he expect more sex?

Careful not to wake him up, I rotate around to face him, which feels like a game of body Jenga. He looks so appeased, almost like a different person. Awake, he's always tense and severe, but right now, the perpetual crest between his brows is gone, and the line of his mouth is relaxed. His hair is messy, and I'm almost tempted to brush it with my fingers. But I can't take the risk of waking him up.

I remain unmoving for a few seconds, secretly enjoying the moment.

The deed is finally done. I fucked Alexander, and now I'll be free to resume my life without the constant lust and tension.

I'm not inactive in bed, but I'm not very enterprising, either. With Lex, however, I ended up begging and pushing back against each of his thrusts. I demanded more, endured, enjoyed … Sex was never like this for me. Not even close.

Slow but steady, I maneuver my way out of his embrace. As I untangle myself from his hold, he barely moves, his sleep particularly heavy. I quietly wriggle to the edge of the bed to sit up with my feet on the floor.

Ouch, I'll feel him *there* for a while. My core is sore and overworked, and the tendons inside my thighs are tender, not used to being stretched for that long.

I notice a large glass of water on the nightstand on my side of the bed, and I immediately quench my thirst with it. When I'm done, I glimpse at the sleeping form behind me, thankful he placed it there.

Just as I stand, I hear the ruffling of the sheets as he moves. Very slowly, I spin around, worried he's waking up. To my great relief, he's still deeply asleep, now lying on his back. He seems more tanned in the darkness. The duvet is low on his abdomen, and I can admire the shapes of his shoulders, arms, and torso. A shallow and superficial wave of pride invades me. I, Andrea Walker, was the center of such a man's attention. *Lucky, lucky me …*

On my way to the kitchen, I feel out of place, naked as I walk around an apartment I barely know. My things aren't on the kitchen floor anymore but folded on the dinner table. It's ridiculous, but knowing he picked my things up and arranged them feels more intimate than him eating me out. Especially when I find my underwear also neatly folded.

I get dressed and check the time on my phone, 5:47 a.m. Shit, I also have a bunch of texts. I completely forgot to text Tami, too absorbed by everything going on. Because she must be worried sick, I immediately text her to let her know I'm alive and well.

As tempting as it is to disappear without a word, it doesn't feel right. After his performance, Lex deserves a standing ovation. So, I open a few drawers from the console near the entrance to find a notepad and a pen. I detach a sheet and lay it on the wooden surface. What should it say?

Thank you for the best night of my life.

As true as it might be, it's way too pathetic. **Thank you**, will be enough.

I leave the note on the dinner table, orienting it where I think he'll come to find it. Then, after one last look toward the corridor that leads to his room, I vanish into the night.

It's early, but there's already some activity outside. I order an Uber since I can't be bothered with bus routes so early in the day. Four minutes until it gets here.

As I wait for it, the gravity of my actions slowly sinks in. *Jesus fucking Christ.* I'll have to share an office with the best lay of my life and pretend it never happened. Somehow, it's even worse than everything I've had to endure until now.

How could I be so stupid!? Why did I trust Kate with this? Even now, I know perfectly well that my lust-filled thoughts for Lex aren't gone. I'll still drool over him as soon as I see him at work in … three hours. *Fuck.*

I won't have to wonder how it would be because I know exactly what sex with Alexander Coleman is. It's a cataclysmic experience I'll never forget. Once you try *slex*, you can never go back to sex.

I'm still wallowing in self-pity when the black sedan arrives, and after a quick confirmation, I slip inside the car.

On my way home, I read my missed notifications. The messages from Tamika span over four hours, and I can tell she was more anxious with every text.

TAMTAM

Hi girl. I'm wondering if you know when you'll get home. I want to order some pizza.

So, I ordered anyway. You'll reheat your slices if you want some.

Are you with Oliver?

He just told me you weren't. Where are you?

Answer me. Even if it's just a 'k.'

Is everything okay?

I'm legit worried now. Call me whenever you can!

Shit. Shit, shit, shit … She thinks I'm into Oli, which I kind of am, but now I spent the night with another man. With our *boss*.

Feeling like the worst friend in the history of mankind, I check Kate's messages.

KATE

Tamika texted me. She's worried about you. Where are you?

She told me you're not with Oliver. Are you with you-know-who?

Babe, if this is happening, I'm going to need ALL the details.

Still at it?

Okay, it has to be some sexathon record by now ...

Omg, are you guys seriously still fucking, or did you pass out?

I bet you passed out, you lightweight.

At least someone is pleased about this … I take a deep breath and force my thumb down to open Oliver's messages.

OLI

Hey, Hulkette. Tamika told me she couldn't find you. I hope everything is alright.

Starting to worry a bit here. Text me when you get home.

Welp, I'm not winning any friend-of-the-year award this time around.

As amazing as the night was, now that I have to deal with the consequences, it almost isn't worth it. *Almost.*

The experience will definitely outweigh whatever aftermath I have to handle. And the memories of it will warm me up at night when I lie alone in my cold bed.

is_new_chapter = True

chapter_number = "19"

pov_name = "Andrea"

As expected, Tamika doesn't take my nocturnal activities very well. It's still somewhat tense between us when we arrive at work. She can't understand why I'm not taking Oli seriously, to the point where I slept with someone else. Since I can't tell her about my overwhelming attraction to our boss, we're at an impasse. All she knows is that it was a one-night stand.

One I'm seconds away from seeing again.

A massive lump clogs my throat as I stand before the door, and swallowing it away does nothing. "Everything will be fine," I whisper to myself.

We're adults who shared a night of passion and lust, and now we'll move on. *Shit, this is so fucking awkward.*

The sooner I'm done with it, the better, so I knock twice and open the door. I spot Lex instantly, standing in the middle of the room, along with Kevin. They stop talking as soon as I enter, and Lex's eyes immediately find mine. I barely notice his dark mood and irked glare, prone to a surge of unwanted memories and feelings. I hold his gaze for a moment, feeling my face and body heat up under his intensity.

Flashes and images of last night flood my brain. His grunts of pleasure, the touch of his strong hands over my skin, the deep and rough ramming of his dick in me, the warmth of his tongue, the filthy words it uttered in the throes of passion …

Tell me, Andrea … Tell me how much that tight little pussy of yours wanted my cock.

Fuck, I can't do this.

He knows too much about me. My taste, my naked body, the sounds I make when I come, that I've touched myself with him in mind, that I get so fucking wet for him … Fuck, I also know way too much.

Two seconds in, and sensual hunger is already overtaking me. Before Kevin can grow suspicious, I force a smile on my face.

"Hi, boss," I tell Kev on my way to the desk. Lex gets a small "Hello" from me before I sit down. The ache in my overworked core has me wincing.

"You were the one who wanted the slot. And now you're telling me you won't be coming?" Lex says with irritation, resuming their talk.

"It's a great marketing opportunity, and you know it," Kevin replies patiently. Okay, so this is about the upcoming convention.

"You were responsible for it. It was your idea to present whatever my team would come up with."

"And now I'm telling you I can't come. Just get over it." Kevin is now growing annoyed as well. "Michelle could have the baby any day, and I won't be eight hundred miles away when it happens."

"So, what? We cancel the slot you booked?"

"No. Absolutely not. The brochures and flyers with our names have already been sent out. You can do the presentation with whoever you want from your team."

There's a moment of silence, and I remember I'm not supposed to listen so avidly. I open a random script to pretend I'm working.

"You know perfectly well I'm not doing this," Lex resentfully answers.

"Well, then your guys will have to manage on their own. Who were you thinking of?"

"Brian and Steven, for the braille phone case. The prototype works perfectly, and the app is polished and ready to be shown."

Oh, that's my favorite one from Kelex. They developed a case designed for low vision and blind users, with an embossed front and a back that modulates to display braille. It's Steven and Brian's pride and joy, and I can understand why.

Since there's a deafening silence all of a sudden, I click and scroll randomly to give the illusion that I'm actually doing something.

"Andy, how long until your app is ready?" Kevin asks.

At the mention of my name, I let go of my mouse and slowly spin my chair around. They are both focused on me, and I strategically avoid looking at Lex.

"Uh … The alpha version is on schedule for Thanksgiving, as intended. But we have three to four weeks of work on it before we can even consider showing it around," I explain. Lex nods in confirmation, agreeing with my prognostics.

"What's the biggest task you guys have to work on to make it presentable?" Kevin insists.

"We're trying to improve the hand recognition algorithm to get rid of the nail polish. As long as the app needs flashy nails to work, it can't be taken seriously. Oh, and we're still waiting on NAD's data. We're currently using something Oli got for me, so it's not entirely legal. But they agreed to send us the files anyway, so it's technically fine. We just don't know when we'll officially get them."

"Can it be done in the ten days we have before the convention?"

I'm tempted to look at Lex to see what he thinks of this. Ten days is tricky but possible. "Hypothetically, it could be done," I venture. "But we're looking at some serious overtime and more coders working on it."

"Lex, do you think you and your team can make it?"

"Facial and voice recognition took decades to reach where it's at now, and that was just the face. We're talking about ten fingers, two palms, wrists, upper body position, and a face. Mannerisms can also be as potent of an issue as an accent. The multiple ways the same sentence can be expressed also makes it all complicated."

"Ok, bear with me here, guys. I'm not asking for the app to be finished and polished. I'm asking if it can be good enough for a demonstration. There will be investors there, people who matter. This could be a springboard for Kelex to become international."

"Kev, the only thing I can tell you right now is we'll try and do our best to make it work," Lex proposes. "But it's safer to keep the braille tool in mind. We can't ridicule ourselves with an unfinished product."

Kevin's reasonable enough to recognize that Lex is right. Sourly, the man nods. "Andy, I know you've already worked a lot for this, but would you be willing to do extra hours?"

"I … guess? But I can't promise it'll be ready."

"That's alright. If it's ready by then, it's great. If not, it'll boost the project," he suggests. As I nod, I'm already trying to organize all this, determine the priorities, what can be left out … "Lex, are you fine with working overtime too?" Kevin then asks.

I can't help it. My eyes go straight to Lex, eager to know his reaction. As compelled as I am, his gaze finds mine, and we stare at each other for a moment. Overtime means we'll be the only ones in the building every evening. It means we'll have even more hours together.

This is terrible. I can't spend so much time with Lex alone in his office. I can't handle my cravings during the daytime, and it certainly won't be better at night or on weekends.

I can't be trusted near him, knowing I'll fantasize about being bent over the desk and fucked. He could also lift me against a wall or a window, hoist me up on the furniture, ravish me on the floor … Damn, I'm so hooked that even the uncomfortable couch seems like a good spot for some *slex*.

He catches up with my chain of thoughts, his eyes darkening. His jaw clenches before he turns to Kevin.

"It's nothing I haven't done before," he answers.

When his attention returns to me, I don't know how to interpret the dangerous promises I discern on his face. The abundant hunger with which he demanded more of me last night isn't debatable. He enjoyed fucking me so much that he got hard again mere minutes after blowing his load. Twice.

At the memory of last night, my skin warms up and my cheeks flush. I avert my eyes when I remember we aren't alone in the room.

Thankfully, Kevin isn't paying attention to me. His eyes are locked on his friend, his brows slightly frowned. "Lex, can I see you in my office?" he asks bluntly.

Alexander looks away from me. "Sure." They exit the room without another word, leaving me alone with my paranoia.

We're so busted. It lasted barely ten minutes before boss number two realized I fucked boss number one. Maybe now is a good time to go herd those llamas in Peru.

Focusing on work is hard, especially since Lex can return any second. I'll have to face him alone and pretend like he didn't tongue-fuck and dick-fuck me. I'm distractedly reading the same line for the tenth time when someone knocks. For a brief moment, I freeze, worried the time has come. But Lex doesn't knock, so my shoulders relax.

"Come in."

To my surprise, it's Aditya, our IT guy. I met him a few times, as he likes hanging out with the guys in the Lair. He's shy, especially with women, but we've spoken once or twice.

"Hi, Adi," I greet him with a smile. "What brings you up here?"

"Good morning, Andy. I got an email from Alexander saying I have to move your computer back downstairs."

My heart sinks down to my stomach. So, that's it? Lex got what he wanted, and now he's getting rid of me? I never expected much from him, but maybe a little more consideration. I feel so … used.

Fuck the man. Seriously.

pou_name =

"Alexander"

"DID YOU SLEEP WITH ANDREA?"

Irritated, I look around at my business partner's office. It's nearly the same as mine but with more colors and wooden furniture.

"I won't let this go, Lex, so answer me."

I meet his inquisitive eyes with unmasked annoyance. "Mind your own business, Kevin."

"That's exactly what I'm doing. Minding my own business; the one we built together. Did something happen with her?"

We stare at one another for several seconds before I cave in. "Yes."

His grin isn't what I expected. I'm still confused when he wraps his arms around me. "Mazel Tov, Lexi."

I push him away, disliking the intrusion in my personal space and life—which he knows I hate.

"It was a one-time thing, so cool down."

"Oh, really? I thought it w—"

"You thought nothing. It happened, it's done, it's over. Period. Now, if you'll excuse me, you just unloaded a shit ton of work and responsibilities on us, so I have to get to work."

"Yeah, yeah, whatever you need to tell yourself."

I glare at him, unamused by his teasing. "Don't tell your wife."

He snorts, and I know he'll text Michelle as soon as I'm out. "She's been asking if it finally happened every day since our dinner with Andrea. Of course I'm telling her."

I roll my eyes. Were Andrea and I really that blind? How did Shelly and Kev know something was bound to happen when we didn't? Ruminating on that, I return to my office.

With the night I had, I should be relaxed and amiable. That's one of the perks of sex—especially great sex. But waking up and finding her gone left a sour taste in my mouth. The sheets still smelled of her, a heady scent of sweat and jasmine, and being unable to have her again brought all the frustrating needs back. I quickly realized that one night wouldn't be enough to satiate my hunger for her, but I at least hoped I would have a few days of respite.

Everything's even worse now.

"Alexander," someone calls behind me. I turn around, finding Beatrix from accounting hurriedly walking up to me.

"Yes?"

"I'm booking the plane tickets for HWC," she explains. "And I was wondering if you have a preference for who should sit next to you."

I think about it briefly, but I'm afraid there's only one logical answer. If we pull this off and get the app ready on time, I should be seated next to Andrea so we can work on the presentation during the flight. Reluctantly, I answer, "Sit me next to Andrea."

After a nod, Beatrix is off again. When I reenter my office, I spot Aditya and am reminded of the email I sent him earlier. Fuck, having her back downstairs isn't an option anymore. I'll have to endure having her here with me.

"I'm afraid I've wasted your time, Aditya. Things have just changed, so Andrea will remain here for now."

"Alright, no problem." Adi shrugs before leaving us.

I don't spare her a glance as I sit on my chair and start working. A few minutes pass until annoyance makes me ask, "I can tell you're angry from the way you bash in each key. What is it?"

Her hammering fingers stop, and she answers, "You wanted to move me back downstairs."

By leaving in the middle of the night, she made her desire for distance very clear. So what is this about? I look over our screens, confused by her temper.

"Is it your Stockholm syndrome talking? Are you enjoying being 'kept hostage' up here?"

She looks embarrassed, as though she forgot what she said yesterday. I continue, petty, "I didn't realize being up here was such a traumatic experience for you, so yes, I messaged Aditya."

I get up from my chair and walk around the desk to stand next to her. She looks spellbound as I bend closer to her, my face inches from hers. "It's only for a couple of weeks, and since we took care of your *little problem* last night, things should be fine until then, right?"

Although I shouldn't, I hope she says it wasn't enough and she needs more—like me. When she opens her mouth to answer, I'm tempted to travel the three inches separating us to claim it. But I hold back, and she swallows her nervousness away.

Eventually, she nods and says, "Yes, of course."

Something twinges in my chest, my hopes to get more of her crushed. But it's better like this. Better for both of us.

pov_name = "Andrea"

My "little problem" is nowhere near fixed. I'm in deep shit.

Things were never smooth between Lex and me, but we've reached a new low. If it wasn't for the ache lingering between my legs, I might believe I imagined last night.

I'm so reluctant to talk to him that I stay stuck for an hour on a glitch I can't fix. But the stakes are too high now, so I swallow back my pride and ask. When the problem eludes him, too, I feel less stupid. After a few unsuccessful minutes, he gets his chair to sit beside me. And that's enough to hijack my brain.

Those damn glasses. I can't get over how sexy and intelligent he looks.

Ten days until the convention. Ten fucking days.

I'll never make it.

His scent surrounds me, and the smell of his skin is intoxicating. Every time he types something, I glimpse at his powerful hands, remembering those thick fingers inside me. Behind his glasses, his eyes are focused on the lines of commands. He looked at me with matching intensity when he extracted shameful confessions out of me, taunting me with an incoming orgasm.

It's hard to keep in mind that we're at work when twelve hours ago we were naked and panting, blissfully enjoying each other's bodies.

We end up working side by side for most of the morning. Undeniably, the combined power of our brains makes things incredibly fast. We're still elbow-deep into it when lunchtime arrives, and while I normally would stay until we get it fixed, I practically jump to my feet. "Sorry, I'm starving," I lie. "I'll be back after the break."

His answer is a mere nod, but I don't care. I need to be anywhere but right by his side.

Just as I exit our shared office, my phone vibrates in my pocket. When I look, I see it's Kate. Was she waiting for my break to call?

"So, how was it?!" she practically shouts into my ear when I pick up.

"Hello to you too, blondie."

"Andy, tell me!"

"It was amazing," I comply with a sigh. "I've never experienced anything like it before."

"Ah! I knew the man was a sex god! How big is his junk?" I can't help but look around, worried someone could be witnessing this.

"Kate! What the hell kind of question is that!?"

"Girl, I need to vicariously live my sex life through yours. Give me the deets, or I'll date the first asshole I come across."

While we often have these sex talks, they are usually the other way around. Kate loves entertaining me with her exploits, and I listen out of genuine interest and curiosity. I'm not as comfortable as she is with all this, though, so returning the favor is hard.

"So? How's Lex Junior?" she insists, unwilling to let go.

"Well, 'junior' isn't the word I'd use for it."

"Meaning?"

I roll my eyes, both annoyed and amused. "Meaning he's Brazzers-sized."

"Oh, my … You lucky bitch. Did he give it to you this morning, too?"

"No."

"Oh? Did you give it to him, then?"

"I wasn't there in the morning," I explain, ignoring the twinge of remorse that hits me.

"Oh, no. Don't tell me you left in the middle of the night!"

"Of course I did. You're the one who told me about one-night stand etiquette."

"Babe, no! A one-night stand is someone you picked up at a bar and will never see again. Sleeping with your hot-as-fuck boss is more than that."

I frown, not getting the nuance. What I did wasn't offensive or wrong. I slept with him and left, which was our agreement. I'm pretty confident he would have done the same had things unfolded at my place.

Since I'm not answering, Kate becomes more inquisitive. "Was he okay with you leaving?"

"We didn't exactly talk about it," I sarcastically answer.

"Have you seen him this morning? How are things between you two?"

Something's off, but it isn't because I left, right? Things are just understandably weird. The man sucked on my clit, so how are we supposed to pretend nothing happened?

I don't want to dwell on it and get more of her intrusive questions. "Kate, I have to go."

She sighs, clearly disapproving. "I know it's all new to you, and you like Oliver. But please remember that Alexander is also his own person. Try not to hurt him."

A graceless snort escapes me. I highly doubt I can hurt the man. He's way more experienced than I am, and surely I'm far from being the first casual sex he's had. Nevertheless, I reassure Kate before we hang up.

As soon as I enter the break room downstairs and spot Oliver, I curse my goldfish memory. He's with the other nerds, and he sees me right away.

We exchange an awkward wave before I get my Tupperware from the fridge. Because of whatever text Tami sent him, he knows I spent the night with someone. But I told him I'd come back to him once I was ready, so it makes it all so weird. Will he think I'm whoring out before settling down with him?

Because I can't keep staring at the yogurts and meal boxes like this, I grab my Pad Thai and straighten up. I jump at the sight of Oli right on the other side of the fridge door. "Hi," he greets with a forced grin.

"Hi." My smile probably looks as fake as his.

He follows me to the microwave and says, "I'm glad you're fine. Tami seemed very worried yesterday."

"Yeah, I messed up. I should have warned her." I shove my opened box in the microwave, which smells like fish once more. *Dammit, people. Stop with the weird dishes already.*

"You know, you shouldn't microwave your things in plastic. It's carcinogenic."

I stare at him with a blank expression. Small talk won't make this any less weird. "Look, Oli, I—"

"It's fine. You don't have to justify yourself," he cuts me off. He stops and passes his hand on the back of his head to distractedly scratch it, looking at the floor. "I won't pretend I'm not a little hurt. I really like you, but it's your life and your choices. I keep thinking about our date, and I can't help but regret not going upstairs with you. And I feel like shit for it because I know you told me how overwhelmed you are and all."

I'm tongue-tied when he meets my eyes again, unsure what to say or do. Like him, I wish we could go from great friends to great lovers, but things aren't that simple.

"I never wanted to hurt you," I say, hoping it can ease his bruised emotions.

"I know. I'm not blaming you; just trying to make peace with it. It doesn't matter what you do now, as long as you're over it when *we* happen," he explains, his hands tucked in his front pockets. I nod, my brows twisted with unease.

I'm such a selfish asshole.

My food rings behind me, so I take it out rapidly. With my cancer-infused meal in hand, I wonder how the hell I can make this situation better.

"I can't promise I'll ever be ready. I like you, Oli, I really do. But I can't be sure I'll ever like you like *that*," I say with my free hand on his shoulder, trying to be as gentle as possible.

Oli processes my words for a moment, his expression slightly confused and worried. "I get it, don't worry. I can handle that sort of thing."

I can almost believe him, but his eyes look so sad.

With a heavy heart, I give him a small smile and go sit with Dakota, Tami, and a few others. I eat in silence, my mind preoccupied. Something tells me I'll never desire Oliver like I desire Lex.

I've never come even close to what the latter makes me feel.

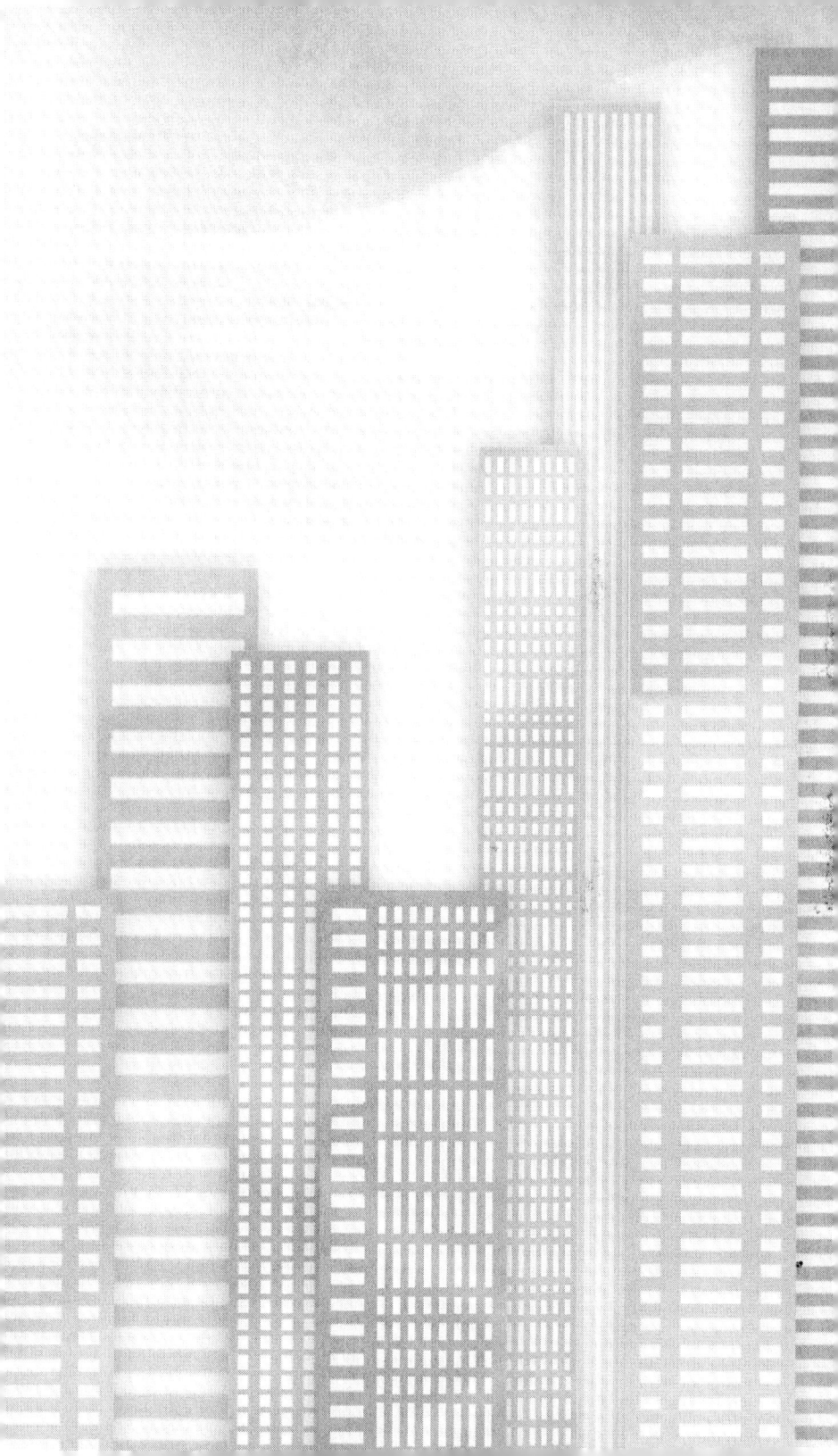

is_new_chapter = True

chapter_number =

"20"

pov_name =

"Andrea"

THE MASSIVE LOAD OF WORK that we have to take care of leaves little to no room for distraction. By the end of each day, my brain is fried, so I leave for home as soon as I can. I'm too tired to want anything other than to go to bed. Alone.

As time passes, I can't help but try to rationalize things. It's logical that after ten months deprived of physical contact with men, I was particularly receptive to Lex's ministrations. Sure, he knew precisely what to do and how to do it, but my intense reaction to him was most likely due to my prolonged abstinence.

And anyway, Lex doesn't give me more of these intense, bone-melting moments where I'm reduced to putty. No, he remains cold and distant—which he's tremendous at. I'm left alone with my fantasies and desires, discreetly looking at him when he isn't paying attention, getting all horny with the lewd flashbacks my mind conjures on an hourly basis.

So, I drown myself in work since it's all I have left at this point. Everyone from the dev team works on my app now, and by the end of every workday, an incredible number of tasks have been completed.

Today, however, will be different. Today is Saturday, and the guys are enjoying their well-deserved weekend.

Lex told me to come in later than usual, arguing I deserved some rest after all that work. But I was up at dawn and figured I might as well go to work.

On my way up, I wonder if Lex will already be here or if he took his own advice and lingered in bed. My mind flashes to an image of him naked, the soft duvet not hiding much of his perfect anatomy, lazily stretching in the light gray covers. Damn, I'd stay in bed in the morning if I had such a comfortable mattress and Lex in it.

I disapprovingly shake my head at the thought. Lazily sleeping in with Lex isn't an option.

It's odd to be in the silent hallways like this and even more strange to use a key card to unlock doors. As I'm about to enter the office, the door swings open before me.

My eyes widen as Lex appears on the other side of the panel with a folder in his hands, oblivious to my presence. Behind his glasses, his eyes are focused on the papers, like a man on a mission. He notices me right before he crashes into me. Frozen in his tracks, he looks down at me, less than a foot away.

After a moment, his surprised expression fades into his neutral self again. "No sleeping in?"

"I was awake, so I thought I might as well come and get the day started."

He nods and moves aside to allow me to come in. "Alright. I need to make some copies, but you know what you have to do."

The morning turns out to be pretty ordinary. The only difference is that people would typically drop by to talk to Lex or ask for his advice or approval. Music is my best defense against awkwardness, so I'm intently listening to a playlist I curated with my abuela. It's full of what she considers the best Latino classics, and it never fails to improve my mood.

I'm taken out of my working trance when Lex's head pops up over my screen. I push my headphones away, guessing he wants to ask me something.

"Yes?"

"I—hm, I don't know if you have plans," he says, visibly uneasy. "For lunch, I mean. I'm off to grab a bite at the Italian place around the corner. I thought the least I could do to thank you for coming in on a Saturday was to treat you to a decent meal."

I stare at him, properly dazed. He wants us to go … eat outside?

At the thought of creamy pasta, my stomach wakes up. Yes, some Italian sounds great. But it means a one-on-one meal with Lex. Not ideal at all.

But … *pasta.*

I frantically try to figure out what I should say. I could lie and say I'm not hungry. Yes, it's a solid plan. That'll work.

I'm literally opening my mouth to politely refuse when my stomach makes a loud, hungry noise. There goes my alibi.

Because I was silent for too long, I worry he'll lose his patience. "I, um, yeah. Italian sounds great," I let out, panicking. *Fuck.* "I'm almost done here. Just give me a minute," I quickly add.

I take a deep breath as my hands tremble with nervousness. It's fine. It's just lunch. The restaurant is always packed, so we won't be alone. We'll share a professional meal, like last time.

Well, we did end up almost fucking in his car last time.

Shit.

I can't drag this out infinitely, so I eventually tell him I'm good to go. We leave in silence and only exchange a look when he holds the door for me.

"Have you ever eaten there?" he asks once we're outside.

"Yes, a few times already."

"Alright. They have the best prosciutto risotto I've ever had."

I can tell small talk doesn't come easy for him, so it's clear he's intentionally being diplomatic. "I haven't tried it, but their gorgonzola tagliatelle is to die for."

"I've never had that, actually." We walk in silence for a few seconds until he says, "The weather is very nice."

This further attempt at jumpstarting the conversation makes me smile, but I bite it back. I indulge his efforts, and we carry an entire conversation about the weather all the way to the restaurant.

The place isn't as packed as I'd hoped, and we get seated near a window, a little isolated from the rest. I go over the menu, using it as an excuse not to have to talk or look at him. I really, *really* want to have pasta, but a shallow part of me considers ordering a salad.

It's not like Lex hasn't already seen me naked and doesn't know I have a fat ass and love handles—which he used to pull me back onto his dick that night. Still, I don't think it's something the women he usually dates have.

This is ridiculous. I never worried about what I should eat in front of a man before. It's so unlike me to be this superficial. Of course I prefer cheese over lettuce, like every single person on this planet—even the ones that are lactose intolerant.

"Have you made your choice?" the waiter asks when he returns, pulling out a notepad from his black apron.

Lex turns to him, closing his menu. "I'll have the tagliatelle al gorgonzola."

Oh … He's trying my thing. A small smile stretches my lips as I realize he just gave me the perfect excuse to not eat salad. "I'll take the prosciutto risotto, please," I ask, grateful for Lex's unknowing rescue. The waiter then asks for drinks, and we settle on sharing a bottle of San Pellegrino.

"So, how did you get into the world of coding?" Lex asks once we're alone again, leaning comfortably in his chair.

"My father," I explain, unable to hold back a grin. "He teaches computer science at a high school. Early on, he used my mom and me as guinea pigs to prepare his classes. I got into it quickly, but my mom gave up after three lessons. My dad gave me special lessons from there, and I think after the first year, I was already better than him at it. I got better all the way to college, where I didn't really learn anything, but I needed the diploma," I explain. Lex listens to me keenly, his gray eyes locked into mine. "What about you? How did you become so good at it?"

He takes his time answering, fidgeting with the napkin before him, his eyes absently gazing at his empty glass. "I was always more comfortable with computers," he eventually says. "I was never very social and rather isolated, so the internet became my shelter from boredom. It provided an inexhaustible source of knowledge, and I couldn't get enough of it. Video games became a great way to pass the time. I looked into how it was done and attempted to make one myself. That's how I started. I think I was twelve."

"You built a whole video game?" I ask, impressed.

"I built several, actually," he says proudly. "It wasn't anything impressive, and I clearly had more fun building them than playing."

The waiter arrives to give us our sparkling water and a breadbasket.

"You have a brother, right?" Lex then asks.

"Yes, Rafael. He's my polar opposite, outdoorsy, hyperactive, and can't sit for two hours straight without going mad. He's a photographer," I explain. "He's been in New York for the past three years, but he's moving back to Portland this month." After a moment of talking about my brother, I ask Lex if he has any siblings.

"I have three older sisters." My surprise is almost impossible to mask, and he notices it. "What?"

"I didn't think you were the youngest."

"Why is that?"

"In my experience, younger siblings tend to be more … carefree. You're so serious and responsible all the time. I thought you'd be the eldest or maybe an only child."

"Ah, yes. I'm afraid my rigidity is a factory setting," he humorously says.

We talk more about our siblings, and then our plates arrive. I hold back a moan at how good my risotto smells but can't prevent an appreciative groan at the first bite. Damn, that is delicious.

"Okay, you were right. This is so, so good," I admit, taking another bite.

Lex eats a forkful of meticulously wrapped tagliatelle and nods once he swallows it. "The pasta is good as well."

"Not as good as this." He doesn't say anything, even though I can tell he agrees.

As we eat, I learn more about his sisters. Two of them are married, and one is engaged. The eldest is Lucy. She's nine years older than him and has two boys, fourteen and twelve. The second one is Emilia, and she has twin daughters who are five. The youngest of his sisters, Julia, divorced about three years ago and is now getting married again in the spring.

I can tell he's fond of them. He has a lingering smile on his face, which I find charming. He barely mentions his parents, though, and I don't ask. Something isn't quite right there. By the end of the meal, he knows a lot more about my family, and I know a lot more about his.

"I can't believe you grew up surrounded by women," I say on our walk back to the office, still surprised by that revelation.

"Why is it so shocking?"

"You didn't strike me as a women's advocate the first time we met," I say boldly. He doesn't seem annoyed by my statement but rather reflective.

"My initial reaction to you had nothing to do with the fact that you were a woman," he ends up saying. "Admittedly, I didn't foresee you would be one, but it's not what caused my distrust. I was expecting someone in their late thirties, maybe early forties. I designed the test myself, and I was stumped when I saw your results. Ninety percent of the applicants scored under fifty out of a hundred points. You were at ninety-two. I think the closest one right after you was sixty-one."

I stare at him with utter shock. "Really? I scored that high?"

He nods. "I triple checked, reread your cover letter, and sent your profile to HR, telling them to hire you. That's why I never got a chance to realize you weren't an Andrew."

"I may or may not have used 'Andy' to make sure I wouldn't be discarded on the count of being a woman," I confess.

"And I understand that. I know I reacted poorly, and once more, I'm sorry for the accusations," Lex adds. "But you were standing there, looking like …" He thinks briefly before continuing, "Looking fresh out of college, and my rational mind couldn't accept you were the same Andy who nailed my test—regardless of your gender."

I kinda get why he was so harsh back then. I look younger than I am, especially when I wear my nerdy T-shirts. Between that and my impressive score on his test, I can understand why he thought I cheated my way in, somehow.

"But you quickly proved me wrong, and I'm glad you turned out to be the real deal," he continues, his intense gaze capturing mine as we wait for the elevator. The mood switches and the amiable conversation now slides into something more intimate. His magnetic aura slowly envelops me, my body warming up at his words.

"I'm glad I did, too."

I'll forever be grateful for the opportunity to work here, meet the team, make such great friends … And no matter what I tell myself, I'm glad I met *him*. Lex is a revelation of the flesh and of the mind.

I silently process all the information he gave me on our way up. Thanks to his newly discovered humanity, I'm even more attracted to him.

As if the man needed any help in that department.

pov_name = "Alexander"

It's like our cordial lunch together unlocked something. Now, our exchanges are somewhat free of tension, and we're not as disinclined to talk. We even arrange our screens so it's easier to speak.

We have until Wednesday to polish the app before San José, and I doubt we'll manage. While we're reaching a ninety-five percent accuracy with colorful nails, we can't get over forty-five without it. It's doable but requires much more time than we have.

At some point in the afternoon, I hear her let out an annoyed growl, so I ask, "Anything I can do to help?"

"I have to make some adjustments, but I need to check the algorithm while it's running for that."

"Do you want me to sign while you inspect?"

"Uh … It would help, yes," she hesitantly answers. "But are you fine with wearing nail polish?"

The fact that she even doubts it is a little insulting. Does she think I'm one of those toxic alpha men?

"I've heard red suits me best."

Her slight shock barely lasts a second before she smiles and looks into her bag. "I don't think I have any. I have a pretty nice fuchsia. It's not great quality, but it dries fast, which is all we need," she explains after some shuffling, brandishing the small bottle.

"Do you want me to apply it?" she offers, failing at hiding her amusement.

I should say no and handle it myself. It doesn't need to be perfect for the test, and it would be the reasonable thing to do. But I've been craving her touch for days, and we're in some kind of peaceful truce, so I roll my chair to her side of the desk and rest a flat hand in front of her.

The absurdity of the moment has her giggling every few seconds as she meticulously applies a coat of cheap fuchsia on my nails.

"Stop giggling," I dryly order, feigning offense before I add, "you'll make a mess."

That makes her laugh softly, and I smile at the sound. Something indeed shifted during our lunch, didn't it?

Once she's done with my left hand, I blow on the nails while she handles the other. The switch brings us even closer, and I can't stop myself from admiring her pretty profile as she works. Since that night we shared, I've been drawn to her lips on more than one occasion. They've been haunting me, making me wish I could enjoy their softness again, sample their taste, experience their greed again … My cock swells in my jeans as I envision them wrapped around it, all pink, wet, and plump. I adjust my position, hoping she won't notice.

With her hands on me and her scent in my nose, it becomes painful by the time she finishes.

"All done," she proudly says, letting me go and straightening up. "You like it?" she teases.

"Not my best color, but it's still better than green." Her puzzled expression compels me to explain. "My sisters practiced all kinds of things on me—hair, makeup, nails … Between the age difference and the fact that we barely shared any interests, I took every opportunity I had to spend time with them."

"That's adorable."

During the following hour, she has me signing various sentences repeatedly while she focuses on the code on her screen. She corrects a few things, and once we're done, I walk over to check the results with her, slipping my glasses on as I do.

We read the lines, scan the script, and when we reach the bottom, I say, "Good job. We'll have to run some tests, but I think it'll help with the final version."

Still looking at the screen, I feel her gaze on my profile. When I turn to her, she swiftly looks away. Her cheeks have a pink tint, and her hands fidget on her lap. And that's when I realize she's just as tormented as I am, desperate for more of what we shared that night. Deep down, I knew there was no way I'd be the only one craving more.

But even now, nearly certain she does, I know we can't indulge. I'm not the relationship type, and she doesn't strike me as someone who can have a casual affair with her boss. She's too intense for that, and she would probably expect so much more than I can give her. And then what? We break things off, and I lose the best programmer I've ever hired? What if she quits and I never see her again? A sense of sadness overwhelms me at the thought.

As tempting as Andrea Walker is, this path will lead to nothing but sour disappointment.

She almost looks upset as she says, "Thank you for your help." She doesn't wait for an answer and turns to her computer.

"Andrea, I …"

I what? I need more, too? I'm not over what happened between us? I've been dreaming of you relentlessly, of your taste, of your moans, of how gushing wet you were for me?

She can't know that. It's too dangerous.

"Can I have the polish remover?" I say instead.

Disappointment twists her pretty features, as if she expected me to say something else.

I ruined it. The lightness of the afternoon is gone because I don't know how to gently let her down. It rarely happens anymore, but I find myself wishing I were better with people, better at anticipating their emotions, so that I could say whatever she needs to hear to move on. So that I could free us of this unwanted need that strains our every interaction.

The day ends like it started—in tense silence. Then it's time to leave, and I'm thankful for it. She isn't coming back tomorrow, so I'll work from home. All this overtime and moments alone with her are driving me to the brink of insanity.

So why the fuck do I offer, "Do you want me to drive you home?"

"I'm good," she says, hooking her bag over her shoulder.

We walk together to the elevators and patiently wait for one to arrive. "Thank you for coming today, Andrea."

"It's okay. I didn't have anything planned anyway."

When she looks up, I'm already looking down at her. I don't have to wonder why she looks somewhat sad because I feel the same way.

I wish there could be more to this. I wish we didn't have to behave. I wish I knew how to handle this. I wish I could kiss her, just one more time. One *last* time.

Don't do it, I tell myself. In a few weeks, the lid will be back on Pandora's box—tightly screwed shut. I need to stay strong for a little longer and resist the tempting call of her parted lips and the silent hope in her brown eyes. But I'm only human, and there's only so much I can endure.

"Fuck it," I grunt to myself.

Like an itch I can't resist, I grab her nape and bend forward. Before she can realize what's happening, I press my mouth on hers for an ardent, urgent kiss.

She's so stunned that she doesn't react, recoil, or say anything. She stands there, her entire frame taut, trying to process what's happening. And then she relaxes, her hand lifting up to rest on my jaw.

It isn't like any kiss we've shared before. It isn't lust-filled. We aren't devouring or seducing each other … It's just an irrepressible need.

I move away from her, but only to admire her flushed face. The wonderment in her eyes makes something clench in my chest. Because she's irresistible, I bend to steal another hungry peck, slipping a greedy arm around her waist to pull her in.

It feels so fucking right to hold her like this.

Her jaw unlocks when my tongue demands access, and the kiss grows more intense. *A few more seconds*, I tell myself. And then I'll pull away for good, and we'll learn to stay away from one another.

The elevator makes a loud "ding," but that isn't enough to break the spell. Not for me, at least. Andrea immediately reacts to it, though, pulling away, so I let go of her as the doors open.

I'm not sure if I'm relieved or not that a few people are already on it. It's probably better that way. I would have kissed her again on our ride down, and that would have resulted in inviting her back to my place.

As I stare into her lust-filled gaze, I know without a doubt she would have accepted.

is_new_chapter = True

chapter_number =

"21"

pov_name =

"Andrea"

I DON'T KNOW WHAT TO expect when I return to work on Monday, but I feel electric. I spent my Sunday reliving our quick but intense kiss. Over and over and over.

There's no more hiding. Our desires are out.

Lex is already on his computer when I enter the office, as always, but my eyes are quickly drawn to an unfamiliar shape in the corner of the room. There's a desk set up there with a computer on it. My own computer is still next to Lex's, so what is that for? I'm about to ask when someone arrives behind me.

"Hey, Andy," Brian very enthusiastically says. He passes by me, his bag hanging on his shoulder, and sits at the newly added desk.

"Hi … Brian." Confused, I look at Lex, not understanding why he would set up Brian in here. Is it out of necessity, or is it to cockblock us? I need to know. Lex has to explain this abrupt change, or else I'll dwell on it endlessly. "Why is Brian here?" I ask once I'm at the desk.

"It's Brian this morning, but the others will take turns working here, depending on the tasks we need to complete. It's either that or we'll never finish on time," Lex explains, finally meeting my eyes.

I decide to believe his answer is honest. We're far from being done, and it makes sense we have to do everything we can to finish by Wednesday. Our kiss doesn't have to be the reason for it.

Having someone else with us only highlights how silent Lex and I usually are. It's nice to work with the guys again, even though it's one at a time. Brian helps on Monday morning. Then Mason is here in the afternoon. Having them nearby is undeniably helpful. On Tuesday, it's Steven and then Joseph. The closer we are to D-day, the more intense the pressure gets.

With every passing hour, I grow more certain we won't make it. The one thing actually ready for the demonstration is the double phone holder, which was 3D printed after a few prototypes were built. But as Kevin said, this gives the app a nice boost.

On Wednesday, I'm delighted to hear that Oliver will spend the afternoon with us. Even if I see him less and less as a romantic interest, he's still a dear friend, and I miss goofing around with him.

Most of the afternoon is spent testing the app's latest version and trying to correct some remaining errors. Oli and I are settled at the coffee table in Lex's office with our testing phones in the holder. We're both signing without nail polish and trying to edit the code as we go. Although it's terrible for our self-esteem work-wise, it quickly turns out to be a fun endeavor. We've been doing this for about thirty minutes, but the amusement isn't fading.

The recognition tool struggles, so the sentence-formulating AI barely has anything to work its magic.

"The milk boy is in my garden?" I ask, confused.

"That's what it says?" Oli turns the device to read it himself. "That's hilarious. It was supposed to be that line from *Milkshake* by Kelis."

I can't help but giggle at the absurd translation. "Oli, you know your classics."

It's my turn to sign, and I follow his little game.

"Done," I say. He reads it with attention, and a smile stretches his lips.

"That's too easy. It's Eminem, *Lose Yourself*."

"What did it write exactly?" I ask, twisting it to see for myself. "There's spaghetti vomit on Mom." I chortle and return the phones to their proper positions. After a few more quotes from rap classics, we decide to do some actual work.

Oli's with me the whole afternoon, and if we bother Lex with our antics, he doesn't let it show. In no time, the end of the workday arrives. Oliver leaves at five-thirty while I stay, waiting for the last build to be over. We have officially accepted that the app isn't the one we'll show during the convention. Thanks to Lex's foresight, Brian and Steven are ready to present their work. Although the failure hurts a little, I see it as a win. This past week was worth an entire month of work, at least.

"You should go home and get some rest for tomorrow," Lex suggests after a while.

"The results might come in any time now. I'm good."

"There's no need for us both to stay late," he insists. I'm too tired to argue with him, and I desperately need a shower and my bed.

Leaving my computer on, I gather my things, ready to go. He stands up at the same time I do, and I give him a sheepish smile. "I'm sorry this was all for nothing."

"It wasn't a complete waste of time," he says. Something about the way he looks at me leads me to believe he means me, *us*, even though the thought is ludicrous. There is no "us". There's him, there's me, and there's a steamy night. It doesn't make an "us".

As if to prove me right, he adds, "The alpha version will certainly be ready by Thanksgiving now, and we'll be able to seek out investors."

It stings, but that's on me for being so foolish. "And when we return, you'll finally get back downstairs," he bluntly continues.

The ache under my ribs intensifies, as well as an overwhelming sense of confusion. Why does it have to be this way with him? One step forward, two steps back? He kissed me, and now he's rejecting me. He goes from hot to cold all the time, and I can't keep up with his mood swings.

"Where did that come from?" I ask, trying to conceal my hurt feelings.

"It will be better that way." The topic definitely shifted, and we aren't talking about work anymore. "Whatever this is," he says, his hand going back and forth between us, "this chemistry won't lead to anything good. I don't do relationships, Andrea. And you don't seem like someone who does what I do."

I don't know exactly what he means, but I still feel insulted. Who am I? Laura from *Little House on the Prairie*? I'm not some naive girl who can't make her own choices.

"How do you know what I do or don't do?" I ask, holding myself straight and my chin up.

"I spent the afternoon watching you interact with Oliver. That's what you do. Cute relationships with someone who shares your interests."

Is that resentment in his voice? Is he jealous of Oliver? The afternoon was friendly and nothing more—I made sure of that. Did Lex imagine something that wasn't there between my colleague and me?

"It's not Oli that I want," I boldly state. His gaze darkens, and I know I got to him.

"I'm sorry if I gave you the wrong impression, but I'm not interested in you, Andrea," he says cruelly. I might have believed him, but I see the way his fists are clenched with restraint. Out of pride, I refuse to let him do this, so I step closer. "You'll end up hurt, no matter what," he insists.

The fact that I was hurt moments ago proves he's right. Even if all I want for now is cataclysmic *slex*, my needs will evolve until I'm in too deep. But who knows? Maybe I'll be great at this no-strings-attached thing. Maybe I'll ace it and get out of it unharmed. The urge to prove myself floods me. I have to show him he's wrong about me.

And anyhow, we both know what happens when we try not to fuck each other. We fail miserably.

"We'll have to make the hurt worth it, then," I utter, taking him by surprise.

Before he can react, I'm bringing his face to mine because this is what we both want. He doesn't ravish me, but he doesn't push me away either, so I take it as a good sign.

Persevering, I press my body against his. When his hands come to rest on my hips, I lasciviously lick the sealed line of his lips. It always works when he does that to me. To my great relief, a low groan rolls in his throat.

But then, he rips his mouth away from mine to mutter, "Andrea, it isn't a good idea."

"I think it's a brilliant idea."

The taste of his skin is addictive as I trace a line of heated kisses down his neck. A vein's pulsing there, so I lick it. He swallows uneasily when I kiss his Adam's apple, making it bob under my lips, and I can't help but smile. I mirror my ministrations on the other side of his neck, coming back up, and rip another groan from him when I nibble on his earlobe. I can't get enough of this man, and he feels the same way about me.

He's getting hard against my lower stomach, so I'm doing something right, but not right enough. I let go of his ear to whisper, "I can't stop thinking about that night."

His hands slide from my hips to my lower back, and he presses me harder against him, making me feel that he wants this, too. My insides clench at the blunt contact, and a veil of lust clouds my thoughts. I move back to meet his eyes, and the want in them traps my breath in my lungs.

"I've been dreaming of you, Lex. I wake up panting, trembling, and wet. So fucking wet …" I tilt my head to the side, my lips parted, ready to administer the final blow. "Do you ever dream of me?" My hand slithers between us, down the plane of his torso, and I mold it over the hardness of his erection. "Do you wake up hard, aching to be inside me?"

He bends slowly, stopping only when his lips graze mine, his warm breath mixing with my own. "You have no fucking idea."

This time, he doesn't resist and lowers to take possession of my mouth. Our tongues dart out simultaneously, and I can't hold back a moan at the electrifying sensation. My knees are already growing weak under the intensity of our embrace. We kiss, standing in the middle of his office, the magnitude of it ever-growing.

Only the sounds of our ragged breaths and the wet noises of our kiss break the silence surrounding us. He's hungrily devouring me while his hands move up and down my body, greedily wanting to touch every accessible part of me. Because I want the same thing, my hand slips underneath his T-shirt to graze the rippled muscles of his stomach, my palm teased by the thin line of hair that runs up his torso. When both his hands knead the soft mounds of my ass, lifting me up on his impressive erection, I get impossibly wet.

Oh, we aren't just kissing. We're going to fuck again.

"Take me to your place," I demand as he kisses the slope of my neck, getting a husky moan out of me. I shiver when he licks the spot where my throat meets my shoulder right before gently biting it.

"I'm not waiting ten minutes to be inside you again."

I wrap my legs around his hips when he lifts me, and a wave of pure, raw lust roams through my frame when my core settles against his hardened dick. My tongue is shoved into his mouth as he carries me across the room, kissing him with ardor.

Once the door is locked, he kneels in front of the couch to lay me down on it, his massive body pressing me into the cushioned seat. I marvel at the rigid muscles of his back that I can feel under the thin layer of his T-shirt. I pull on the fabric, and he lets go of our kiss to remove it, dumping it on the floor behind him. Within half a second, he's already back on me, reuniting our lips.

His hands move down my ribcage, waist, and hips before coming back up, lifting my top—an oversized red sweater with "Bazinga!" written in yellow letters. He pushes it up until my bra is revealed. I observe him back with hooded eyes for a moment, and then he lifts my bra up as well. To make things simpler, I help him remove it, along with my sweater.

Once my small mounds are freed, he covers each with a hand, his eyes dark with hunger. When I'm lying down like this, they become practically nonexistent, flattening on my chest and giving my upper body a boyish look. But he doesn't seem to mind, given how he intently fondles them. He pinches both my nipples, sending an electric jolt all the way to my clit, which makes me moan and press myself on him.

A trembling breath welcomes his next enterprise as he takes one of my brown tips into his mouth. He bites, just enough to make me cry with pleasure and pain, and then soothes the attack with a soft lick. After a thorough treatment of my left breast that leaves me panting and begging, he moves on to the right one and gives it the same torturous attention.

I'm so turned on that I suspect I'm drenching my jeans as well as my underwear. His licks, bites, and kisses bring me a ridiculous amount of pleasure. I can't help but grind against him, rubbing my aching pussy against his hard length. It's all too much, and I'm about to come just from him teasing my nipples. But I don't want to find my release like this. I want him to be buried deep inside of me when it happens.

"Fuck me … Please," I breathe out.

My lustful demand gets him to groan, and he pulls on my pebbled nipple between his teeth one last time before straightening up. He's quick to lower my jeans, throwing my Vans behind him with his shirt.

"No themed socks today?" he teases when he sees the plain white cotton.

"No. I relocated my funny socks to the bottom of my drawer."

He let out a small laugh. "A shame; I was eager to discover the surprise of the day."

"I'll keep it in mind for the future."

That is, if there's a future. I hope this second time means our sexual escapades will become a recurring thing, but until we talk about it, I genuinely have no idea what the future holds for our illicit affair.

I lie here, wearing only my underwear while he gets naked. It's like a little show just for me, and I revel in his perfection, sensing myself growing wetter with every inch of skin he unveils.

I'm so affected by his magnetism that it takes a moment for my brain to process what I just saw. "Why did you have a condom in your back pocket?"

He doesn't answer right away, embarrassed—an unusual sight coming from him. "I wanted to be prepared, just in case."

"You expected this to happen?"

"Not expected, no. But part of me hoped it would."

And he tried to pretend he wasn't into me …

Once the protection is on, he grasps my hips and bends to lay a kiss on my cotton-covered pussy, right on my demanding clit. The hunger of the gesture has me shivering from head to toe. Then he pulls my panties down my legs, revealing my intimate folds. When his eyes settle on my dripping slit, he smirks with pride and cockiness.

"Andrea, how are you always so wet for me?" Without any warning, he shoves his middle finger inside me, making me arch with a moan. Fuck, it feels so good. He pumps it in and out, bending it so it rubs on my front wall, knowing precisely what he's doing. I cry when he adds another finger.

"Come for me, Andrea. Come on my finger so I can fuck you properly."

Given his impressive size, I understand why he wants to do it that way. I consider arguing, but I can already sense my orgasm building up. It won't be long before he's buried inside me to the hilt. Especially with the way his thumb rubs my clit. With his other hand, he plays with my nipples, adding to the delight.

Absolutely helpless, I yield to the pleasure. It's growing so quickly that it's almost unbearable. The drenched sounds of his fingers fucking me hard and fast are almost embarrassing, but they're covered by my moans and whimpers. Before I can even understand what's happening, I come apart with a confused cry, crawling up on my elbows to escape the overwhelming stimulation. Mercilessly, his hand follows me to push my orgasm further, making me quiver and tremble.

"Aah, Lex …" I whimper, hoping he'll stop his torturous ministrations.

When he finally removes his hand, the relief is short-lived. He pulls me back to him at the edge of the couch, and the round head of his cock takes its position at my pulsing opening.

He pushes himself inside of me with a careful yet firm thrust until he's all the way in. Despite the orgasm, some discomfort lingers, but the ridiculous amount of pleasure makes it barely noticeable. Is there a better sensation in this world?

"I can't wait until I've fucked you enough to mold you to my cock," he says with a low voice.

There it is … The confirmation that there'll be more of this. Like me, he accepted we'll reiterate in the future.

His hands travel up from my parted knees, finding their place at my waist, circling it. "Should we count how many times I can make you come before I do?" he suggests.

My eyes widen. I should refuse because I'm no match for his stamina. But some combative part of me is curious. Boldly, I look up to meet his eyes, and after a moment of us studying each other, I nod.

He shakes his head, a ghost of a smile lingering on his mouth, and pulls out slowly before thrusting back with a deep shove. My confidence already wavers as I involuntarily moan. He does it again and again, and I quickly lose my ability to think. Adding to the physical satisfaction of being so perfectly filled and having the base of his cock hit my clit with each thrust, I'm also overwhelmed by the meaning of the moment.

I'm having sex with Lex again. He's right there, all magnificent and intense, the muscles of his arms and upper torso flexing every time he pulls me onto his hammering cock. His abs also contract each time he moves forward, making me salivate with need. He's so fucking attractive.

Keeping one hand against the armrest to make sure I won't slide up, I lose control of my body. My hips are now moving in harmony with his, my fingers digging into the solid muscles of his arm, my back arching of its own will …

"Are you going to come for me already?" he rasps.

Something inside me rebels at the thought. I don't want to be such a lightweight, but I can't help how intense it all is. I stubbornly shake my head and close my eyes to focus on not orgasming. For fuck's sake, it hasn't even been five minutes.

Lex takes it as a challenge, his rhythm intensifying and his thumb teasing my swollen clit, rubbing it with just the right pressure. As much as I try to hold back, the double assault of his thumb and dick is too much for me to resist. My legs twitch on each side of him, and my eyes whip open.

"Aah, fuck!" I cry out as I tilt over the edge. Anticipating that I'll shake uncontrollably, he pins me firmly on the couch's seat, never stopping his maddening thrusts.

My pleasure explodes as I desperately moan his name, my back arching until only my ass and the back of my head are left on the cushion. Endless ripples of intense ecstasy make my body tremble, my cries filling the empty office. He's still ramming into me, expertly dragging out my climax, but at least he slowed down, showing mercy to some extent. It takes forever for bliss to settle down, and by the end of it, I'm feeling weak and helpless. My nails are planted into his forearm, and I'm glad they aren't long or sharp. One by one, I lift my fingers to release him, revealing small crescent-shaped dents.

Lex is now unmoving, seemingly very proud of himself. "That's two."

Fuck, I'm so losing this game …

pov_name =

"Alexander"

Andrea welcomes my lips when I bend down to kiss her. I can't believe this is happening again. And I can't believe how good she feels—even better than I remembered.

I guess we were fooling ourselves, thinking we'd manage to keep things platonic and professional. This was always bound to happen. I want her too much.

After a few more seconds of intensely making out, I rearrange myself with a knee on the couch so I can push deeper, and thrust again. The slow pace quickly increases, and she rips her mouth away to take a deep breath before she moans.

"I can feel you clench around me already," I say, inches from her ear. "Tell me you're not about to come again so soon."

Fire ignites behind her brown irises, and she lowers a hand between us to make a tight ring around my cock with her index and thumb. The added pressure has me buckling with the need to come.

Before she can take it further, I grip her wrist and force her hand over her head, giving her a warning frown. She immediately tries to do it again with her free hand, but I intercept it before it reaches my cock.

Seeing her restrained like this, with her slim wrists imprisoned in my hold, brings out something primal in me. She's at my mercy now, and there's nothing she can do to stop me from making her come again. And again. And again.

"What will you do now?" I ask, rolling my hips sinuously to make her feel helpless.

Her rebellious smile isn't the answer I expected. Nor is the way her walls suddenly clamp around me.

"Ah, fuck," I mutter, hips jerking.

Victorious, she playfully bites my chin. "What is it? Are you scared you'll lose?"

"You seem pretty confident for someone who came twice in barely five minutes."

"If you're so sure of yourself, just keep fucking me, Alexander."

I accept the challenge, adjusting my position over her, and resume the fucking. My confidence wanes as she clenches again.

"You're so fucking tight already. It feels fucking insane when you do that." That only makes her clench harder, so I curse. "I'm going to relentlessly fuck you for hours one day, Andrea, and you'll only have yourself to blame for it."

I see the way her pupils dilate at the threat, so I make a mental note of actually enforcing it. With my face less than an inch from hers, I keep up with the merciless pace, rubbing the base of me on her clit with each deep thrust. When the first signs of her pending orgasm arrive, I can't even rejoice. I'll be coming with her, there's no doubt about that.

Just as the first spasm of her cunt chokes my dick, she begs, "Kiss me."

I let go of her hands and grab her jaw instead, pulling her in as I comply. Her cries vibrate against my tongue as her hands grip my ass to pull me closer.

Her involuntary twitching, the way she screams my name, and how she spasms around me bring my stamina to its knees. With a savage roar, I follow her in bliss, cum jetting out of me with so much force I can feel it in my bones. Her walls milk it out of me, compelling more rope of cum to surge out until I feel empty and satiated.

We're still like this long after the last shivers ran through our overheated frames, our bodies still joined. Again, the pleasure she brings is beyond anything I've known before. After a few minutes, though, she softly mumbles, "Lex, I can't breathe."

I maneuver us around, dislodging my semi-hard dick from her warmth. In the process, I tug at the condom and throw it on the coffee table. Within a few seconds, I'm the one lying on the couch, and she's sprawled on top of me. My fingers move on their own to draw mindless patterns on her back, which is veiled with a thin film of perspiration.

She did this to me last time, and the shivers it triggered were among the most pleasant sensations I've ever experienced. When she practically melts onto me with a sigh, her temple on my chest and her legs entwined with mine, I gather she likes it as much as I do.

"You cheated," I say after a while of this.

"You never mentioned any rules."

I grunt my disapproval and hold her tighter against me. "It wasn't very fair play of you."

"It was survival instinct." That makes me chuckle.

Although I wish we could stay like this for hours, basking in the moment, the couch underneath me becomes uncomfortable. I wriggle under her, trying to find a better position. "This couch is horrible."

She looks up and meets my eyes to ask, "You didn't know?"

I shake my head. "I've never spent enough time on it to notice before."

"Well, now you're aware," she says, kissing my chest before resting her head on it again.

"Come on. You'll be in your bed in half an hour," I encouragingly say. "We have a plane to catch tomorrow morning and things to prepare before that."

She reluctantly cooperates to stand on wobbly legs. Like the greedy little woman she is, she turns around to look down at me, sprawled naked on the sofa. I don't work out to look good for women, but my rigorous way of life seems to have that effect. I never really cared what my sex partners thought of my body, but Andrea's appreciation makes all the hours of lifting weights, swimming, and playing basketball worth it.

"Like what you see?" I arrogantly ask.

Because she can't help being a brat, she shrugs and says, "Meh …"

I'm not fooled, though, and her grin confirms my suspicions. I'm very much to her liking.

Twenty-five minutes later, after getting dressed and leaving the building, I'm parking in front of her place. I'm still not over what happened in my office, almost lightheaded from it.

"Lex?" she softly calls.

"Hmm?"

"What are we doing?" The question surprises me, even though it's to be expected. "I mean, it's pretty obvious we're amazing at this sex thing. And I'm definitely up for more of it. But is it a thing now? Are we, like, sex buddies, or whatever it's called?"

There's no point in saying we'll keep our distance anymore. We've been shit at it so far, and it only worsens the tension and angst. That's why I say, "I'm not opposed to it. It seems I can't stay away from you anyway. But the situation is delicate, so we should take a moment to establish some ground rules. I doubt we'll find the time during the convention, but we can work on that when we get back."

"Okay, I'm good with that. Anyhow, I'll see you tomorrow at the airport. Also, Lex?"

"Yes?"

"Thank you."

"For the sex or for driving you home?"

She laughs. "For both, I guess. And for the kiss, too."

"Which ki—" I don't even have the time to finish my sentence as she traps my mouth under a hungry kiss. It's as intense as it is short, and she moves back, licking her lips like she can't get enough of my taste—a sentiment I share.

Hm, maybe we can have a quick fuck in my car before she goes. God knows I'd be up for that.

"One of these days, we're going to fuck in your car," she promises, making me think she might be a mind reader. "In the meantime, sleep tight."

She's out before I can stop her, and she disappears behind her building's entrance after one last look back. When my phone vibrates, I rip my eyes from the door to check on it. It's a random news notification, but I then see several missed texts from Kevin.

HE-MAN

It's happening again, isn't it?

Next time you two give it a go at work, maybe make sure no one's doing overtime in the adjacent office ;)

Just a one-time thing, eh?

Okay, this feels like I'm cheating on my wife. I'm leaving.

I suppose we're lucky he was the one doing overtime and not someone from HR.

Next time, I'm driving her to my place. That way, she can stay the night, and we'll get more time to ourselves.

is_new_chapter = True

chapter_number =

"22"

pov_name =

"Andrea"

THE MOMENT I ENTER THE terminal where we're supposed to meet, I spot the tall, dark, and handsome man who occupies my every thought. Just for him, I got up an hour early to pluck, wax, exfoliate, hydrate … I'm ready for whatever will go down in San José.

Rolling my suitcase behind me, my backpack heavy with my laptop, I join Lex and Steven—the only ones here so far. Lex notices me when I'm about ten steps away, and his eyes lock on me, not letting go until I reach my destination. "Hey, guys!" I greet.

Strategically, I avoid looking at Lex, fearing I might spontaneously combust. He's wearing a black button-up shirt tucked in his jeans and a dark blue blazer. I'm wearing a white dress shirt with a red leather jacket I barely ever wear, brand new jeans, and my black Chucks.

Since we'll represent Kelex there, we were told to step up our game. That's why my suitcase is filled with blouses, professional-looking tops, two skirts, fancy jeans, dress pants … I have some more comfortable items too, but not much. There's also a pair of modest heels in there.

Steven is still sporting one of his plaid shirts, but it's ironed. "Hi, Andy," he says with a smile, adjusting his glasses on his nose.

"Hi, my dudes!" Brian barges in, visibly very happy to be here.

Before long, Mason arrives too, looking so stylish he could be on the cover of Vogue. Then it's Oliver, charming in his beige pants and a mossy green long-sleeved shirt. While Lex is busy talking to Brian and Steven about their presentation, I greet my ginger friend with a smile.

Our little group is energized, and we share an exciting conversation about our hopes and expectations. The whole thing feels more like a fun trip with friends than a work trip, and I cannot wait to get there. The computer nerds in us are thrilled. I'm confident it'll be amazing, especially if I score some *slexy* time while in San José.

Joseph arrives about five minutes later, dressed like his usual professional self.

"Everyone," Lex calls once we're all here. He takes out a large envelope from his laptop bag and pulls out our plane tickets before distributing them.

Twenty minutes later, we're boarding our plane. With some resentment, I look up at the compartment I'm supposed to lift my suitcase into. "Okay, let this not be too humiliating," I whisper.

I'm struggling to make it fit when a familiar hand comes to my rescue. Lex is right behind me, standing a little closer than he should, and he effortlessly settles my luggage in there.

"Thanks," I say, feeling even shorter than usual.

"No problem."

I take my seat by the window and frown when I see Lex settle his suitcase up there with mine. He then removes his jacket, folds it in half, and lays it over our things. My confusion deepens when he sits beside me, setting his computer bag at his feet.

"Did you … Did you plan this?" I stammer, gesturing at our seats.

His unfazed look makes me feel stupid for some reason. "Of course. I asked Beatrix in accounting to get me a seat right next to yours when she bought the plane tickets," he sarcastically answers.

It's only fair to get stupid answers when we ask stupid questions, but still, I don't exactly like his tone. "Okay, no need to be a jerk."

He surprises me by resting his hand on the inside of my knee, sending a shiver up my thigh. "Sorry. I'm not a big fan of planes."

The guys are somewhere in front of us, so I doubt they can see Lex's hand, which is why I don't swat it away. The intimate gesture does all sorts of things to my brain and body.

I don't know how to make him feel better, but having a view might be a nice distraction. And most people prefer the window seat, right? "Do you want to switch seats?" I offer.

"I have more legroom here."

Since that didn't work, I try something else. "You know, planes are the safest form of transportation. Then I think it's buses, trains, ferries, cars, and way down there, motorcycles. I can't remember where bicycles stand."

He looks down at me with a crooked smile and a soft chuckle. "I'm not scared of the plane crashing. I just don't enjoy being stuck in it with people," he explains. "I find it overwhelming, with the noises, vibrations, uncomfortable seats …"

Oh, yes, that makes sense too. "Well, at least it isn't a long flight," I say with optimism.

He squeezes my thigh gently. "Something tells me I'll enjoy it."

Letting go of my leg, he unbuttons the wrist of his sleeve before rolling it up, revealing his muscular forearm. Hypnotized, I follow the movements of his hand, methodically folding and tucking the fabric before doing the same on the other side. Those long and thick fingers fucked me to bliss yesterday evening.

Ugh, why does everything about this man have to be so hot?

Two hours this close to him is a bad idea. A hundred witnesses—five of them being colleagues—and a very hot Alexander is a dangerous combination.

As if sent by the gods themselves, Mason pops up next to us. "Hi, fam. Andy, would you mind changing seats with me? I wanna show Lex something, and I thought we could use this time to do that," he asks. His voice contains so much hope that I know I can't refuse. "I mean, if that's okay with you," he adds to Lex.

Our boss cocks an arrogant eyebrow but says nothing, so I understand that I'm in charge of making the call. Mason looks like he really needs this time with Lex, and it would be weird of me to refuse such a simple favor.

"Yeah, of course," I say, picking up my bag at my feet. I can feel Lex's disapproving glare but ignore it, biting my lips to hide my amusement.

"Okay, great, you're saving my life, girl. I'll go get my stuff," Mason says before leaving us.

Once we're alone, Lex turns to me, his eyes dark with annoyance. "Seriously?" he coldly asks.

"It'll help pass the time. Mace is very talkative."

Aware that I'm being a tease, I stand from my seat with my handbag. Lex moves his knees to allow me to get to the aisle, and while I'm squeezing my way there, his large hand clasps my ass. It's his second intimate touch within five minutes, and the sexuality of this one sends a flash of lust straight to my core. It's ridiculous how easily he can make me horny.

"This would have been more efficient than Mason's blabbering," he mutters, his fingers squeezing with eagerness before releasing me altogether.

Pretending to have barely noticed his adventurous hand, I don't say a thing until I'm in the aisle. "Please enjoy your flight, sir," I say with my best flight attendant voice, "and thank you for choosing our airline." He shakes his head as if unamused, but I can tell he's holding back a grin.

Mason's already coming back, holding his bag before him. "Thank you again. I owe you one, boo," he tells me before giving me his seat number.

Behind me, I hear Lex say, "I'm taking the window seat."

A silent giggle rolls out of me as I walk to 26B. To my great surprise, Oliver is in the seat next to it. "Hi, stranger," he says upon seeing me.

"Hi, yourself."

"I saw you were with the boss, and I thought you'd prefer my approach," he explains as I sit down, taking out his Nintendo Switch.

I'm a little lost at first, but then I get it. "You sent Mason?"

"Well, he was telling me how he needed to find some time with Lex during the convention, and I pointed out that now might be a great opportunity."

"I see … Pretty smart, Paulson. What games do you have?" I ask, pointing at his Switch.

The plane takes off shortly after my relocation, and Oliver sets the screen on a tablet in front of us, handing me the red controller. We play games on it until my bladder decides it can't last a two-hour flight without a purge.

On my way up the aisle, I smile at Lex and Mace, intently focused on the laptop in front of them. I would have preferred being seated next to Lex, but I'm happy Mace is making the best of it.

pov_name = "Alexander"

"I NEED TO GO TO the bathroom," I tell Mason. He stands to let me pass, and I follow the faint trail of jasmine Andrea left behind as she walked by.

I barely even caught a glimpse of her, but it was enough to set my plan into action.

Once I reach the toilets, I discreetly close the partition curtain and wait. I hear the flush, the tap, and the lock being turned. The door folds open, and Andrea's eyes widen upon finding me right there. She looks to my right, notices the curtain is shut, and a knowing smile stretches her tempting lips.

Not wasting another second, she fists the front of my shirt and pulls me in with her in the confined space, tilting her head to the side. Our lips connect before the door is even closed behind me. Our embrace is full of impatience, as if we haven't done it for weeks instead of twelve hours.

"Good morning," she breathes into our kiss.

"'Morning," I impatiently reply before taking her lips again.

We're too voracious, almost brutal, and my glasses between us become an issue. I throw them in the sink, and we resume. I can never get used to how good this is. Our tongues are meant for one another, and despite the height difference, we're always in perfect harmony. Kissing her feels like sex, like sin, like our souls are set ablaze. The dripping lust between us has to be a one-way ticket to hell, but it's a price I'm willing to pay.

My hands slither down her back to grope her thick ass, lifting her against my hardening erection and making her moan in my mouth. Wishing I had more hands to enjoy every part of her at once, I then cup the space between her legs, sensing her heat seeping into my palm. This insatiable hunger can't be normal. Something's wrong with me. With us.

Still kissing her, I slip my hand into the waistband of her jeans, past her underwear, and push it down until my fingers graze the curls of her soft mound. Purposefully, I ignore her clit and slide two fingers along her drenched opening, scooping as much wetness as I can.

"I didn't take the time to taste you yesterday, and it's been driving me insane," I groan.

Shock spreads on her face as I bring my two glistening fingers to my mouth, sucking them clean. Fuck, she tastes good. The flavor of her cunt is quickly replaced by that of her tongue as she kisses me again with savagery, hooking a leg over my hip in an attempt to be closer. After stumbling a few times, she ends up with her back to the door while I press her onto it.

I'm unsure how she does it, but she manages to unlock the door behind her. Before I can stop her, she opens it and steps outside. We're both slightly panting, and I consider pulling her back in. We can be discreet and quick. No one would know. As a last resort to counter the insanity that is us, she opens the curtain, exposing us to the passengers.

"This should help you last until tonight," she states. Then she looks down at my hard-on and grins. "Good luck getting rid of that."

Then she's off, leaving nothing behind but a raging erection, frustrated needs, and a lingering aroma of jasmine.

I don't care if it's in my room or hers, but I'm fucking her through a mattress tonight.

is_scene_break = True

"ALRIGHT. I have one room with twin beds for Brian and Steven, in case you two need to work on your presentation, rehearse, or prepare."

We're all gathered in the hotel hall after our ride from the airport, and I'm handing out the keycards. The sun is shining outside, the weather is warm, and I can tell they're all overjoyed to be here.

Once they have their cards, I hand the next ones to Oli, Mace, and Joseph. "This one has two twins and a queen for you three."

"Dibs on the queen," Mason quickly chimes.

"As if there would be any confusion," Oliver jokes.

"This is a professional trip, so childishness should be kept to a minimum," I remind them. Finally, I give the last one to Andrea. "You have a single room with a queen bed."

"And what size is your bed, then?" Her question is innocent enough to not raise suspicions. But we both know why she's asking.

"King-size," I answer, eyes planted on hers.

Heat dances behind her irises, and I guess I have my answer. I'll be fucking her through *my room*'s mattress later today. Especially since hers is on the same floor as three of her colleagues while mine is isolated from everyone we know, a few floors up.

They all get fifteen minutes to freshen up, and then we gather again in the hotel's lobby. This time, I hand them their badges, and we're off. The convention center is a ten-minute walk from the hotel, so we're on foot. When we arrive, I barely look at the space and the stands. I've been coming here every year for over a decade, so it's lost its charm. I observe Andrea, though, and the way she marvels at everything. She looks thrilled to be here, and it warms me from within. She's the reason for this change of plan, after all.

"Everyone," I call, demanding my employees' attention. "Some ground rules before I let you run around like kindergarteners. Don't go near Avoss, or they'll try to poach you. It's happened in the past."

I check my watch and look back at my team. "The day ends in a little over five hours. Keep the receipts if you get food or drinks so Beatrix can reimburse you. Alcohol is on you, and keep it light. I will not have Kelex's image tarnished because you can't control yourselves. We will all meet back here after the last conference ends. Warn me if you leave before that."

They nod impatiently, ready to explore the stands, energized like overcharged batteries. With a wave of my hand, I set them free. Brian, Steven, and Joseph immediately walk away together while Oliver and Mason encourage Andrea to follow them. She gives me a sheepish look and takes off with the duo, leaving me alone.

I know we need to be discreet, but this isn't how I envisioned today to unfold. We were robbed of our plane ride together, and now this …

With a disapproving mumble to myself, I make my way to one of the smaller rooms, where it isn't as crowded and noisy. If I don't get to spend time with Andrea, there's no point in exposing myself to so much stimuli.

pou_name =

"Andrea"

THIS PLACE IS INCREDIBLE, AND I can't get over the fact that I'm finally here. Hanging from the high ceiling, some banners and installations show the location of the biggest companies, like Google, Facebook, Avoss, Blizzard, Microsoft, Apple … Every single tech giant is here. The immense hall is divided into booths of various sizes, and the companies range from international tycoons to family-sized businesses. Some develop dozens of apps per year, while others only have one software program.

A few stands offer games or tests, and we stop in front of one that challenges the passers-by to code a game of snake. Mace, Oli, and I take three of the available computers, and when we're ready, they set off a timer. It's like some thrilling race, the surrounding people cheering us on. Oliver finishes first, me second, and Mason third. It turns out Oli forgot that the snake dies when touching itself, so he's disqualified. I'm crowned champion of the round, and I happen to be their best score today. I have no illusion I'll be dethroned soon enough, but it feels good.

When Lex finds all six of us, we're all settled in the Avoss lounge, too curious not to venture there. This company is an impressive conglomerate, nearly as big as Google, dabbling in almost everything online. Both a search engine and a social network, they are everywhere. They're also the fastest-growing internet tycoon, and working for them is every programmer's dream, mine included. Or at least, it was before my incredible position at Kelex.

Lex gives us an irked glare, shakes his head, and joins us. We're talking to someone ranking relatively high in the company, and when he sees Lex arrive, he stands up.

"Alexander! It's been a while," the man says, extending his hand.

"Hugh." Lex shakes the man's hand, visibly squeezing it harder than necessary. "Last time was when you took Gregory from us."

The name Gregory rings a bell, and I try to remember why.

Oh! Right! Gregory is the former employee the guys suspect to be Nammota. Oli mentioned how the timeline of his departure matched the high scores appearing in the *Donkey Kong* game. So, Nammota is possibly working for Avoss now? It makes sense.

"It's a nice herd you've got here," Hugh says while turning our way, ignoring Lex's animosity. "Is this your programming team?"

"Yes, the company has been doing very well," Lex answers. "Mason has been with us for about three years. He's particularly good with visual programming. Brian is our C and Java expert. He joined us about two years ago. Our last recruit is Andrea. She dabbles in everything, particularly Python, and we're currently working on an app we bought from her." I can hear the pride in his voice as he introduces his A-team like this. Clearly, we aren't as big as Avoss, but we're the shit.

"Oh, really? What does this app do?" Hugh asks, turning to me.

"Hm, it's … um …" I hesitate, unsure of what I'm allowed to say.

Lex is quick to rescue me. "We're still working on it. You'll understand we'd like the information to remain private until we're ready to go public."

I'm used to seeing business-Lex. This version of him is pragmatic, efficient, and cold. He's concise and doesn't leave any room for contestation. However, there's something more going on here. Lex despises the man. Hugh doesn't insist and just nods, accepting that he won't get anything.

"There's a conference about to start, and I'd like my team to be there," Lex says. We all spring off the couches, ready to follow the will of our fierce leader.

"Of course. I guess I'll see you around," Hugh responds haughtily.

Lex doesn't scold us on our way to the conference, but there's no need. We can all sense how much he disapproves. The hall is almost full when we arrive, and my colleagues spread out to find empty seats. I'm about to do the same when a firm hand clasps my arm.

"Over there," Lex says, pointing toward a spot where two seats are available. The room is dark, and the guys are already seated. It doesn't seem risky, so I follow him.

"So, what happened between you and Hugh?" I ask once we're settled.

"Nothing in particular."

"Yeah, right. You wanted to strangle him, but nothing happened."

"We didn't get along when we worked together."

"He worked at Kelex?"

"No. I worked at Avoss."

Before I can ask more, the lights dim to full darkness, and a few people enter the stage. Out of respect, I shut my mouth and listen to them. I quickly realize I already know their software, and it's rather unimpressive, so I return to more interesting matters.

"When did you work for them?" I whisper to Lex.

"For who?"

"Avoss."

"It was my first job. I was twenty, fresh out of college. Hugh started at the same time."

"Why did you leave?"

"Andrea, I was serious when I said I wanted us to listen to this presentation."

"It's bogus. Their app is just a better-looking version of *Scratch*. It's as limited as the others, and they ask for a ridiculous price." For the first time since the presentation started, he looks away from the stage to stare down at me, inquisitive. "I was a beta tester for it," I explain. "So, why did you leave Avoss?"

"Kevin and I wanted to do our own thing. Also, things were getting out of hand with Hugh."

"What happened?"

"He's an arrogant and entitled prick with a ridiculous sense of superiority," Lex recalls. I don't say anything, but I almost want to point out that he can pass for all those things. It seems I don't need to say it. "It's not the same thing," he argues. "I'm socially inept, and he is an imbecile. Two entirely different issues. Avoss' management even offered to fire him if it meant I'd stay."

"Neat. How long were you with them?"

"Over six years."

So, he left Avoss when he was about my age and then started Kelex. It makes me wonder, "How old are you?"

"Thirty-four."

I nod silently. Eight years older than me. I never thought about it before. It isn't a lot, but it isn't meaningless either.

"Does it bother you?" he asks, uneasy because of my prolonged silence.

I shake my head and gaze up at him. The room is dark enough to shield us from the others but sufficiently bright for me to admire the details of his face. His age doesn't matter at all. Actually, it means he's old enough to make decisions and know what he wants.

Feeling bold, I take his hand from the armrest and press a kiss on the back of it.

"It really doesn't bother me."

I lay our joined hands on the armrest between us. When his palm moves under mine, I think he wants to remove it. Instead, he intertwines his fingers with mine and sets our hands on his lap, his thumb gently grazing my skin.

During the entire presentation, I feel alone with him, as if we're in a safe bubble where no one can reach us. And there's an unshakable grin lingering on my face the whole time.

is_new_chapter = True

chapter_number = "23"

pov_name = "Andrea"

As I MAKE MY WAY to Lex's room, much later that day, I feel like a smuggler illegally transporting some goods. I'm both the smuggler and the goods.

It's past eleven, and everyone's off for the night, which means it's time for some after-dark fun with my boss—something I'm still not getting used to. The day was long and intense, but I'm full of energy as I knock on his door.

I look down at my outfit, aware I'm anything but sexy. I'm wearing sneakers, a pair of black leggings, and my Yoda hoodie with "Do or do not, there is no try" written on it. But it's okay, right? I'll be naked soon enough.

Before I can get in my head too much, the door opens before me. My face is tilted down, so what I see first are his bare feet. As my gaze rises, I suddenly get why women go crazy for gray sweatpants with nothing under them. *Damn, that is all mine for the night.* Trying to get over the distracting sight of the very visible bulge of his dick, I move on to the white T-shirt that fits his shoulders and torso just right. A little higher, I meet his amused gaze behind his glasses. His hair is still wet from a shower, just like mine.

He's temptation in the flesh.

"Hi," I say, almost timidly.

He answers with one of his bone-melting smiles, which causes my heart to flutter. It's good that those are rare because I'm pretty sure that's how babies are made.

His room is a suite with a seating area, a separate bedroom, and access to a small balcony. I spot his laptop on the coffee table and understand he was working while waiting for me.

This is a little awkward because it's nothing like our other times. It isn't in the throes of passion or in the heat of the moment. It's thought through, agreed upon, and premeditated. So, I'm not entirely sure how to proceed.

"Your room is very nice," I say, realizing only too late how mundane it sounds.

But I might as well have said the sexiest thing in the world because the next thing he does is claim my lips. Our gestures have no urgency, as we're aware we have the entire night for this. It's slow and languid as we savor each other and take our time. One of his hands lowers to the bottom of my hoodie, and it comes back up under it, grazing my skin directly. A trembling breath flows out of me as it moves up, leaving a trail of heat in its path.

"Hm … From now on, you must come to me braless every time," he demands when he realizes I'm wearing nothing underneath my hoodie. With another appreciative growl, he fondles the small mound before taking an erect tip between his thumb and index. He pinches it hard, surprising me, before caressing it to soothe the slight pain.

My arms hold on tightly when he lifts me, and I wrap my legs around his hips frame like a vine. I adore the moment, the softness of it, the laziness, almost. This isn't as frantic as the other times we've had sex.

"I don't think I've been fully soft since that moment in the plane's bathroom," he reveals, grinding his erection onto my aching pussy.

"And I don't think I've been fully dry since I met you."

His chuckle comes in the way of our kiss, and I smile broadly at the sound. It dies at once when he suddenly tips over, making me squeal. We land on the soft mattress of the bed, and he makes sure not to crush me with his weight.

Caged under him like this, I slowly undulate, pulling on his T-shirt to remove it.

"Now that I know you don't play fair," he says once it's discarded on the floor, "I have to set some rules."

"Like what?" He pulls up my hoodie to expose my tits and randomly kisses, nibbles, and licks the smooth skin of my stomach.

"I have my pride, and I can't allow more of that clenching."

I pout, refusing to surrender my only trick. "If you take away my only defense, you can't use more than one of your assets at a time."

He halts his kisses to give me a bratty glance. "What do you mean?"

"It's either your dick, your mouth, or your hand, but not several at once."

He doesn't seem to like my demand, as his eyes darken. "Only for tonight, then. I like it when I make you come so hard you tear up."

His crude words have me trembling beneath him. It's tempting to ask him to hold back on the dirty talk as well, but I like it too much.

"Fine then. I won't clench," I concede, hypnotized by his ravenous eyes.

"I'm beginning to think I may not even need two 'assets' to make you cry, anyway."

With that, he bends to take my lips, his tongue brutally invading my mouth to meet mine. Then, he leaves me panting and high on his taste to stand before me. As I lie on the soft mattress, he takes out an orgy-sized condom box from his nightstand.

"A bit pretentious, isn't it?" I ask, pointing at it.

"More like, optimistic."

Lex stares at my exposed tits while sliding his pants down, releasing his impressive hard-on. I take off my hoodie and throw it somewhere on the floor, and then I extend a foot his way. I have a little surprise just for him. He tugs at my sneaker, revealing my sock, which he inspects with interest.

"Is this a winged pig?" he asks, intrigued.

"Or, as I like to call it, a pigasus."

He chuckles before removing the sock and takes care of the other foot. Before long, he's sliding my leggings and thong down my legs, leaving me utterly naked. He joins me in the bed, propped on his muscular arms.

"Should we establish a safe word for when you want to forfeit?" he arrogantly offers before kissing one of my nipples.

The proposal triggers my competitiveness, so I scowl at him. He ignores my temper, leisurely kissing his way down my stomach.

"How about 'you win, Andrea, I'm the weakest' as a safe word?" I suggest.

"That's too many words. You'll barely be able to remember your name by the time you need it." He's still on his slow descent, kissing near my belly button.

"How about 'pigasus?'" I suggest.

His silent laugh teases the skin of my lower stomach. "Perfect."

My last coherent thought, right before he dips his head between my legs, is how Kate always tells me a woman should hold on to a man who loves eating pussy and is good at it.

Lex is definitely great at it, and based on the appreciative sound he lets out right before tonguing me to heaven, he *really* enjoys doing it.

pov_name = "Alexander"

THIS WOMAN WILL BE MY fucking death.

We've used three condoms in the past two hours, and I'm slowly inching toward filling up a fourth one. Actually, I'm dangerously close to it.

How could I not with the way she's riding me? She looks like a pagan goddess with her thick thighs over my hips and her small tits bouncing with every adamant rise and fall on my cock. Her expression is one of pure pleasure, her brown eyes veiled with lust, her cheeks red with the effort and pleasure combined, and her hair wild and damp, like the rest of us.

I look down to where we're joined and groan at the sight. Her drenched curls meet the trimmed hair at the base of my dick, which I can see appear and disappear in rhythm, shiny with her wetness. Jesus fucking Christ, this is too much. She's about to make me come again before she can reach another climax. I can't let that happen.

Just as I'm about to send the tip of my thumb to her swollen clit, which is poking out of under its little hood, I'm reminded that I'm not allowed to do it. Not right now. *Fuck.*

She didn't stop me earlier when I fondled her tits, so I reach up and pinch both nipples between my fingers. The throaty moan she lets out is a good start. Now, we just need a little more to reach the finish line together.

"Touch yourself," I command.

She trembles from head to toe, hips jerking with the need to come. I don't have to utter my demand again as she lowers her fingers between us, flicking them over the swollen crest.

"You're so fucking hot … I'll never get tired of watching you come," I moan, close to losing it entirely.

The pace of her fingers intensifies as she cries out my name. "Lex, I'm so close!"

"I know. Come for me, Andrea. Make me feel your tight cunt throb."

As often with her, my crude words are what get her to topple into bliss. She lets out a sobbing cry, her body twitching over mine, her hands now flat on my chest as she grinds onto me, lost in pleasure. For a brief moment, she shuts her eyes tightly, as if overwhelmed by it all. But she promptly opens them again to maintain this connection between us.

Her orgasm shakes her, so I hold her in place as my hips drill her from under at a fast pace, seeking my own release. She begs for mercy, trying to pull away, but my climax is right fucking there.

"Fuck," I shout at the first rope of cum that shoots out of me.

My hands grip her hips in a bruising hold to keep her down on me as I empty myself yet again in the condom. Seconds stretch until we're both done twitching with pleasure. Completely spent, she topples over on my chest, her breathing hectic.

How is this not getting dull? Why is it so uniquely good every single time? Something about her makes this very different from my past experiences. It's like I've met my match not only when it comes to coding but also in bed. All the yearning, the tension, the friction between us … they were a sign. Or maybe a warning.

My hands softly course over the sweaty expanse of her back, and when I reach her ass, I gently tap it as an encouragement to move.

"Is that a double-tap? If you want to forfeit, you need to say 'pigasus,' remember?" she humors, her voice husky from overusing her vocal cords for the past few hours.

"Not even close. Give me ten minutes to recover, and I'm good for another round."

She mumbles her disappointment and lifts herself, enough to dislodge me from within her, and then flops by my side, properly spent. I pull the condom off and throw it on the floor by the bed next to the other used ones.

Maybe that oversized Trojan pack isn't too much, after all.

"Is it me, or are we getting better at this?" she asks, staring at the white ceiling.

"As crazy as it sounds, I think we are, yes."

I gaze at her, enjoying the sight of her tousled hair, reddened cheeks, and sparkly eyes. Giving into my desire for tenderness, I move to kiss her, and she eagerly welcomes it.

While I know this isn't anything other than a sex arrangement, I can't help but hope it will last. Not only am I curious to see just how good we can get at this, but I also enjoy being around her.

But deep down, I know perfectly well that the longer this lasts, the harder the fall will be. I can't give her more than this—amazing, otherworldly sex. And if my past arrangements taught me anything, it's that she'll soon demand more.

And for her sake and mine, I can't give her that. There's nothing but disappointment and resentment down that path.

pov_name =

"Andrea"

I'LL HAVE TO AVOID STAIRS for the next twenty-four to forty-eight hours. And I'm perfectly okay with that. I'm sore as hell *everywhere*, but it was definitely worth it.

After everything, Lex managed to trick me into shower sex, and then I passed out on his bed. I snuck to my room at dawn, slept some more, and now I'm making my way to the breakfast buffet, looking for my people. I find them gathered at a table, with only Lex missing, so I fill myself a plate and join them.

"Wow, someone's hungry," Oli says when I join them.

With a wince, I look down at the tray. Yeah, I got a bit carried away, but I'm famished. Unsure how to justify my abnormal hunger, I shrug my shoulders and sit down.

"Oh, could it be her?" Brian asks before pointing at a woman who just entered. We all look at the tall brunette, and when a man joins her, sliding his hand around her waist, Steven shakes his head.

"What's going on?" I ask, intrigued.

"We're looking for a good-looking woman with a limp."

"Or one in a wheelchair."

Confused, I glance at Oli. He rolls his eyes, apparently disagreeing with them. "Is it some new fetish you two have developed overnight?" I ask with humor.

"It's a long story," Brian says, dismissing my question with a vague hand gesture to focus on the entrance. I refuse to be the only one around this table excluded from the conversation, so I give Steven a determined look.

"Okay, when we came back from the ramen place yesterday, Brian broke our toilet with his fat ass."

"Hey!" Brian protests with a pout. The comment was clearly ironic, since he's skin and bones, so it's amusing that he takes it personally.

"Anyway. They relocated us to another room," Steven continues. "It was an upgrade, so we felt good about it. But then the people in the room next to us started to have sex like wild animals."

My heart drops and blood leaves my face as a dreadful feeling invades me. I do my best to hide it, hoping my hunch is wrong.

"It went on for the longest time. We actually felt bad for the poor woman," Steven explains while Brian confirms with a grave nod. "Anyhow, we wouldn't have given it another thought, but when we came out ten minutes ago to get down here, guess who we saw, coming back from the hotel's gym, entering the very room where all the crazy sex happened?"

I don't want to answer. I refuse to be right. Please, God, let it be Justin Trudeau, Gordon Ramsay, Santa fucking Claus … Anyone but Lex.

"Our boss!" Brian nearly shouts, stealing the big reveal from Steven, who glares at him.

Shit. Shit, shit, shit.

I feel both hot and cold, my hands clammy and trembling. This is so unfair. What are the odds of those two ending up in the room right next to Lex's?

This is so fucking bad.

In my life, I've known my fair share of embarrassing moments, but this one takes the cake. I want to disappear, to just *poof*, vanish into nothingness. Leaving the table abruptly and showing I'm upset isn't an option, so I have to endure it.

Mistaking my silence for astonishment, Steven continues. "So now, we're trying to guess which one of these ladies was with him last night. We established she has to have some sort of limp going on after what he did to her, so it's our main clue. Also, she's got to be a total babe."

"Maybe a limp is a bit much," Oliver notes, still not on board with this. *A limp really isn't too much, no …*

"Dude, you weren't there. You didn't hear it. It was kind of muffled, but I swear, the man has got to be a sex god or something. It was insane like, bed banging on the wall for two hours straight, and nonstop, 'Aah … Yes! Oh, God, yes! Ooh … Ah,'" Brian imitates with a high pitch. A few surrounding people take an interest in our table, intrigued.

If all the blood hadn't drained from my face, I'd be poppy-red right now. If that's how I sound, how is Lex not shoving my face into a pillow?

The guys won't drop the subject, and I try my hardest to appear unfazed, even though I'm dying inside. Oli tries to veer the discussion to another topic a few times, arguing it's Lex's private life, but it does nothing. My appetite is gone, so I push my food around, eating very little from my massive tray.

"Whoever was that hoe with him," Mason says at some point, sipping on his Earl Grey, "she a lucky bitch."

"Okay, how about we change the subject? Lex got laid. Good for him. Let's not shame a woman for it," Oli intervenes. I could kiss him for always doing the right thing.

"Here he comes!" Brian excitedly says, ruining his efforts.

We turn in the direction he's looking, and I spot Lex, wearing a charcoal two-piece suit with a black shirt underneath, the first two buttons undone. As always, he's stunning.

"Good morning, everyone," he greets us when he reaches us with his tray, suspiciously joyful given his usually stern attitude. He sits opposite me, and while I look away, I sense his gaze on me.

The guys salute him back, and there's a moment of silence while Lex digs into his breakfast. They're all burning to ask him about his night, and I don't even have to wonder which one will break first.

"So, how was your night?" Brian asks. Almost immediately after, Mace kicks him under the table.

Oblivious to the awkward ambiance, Lex drinks a sip of coffee to help swallow his mouthful of buttered toast. "I slept nicely. Thank you for asking."

He's in a remarkably good mood. An evening of sex makes him delightful to be around, doesn't it?

"But you didn't sleep much, though," Brian insists, ignoring Mason, who kicks him again.

Lex scans each of us, now aware that something's off. I can't give even the slightest hint to the guys, but I try to pass on all I can in our silent exchange when our gazes cross. "What do you mean?" he asks Brian.

"Well, Steven and I were moved next to your room, and we heard you had some feminine company."

Mason facepalms, Oli closes his eyes with a sigh, and Steven shakes his head. Joseph isn't missing any of this, reading lips and enjoying the free entertainment. I'm thankful for Lex being so clever and quick-witted because, after a short instant of shock, he doesn't turn to look at me. Thank God for that, because it would have been a dead giveaway.

He stays silent for a moment, seemingly unaffected, his stern face impossible to decipher. I'm starting to know him pretty well, though, and I can sense he's pissed. My suspicions are confirmed when he finally speaks, giving Brian a dangerous glare.

"Was there a fucking question?"

It's the first time I've heard Lex swear in front of them, and the shock on everyone's faces tells me it's a very rare occurrence.

Brian turns pale, torn by confusion and embarrassment. "I, umm … We—No, not really. It's more of a … an observation," he stammers. Lex doesn't answer, but he gives a look that makes it abundantly clear what he thinks of his "observation."

Lex is very private, living in a fortress of an apartment with his own AI to ensure no one knows what happens inside. I can easily imagine how having his intimacy laid out for all to see—or rather, to *hear*—doesn't sit well with him.

The joyful mood is gone, replaced by awkward silence. Eventually, the guys filter out one by one until only Lex and I are left.

He empties his plate with harsh gestures, and when he finishes and puts his cutlery down, I bend forward with an understanding smile, even though I'm not sure I'll ever truly understand the man.

"They didn't mean to be offensive or mocking. It's alright."

"It's not alright," he counters, not any calmer.

"They all know you get some action. It isn't some big secret."

"I don't give a shit if they know when and where I fuck someone."

Offended by his crudeness, I pull away from him. "Then what's the big deal?"

"What's the big deal? The big deal is it was *you*. They heard *you*. They know what *you* sound like when *you* come. They heard *your* cries and moans," he explains, his eyes dark with irritation. I blush crimson at his words and look around to ensure no one's listening. "I had no clue this hotel had walls so fucking thin, or I would have gagged you," he bitterly adds.

The thought of him doing that to me has all sorts of shivers running through my body. I press my knees together to muffle the sensations awakening in my core. *Shit, we'll have to try that at some point.*

I then curse my gutter-minded brain. There's a delicate situation that demands my full attention.

"Let it go, Lex. They have no idea it was me," I insist, bending forward again to rest a hand over his clenched fist. "They think it was some stunning woman worthy of sharing your bed. I'm miles and miles away from their suspicions."

"It was still you, whether they know it or not." Although there's still some annoyance in his tone, he sounds less irritated.

"It was so muffled they could barely hear anything," I pretend. The guys won't speak about the matter again, and if a tiny lie can help save the day, I'm willing to do it. "Seriously, you're the only one who knows the sounds I make when I come."

It gets his attention, and the last remaining traces of anger disappear from his handsome face. "What about your exes?"

"Now you're fishing for compliments, and I won't feed that colossal ego of yours," I respond, getting up. "I need to go get a few things from my room. Meet you in the hall?" I offer. He nods, pensive. "Also, you're the boss, and it's your call, but maybe have a talk with Brian. This trip is too important to let something like this ruin it for everyone."

He nods again, and I can tell he's genuinely considering it. Maybe he can be saved after all.

Who knows? With time, his heart might even grow three sizes.

is_new_chapter = True

chapter_number = "24"

pov_name = "Andrea"

DESPITE A ROCKY START, THE day unfolds splendidly. Lex follows my advice and talks with Brian to appease the tension that accumulated during breakfast. We get to enjoy more conferences, discover more companies, and then return to the hotel for the evening.

It's apparently tradition to participate in the nerdy trivia held in the hotel's bar, and for the first time ever, there's an all-Kelex team.

"Oh, wow. You look like a woman," Brian says when I arrive in the lobby, ready for the evening.

"She *is* a woman, you moron," Mace defends me with a confused expression.

"I know, but she looks like one right now."

I get what he means, so I'm not offended. My black dress has a scoop neck and tight sleeves to my elbows. The skirt's hem goes mid-thigh but is loose enough to not look too audacious. I tried wearing the heels I brought but ended up in my black Chucks. My hair is up with loads of pins, and adding to my winged eyeliner, I have bold red lips.

I feel like a woman. A desirable one, I hope, knowing Lex is joining us for trivia.

"Gentlemen." *Speak of the devil* … Startled, I spin toward him. His smoldering eyes scan me from head to toe, which means I succeeded. He quickly regains control of himself and bows his head slightly. "Andrea."

I nod back, sure my voice will fail me if I talk. Fuck me dead and bury me pregnant. The man is temptation incarnate.

If there's one thing I like more than Lex wearing a suit, it's Lex doing it *casually*. He's still wearing his charcoal pants and black shirt, but he ditched the jacket, rolled up his sleeves, and opened another button, revealing a triangle of chest hair. Also, his glasses are poking out of his chest pocket, and if he whips those out during the evening, I'll lose it.

Before I can get too much into my lust-filled thoughts, the others arrive. Upon seeing me, Oli gives me an appreciative grin. Not wanting to encourage him or let him think this is for him, I give him the slightest smile and focus back on the others.

I'm the first to enter our designated booth to the right. Lex enters via the left, and it's only when we're both seated that I realize we'll be this close the whole evening.

I flash him an alarmed glance, unsure this is a good idea. Either he doesn't notice, or he doesn't care because he does nothing about it. Alright, I'll just have to focus on the questions, the people around us, and my very near colleagues. Anything but Lex.

The trivia organizers hand every team a tablet. Steven takes charge of it, and the evening of fun starts. Our ultimate goal is to beat the Avoss team—the usual winners. Sipping on my beer, I lean back in my seat, amused by how determined to win everyone is. Shortly after, Lex does the same thing and nonchalantly spreads his knees, as if he's relaxing. It results in our legs touching, which sends a shiver up my body. When I send him a disapproving look, his knowing expression makes it clear it's on purpose.

The table hides our illicit contact, but I still don't feel comfortable with it. Just a little, I move away and break the connection, imperceptibly shaking my head at him.

Before he can attempt something else, the game begins.

Bill—tonight's host—asks the questions, and then we have one minute to discuss it, plus an extra fifteen seconds to enter our answer on the tablet.

With our seven brains put together, we're doing pretty good and getting every answer right. All this enthusiasm could almost have distracted me enough to forget about Lex's closeness. But his fucking brain is in the way.

While he sucks at most pop culture questions, he's extraordinary with everything else. I'm amazed by his knowledge, as he doesn't just give answers but also shares dates and facts for each of them.

By the end of the first series of questions, we're on top, tied with Avoss and another team.

"You're doing great," someone says behind us. I hear Lex grunt with annoyance and know it's Hugh before I even turn around. "How about we make it a little more interesting?" the Avoss executive offers. "The swag bags are nice, but they're low stakes."

"What are you suggesting?" Lex asks, unimpressed.

"We all know how these business trips only pay for basic expenses, alcohol excluded, so how about the losing team pays for the winning team's drinks tonight?"

Lex considers it, gauging our team and Hugh's. "Deal," he eventually accepts. They shake on it, and Hugh confidently goes back to his table.

If I thought Lex was brilliant during the first round, it's nothing compared to the second one. The man is a fucking encyclopedia, and I enjoy his display of gray matter a little too much.

The sapiosexual in me melts a little more with each of his answers. To the point where it becomes harder and harder for me to focus on the game. Every time the man opens his mouth, I have to clench my legs to hush the growing need between them.

I'm in serious trouble.

My head drifts out of the game, and my mind goes into some blurry state. I'm feeling hot, almost feverish. Pure lust is running through my veins, and the need to be alone with Lex grows stronger with every passing moment. I can hear the guys' voices around me, but I can't make out what they're saying.

I'm uncharacteristically silent, and Lex notices. "Are you alright?" he whispers, bending slightly. Our shoulders touch, and I need him to back off. My hunger for him is too fucking great for even that. Not meeting his eyes, I nod.

"What's wrong?" he insists, not duped.

With clenched teeth, I dare to look up at him. He studies my face for a second, and then understands what's happening to me. A triumphant smile drags the corners of his lips up, his pupils tripling in size.

His attention seemingly returns to the guys, but then his large hand settles on my inner thigh, just above my knee, making me jump. I squeeze my thighs together before he can go any further, careful not to make a fuss. Bill is talking again, and the guys aren't paying us any attention.

Lex looks remarkably smug as he slides his hand higher up my leg. Since my threatening scowl isn't enough to make him stop, I cross my arms before me on the table and lean forward so no one can see what's happening down there.

My overly aroused state and the thrill of being caught causes intense shivers to run through my body. Bill is done with his question, so the guys all focus back on the center of the table. With his hand still slowly trying to push itself between my clamped legs, Lex leans forward, his attitude inconspicuous.

Under the table, his tactics change, and instead of aiming for the sealed space between my thighs, he moves up and slips his fingers over the covered mound of my intimacy, trying to gain access. "Star Trek II, The Wrath of Khan, in 1982," he tells the group.

When the tips of his fingers get to the soaked lace low on my panties, his advance halts, as do his words, but after a second, he resumes. "Graphics Group did it, from Lucasfilm, now known as Pixar." It's uncanny how inconspicuous he can sound while his fingers graze the front of my core.

This is crazy. I enjoy his touch too much to fight him, but every brain cell not focused on him is screaming I should stop it.

Lex presses a little harder, right where my clit is, and I almost let out a moan, biting the inside of my cheek.

The guys are now talking about something else, but I can't say what, as Lex's fingers are now torturing me with slow rolls. My legs are still tightly clenched, and it's hard to resist the urge to spread them.

Bill talks again, and Lex uses this distraction to slowly bend toward me to pour the most scandalous request into my ear. "Open for me, Andrea. Your cunt is starving for my touch, isn't it?"

His crude words hit me hard, and I almost whimper from the acute shiver they unleash. Powerless, I send him a pleading look, utterly disconcerted by my overwhelming desire for him.

"I know," he whispers. "Spread your legs so I can take care of it."

This time, I helplessly obey. My knees part, a glimmer of victory flashing in his gaze. As the guys try to find the next answer, Lex toys with the elastic of my underwear. He tugs it to the side, and I shiver from head to toe when two of his fingers slide along my molten slit, sensing just how turned on I am. In the corner of my eye, I see his jaw clench, his hand tensing under my dress.

He isn't destabilized for long, and his two fingers lower and dip inside my tight entrance. Miraculously, I don't make a sound, but I poorly hide the small jolt my body does.

Fuck.

I can't believe this is happening. He's slowly, leisurely thrusting his thick fingers inside me while the guys are right there. Terrified that someone might know, I peer at my colleagues. When I meet Oliver's gaze, my heart tightens as my entire body freezes.

Shit, I'm the fucking worst. Lex's fingers are fucking me under the table while Oli is almost at arm's reach. To my great relief, the latter has no clue what is happening. It gives me the determination I need to shove Lex's hand away in a manner I hope isn't obvious.

The guys are still busy debating over our next answer, so Oli returns his attention to that instead.

As for myself, I look up at Lex and observe with widened eyes as he casually brings his hand to his mouth. Stunned, I stare as he engulfs his fingers one by one to taste me, licking off my juices from them. It isn't suspicious, as we've been doing the same thing all evening, licking away Doritos dust from the tips of our fingers.

But it isn't Doritos on his tongue right now.

My clit throbs even harder than when he was teasing it.

A new question is asked about a minute later, and the guys focus back on us. "Ronald Wayne owned ten percent. He sold it for eight hundred dollars in 1976," Lex answers, not wasting a second. "Now, if you'll excuse me, I'll return before the game resumes." Steven and Joseph move so he can leave.

Oh, we're already at the twenty-minute break? Somehow confused, I stay seated, trying to think through my arousal. What the hell just happened?

My phone buzzes in my bag, and I take it out. It's a message from Lex.

LEX

Your room.

Is this … Are we doing this? It doesn't sound reasonable, but neither does sitting there in my wetness, unable to contain myself.

The phone buzzes again.

LEX

Now.

Oh, well …

ME

On my way

Minutes later, I'm with him. We enter my room, and Lex impatiently plasters me against the door. He bends to take my lips, but I turn my face away. I can't go back downstairs with smudged lipstick.

Before I can explain my refusal, he catches my drift and opts for my throat instead, tasting the soft skin there. Before I know it, my underwear is on the floor, his dick is sheathed in latex, and he impales me on it with a firm thrust.

"Aah … Shit," I whimper at the sudden intrusion. It's the first time he's entered me without lengthy foreplay, and I understand why he's always so adamant about making me come before penetration. It's painful but in a good kind of way. The ache of the stretch almost adds to the pleasure, even.

"Are you alright?" he asks with worry.

"Yes. You're just … so fucking big."

"And you're so fucking tight."

He attempts a few small nudges, and the discomfort recedes fast, almost entirely gone already. Writhing my hips against him and tangling my fingers in his hair, I encourage him to go harder. His momentum builds up, and he gives me longer thrusts, implacable. *Damn, I'll never get enough of this …*

"Tell me. How did you get so wet back at the bar?"

I'm tempted to kiss him, so I voraciously settle my tongue in the hollow spot between his collarbones. With one lascivious motion, I drag it up the firm column of his throat, passing over his Adam's apple, which bobs uncontrollably. I lick past his chin, his stubble tickling my tongue. His taste is intoxicating, a little salty and earthy, and it works on me like the most potent of aphrodisiacs.

"Answer me," he commands with a harsher thrust.

"Some smartass with a big brain triggered the sapiosexual in me." His satisfied, wicked smirk has me pulsing around his hammering dick.

"Is that so? Intelligence gets you off?"

"Perhaps that's why you're so good at making me come," I reply with fierceness.

He chuckles hoarsely and then brings his lips right against my ear, still thrusting inside me, still pinning me onto the door. "Three," he rasps. "One. Four. One. Five …"

With each number comes a punch of his cock, and they grow faster and deeper as he goes. When I understand what he's doing, a breathy laugh pours out of me, quickly dismissed by throaty moans. As hot as it is, I end up focusing on the numbers more than the sex to make sure he isn't messing up Pi.

Eventually, I put my hand over his mouth to make him shut up. "Less talking, more fucking," I order, panting.

He smiles under my palm, his amused eyes locked on mine. He braces himself, repositioning his feet, and I know it means shit is getting serious.

He plows into me hard, shoving the entirety of his length inside of me each time, hitting my clit with the base of it. I'm so wet we can hear it, along with the rhythmic sound of our embrace, the ruffle of our clothes, the metallic buckle of his belt slapping between us …

It's freakishly hot that we're both fully dressed, with only my underwear off. It's the first time in my life that I'm having sex like this. Like it's impossible to stop. Like we have to do it or implode.

"Fuck! Yes! Aah … Don't stop!"

He keeps thrusting as I shatter in his arms, his weight heavy against me to contain my blissful convulsions. While he seeks his own climax by ramming into me with intensity, he triggers a second orgasm, less intense than the first one. My shaky cries answer his loud groans as he comes with jerky moves.

For about a minute, he keeps me pressed on the door while we both pant, trying to get back to the land of the living.

His eyes linger on my lips when he looks down, and I know what he wants. A peck won't smudge my lipstick, so I extend my neck to press my mouth on his. I stay there for several seconds and move back. He licks his lips with hunger, clearly wishing there could be more to it.

He lowers me to the floor, only letting me go when he's sure my legs will hold me. I watch as he slips the condom out and ties a knot. We're not doing the environment any favor with how much of these we go through, are we?

"I couldn't wait until later tonight to have you. You're so fucking alluring when you're horny," he rasps, softly kissing my temple.

The notion of a "later tonight" brings an unwelcome realization. "Shit … I can't come to your room anymore. And you can't come here either—the guys are just down the hall."

He fishes out something from his back pocket, his pants still low on his hips, and hands me a key card. My eyes widen when I see the number on it. 504.

"You booked another room?"

"I did."

Knowing he's as eager as I am to share more of these intimate moments fills me with joy and contentment. I throw the card on the bed behind him, giving him a delighted grin. As I walk toward the bathroom, he stops me, grabbing me by the waist and pressing my back onto his front, his lips grazing the length of my throat. I'm tempted to give in, even though it isn't reasonable.

"Lex … We need to get back downstairs," I protest.

"We still have six minutes to be there on time," he argues, his tongue leaving a burning wet line along my jugular.

"We already used your emergency condom," I try.

"I have two more in my wallet."

I laugh, amused by that fact. "Overkill much?"

"Not with you, no."

I'm pressed onto the door again, but with my front this time, and he greedily pulls on my dress to unveil my bare lower half. "Don't you ever get soft?" I complain when he presses his hardening dick between the mounds of my ass.

"Not when you're around."

He grinds into me, getting himself fully hard again, and I allow it, too weak to refuse him. But just as I accept that we'll fuck again, everything comes to an abrupt end.

Not only do the three knocks on my door resonate loudly in my ears, but I also *feel* their vibrations on my front.

We both instantly freeze.

"Who is it?" I hesitantly ask.

"It's me," comes Oliver's voice.

"The fuck is he doing here?" Lex mutters right before I push myself away from the door. Filled with dreadful panic, I turn around to meet his irritated scowl.

"Give me a moment," I answer to Oli.

I hastily pick up the discarded condom that Lex dropped on the floor and then push him all the way to the bathroom despite his irked glare at the door. Once in there, I shove him into a corner, throw the condom in the trash, and grab a small towel. Ignoring any sense of elegance or class, I quickly drag it between my legs to wipe the wet mess Lex conjured. I throw it toward the bathtub, but Lex intercepts it and uses it to wipe himself as well. My heart is in my throat as I return to the room.

"Stay here, don't make a sound," I command. He looks pissed, his jaw clenched, his eyes dark, but I don't have time for this.

"Are you alright?" Oliver asks from outside.

"Yes! I'm coming!"

"You already did, actually. *Twice*," Lex mutters from the bathroom. "All over my cock."

Unamused, I give him a warning glare, which he answers with an eye roll. I rush to a drawer and grab the first pair of underwear I can find. After swiftly putting them on, I spot my previous pair lying there, drenched and rolled up. Mindlessly, I throw them toward the bathroom. Lex cocks his eyebrow at me when it lands on his chest, his hand grabbing it out of reflex. When I gesture for him to move back, he gives me another one of his disapproving scowls before complying.

After a quick and deep breath, I grab the handle. The whole thing was quick, so I'm not sweaty and don't think I reek of sex. Hopefully, I also don't have Lex's scent on me. I'm undoubtedly still flushed, though. I open the door, doing my best to control my breathing.

"Hi! I'm good to go."

"Where's your jacket?"

Fuck. That's the excuse I gave the guys when I came up here.

"Oh, right. I went to the bathroom and forgot. Good call."

I fetch my red jacket and return. "*Vámonos*," I say enthusiastically, eyeing the half-closed door of my bathroom one last time.

The elevator's mirror informs me that my face isn't overly red, my hair isn't a mess, and apart from my sparkly eyes, one could never guess I was just thoroughly fucked against a door.

Because I'm so preoccupied with my situation, I don't even wonder why Oli came up to get me, and it doesn't occur to ask. A few steps into the lobby, he stops me, reaching for my arm.

"Are we okay?" he asks.

"What do you mean?"

"You've been avoiding me since we left Seattle. Things are weird between us."

I avert my gaze, looking around and wondering what to answer. Yes, I've become distant—not because I don't want to spend time with him, but because I'm unsure how to act around him. I told him I might never be ready for him, and I don't want to hurt him by insisting we might never become a thing. He'll just get over me on his own at some point.

"It's because you've met someone, right?" he asks. I say nothing again, but my silence is an answer in and of itself. In his eyes, I read the pain I'm causing, and I hate myself for it.

Because I must have been Hitler or Zedong in my previous life, my terrible karma acts up, and Lex notices us on his way out of the elevator. His eyes lock on Oli's hand, still on my arm, and his chiseled jaw clenches with anger. *Fuck.*

"Is it serious between you and that guy?" Oli asks, oblivious.

Lex is close enough to hear that, and if I had any doubt, the way his brows furrow confirms that he did. He stays there, pretending to check something on his phone. Why is this happening? How did I go from some incredible *slex* to this? Five minutes ago, I was swimming in ecstasy, and now all I want is to dig a hole and disappear into it.

It's a great fucking dilemma. I can't tell Oli it isn't serious because he'll get ideas and think there's still a chance. But I also can't tell him it *is* serious because Lex is listening, and all I can think of are the harsh words he said back in his office.

I don't do relationships, Andrea. And you don't seem like someone who does what I do.

"No. It's not," I bluntly say. Oli finds my answer reassuring enough to let go of my arm.

As for Lex, his stoic expression is unreadable when I peek at him. He puts his phone away and resumes his walk to the bar. That's what I was supposed to answer, right? We're just having fun. The opposite of serious.

Oli interrupts my overthinking with, "So you're not actually seeing someone?"

"Oli … I told you I might never be ready for you. You can't wait for me because I can't promise anything."

"I want to wait."

"And I'm telling you not to," I retort, hoping it isn't too harsh. "We should get back. I don't want to miss the next round."

Not waiting for his answer, I return to the bar. The guys move to let me get to my seat, and I'm back next to Lex. He doesn't even glance at me, probably still in a dark mood from being abandoned with a hard-on. It can't be good on the nerves, but he has to understand I didn't have a choice.

The three of us are completely out of it. I'm preoccupied, Oli is pensive, and Lex is ruminating. Thank God the other four members of our team are still focused enough so that we win by literally one point. The *Lex-Men*—as Steven registered us—are this year's trivia winners, and our drinks are on Hugh.

The other teams in the bar applaud, we stand up to thank them, and the effervescence slowly tones down. We all end up exchanging congratulatory hugs, and when it's Lex's turn, I swiftly change my mind. Instead of hugging, we share a very impersonal handshake, barely meeting each other's eyes.

Something is wrong between us, but I don't get it. What's his problem? He's acting as if I asked Oli to come up to my room. If he's mad because I prioritized Oli over him out of some sense of possessiveness, then it's not my problem.

He made it clear this wasn't a relationship, so what's his deal? We aren't together; he can't expect anything from me unless he's being my boss. That's the deal. He didn't believe I could do this no-strings-attached thing, but I'll prove him wrong.

"Oh! He's coming," Mason whisper-shouts. We all try to act inconspicuously as Hugh walks up to us.

"I guess I misjudged your team, Alexander," the man says, sounding arrogant even though he lost his bet.

"You did."

"I'll go pay for your drinks. What was it? Fourteen beers and three servings of nachos?" Shit, we should have ordered more to make the asshole regret his haughtiness.

"I don't think so, no," Lex stops him, spreading confusion around our table. "We shook on the evening's bill, and the evening is still young. We'll send you the bill when the bar closes."

After exchanging some excited looks at each other, we bite back our grins. I regret facing away from Hugh because I'm dying to see his face. He doesn't say anything for a while and eventually clears his throat. "Alright, it's only fair. I'll tell the bar to put your tab on my room," he agrees with annoyance.

With that, he leaves us. When he's far enough, the guys turn to Lex, who sits down. "Before you all ask for top-shelf bottles, I'll set a limit," he explains. "I don't want to have to argue with the prick. Don't let the amount exceed two thousand dollars."

It's a lot for seven people, despite the hotel's high prices, and we'll surely get shit-faced with all that. Which isn't exactly a great idea, given we're on a professional trip. As if he can hear my thoughts, Lex adds, "You can have your morning off to recuperate, but be in the C hall at two for the conference about the future of algorithms."

His proposal is received with enthusiastic nods, and some of us don't waste time ordering drinks from a waiter who passes by. "I'll leave you be. Don't make a scene."

I watch him leave the bar, wondering what I should do. Somewhere in my room, I still have the 504 key. I'd rather celebrate with him there than get drunk. But he clearly has a problem with me for some reason, all broody and aloof. For once, I'll stay strong and not give in until he apologizes for being a distant ass.

He doesn't deserve sex right now.

pov_name =

"Alexander"

I SHOULD HAVE SWALLOWED MY pride and stayed downstairs with the others. But if I did, I probably would have done something we would both have regretted.

How could Andrea be so blatantly disrespectful? We're not serious, no, but how could she make herself available to Oliver right in front of me? And minutes after I fucked her, probably still sensing me between her legs.

I've always known that if it were her choice, she'd rather be intimate with Oliver than with me, but one cannot always choose who their body longs for. And as much as I hate to admit it, he's much more suited for her than I'll ever be. I've seen them interact, so I know they get along better than we do. We're fucking until one of us gets over it, and then we'll move on. And if things go according to her wishes, she'll move on with *him*.

The thought angers me infinitely more than it should. She isn't mine, and I don't want her to be. But the thought of sharing her has a ball of rage coiling in my stomach.

The sex is so fantastic that I can't even fathom being interested in another woman at the moment. I won't be entertaining the idea for a while, actually. So, I despise the fact that she's still keeping Oliver close, already thinking of what comes after us.

With a dry slam, I shut my laptop and throw it on the couch next to me. I've been trying to work since returning upstairs, but my mind is too clouded. When I check my watch, it's later than I expected. I've had no news from my team downstairs, but I imagine the bar is closed by now. Or it will be soon enough. Should I go check?

But then, I'd have to see Andrea again, and I'm not sure how to act around her.

They're grown adults. They can handle themselves.

I'm on my way to the bathroom when my phone buzzes in my pocket. My eyebrows come together when I see it's a text from Andrea. I open it, and the message that appears only deepens my confusion.

ANDREA WALKER

Goinh to the.secrt room

Just how drunk is she, exactly? I'm still trying to decode whatever the emojis mean when another text comes in.

ANDREA WALKER

This makes even less sense. Three more messages rapidly appear, though.

ANDREA WALKER

That, I understand.

She really expects me to come crawling after the way she behaved? We're into this for the sex, but I'm not a sex toy that can be discarded and summoned whenever she needs a good fuck.

I dismiss her messages, adamant to leave her hanging. But by the time I'm in bed with my laptop in another attempt at being efficient, remorse has made its way into my mind. Her texts indicated that she was heavily intoxicated. The hotel's hallways are probably empty at this hour, and anything could happen to her. I need to check on her and make sure she's alright.

With my jeans back on, as well as my sneakers, I exit my room and walk to the elevators. As I suspected, the place looks deserted. Snatching up a petite woman like her would be child's play, and no one would notice until it was too late.

My guts are twisted with anguish by the time I reach room 504. If something happened to her between her text and now, I'll never forgive myself. I should have at least responded to let her know I wouldn't come, so she would have stayed in her room.

The door unlocks with a *blip*, and I quickly step in. The lights are on, and I immediately spot her lying on the bed, brown curls sprawled around her sleeping face. She's still wearing her clothes, except for her shoes—kicked at the foot of the bed. There's a slight snore that filters out of her parted lips, in rhythm with the ups and downs of her chest.

As soon as I see she's alright, I let out a reassured breath.

Although I should spin around and return to my room, I let my feet carry me further in. The tip of her nose is an adorable shade of pink, I suppose because of the alcohol.

It's no wonder she drives me insane. She's the prettiest woman I've ever seen, with those lips, the thick fringes of her lashes, the freckles sprinkled on her nose and cheeks … I lose my mind around her because, like most men, I'm genetically engineered to want the most beautiful women for my progeny. It's a future that'll never happen for me, but the primitive side of my brain doesn't know that, does it?

When the perfect arches of her eyebrows twitch and frown, I lower myself to one knee and pass a soothing thumb over it.

Andrea's frown dissipates, but then her eyes flutter open. *Shit*, I curse internally.

"Hey, Clark," she mumbles with a naughty smile.

Who the fuck is Clark? I knew about Oliver, but is there a third man in this race, battling for her affection?

Before I can let this new surge of jealousy bring back my anger, she drunkenly reaches for my glasses and pulls them away from my face. "Hey, Kal-El," she giggles this time.

Oh … I'm Clark. Or I'm the fantasy of him.

Ever since I was eleven, I've been going by Lex, after Superman's nemesis, Lex Luthor. Already then, I was cerebral, calculating, and out of touch with my classmates, easily discarded as a weird child. I've always been more like the villain than the superheroes who bravely fight him. But Andrea doesn't see me this way, does she? For some reason, she associates me with Superman, one of the most virtuous and beloved superheroes.

I'm not sure what to make of that or what it means. Am I not weird to her? She disliked me so much during the first few weeks that she shouldn't see me as the hero, should she?

"I knew you'd come," she whispers with a smile, rising to her elbow for a kiss.

Her attempt is slow and imprecise, so I could easily stop her. But I let her, smelling and tasting the alcohol on her tongue.

"Couldn't resist this bomb pussy, could you?" she then whispers, dragging her lips to my jaw.

"I just came to make sure you were alright. I'm leaving."

"I'm not alright, Lex. I'm so needy …"

She grabs my hand to guide it between her legs. Before it reaches its destination, I pull my wrist free. "I'm not fucking you drunk, Andrea."

I stand and take a couple of steps away from her before she can do anything else.

"You almost fucked me drunk that first time in your car," she reminds me with a pout.

"But you weren't drunk, were you? You were tipsy."

To shut her up, I bend forward to give her a quick kiss as I snatch my glasses from her loose grip and then turn on my heels to leave her there. She calls out my name, but I ignore her. This isn't happening, no matter what she says. Not only is she too intoxicated to give genuine consent, but I'm also still mad at her for her behavior with Oliver.

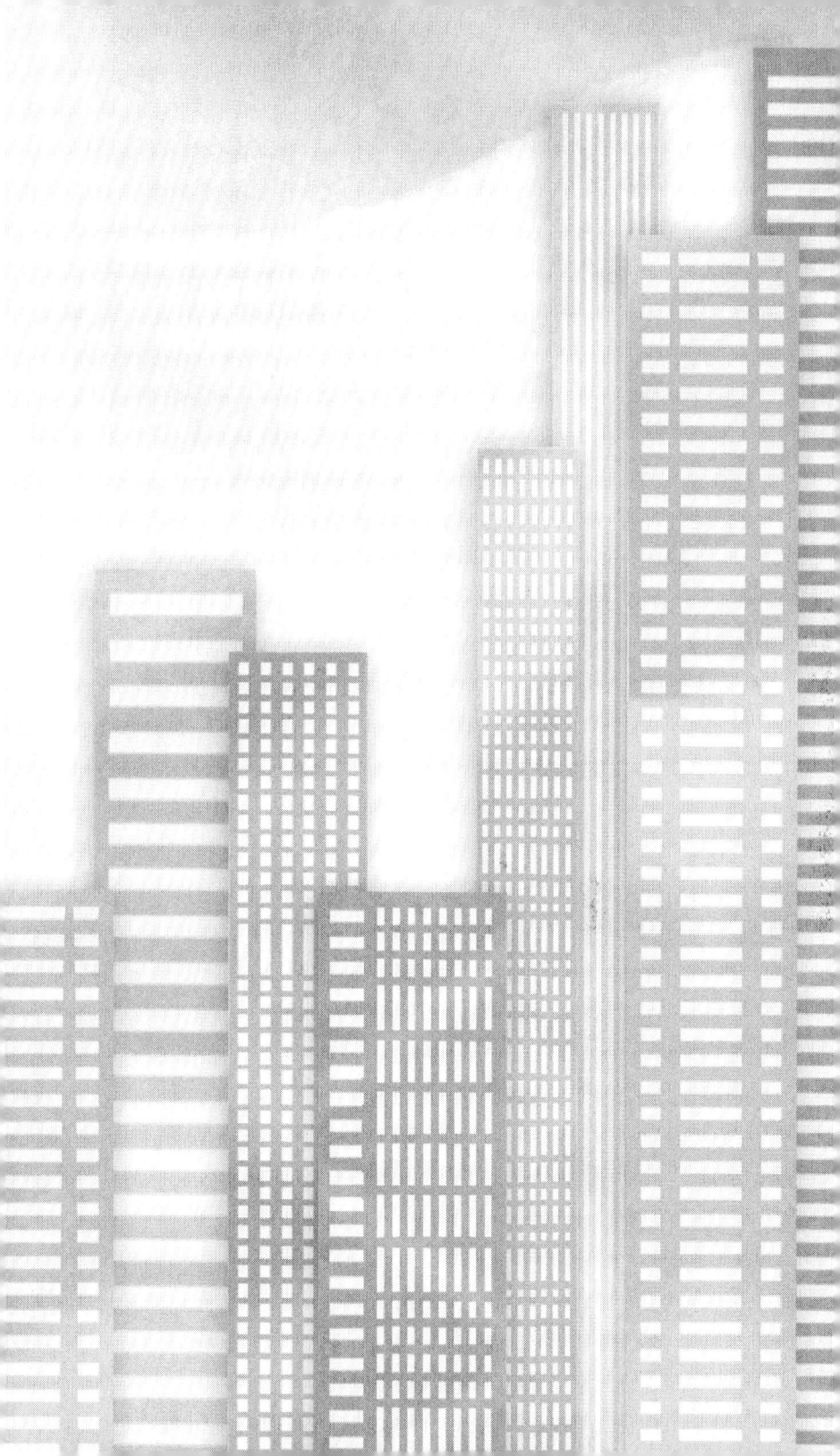

is_new_chapter = True

chapter_number =

"25"

pov_name =

"Andrea"

I. Am. In. Pain.

My eyelids are heavy, and the room is too bright. I stretch my limbs, groaning at the ache running through them. The fuck …? Did I get hit by a bus? My head's killing me, and my muscles are sore. What's happening?

Oh shit. I got drunk. *So* drunk. We stayed at the bar until they basically threw us out. I vaguely remember a heated debate about Star Wars versus Star Trek, ending with Joseph and Brian making everyone in the bar vote for the best franchise.

I try to move again with a grunt. Shit … Twenty-six is too young to be this wrecked by a hangover. I roll over in search of my phone and freeze.

This isn't my room.

What the hell?

Two keycards are on the nightstand by my phone, and then I remember. I went to my room, changed my mind, and went to room 504. As I grab my phone, I suddenly recall something else.

Oh, fuck. Oh, no. I sent texts. *Booty call* texts.

Utterly mortified, I summon the courage to read what I sent to Lex.

Oh, this is bad. This is so. Fucking. Bad.

With my face buried in the pillow, I let out a scream of frustration. I'm never touching alcohol ever again. Drunk Andy is a fucking idiot. I can't tell what's worse. The ridiculous emojis, or how he left me on read. But even I want to ghost myself, so I can't exactly blame him. I'm so pissed that my pounding headache becomes irrelevant. *Holy shit, I hate myself.*

How the hell do I keep putting myself in these situations?

I roll on my back to stare at the fixture above me. I can't face him after this. I simply cannot. I need to be on the next flight to Peru.

With a tearless sob, I drag my ass out of the bed to take an ibuprofen tablet from my bag. "What the—"

It's filled to the brim with loose peanuts. My face is frozen in confusion as I stare at the weird contents for a moment. Last night was really wild, wasn't it? I shuffle through them to find what I need and head to the bathroom for a glass of water.

Then, I sneakily make my way back to my room, praying to God I won't encounter one of the guys. Thankfully, I don't, which allows me to relax a little. I proceed to get ready as fast as I can in my incapacitated state. Since I can't find it, I suspect that Lex took off with the thong I threw at him yesterday, and I don't know what to make of it.

When I arrive at the breakfast room, I instantly spot my colleagues, thanks to Oliver's red hair. Once closer, I see Brian and Steven are the only ones missing. I fill a plate with whatever feels edible—so, not much—and sit with the group in one of the empty chairs.

"Hey, guys," I say, avoiding Lex's gaze at all costs. They greet me back as I take a bite of my English scone.

"So, last night was pretty wild, eh?" Oliver says to me. Why me in particular, though? He senses my confusion and chuckles. "How much of it do you remember?"

"Bits and pieces."

"Well, I don't remember everything, but I sure remember you clapping back at that dude who groped your ass," Mace states with esteem. I stare at him blankly, failing to remember that moment. "Queen shit right there. I never want to be yelled at in Spanish. What was it you said when he told you to calm your tits?"

"Uh … Probably something like '*no voy a calmar mis tetas, pendejo.*'"

"I need to remember that one," Mace continues, still grinning.

I finally dare to look at Lex. His darkened gaze is on me, and it's easy to guess he's pissed. Well, today is going to suck.

"How much was the tab again?" Joseph signs.

"Hmm, I think it was $1998.75," Oliver answers.

"Yeah, something like that. We were missing around thirty dollars when they stopped serving alcohol. That's when Andy thought of ordering peanuts."

Oh, that explains my bag. "I, hmm … Maybe I went a little too hard on the tequila shots," I say, looking at the guys sheepishly.

"You certainly did," Lex mutters. I offer him a warning glare.

He better not start right now. First, he was pissed at me for no reason last night. Second, he asked us to make Hugh pay up, so he can't blame me for my alcohol intake. Third, he ignored my drunken, pathetic attempt at sexting.

"How's your head?" he then asks, having the audacity to look like he actually cares.

Because I'm still a little drunk and feeling petty, and because of my obsession with *RuPaul's Drag Race*, the first answer I come up with is, "Haven't had any complaints."

I regret the words the instant they come out of my mouth, but it's too late. Mace spits his mouthful of tea back into his cup, trying his best to keep it from spilling out. "Girl, you didn't!"

Lex takes barely longer to react, but when he understands what I meant, danger flashes in his gaze. Clearly, he doesn't like to be made fun of. Before we can dwell on it, my unknowing saviors arrive. Steven and Brian sit with their trays, instantly becoming the table's new concern. Brian's wearing sunglasses, and Steven looks eerily anxious.

"Hey, guys. Everything alright?" Oliver asks.

"Peachy," Brian says.

"What's with the glasses?" Mace wonders.

The two of them look at each other for an instant, hesitating. "It's a long story."

"We have time," Lex stoically replies.

"Well …" Brian starts, "yesterday, after the bar, Steven and I were the last ones to leave, and we kind of did something stupid." He looks so sheepish and ashamed that I take pity on him without even knowing what it is.

Lex, on the other hand, doesn't. "What did you do?"

"You know the grand staircase in the lobby? We, uh, raced each other to the bottom. Sliding down the railing."

His hand slightly trembles as he removes his glasses, revealing a nasty black eye so swollen he probably can't even see through that side. We all stare in shock at his injury, utterly silent.

"Did something happen to you as well?" Lex asks Steven, his tone ice cold.

"Yeth. I broke a tooth," he says before offering a tentative smile to show us. He lost an upper front tooth and a chunk of the second one.

Oh, shit …

A surge of laughter bubbles in my chest, probably because I didn't sleep enough and still have alcohol in my blood. My eyes meet Mason's to my right, and I see he's also fighting for his life. Trying my hardest not to laugh, I bury my face in his shoulder.

"The sliding was fine. It's the landing that sucked," Brian explains.

I explode at the same time Mace does, and our hysterical fit of laughter fills the otherwise quiet room. I can't contain it. It's just unstoppable. Through tears of hilarity, I glimpse at the odd pair, chuckles spilling out of my mouth. Shit, it isn't funny. They actually got hurt. But every time I look at them, I envision them gliding down the railing, giggling like little kids.

I'm literally just calming down when Oliver amusedly asks, "Who won?"

"I won the first time," Brian says.

"You did it more than once?!" Mason shrieks.

"Three timeth," Steven corrects with a lisp. "Then they made uth thtop."

Just like that, it starts all over again for Mace and me. I can't even breathe at this point. "Bitch, we finna ask the hotel for the security feed. I gotta see that," Mason says through tears of laughter.

Oliver is amused as well but isn't laughing, just like Joseph. Lex, however, looks furious. "You can't do your presentation tomorrow," he states, barely containing his anger.

It kills our laughter at once. Shit, that is true. The presentation.

"I can wear makeup," Brian proposes. We all know the swelling won't recede enough for that by tomorrow morning.

"And maybe I can get my tooth fixthed."

"Do you have the missing piece?" Oliver asks.

"Uh … I think I thwallowed it."

Mason makes a strangled noise next to me, and I do my damned hardest not to laugh, either. Shit, this is ridiculous.

Lex pinches the bridge of his nose, struggling to remain composed. We wait while he thinks about all this intently, his clever mind searching for a solution. When he figures out the proper course of action, he's serious and contained.

"Oliver, you know the app well, right? You worked with them on it."

"Yeah, I think I could present it."

"Good," Lex approves with a nod. Brian lets out a high-pitched noise, halfway between a squeal and a whimper. Our boss immediately turns to him with a hard glare. "What now?"

Steven is the one to explain, "Maybe I had the prototype with me, becauthe we thought we'd work on it. And maybe it kind of broke when I landed on it."

"You broke the prototype."

"Yeth."

"The $150,000 prototype," Lex insists, eerily calm about it. We all wince at the reminder of the price.

When Steven nods, Lex closes his eyes with barely contained frustration. "That's my fault," he mumbles to himself. "I shouldn't have encouraged them to drink."

I genuinely don't know how he does it, but when he opens his eyes again, he doesn't blow up at the guys, almost composed. "Brian, get your eye checked before heading to the convention. Steven, you decide if you'd rather see someone now or when we return to Seattle. Andrea," he continues, taking me by surprise, "you'll have to present your application."

Hold up. "What?"

"You'll present the ASL app tomorrow."

Shit. No. No, no, no. I'm not ready. The app isn't ready. I can't do it. I can't prepare a presentation for three hundred people overnight. I can't even speak in front of that many people.

"Lex, no. Please," I beg.

"We don't have a choice," he insists. "Canceling now would be unprofessional and poorly received. That's not even considering the missed opportunity. I'll help you get ready this afternoon. We can't miss that chance, Andrea." I can see he's sorry for the turn of events, but it's clear we're cornered and have no other choice.

Shit, I don't want to do the presentation, but I also don't want to let him down. I can't tell if it's because he is my boss or because of the intimacy we share, but I don't want to disappoint him.

Slowly, I nod, my eyes fixed on his.

is_scene_break = True

BECAUSE OF THE CHANGE OF plans, I have to meet with Lex later this afternoon so he can help me prepare for the presentation. I'm not looking forward to it, but it's not like I have a choice. The positive thing about him being a jerk is that I won't be tempted by him. If he remains insufferable, I'm certainly not going to let him touch me.

He has his glasses on when he opens the door, and his hair looks like he's passed his hand through it over and over. Given his frown, I can tell he's preoccupied. Although it isn't a particularly sexy mood, I always like him better when he seems less perfect. He's wearing a simple gray T-shirt with jeans, and his sneakers are immaculately white.

"Come in," he invites, moving to the side.

My face flushes as I look around, memories of our first night in San José flooding me. My eyes slide to the half-opened bedroom door, where I can see the bed we fucked on for hours. Well, there goes my determination not to be tempted.

He points at his laptop on the coffee table. "I already started a list of everything we need for tomorrow."

This is pathetic. I can't even be in the same room as him without getting the naughtiest thoughts while he's effortlessly keeping it to business. I sit beside him on the couch, ensuring our legs don't touch.

"We'll need visuals for the two screens over the stage. Videos, screenshots, diagrams, numbers … That sort of thing. We'll also set up a live feed of the phones while they are being used so people can see the app in action. Right now, I'll work on those, with the help of the design team back home, while you prepare what you want to say," he explains very professionally.

He smells so good, and his large body radiates warmth. My nipples harden under the thin layer of my bra, and I hate myself for how my core rouses. I'm so fucking whipped.

"Andrea," he starts, with his low, masculine, and ever-so-sexy voice. Worried my naughty thoughts are showing, I stare at the screen. "We need to talk about what we're doing," he says gravely.

"You mean the presentation or the … other thing?"

"The other thing."

"Okay."

"I know now isn't the time, but it'll be in my head all afternoon, and I won't be able to focus." He passes a hand in his hair with a sigh, uneasy. "I'm not sharing you," he bluntly says.

I gape at him, baffled. What? Is he asking for exclusivity? What happened to his whole liberal and carefree attitude about sex?

"What do you mean exactly?"

"I mean, you can't see other people while we're fucking." Well, whoever said romance is dead was absolutely right.

I remain silent for a while, digesting the information. It's not even that I want to sleep with other men, but rather principles. This isn't what we agreed on. There is no such thing as exclusive casual sex. Also, I goddamn hope he means it both ways.

"Okay, first of all, what happened to 'I don't do relationships, Andrea?'" I ask, poorly imitating his low pitch.

"I'm not asking for the whole dating thing." He sounds almost appalled. "I just won't tolerate you seeing other men."

"Is it out of selfishness, entitlement, pragmatism, or jealousy?"

"We work together, and I don't want this to become a bloodbath." His answer disappoints me. I hoped it would shed some light on his attitude lately. "Speaking of which, HR will have my head if we don't sign a consensual relationship agreement."

Oh, hell no. I don't want anyone to know about my affair with my boss. Especially not HR. "Lex, this sounds like a lot."

"I know, believe me. But I can't take risks. It's my safety net if things end poorly and you decide to retaliate." Outraged and insulted, I open my mouth to protest. "I'm not accusing you of anything. But Kelex is still young, and a sexual harassment lawsuit could cause irreparable damage. No one needs to hear about us outside of Karen in HR. I'll make sure the information isn't disclosed."

"Do you plan on ending things poorly with me?" I ask, unsure what answer I'm hoping for. *That he doesn't intend to end things at all.*

"I don't. But I can't know how things will evolve down the line." He's right, of course.

"I'll think about it. And for the no-sleeping-around thing, does it go both ways? Like, I can't, but you can't either?"

"I wouldn't ask something of you that I can't handle myself."

"So, you won't?" I insist, despising the faint hope I can hear in my voice.

"I won't."

Trying to hide my satisfaction, I nod. It may be stupid and sentimental, but knowing he is all mine for now is incredible.

But that's the problem, isn't it? He isn't mine, and I'm not his. We're just fucking each other. Exclusively. And we'll make it official with a legal contract.

That's … something.

"So, just so we're clear … We'll keep fooling around, we won't see other people, we will make it official with HR, but we aren't actually together?" I summarize.

Just then, he sees it. What he's asking for isn't casual anymore. It's the beginning of something.

"Fuck, this is a mess," he mutters, removing his glasses to pass a frustrated hand over his face. "I told you I don't do relationships because I'm terrible at it. I'm a workaholic, don't have a romantic bone in my body, and never cared for someone long enough to commit to anything serious."

I'm not expecting a relationship out of this, but knowing I'll soon be back to Idris and loneliness hurts a little. He notices my pout and raises his hand to rest it on my jaw. His warm eyes travel down the length of my face, and I melt into a puddle when his thumb gently grazes my lower lip.

"I'm not used to the things you trigger in me. I've never been the jealous type, but when I see you with Oliver and how easy things are between the two of you, it makes me irrationally mad."

My heart beats so hard in my chest that I worry it might break a rib. Shit, he can't say things like this. It's easier if I can't sleep around because we work together and not because he's jealous. He can't expect me not to get overly attached when he says that while looking at me with those incredible gray irises so full of … something.

At this precise moment, I know he'll break my heart one day. It's clear now more than ever. I'll fall head over heels for him, and the ending will be excruciatingly painful. Maybe we should put an end to it right now. It's the smart thing to do. He's my boss, so I'm not only risking my heart but also my career.

"No matter how much I get, it's never enough. I constantly crave you, Andrea," he confesses, his voice barely a whisper.

His vulnerability gets the best of me, and I plunge in for a kiss. In seconds, we're heatedly making out, and I'm straddling him on the couch while he leans on the backrest. I devour him with all the passion I hold, enjoying his taste, the touch of his hands on my lower back, the warm wetness of his tongue …

"Fuck … I really meant for us to work," he groans, his forehead pressed against mine, not stopping me from unzipping his pants.

"We'll work after." My slim hand lowers into his underwear and rips an animalistic growl out of him when my fingers wrap around his thick girth. I massage him up and down, my mouth hovering over his, the tips of our noses grazing.

"You drive me fucking insane," he says with breathtaking intensity. "I constantly think I can't possibly want you more, and I'm always proven wrong."

I tear myself away from him to stand and watch as Lex pushes his jeans down, freeing his magnificent hard-on.

"Shirt off," I command. With a crooked smile, he obeys. Then, he sits there, holding his dick and stroking it leisurely. Shit, it's so hot. One of these days, I'll have to ask him to get himself off like this. But not today.

Deciding that now is time for me to finally taste him, I lick my lips.

His pupils eat away their surrounding grayness when I kneel between his parted knees. The connection of our eyes breaks when I gaze down to admire his cock. It looks even thicker and longer from here. The head is appealingly sitting on top, its shape the most tempting of plums. I trace the prominent veins with the tip of my finger, finishing my exploration with the big one under his length, following it all the way to the crease at his tip. God, I adore his dick.

It needs to be molded and mass-manufactured into dildos.

"Are you torturing me on purpose?" he asks in a raspy voice.

"I'm trying to decide if it's safe to take you in my mouth." Choking to death on him wouldn't be the worst way to go, but I'd rather avoid it.

"I got tested after our first time together, and the results came back negative for everything," he says, misunderstanding me. "Since we won't sleep around, I thought we might discard the use of condoms."

A shiver runs down my stomach as I remember how he wanted to take me raw back in his kitchen. "Why do you so badly want to have me without protection?"

It's a big step, clean or not. Despite my IUD, there are pregnancy risks I don't want to take.

"I never tried before, and it's been in my mind ever since that moment in my car when you wanted me to fuck you raw," he casually explains.

"So, you want me to be the first woman you've had without a condom?"

He nods, his eyes caressing my confused features.

Somehow, that's the straw that breaks the camel's back. I can't do this.

His meaning of casual sex won't work for me. It's too easy to get attached and get my hopes up. With trembling legs, I push myself up. The moment is gone.

pov_name = "Alexander"

"WHAT'S HAPPENING? What did I say?" I ask as Andrea gets up, completely blindsided.

"You need to take a moment to think long and hard about what you want from me," she explains. "When we started, you told me we'd just fuck around, nothing more. Then you ask for exclusivity, a signed document, this … It means something, whether you admit it or not."

I pull up my pants, not bothering to fasten them, but say nothing. When she continues, her voice trembles slightly. "I'm going to get hurt—we knew it from the start. But you aren't making any effort to protect me. You're charming when you're not being a jerk, incredible at sex, humorous, caring … And now you tell me I make you jealous for the first time in your life, that you can't get enough of me, and you ask of me things that are meaningful and important. How am I supposed to not get attached when you're like this?"

"Would you rather I treat you like shit?" I ask, irritated.

"No, I'd rather you treat me like your booty call and not like I'm your—" She stops and pinches her lips.

"Like my what, Andrea?"

She frowns, displeased, and then says, "Nothing. Forget I even said anything."

"How am I supposed to treat you like my 'booty call' when I see you five days a week? It doesn't work like that."

"Then how does it work?"

I rake a nervous hand through my hair, my mind wrenched with confusion and frustration. Ending what we have seems impossible despite knowing I should.

"I don't fucking know! I can't bring myself to end it. I don't know where it's going. I don't know where I want it to go … I can't fucking think straight when you're around."

I take a moment to breathe in an attempt to think this through. I need the rational side of my brain to take over. "It hasn't even been two weeks yet," I continue. "I think we should wait more before trying to label it. We'll have a better vision of things a month in."

"So, we keep it light and breezy for another two weeks, and then we see where we're at?"

I let out a low chuckle, some of the tension vanishing. "I don't think we've ever been 'light and breezy,' but we can try."

"You can't keep saying those meaningful things to me, then."

"I won't. Feel free to whack me if I do."

She's the one to laugh softly this time.

We look at each other for several moments and something meaningful passes between us. She puts an end to it when she offers, "We should use this time to start working on the presentation."

I release a hoarse groan, fastening my pants. "I don't think anyone has ever left me with blue balls as often as you have, Andrea."

"They match my blue ovaries."

I laugh at her bad joke, and we quickly return to work. Since we're used to being in tandem like this, we accomplish a lot in the little time we have. I handle some back-and-forths with Seattle, and she prepares her pitch, showing it to me as she goes.

"Who did you have in mind for the live demo?" I ask at some point.

"Well, you."

I tense, the mere idea of it making my skin crawl. "I don't do public speeches."

"Really? Are you secretly shy?"

"Something like that."

For some reason, that earns me a smile. "It doesn't leave that many options. It's either Mason or Oliver with me on stage." My jaw clenches before I can stop it, and she notices, her lips pinched in a displeased line. "I'll go with Mason."

"Pick whoever you prefer."

"I'm fine with Mace. He's charismatic, and we get along well."

"I don't expect you to cut ties with people because of how I feel. Go with Oliver if you want to."

Again, she offers me a soft smile. "I'm happy to do it with Mace."

We order food when the evening comes and take a much-deserved break … At some point, when I'm unfamiliar with some pop star she mentions, she forces me to listen to a few of her most famous songs. It rings vaguely familiar, so I suppose I've heard them in the past. In the evening, I meticulously paint the nails on her right hand after she did the left one, and she uses that time to review the visuals Seattle sent us back.

"Alright, I'm done," she sighs as she leans back. We're nearing midnight, and she looks just as exhausted as I am. "All work and no play makes Andy a dull girl. If you don't want to be chased with an axe, we better stop," she says with amusement.

Fuck. That also rings somewhat familiar, but I don't know what it's from. "Before you get all angry at me," I cautiously start, "I realize it's another pop culture reference. I just don't know which one."

"Lex, no! I didn't say anything earlier when you didn't know Britney Spears, but—"

"You said plenty," I cut her off.

"But I didn't scold you. How can you not know *The Shining*?"

"I never saw it," I defend myself, shrugging my shoulders. Instead of insisting, she walks up to me and sits on my lap. I welcome her with warmth, circling her hips with my arms.

"Okay, I have a deal for you, Coleman," she gravely says. "If you'll have it, it would be my greatest honor to introduce you to the joys of classic movies."

I grin as I take in the details of her beautiful face. "I'd love that. But what's my half of the deal?"

"Well, you have very limited experience with movies, and mine is mediocre when it comes to sex. So I thought we could come up with an exchange of knowledge," she suggests, her mouth so close to mine I can almost taste her.

The mood shifts as I slowly caress her curves. Maybe I'm not as tired as I thought. We don't kiss, delaying the moment our lips will meet. We play with the idea, though, our mouths barely grazing each other's.

"Sounds like a lot of work. I don't know if I'll be up to the task," I tease.

"What about me? You haven't even seen *The Shining*."

"You're definitely better at sex than I am at movies."

"That's hardly an accomplishment. I don't even know where to start your education."

"How about you show me your favorite movie first?"

"Nah, you wouldn't like it."

"I'm feeling quite open-minded at the moment," I argue, shifting so she can feel my erection against her thigh.

A naughty smile stretches her lips. "You can't be that indulgent. What if I told you it's *Dirty Dancing*?"

"I have three older sisters, remember? I know it by heart."

"Really?"

To prove my point, I recite a whole section of the movie with the intonations and facial expressions. She gapes at me at first, but then it turns into a broad smile. For both our sakes, she shuts me up by plastering her lips over mine. I embrace the distraction until she pulls away, still grinning.

"I can't believe you actually know *Dirty Dancing* by heart."

"I think I've watched it thirty times. And as soon as I was strong enough, my sisters made me learn the dance with the lift and all."

She fails to contain her laughter.

"Are you making fun of me?" I wonder, a little offended.

"I swear I'm not. You're just … adorable."

"I don't think anyone has called me adorable in twenty-five years."

"It was about time I came along, th—"

A couple of knocks interrupt her. On reflex, she jumps away from my lap. "One day, we'll lock ourselves somewhere for a week where no one can interrupt us," I say in a way that's closer to a threat than a promise. "Who is it?" I bark, standing up.

"It's Hugh," the person at the door answers. Fuck, what's that asshole doing here?

"I swear I might just kill the man," I mutter.

Andrea swiftly gathers her things as I walk to the door to open it.

"I'm sorry. I didn't know you had company," Hugh says when he notices her, not seeming sorry at all.

"We were getting ready for our presentation tomorrow. What do you want?" I coldly ask.

Andrea is done packing her computer and shoving the rest of her belongings in the bag with it. She grabs her phone on the coffee table and joins us.

"Good night," she mumbles, eyes on the carpet as she passes us.

I wait for her to be far enough and then turn to the unwelcome intruder. "The fuck do you want, Hugh?" I ask, not even bothering to contain my irritation.

His attention is still on Andrea, walking away at a fast pace. When he looks at me again, there's something cunning in his eyes. "Working late, were you?"

"That's none of your business. What do you want?"

"Well, I thought we could catch up. It's been a while."

"I have nothing to say to you, Hugh. Now, if you'll excuse me, I have a long day tomorrow."

Eager to be done with this, I go to close the door. He stops me with a firm hand on the panel.

"I looked into that new recruit of yours. She doesn't sound like the coding genius you implied. Her last job was shit. But then again, you've always been great at finding rare gems … Maybe I should make her an offer and get her to work with us so I can judge for myself."

Again, the irrational anger that only seems to come out when Andrea is concerned warms up in my chest. My hand reacts before my mind can stop it, and I fist the fabric of his crisp white shirt to pull him closer to me. Fear flashes in his eyes despite trying to keep his composure.

"You stay the fuck away from her, you pathetic weasel."

"Alexander, there's no need for—"

"Oh, there's need. You will stay away from Andrea, or I'll do what I should have done all those years ago and break your fucking teeth," I threaten. He blinks, still frightened by my show of strength. "Nod if you understand," I command.

He complies with haste, so I release him. "Now, again, I have a long day tomorrow. So, if you don't mind …"

He doesn't need to be asked again as he turns around to return to whatever hole he crawled out of.

As soon as the door is shut, what I just did dawns on me. Fuck. I should have been more clever about this. As stupid as I believe Hugh to be, he isn't dumb enough to not figure out why I'm so possessive of Andrea. My fit of anger disclosed feelings that a boss shouldn't have for an employee.

I'm still not over the idiocy of my impulsive reaction twenty minutes later, lying in bed. My eyes wander to the emptiness at my side, and I can't help but wonder.

Would Andrea have ended up here with me if Hugh hadn't interrupted us? Brian and Steven are still in the room next door, but I could have fucked her gently so that the bed wouldn't bang on the walls. I would have swallowed her whimpers and moans with my mouth and then muffled them with my palm as she climaxed.

It seems I'm not the only one thinking of that because my phone lights up on the nightstand, and I see a text from her.

ANDREA WALKER

Do you want to meet in the room?

ME

No fruits or vegetables to illustrate?

ANDREA WALKER

Emojis are my drunk alter ego's signature. I have way more class.

ME

Looks like both of you want the same thing.

ANDREA WALKER

We sure do. So?

As tempting as it is to accept her offer, I know we'll lose ourselves in each other for much longer than we can afford. It's already past midnight, and I need her on top of her game for the presentation.

ME

I would, but you need to rest. Big day tomorrow.

ANDREA WALKER

But I want you now :(

ME

Consider it your reward for a job well done. I'll fuck your brains out all you want after the presentation.

ANDREA WALKER

But I can't sleep without a good night kiss.

This fucking greedy woman …

In less than two minutes, I'm in front of her door, knocking. She eagerly opens it and poses with a hand on her hip and her elbow on the door frame, looking triumphant. Her flannel shorts and mismatched T-shirt are nothing like the delicate nightwear I'm used to, but I still find myself craving to rip them off of her.

Without wasting a second, I dominantly give her the kiss she begged for. I practically fuck her mouth with mine, one of my hands slipping under the elastic of her shorts to grope and fondle her perfect ass. She moans and clings to me with an arm thrown around my neck.

Before it can derail, I rip myself from her and step back. Her cheeks are flushed, her lips temptingly wet, and I want nothing more than to carry her to the bed behind her and fuck her.

Instead, I say, "Now, go to bed, Andrea."

Utterly shocked, she tries to negotiate. "Lex—"

"No, no more pleading. I gave you your goodnight kiss. Now you can sleep."

She looks almost scandalized to hear that I won't give in to her demands. "Good night. And enjoy the blue ovaries, Walker," I say before leaving, struggling to contain a smile.

It's about time she remembers who's the boss. Though, if I'm being honest, she could probably bring me to my knees without having to try hard.

I might be her boss, but she holds the reins in this thing between us.

And I'm not even mad about it.

is_new_chapter = True

chapter_number = "26"

pov_name = "Andrea"

As we're all having breakfast together, two and a half hours before the conference, what's about to happen really hits me. The guys are doing great, aside from Mace, who looks a little off, and I sit here, alone in anguish. My breathing grows short, the lump in my throat so intense it's painful to swallow. My vision's blurry, and I understand my eyes are watering. I'm having the worst case of stage fright, even though I'm far from being near the stage.

Oliver's the first one to notice. "Andy, are you okay?"

I look up from my bacon and eggs, only to see everyone's attention is on me. Pride wants me to say yes, but playing it off doesn't feel right, so I shake my head. We need to find another solution. I can't do this.

"Anything we can do to help?" Brian asks. As suspected, his eye is still swollen and even darker than yesterday. It serves as a harsh reminder that there is no other solution.

I look at the guys, wishing they could help, but only one person might be able to do that right now. Whatever silent plea I give Lex, he gets it.

"Shit," he mutters, getting up from his chair. "I'll take care of this. Everyone else, you can head to the convention center. We'll meet you backstage half an hour before the presentation." Ignoring the guys, he wraps his hand around my arm. "Come with me." I obey, a surge of anguish overtaking me. He lets go once I'm up to press his hand on my upper back instead.

"Do you want me to come?" Oliver offers.

Lex doesn't answer for a moment, and it takes me a few more seconds to get that Oli isn't asking him. He's asking me. I shake my head and smile reassuringly, not trusting my voice.

The professional and detached facade stays on all the way to the elevator. However, as soon as the doors close behind us, Lex pulls me close and wraps his arms around me comfortingly, resting his chin on top of my head. In his strong embrace, I rapidly relax, his warm and solid form reassuringly familiar.

"Andrea, I don't want to force you to do this if it's too much," he whispers. "I thought you had it in you, or I would have never insisted."

"I—I'm sorry. I can do it." I pause, wrapping my arms around him. "I'm just so scared I'll mess something up and bring shame to the company, myself, or you."

"You can do no wrong," he promises, moving away to meet my eyes. "I've heard your pitch twice already, and it's brilliant. You'll nail this, Andrea." I nod, already feeling a little better about all this. "What can I do to help?"

I can't believe what I'm about to say, but here I go. "There's one way you can help me unwind."

There must be something in the look I give him that's very eloquent because he instantly gets what I have in mind. The elevator doors open to the seventh floor, but we stay in it as Lex presses the fifth button.

My phone dings with a notification, and I see it's Joseph in the group chat.

JOSEPH

Let us know if there's something we can do.

ME

Thank you, guys. We're going on a walk to clear my head. That should do the trick.

"You clever little thing," Lex amusedly mumbles while we walk out of the elevator.

As soon as we're in room 504, he grabs me, pulling me harshly against him to kiss me. Based on the demanding strokes of his tongue, I guess he's been dying to fuck, too, just as deprived as I am from yesterday's dry spell. We undress each other on our way to the bed, ripping away clothes, popping open buttons … Our refusal to let go of each other's lips for longer than a few seconds makes our advance slow. Still, we manage, leaving a trail of discarded garments on our way to the bed.

Lex pushes me, and I let myself fall on the mattress, crawling up the comfortable surface before taking care of the clothes I have left. He watches me slip my pantihose along my legs while he finishes removing his pants.

"I'll fuck you hard until you can't take more of me," he says, his voice dripping with sin. "And then I'll fuck you some more, just to be sure."

It probably isn't a good idea to get on stage with a limp, but I can always pretend I twisted my ankle during our walk.

Mumbling something inaudible, he grabs my legs and pulls me toward him until my ass is near the edge, kneeling in front of me in the same move. He settles between my parted thighs, slips his arms around them, and I tilt my hips, ready for the touch of his tongue on my dripping core.

"Always so fucking wet …" Taking his time, he drops a kiss on my inner thigh, then licks the spot gently. "You never told me your favorite movie."

"Lex, we don't have time for this," I protest, tangling my fingers in his thick dark hair, determined to bring him where I need him.

"We're multitasking. So?" More butterfly-like kisses, but not where I need him.

"You'll make fun of me."

He tightens his hold on me, determined to make me talk, and gives me the faintest little flick of his tongue right on my clit. "What's your favorite movie, Andrea?"

"It's … *Toy Story*," I give in, my breath short.

That earns me a slow, precise circle around the swollen crest. "So, according to you, the greatest movie of all time is a cartoon?"

"Animated movie. And it *is* the greatest movie of all time."

"Why is that?" He's giving me what I need, but not enough of it, keeping me on the edge of pleasure and frustration.

"It's—Well, the kid is named Andy, so, best name ever, great start, obviously," I half-joke, letting out a nervous laugh when Lex's tongue enters me.

"Keep going."

Swallowing the lump in my throat, I nod docilely. Shit, he's making it hard to form sentences. "Also, the plot is amazing. I spent months spying on my toys after that, hoping I'd catch them moving when they didn't know I was looking."

I buckle under him as he plays with my clit again, my skin tingling from his teasing, my body feverish. "Keep talking, Andrea."

"Lex, I don't want to talk anymore," I whimper, tightening my fingers in his hair.

"A lesson for a lesson, remember?"

Fuck, right. He teaches me sex, and I teach him movies. Forcing my two functioning brain cells to rub together and form a proper sentence, I say, "The technical prowess of the movie is just—Aah!"

That teasing asshole is doing this on purpose. "The prowess is what, Andrea?"

"It's very commendable. And it is the first of its—Oh shit," I moan when he pushes a finger inside my drenched slit, his tongue flicking and his lips sucking. "Yes, don't stop!"

"You're terrible at this," he jokes, his voice muffled by the way I keep him pressed there.

"Stop talking! Just—Ah! Fuck!"

The rhythm of his tongue grows faster, flicking over my clit with just the right pressure. His free hand slithers up to pinch my nipple, twisting it gently, and the flash of pleasure is enough to make me orgasm. My hips jolt from it, and the involuntary contractions of my abdomen make my upper body convulse.

His wicked, *wicked* tongue lowers to where pleasure is gushing out of me, lapping at it with eagerness. When I'm clean of any excess wetness, he moves away from my throbbing pussy, wiping his lower face on the smooth skin of my inner thigh. The carnivorous expression on his gorgeous features releases an ultimate shiver in me.

"Alright, mission accomplished," I pretend. "I'm all relaxed and ready to go."

He doesn't seem to get the humor in my tone because his face is terribly serious when he says, "I don't think so, woman. Turn around and get on your knees."

Despite my heavy and clumsy limbs, I comply as fast as I can. Propped on all fours before him, I hear him shuffle with his discarded jeans, and then comes the tearing of a condom wrapper. That brings me back to our conversation yesterday. I want to be the first woman he'll enter without any protection because it'll mean I'm his first for something. But it's too soon for that.

The mattress dips as he positions himself behind me. It's insane. Two days since we last had sex, and I'm craving him like my life depends on it. I'm addicted to him. Heroin has nothing on this man. Meth who?

"Tell me if I'm going too hard," he says, his low voice making my insides flutter.

He doesn't wait for my answer and pushes himself in with a firm shove. I let out a throaty sound, half-cry, half-moan, the sensation of his massive cock fulfilling my every need. He holds my hips with both hands to make sure I won't try to escape his onslaught—as if I would try to get away from any of this.

He slowly retreats and then harshly fills me again, making my ass jiggle when his hips meet it. "Words can't express how much I adore your ass."

By his third mighty shove, I can't control anything, pushing back in rhythm with him. Soon, he's plowing me with intensity, granting me the hard fuck I was so desperate for. Shit, I still want more. I want him to dominate me in every possible way.

"Pull on my hair," I demand with a trembling voice, remembering how amazing it felt when he did it during our first night together.

As he obediently complies, a shaky cry rolls in my throat, his fingers tightly clutching a handful of my curls. The gesture sends a flash of pleasure mixed with pain that travels down my nape, spine, and then ends right in my aching clit, where he's still heavily ramming into me.

"Aah, baby, yes! Don't stop …" I moan, sinking my teeth into my lower lip.

Everything stops, his grip on my hair loosening. After a moment without him resuming, he releases my hair, and I realize something is wrong. With a frustrated sigh, I turn around, meeting his perplexed face.

"Did you just call me 'baby?'" he asks after a few more seconds pass.

Shit, I have no idea. That could have slipped past my lips in the heat of the moment. "I did?"

"You did."

I look forward, unsure if it's a good or bad thing. Clearly, it's an endearment, which means I may harbor tender feelings toward him. But, understandably, my brain acts up when he's fucking me silly.

"What should I do to make you say it again?" he asks. There's an unmistakable smile in his voice.

I let out a relieved sigh. It's not a bad thing, even though it's too early. "I don't know, maybe keep doing whatever you were doing?"

To my relief, the incident is left behind, and we return to more pressing matters—like relaxing me before the presentation.

His initially slow momentum increases, the shoves growing deeper and faster, pulling me back harshly each time. He returns his hand to my hair and tugs on it again, intensifying my enjoyment of his ministrations. Shit, he must look so, so hot right now, with the long and fast thrusts, the firm hold on my hip and hair … Good God, his ass must look divine as he plows into me like this.

He removes the hand on my hip to get it under me, bending over, and he places the tip of his middle finger on my engorged clit, never halting his thrusts.

"Yes, make me come," I beg. With just the perfect amount of harshness, he pulls my head back. My spine is arched to the maximum of its capacities, my ass and face tilted up.

"Make me come, *who*?" he demands, his lips against the shell of my ear.

"Make me come, *Lex*."

"Not that one," he insists, teasing my greedy nub just enough to make me frantic. He also tugs on my hair roughly, like a silent, disapproving punishment.

He always finds the most wicked ways to tease me, and I'm *not* calling him "baby" again.

"Alexander," I warn, reaching over my shoulder to clasp his hair.

"Not that one either."

I try to deny him the satisfaction of caving in too fast, but he's incredibly cunning, expertly teasing my sensitive bud to bring me as close as possible to my climax, keeping me there, helplessly balanced on a razor's edge.

"Make me come, *baby*," I end up begging after less than a minute of this treatment.

"What was that?"

"Make me come, *baby*," I repeat louder.

A low and approving grunt rumbles in his chest just before he kisses the side of my neck. "There. That wasn't so hard, was it?"

I'm about to tell him to go to hell when he finally gives me what I want. His finger strokes me with precision, and I let go of his hair to grab onto the covers. His shoves are even rougher than before, and he uses his hold on my hair to pull me back with each of them.

"Yes! Fuck—Yes!"

I come hard, my insides pulsing feverishly around his throbbing length as I scream his name. The pleasure is so intense I think I might pass out. Behind me, Lex tenses before biting on my shoulder with a groan. The pain of it strangely adds to my orgasm, mixing well with the waves of bliss. We come apart together in a mass of legs and arms, undulating and holding onto each other, our wet skin glistening, our ragged breaths filling the empty space.

By the end of it, he's lying over me, pressing me into the soft mattress, his dick buried inside me as far as it can go.

"Shit, it was so, so good," I moan, my hoarse voice muffled by the duvet.

"It really fucking was …" The sultriness of his voice makes me clench one last time. "Jesus Christ, woman. Give me five minutes, and I'll be ready again."

Hot damn … If I'm not entirely relaxed by the time I get on stage, it won't be for lack of trying.

is_scene_break = True

"AH, THERE YOU ARE. We were starting to worry," Oliver says, putting his phone away and coming to me when I enter the backstage room where we're supposed to meet. We're slightly late, which I blame on our inability to take a shower together without it turning into extra sex.

"Sorry, halfway to here, I realized I forgot something back at the hotel, so we wasted some time," I lie.

"Well, at least the walk helped. You look much better."

"It really did," I agree, trying not to blush—a lost cause. *Dammit.* "Okay, we need to check a few things before it starts."

Everyone knows their role, and they are all ready to ace it. Mace looks a little pasty but promises he'll be fine. It's the last time he eats sushi at an all-you-can-eat buffet, he swears.

"It starts in a little under five minutes. People are already coming in. Half the seats are taken so far," Lex says as he joins us. I nod with a grimace, letting out a small sigh.

I can do this. I just have to not let it go to my head.

"We should go," I suggest, ignoring the lump in my throat. We leave the room, back to the outside's agitation. It'll be fine. Lex thinks the presentation is great, the team at Kelex made some incredible visuals, and I have Mason backing me up.

Oli, Steven, and Brian are in charge of handling the screens' content, so they leave for the control room. The rest of us—Lex, Mace, Joseph, and me—walk to the stage's side entrance. My nervousness increases more with each step.

Lex senses my gaze when I look up at him, but instead of turning to me, he grazes my forearm with his knuckles in a reassuring gesture. The simple contact appeases me. He trusts me and has faith in my ability to nail this. And he's the most intelligent person I know, so if he thinks I have it in me, he's right.

When we get there, someone from the sound department comes to pin a mic on my shirt and hands me the wireless transmitter, advising me to tuck it into the back of my jeans under my blazer. Joseph helps me do that, and I watch as Mace gets the same treatment.

"You'll be great," the latter assures. His eyes are glassy, and his dark skin is pasty. *Damn, that must have been some awful sushi.*

Lex comes closer to me to put his warm hand over my shoulder, encouraging more than intimate. "Don't stress about it. This morning, I read that focusing on some random point across the room helps."

It's surprisingly sweet to know he's been doing research for me, and I listen as he tells me everything he can remember. His voice has a soothing effect that I can't comprehend.

"Everything's ready," the sound guy interrupts. "You can go whenever."

I can do this. I'll nail this for Narnia and for Aslan. And for Kelex, too. Lex gives my shoulder one last gentle squeeze and lets me go.

Before I know it, I'm walking on the stage, trying to look casual despite my overbearing nervousness. A surge of adrenaline peaks through me, making me almost shake. Lex suggested getting in a good headspace, so I summon the memories of this morning, away from the world, with just him, me, and a bed. It works wonders, and I now dare to look at the people in the room. Oh, three hundred people aren't that many. For some reason, I thought it would be way more.

"Hello, everyone. I'm Andrea Walker, junior developer at Kelex," I start with a smile, my gaze fixed just above the public's heads. "So, there's been a slight change of plan, and I'm not here to present the amazing braille solution my colleagues developed as it says in the leaflet, but a revolutionary app meant to help out millions of Americans, as well as dozens of millions of people worldwide once we expand."

Before I dive into my app, I give a quick presentation of Kelex, the company's goals, purpose, values … It's the polished PR pitch the communication team sent me.

"In their pursuit to improve the lives of people with disabilities, Kelex recently acquired an app meant to act as American Sign Language's Rosetta Stone. ASL is one of the numerous sign languages that exist around the world. With one million Americans who are functionally deaf, over ten times more who are hard of hearing, and one in eight who has measurable hearing deterioration in both ears, hearing loss is the third most common chronic health condition in the US." I take a short break, remembering I should move around.

"These stats are growing because of various factors—including exposure to loud noises. And they are growing fast. The number of Americans with hearing loss grew by over 100 percent from 1971 to 2000 when the population only increased by 30 percent. And it's not only aging people who are becoming deaf. One in five kids suffers from some form of hearing damage, and the numbers are also increasing for teenagers.

"Some of those kids will be lucky enough to grow up in families who will learn ASL to interact with them. But ninety percent of deaf children are born to hearing parents, and an alarming number of families will never bother to learn it. It can be out of denial or because they want to raise their child in an environment they deem 'normal.' This results in isolation and a secluded childhood," I explain, feeling myself grow a little emotional. Thank God we never did this to Rafa. "What we aim to do here is to not only help people learn ASL with a process that will make it easier for everyone. It'll also allow deaf and hard of hearing people to communicate with whoever, whenever they want, via a solution more organic than writing their words down."

I'm actually feeling great. The adrenaline is doing its job, and I'm speaking with ease and clarity, addressing the public, moving around, smiling … I get into some coding technicalities, and I can see the subject interests most of them. *Those nerds* … Most of my jokes land, and I decide it's thanks to my fantastic sense of humor, rather than being a woman when most are men.

"We all know hand recognition is particularly tricky. Facebook has worked on it for a while for their controller-free Oculus experience, so if any of you work for the social media titan, you'll get what I mean. Now, you have to realize ASL actually uses way more than hands. We are talking movements of the face, torso, and arms as well," I reveal, feeling quite proud of myself for developing such an app. I'm not exactly bragging, but almost.

Time flies by, and everything goes as smoothly as it can. The visuals are displayed without an issue, I don't forget anything, no one is getting up and leaving …

The live demo approaches, so I peek at the side of the stage to make sure Mason is ready. Instead of seeing him about to come up here, I catch him ripping his mic off and shoving it in Lex's hands before running away with a hand over his mouth, about to be sick.

What the shit?

What's happening?

Oh God, what am I supposed to do now?!

pov_name = "Alexander"

I ALREADY KNEW IT, BUT fuck, this woman is incredible. She was a little tense earlier, but it's all gone now, and she moves with confidence around the stage, her brilliant mind shining for all to see. The crowd is mesmerized by her presentation, just like I am—even though I've heard it several times already.

My chest is full of what must be pride as I watch her explain her application to the world. She has never felt as uniquely brilliant as she does now, and I find myself wondering how I got lucky enough to have her on my team. More importantly, I wonder why this woman somehow wants me to the extent she does. She could have any man she wants with her incredible physique and even better mind, yet I'm the one she picked. For now, at least.

I'm entirely absorbed by her performance when Mason suddenly slams his mic system on my chest and bolts off with a hand plastered on his mouth. Andrea notices, and shock widens her eyes. Fuck, he was supposed to join her on the stage in a minute.

"Go get Oliver," I hurriedly sign to Joseph, who immediately complies.

Andrea's panic makes her stumble on her words, her speech now stilted. Oliver will take too long to arrive, so her stellar presentation will now be remembered as a poorly organized failure. I can't let all her hard work go down the drain like this.

"Put this on me," I ask one of the stage managers, showing him the mic.

He swiftly moves into action and pins the mic on my jacket, and I help him slip the transmitter into the inside chest pocket. Just as he turns it on, Andrea looks to the side again and sees what's happening. Once more, she isn't very good at containing her surprise. But she recomposes herself quickly and clears her throat.

"Alright, enough chit-chat," she tells the public. "We're going to proceed with a live demonstration to show you the extent of the application's capacities."

After one deep breath, I shake my nervousness away and step onto the stage with the phones and improvised holder. My eyes are fixed on her as she introduces me. "This is my boss, Alexander Coleman, co-owner of Kelex."

I give the crowd a vague hand wave, looking above the public, and then back at her.

"So, who in the room has some basic knowledge of ASL?" she asks the audience. A few of them raise their hands. More than the average. "For the ones who don't know about it, you have to understand that when using sign language, you aren't formulating standard sentences. It is an entirely different procedure that is extremely complex to cram into an algorithm. Even the most basic sentences can be signed in several ways. And facial expressions can also add meaning to what's being said."

Andrea explains what's happening as I settle the phones on a high table someone from the backstage crew brought. "Now, we could be in a bar, workplace, public service building … The idea is that all you need are two smartphones and a holder. Or not even if you're a bit of a MacGyver and can improvise something to keep them standing."

All of my focus is on her, and it somehow helps with my nerves.

"Hi, Alexander," she says softly, signing as well. The phone translates easily, and above us, the screen captures it.

"Hi, Andrea." Her phone shows the words.

"The weather here is very nice. Going back to Seattle will be hard," she signs as she speaks. The app adjusts for a moment, looking for the right combination of words, and soon enough, the sentences appear perfectly.

"Leaving San José will be hard for many reasons," I reply. I'll miss having her close by. And I'll miss room 504.

"I know what you mean. My boss is so obnoxious," she jokes. Some people laugh next to us, and the fit of humor helps me relax some more. This isn't too bad. It's just us interacting as we normally would.

"I hope he's giving you a raise for all this," I answer with a smirk.

Our back and forth is humorous and lively; our chemistry makes us particularly good at this. The second half of the demo unfolds just as great, and this time, people from the audience give us discussion topics.

Soon enough, we get to the end of our appointed time. Andrea concludes her presentation with the PR speech given to her about Kelex's work, goals, projections …

Some part of me feels compelled to give her more merit in this whole thing, so I turn to the assembly and say, "I'd like to point out that Kelex has only been working on this incredible tool for about three weeks—when we acquired it from Andrea. So, as much as I'd like for my company to take the credit for it, she is, in all honesty, the genius behind it."

Andrea all but gapes at me, utterly blindsided by my initiative. I then take it upon myself to lead us off the stage, resting a hand on her back and saluting the crowd one last time. Once we're backstage, two people take our mics off, and we're sent to the lounge we arrived in to pick up our things.

The sense of relief that I feel is grand, but I imagine she feels even better. The dreaded presentation is over, and she was incredible. We get into the small room, the first ones there, and she shuts the door firmly and turns to me.

Exhilarated, she grips my jacket, taking me by surprise, and brings me down for an ardent kiss. God, how I love kissing this woman.

After a short but intense peck, she moves back to look up at me in wonderment. "Thank you so much. It was … amazing. You were amazing. God, my skin is tingling, and I feel like I could run a marathon."

A lopsided smile twists my lips, and I bend for a hungry peck before moving back up. "It's the adrenaline. It'll go down soon."

"I don't think so. I think it's you," she blurts out, taken by the intensity of the moment.

My heart flutters at her words but even more at the enthralled expression on her face. The way she looks at me is … dangerous. There's more in her eyes than lust or need. There's something deep, meaningful, and undeserved. She shouldn't look at me like this. And I shouldn't like it as much as I do.

But here we are.

Nothing comes when I try to answer. What can I even say?

Because words fail me, I let my body respond to her declaration the way it craves to. I haul her to me again, capturing her lips with a hunger that matches my adoration for her. She clings to me, desperate for support.

I'd kiss her endlessly, but voices suddenly resonate outside. Shit, the others are here. We barely have time to step back and arrange ourselves before the door flings open.

"Guyth, you were fantathtic!" Steven utters first, looking at her, then at me. "You two make one hell of a team!" The others chime in, all agreeing.

I glimpse at Andrea, and when our gazes meet, we exchange a smile.

Yes, we make one hell of a team.

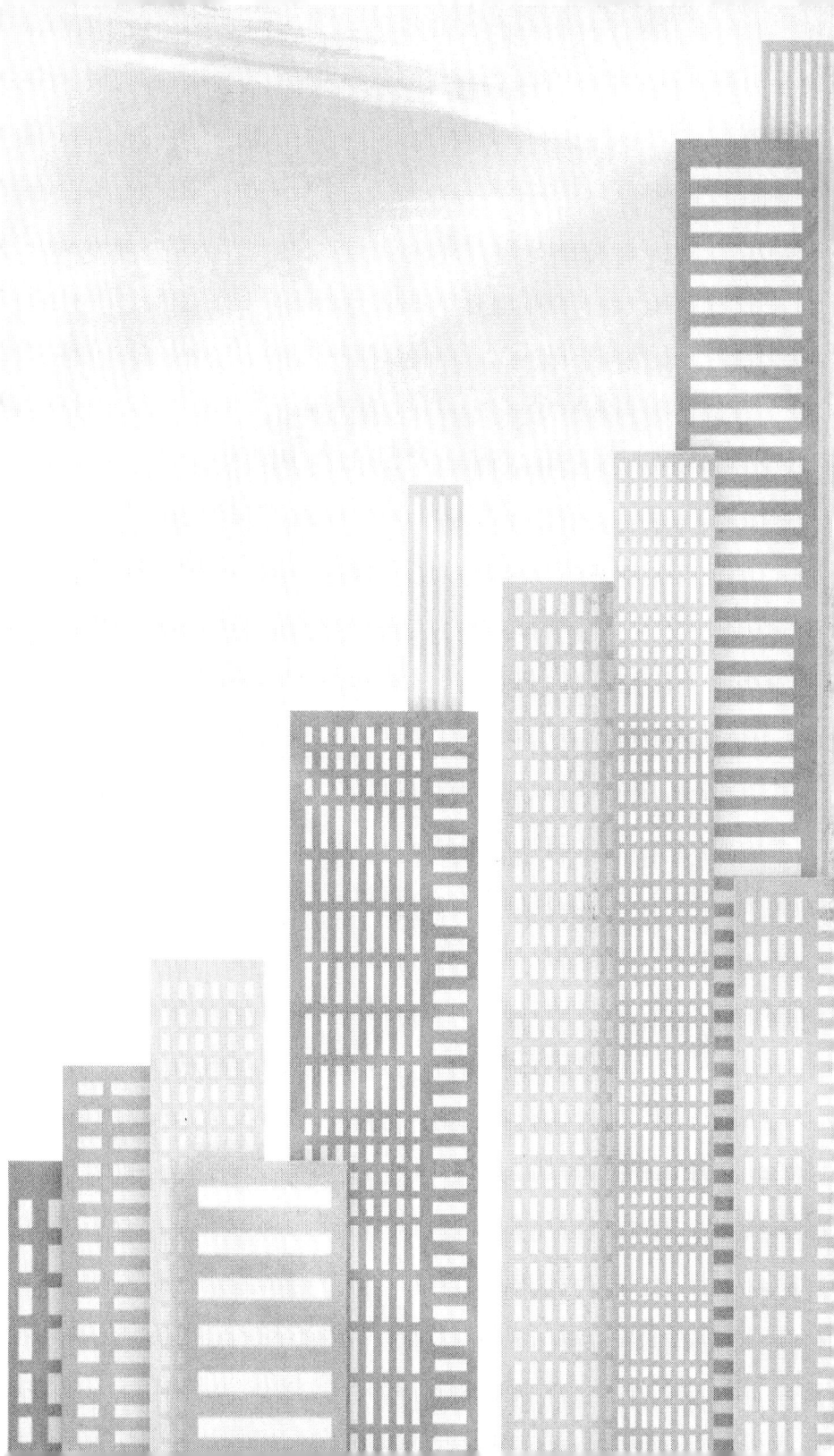

is_new_chapter = True

chapter_number = "27"

pov_name = "Andrea"

THE MOST ANTICIPATED EVENT OF this convention is the robot battle, which happens the afternoon that follows our presentation. It's the perfect opportunity to celebrate our hard work and have fun one last time before heading home later tonight.

It takes place in a separate hall, smaller than the others. There are a few stands there, with companies that are primarily into high-tech electronics or robotic programming. In the middle, there's an arena the size of a boxing ring, surrounded by high plexiglass walls and a net over top.

A stand offers visitors a chance to bet on their champion, and while money isn't involved, we can win some cool merch if we get it right. All the fighting robots—essentially weaponized Roombas with armor—are displayed so we can choose. I go over them individually, examining their shapes and gauging their potential.

I'm debating whether to vote for number twenty-three when Lex's voice says from behind me, "Are you sure about that one, Walker?"

I smile, sensing some teasing coming. "I can't be certain, but I have a good feeling about it."

"It's quite small compared to the others."

"Just because it's tiny doesn't mean it isn't fierce and skilled."

"A fact I'm well aware of," he answers suggestively. He definitely isn't talking about number twenty-three. He gives me a playful side glance. "Do you want to place a bet?"

"Oh, I'm betting on this one. We shorties have to support each other."

"I meant another sort of bet, just you and me."

The promise of some sexy bet makes my skin warm up and my heart flutter. "What do you have in mind?"

"How do you feel about being tied up while I take advantage of you?" he whispers in my ear.

Fuck … My knees turn to mush, a shiver runs up my spine, and heat spreads in my lower stomach. Images of being tied up while Lex finally lets his inner beast free flash before my eyes. He understands how much I enjoy the idea, his gorgeous face veiled with want. Alright. Even if neither of us wins, we're absolutely trying light bondage.

Before he can answer, we're interrupted by Brian. "Guys, the votes are closing in three minutes," he reminds us on his way to Mason and Steven.

"For an hour?" I ask Lex once we're safe again.

"Not enough. Two minimum."

"Two and a half, and you have a deal."

"A little greedy for someone who'll tap out in twenty minutes," he teases, his eyebrow cocked up.

"It's how long *The Shining* is."

"You'd tie me up to make me watch a movie?"

"I would for *The Shining*, Lex."

We place our bets and find the others around the arena, ready to enjoy the carnage. The ambiance is like the Super Bowl but for nerds, and it's surprisingly fun to watch robots demolish each other to death.

After the first series of rounds, while there's a break for the winning robots to get some maintenance, I excuse myself to go to the bathroom. As I come back, a masculine voice stops me in my tracks.

"Congratulations on this morning's presentation," Hugh says, his sneering tone making my skin crawl.

Fighting the displeasure he ignites in me, I face him and force a smile on my lips. "Thank you. It was a resounding success."

"Alexander said the app was mostly your work. Is that true?"

"Yes, it was a personal project until Kelex bought it from me."

"It's impressive. A shame you didn't look at your options before selling. We would have bought it for much more than Kelex could ever afford."

His remark irritates me irrationally. "Not everything is about money," I dryly retort.

"Of course not. But Avoss has the means to make such a tool accessible worldwide with a snap of its finger."

"Well, Avoss also sells private data and supposedly secure information to fraudulent companies, among many other unethical things."

My jab amuses him. "Ah, you don't like us very much, do you? A shame … I wanted to offer you to work for us for double your salary."

Given his tone, I have no doubt that he's dead serious, so I look at him with widened eyes. Working for Avoss is the opportunity of a lifetime. People would kill for such an offer—especially for double my current pay.

"Maybe I misjudged you. Perhaps I can convince you," he notes, mistaking my silence for hesitation.

"No. I'm happy where I am."

"Once more, Kelex won't get you very far. Money-wise or career-wise. Sleeping with your boss may help you climb the ladder, but it's a very short ladder you're working with."

Air leaves my lungs as if he hit me in the guts. How does he know? Did he guess? Did they discuss this yesterday after I left Lex's room in a hurry?

"I'm—I don't know what you—"

"Save your breath. I'm not an idiot. You do whatever you want, but if you'd rather get a job that values you for your actual work rather than your bedroom skills, give me a call," he coldly says, handing me his card.

I glare at it like it's venomous and then at him. Who the fuck is he to say those things to me? When Hugh understands I won't take his card, he slides it back into his chest pocket. "Whenever you aspire to be more than someone who sleeps to succeed, you know where to find me," he concludes, leaving me alone.

He has no idea what he's talking about. I'm not sleeping with Lex to succeed, and he isn't using his position to take advantage of me. We're doing it because we can't help it, because we need each other.

Someone bumps into me, taking me out of my thoughts. With a groan, I shake my irritation away. Hugh is a prick, and what he thinks doesn't matter. But deep down, I know he won't be the only one thinking I'm doing it to get somewhere professionally. For God's sake, Kelex just bought my app for a lot of money.

What about my colleagues? They're reasonable people, but I'm already leading a massive project shortly after getting the job. Shit, they'll imagine things started before the sale or that Lex had me upstairs with him for *that*. My professional image could be ruined by all this.

I feel like an empty shell of myself as I return to my chair before the second round starts. I should have thought about all this before we started having sex. I should have focused on the big picture rather than giving in because the dick was too good.

"Are you okay?" Lex whispers, sensing something's off.

"Yeah, uh … We need to talk." My seriousness apparently translates well because worry flickers in his eyes. "Can you drive me home tonight?" I ask.

He nods, still tense, and I offer a small smile to reassure him.

"Are we fine?" he whispers.

Still looking up at him, I give his thigh a small, discreet squeeze. "Yes."

I don't want to break things off, but we must establish some ground rules. He'll have an HR document to protect him from some potential scandal. But what will I have? What will protect me from the gossip, assumptions, and judging side-eyes?

is_scene_break = True

I CAN'T STOP THINKING ABOUT my brief talk with Hugh. It was like a harsh slap back to reality, and now I have to rethink everything.

Thankfully, I'm seated next to a sweet old lady who's knitting a scarf on the flight home, and while I'm not sure about the color combination, I can't help but appreciate the quality of her work. Watching the repeated motions and hearing the rhythmic sound of her needles is strangely relaxing. This quiet moment gives me the time I need to think about what I'll tell Lex. My affair with him jeopardizes many things, and the more I think about it, the longer the list gets.

It's dark, cold, and rainy when we exit the airport in Seattle, and I already miss San José. Brian doesn't waste time wishing us a good Sunday and hops into a cab. Mace orders an Uber, and Steven tags along with him, since they live in the same area. Joseph's mom is already waiting for him, so he quickly leaves, too.

"Since we're going in the same direction, do you want to share a cab?" Oliver suggests. I glance at our boss, who's checking something on his phone, and then back to Oli.

"Thanks, but I'm good. Someone's picking me up."

"At this hour? That's one devoted friend."

I wince, giving him a contrite smile. "Yes, *he* is quite devoted."

Oliver's amusement fades, and he frowns. "Oh … That's *him*, right? The guy you're seeing?"

I can sense Lex's presence behind me, and I have no doubt he's listening. Fighting the urge to comfort Oli, I nod. The hurt in his eye is evident, but I need him to understand I won't be with him. We're friends, and as much as I may have wanted us to work something out, I don't want that anymore.

"Alright, then. Enjoy your Sunday. I'll see you on Monday," he concludes, waving awkwardly before heading to the line of cabs. I watch him get into one and wait for the car to disappear after a turn.

"So, I'm devoted, eh?"

I'm not in the mood for Lex's taunting. "Don't. It's hard enough that I keep hurting his feelings like this. I don't need you to add to it."

Lex recoils, confused. "So I guess everything isn't fine between us." He passes an irritated hand through his hair, his whole body tense.

"Oli is a friend, and I don't like hurting him, that's all."

He raises a skeptical eyebrow at me, but doesn't comment. "Let's get you home."

His Mercedes is in the parking lot, so we head there. He hauls our luggage in the trunk, and we're on our way. After a few minutes of tense silence, I sigh heavily.

"So, about that talk … Hugh came to me this afternoon. He told me he knew about us and basically called me an opportunistic slut."

As I wait for his answer, I hear the raspy sound of his hands fisting the leather of the wheel with a death grip. "I will punch that cunt the next time I see him. I should have been more careful when I talked to him yesterday."

"Why? What did you two talk about?"

"He made some snarky remarks about poaching you, and I told him to stay the fuck away."

A mix of pride and joy overwhelms me. Possessiveness isn't a trait I should appreciate—it's a Neanderthal thing—but it's different with Lex. "He offered to double my salary if I go work for Avoss," I reveal.

"He did? What did you tell him?"

"I accepted, of course. It's double my pay."

I'm obviously joking, but Lex doesn't get it, frowning and grasping the steering wheel even harder.

"I told him I was happy where I am," I quickly explain, sorry to have distressed him over a stupid joke. "Anyhow, Hugh's an asshole, but other people will think the same and draw those conclusions. Although they probably won't voice it so rudely."

As someone who is always a few steps ahead, he probably thought of that already.

"I didn't really care about it before, because it was supposed to be just a one-time thing. But it looks like we'll be doing this for a while—at least if I have a say in it," I continue, biting my lip anxiously.

"Yeah, I'm … hoping the same."

His confirmation has my chest tightening with glee. "Great. This means we have to be discreet. I don't want people to know about us. It would hurt me if the guys thought all I've accomplished is because we were having sex and not because I'm worthy."

"I imagine you'll want to work back downstairs from now on?"

"It would be wiser, yes."

"I'll have Aditya move your computer. When will we see each other?"

I think about it for a moment. "Maybe keeping it to the weekends is more prudent."

Lex reluctantly mumbles. "I'm all for planning things, but five days is a long wait. I will only agree to this if you stay from Friday evening to the end of Sunday without disappearing in the middle of the night," he negotiates, clearly disliking my nocturnal escapes.

"I don't think I can survive forty-eight hours with you. And I have plans most weekends."

"Fair enough. Then we let it happen as it comes."

I give the idea some consideration. Tamika knows I'm seeing someone, so I can go to his place now and then without raising her suspicions. And barely anyone at work knows anything about Lex's personal life, so I would be safe from that.

"As long as we make sure no one knows, I'm good with that," I agree.

We talk a little longer about logistics, and then I brag about winning our bet. Both our robots failed to be crowned champion, but mine lasted a little longer than his, meaning I'll get to tie him up. He doesn't look too pleased with that, especially since he thought his robot was a sure thing—he personally knows the guy who built it but claims that wasn't cheating.

"I wish you could come up for a quickie," I say with a pout once he's parked in front of my building.

He chuckles and shakes his head. "You live with Tamika, right?"

"Yes, and seeing you sneak into my room would blow our cover."

"We probably wouldn't be quick anyway," he says with one of his wickedly sexy half-smiles.

"Stop tempting me, Coleman."

Despite the coziness of the moment, I force myself to exit his car, and he opens the trunk to take my suitcase out of it. The rain momentarily stopped, which allows us to linger a little. "I'll see you on Monday," I tell him, raising myself on my toes for a kiss. As always with this man, I rapidly crave more, and what's supposed to be a quick peck on the lips turns into a thorough make-out session.

I'm trying to press myself harder on him, our tongues lasciviously grazing each other's, my fingers curled into his jacket, when he pushes me away with a groan. "You should go before I forget about Tamika and drag you to your room."

"Yes, uh … Enjoy your Sunday."

"Enjoy your Sunday, Andrea," he says inches from me, his nose softly brushing mine.

"You too."

His chuckle fans across my face. "You already said that."

"Oh, right … Did we already kiss goodbye, too? I don't think we did."

That's all he needs to kiss me again, and we keep things more reasonable this time. After one last longing peck, I push myself off him and grab my suitcase.

"I want my underwear back, by the way," I demand as I walk away.

"I'm keeping it as payment."

I stop and spin to face him. "For what?!"

"For leaving me high and dry in that bathroom."

I giggle, shaking my head incredulously. As I walk to my entrance, I glance back at him every few steps. He waits, nonchalantly leaning on the side of his car until I disappear into my building.

Damn, I'm one lucky girl.

Tamika is watching a movie in the living room when I come in, and after a friendly welcome-back hug, I head to my room. A while later, ready for sleep, I send a message to Kate, asking if she's still up.

I don't even have to explain myself. She calls on her own less than a minute later. "Hi, babe," I greet her, excited to hear her voice.

"Hey, Deedee. So, how was the convention?"

"It was great. Hello World is seriously awesome. I saw robots fight to the death today. But I know you're not into that nerdy stuff, and it's not why I wanted to talk to you."

"Oh? What is it then?" she asks, curious. She sounds a bit off, almost detached, which I'm not used to, coming from her.

"Are you okay, babe?"

"Yes, of course. Why?"

"I don't know. You sound off."

"No, I just sound tired. And now, impatient! What did you want to talk to me about?"

Her explanation isn't enough to dismiss my concerns, but I decide to give her the time she needs. Whatever's going on, she'll tell me when she's ready. After all, we tell each other everything, which is why I continue with, "I've been having sex with Lex all week."

"Oh my God, yes! I knew you wouldn't be able to resist."

My face is burning with excitement and embarrassment, so I bury it in the pillow. "Yes, you were right. The man is just so … *everything.* I swear, I feel like I'll never get my fill of him. For God's sake, I let him finger me in a crowded bar with my colleagues right next to us."

"Holy shit, that sounds so hot."

"It was. Everything he does makes me want him even more. He's stupid smart, and attractive, and sexy, and handsome … I don't get it, babe. I'm just … me, and he is a human version of some perfect Greek god."

"Stop saying that, dude," she scolds. "You're the fucking bomb. You're pretty as hell, you're smart, you're witty, you have character, you're talented, and so many other things."

"I'm shorter than the average thirteen-year-old, I have a gigantic ass, I have no boobs, my humor is weird, I can't learn fashion to save my—"

"You're literally the average height for Mexican American women, Dee. And who gives a shit about any of that anyway? Did Lex make a demeaning comment about your butt? I will unalive his ass if—"

"He likes it," I cut her off. Heat flashes in my cheeks as I recall his enraptured words from yesterday. *Words can't express how much I adore your ass, Andrea …*

"There you go. Stop worrying about what society wants. All that matters is what *he* wants. Which, quite obviously, is you," Kate scolds. "I'm sure your Lex has many flaws, too. He can't be all that perfect."

"He isn't *my* Lex," I respond defensively, knowing she is right about my inability to love myself.

We spend over an hour talking. I tell her everything I can think of, sparing her the steamiest details. I feel like an infatuated teenager confessing her stories about a boy. By the time we hang up, I'm much more confident about myself, and the future seems to hold great promise.

I fall asleep a few minutes later, a dreamy smile on my face, imagining what's to come with *my* Lex.

is_new_chapter = True

chapter_number = "28"

pov_name = "Alexander"

It's odd to be alone in my office again. Not only did I get used to Andrea's presence, but I also grew fond of it. She fidgets, and moves, and sings, and can't keep an organized desk to save her life. Which are all things I hate.

But the space feels empty now that she isn't in it anymore, and I keep looking at the bare half of my desk, wishing her screens were still there with her mess.

I'm sure she's happy to be downstairs again with the others, so I take comfort in knowing that returning to normal is good for one of us, at least. And I can always join the team in the Lair if the silence becomes too oppressive.

That's exactly what I consider doing when someone knocks on the door. "Come in."

As if my mind conjured her, Andrea appears as the door opens. She's wearing the Hulk T-shirt she had on during her first day here, and it throws me back in time to those first moments in the elevator. But the high-waisted black skirt it's tucked into takes me to a hypothetical future where I rip it off her.

She hesitates, wondering if she should close the door or leave it ajar. Everyone usually does the former, so I say, "Close it."

She complies and walks around my desk to stand next to me. "Hi," she greets, bending just enough to be level with me. I don't need a more vocal invitation to give her a kiss.

"Hi. How was your Sunday?"

"Restful. Yours?"

"I worked." She frowns disapprovingly. "What brings you here?"

"I'm having issues with the deep learning protocol, and I was told you could help me."

"I might, but what do I get in exchange?" I try, playful and seductive.

"An app that'll make you millions," she snorts with an eye roll while moving to get a chair to sit by me.

I chuckle and save what I was doing. We work for a while, miraculously behaving, finding enough satisfaction in our knees touching under the desk. After about two hours of focused work, I'm done correcting the issues while explaining the process to her. Once everything is saved, she returns the chair to the other side before coming back to me. She doesn't seem ready to head back downstairs yet. Which is good because I want more of her.

"So, how does it feel to get your office back to yourself?" she asks, leaning on the desk with her arms folded over her chest. "Do you miss me terribly?"

"It's awfully quiet now."

"I wasn't noisy."

"You got carried away with the music at times," I reveal. Vexed, she frowns. "I'm not complaining. I quite enjoyed it when you hummed a tune or sang a verse. Especially the ones in Spanish."

"I'm not a good singer," she says with a grimace.

"I noticed."

Her jaw drops with amused indignation, and she attempts to move away from me. But I hook my fingers in the waistband of her pretty skirt and tug her closer.

"Good thing we won't have a karaoke machine at the party on Friday." This time, my teasing earns me a weak punch in the shoulder, but she stays right there. "Do you have your costume?"

Kelex's eighth anniversary is right around the corner, and like every year, everyone gets absurdly excited about it. It's always a big fuss, where we treat our employees with an evening of fun.

Since Kevin and I weren't sure about Kelex's official birth date, we picked September 23rd—a significant day for several reasons. Richard Rhodes invented the very first version of the hearing aid, and Nintendo was founded on that same date. Three years into celebrating Kelex's birthday, dressing up as Nintendo characters for the party became a tradition.

Andrea looks very smug when she answers, "I actually won the privilege of being Mario this morning."

Her smile is beyond endearing, so I pull her even closer. "That's a great honor. I'm surprised the team let you have it—they usually have a whole system in place for who gets to be Mario."

"Like I said, I *won* it," she explains, even prouder.

"Oh?"

"Yeah, I beat the shit out of them in the Arena of Doom. One. By. One."

"Really?"

She nods. "We had a foosball table growing up, and I used to kick my brother's ass all the time." She pretends to polish her nails on her shoulder and then blows on them. "It looks like I haven't lost my skills."

God, how I adore this woman. "When can I see you this week?" I ask.

"I have something tonight with Tamika. And I have been invited to my first girl's night with a few other colleagues tomorrow. Other than that, I'm free all week."

"Damn it," I mumble. "My sister is in town from Wednesday to Friday. She has a whole schedule, and I don't think I'll have a minute to myself."

"So … the best we can do is Friday, after the party."

I stand up, trapping her between my desk and my body. I'm not waiting five days to be with her. "Or we could find another way," I suggest, mouth dropping to the side of her throat.

"Lex, we're supposed to be discreet," she protests with little resolve.

My hands sensuously caress her petite body, exploring her curves, squeezing, pulling, fondling … When they reach under her skirt, my palms and fingers grip her ass, skin to skin. What a naughty girl, wearing a thong under that little skirt …

"We can't do this, Lex. It's the middle of the afternoon."

"We'll be fast," I argue before guiding her to the empty side of the desk—the one she used to occupy.

"Lex, your 'fast' is everyone else's record performance."

"I went fast enough back at the trivia night."

I spin her around and press on her back to make her bend over my desk. Fuck, how many times have I imagined doing exactly this?

"Lex, someone might—"

Her words die with a whimper when I eagerly hike up her skirt, bending to press a long and insistent kiss on the birthmark she has there. Then I fondle both mounds, which has her moaning softly. I fish the thong from between them and stretch it to the side, revealing pink folds already glistening with want. With bated breath, she waits for whatever I'll do next, back arched in a clear invitation.

"Fuck, Andrea … I'll never get tired of your—"

Firm knocks on the door pull us out of the erotic trance, and she straightens up in a split second. I spit out a curse and move away as she tugs her skirt down.

As soon as she looks proper again and there's some distance between us, I command, "Come in."

Beatrix from accounting enters and greets us with a smile. It doesn't seem she suspects anything as she hands me a pile of documents. After a few mundane exchanges, she exits the room, closing the door behind her.

"I can't believe I let you do that!" Andrea whisper-shouts with vehemence, pointing at the spot I just bent her over. "This wasn't *discreet*."

"Alright. But just to be clear, you could have stopped me."

"I was telling you we had to stop," she responds, appalled.

"Yes, and you were doing it with such spirit."

"Fuck you! It's not my fault if my brain stops working as soon as you touch me."

"And it's my fault if mine stops the moment you walk into the room?" I ask in the same irritated tone.

That apparently short-circuits her brain because she stays silent, jaw hanging. When she shakes herself out of it, it's to say, "We obviously can't be trusted to be alone in the same room together, like hormonal teenagers with no boundaries. So, from now on, being alone together at work is off-limits."

"I don't like that."

"Well, tough luck, big guy. Ten more seconds and that woman would have found us with your dick inside me," she explains, pointing at the door.

"It would have been my tongue," I refute. "I was going to eat you out first—I'm not a savage."

Heat creeps up her cheeks, and she nearly scowls at me. "I'll tell you when I need help, and you can come downstairs. Or I'll come up here with someone. Or we'll leave the door wide open."

I still don't like that, but I give in with a sigh. "Alright."

She looks satisfied with that, so she walks up to the door. "Let me know if you have some free time while your sister's here." With her hand on the handle, she impishly adds, "I'm sorry for the blue balls."

"And I'm sorry for the blue ovaries."

That makes her giggle, and the sound stays in my ears long after she's gone.

I don't know what Lucy has planned during her stay here, but if I can get even half an hour to myself, I know how I'll spend it.

Buried to the hilt in that tease of a woman.

pov_name =

"Andrea"

WHAT THE FUCK IS WRONG with me?

I lasted ten months deprived of sex, and now I can't even handle five days without it. What has Lex done to me?

I'm a Lexomaniac, a *slex* addict. I need my dose of it before I go insane. If I'm completely honest, my addiction isn't solely focused on the phenomenal dick but on the whole man attached to it. I miss spending time with him, simply talking and being around him.

Work-wise, things are back to normal. The high of the convention wore off, and my old habits with the guys are back—gaming lunch breaks, geeky debates about video games, movies, shows … At home with Tami, everything is smooth as well. We have a furry companion for a few days—friends of hers who are going on a short getaway—and we go through a few rom-coms with the cat by our side.

It's all very nice, but thank fuck it's Friday. As incredible as the party will be, I'm even more impatient for what comes after. The whole office gets the afternoon off so we can get ready while the party planning committee prepares everything.

Tami is dressed up as Sasha from Pokémon, looking cute as hell, and I'm a real-life Mario—red sweater, denim overalls, an alarmingly realistic mustache, and an actual tool kit belt. I regret not being a little more feminine, but I'm still proud of the fit, so I send pictures. Kate says I'm hot, liking the creepy vibe I'm sending off, and my mom jokes that I'm five minutes away from luring kids into the back of a van with candies.

The party itself is '80s themed, which I adore. The desks of the open space have been pushed to the side, hidden by panels covered with graffiti. The color scheme is vivid neons, with accessories, balloons, a giant boombox, a disco ball … It's all very kitsch but also perfect.

And the costumes … Oh, the costumes are fantastic, and it shows that it's been going on for years because people got extra creative about it. Someone dressed up as a GameCube, and their partner is the controller, with a rope tying them together. There's also a banana peel from *Mario Kart*, but the most impressive costume is a pot from *Zelda*, which can break and be reassembled thanks to magnets. Soon after arriving, I'm much less proud of my costume. It's too basic. I don't have time to dwell on it as my eyes catch a flash of bright pink.

"Hi, guys!" I greet them with enthusiasm. Then, unable to hold back a smile, I turn to Oli.

Because we were the finalists in the battle to be Mario, I got to choose his costume for tonight, and I must say, I chose well. He's wearing a Birdo onesie that is several sizes too small for him. The sleeves barely reach the middle of his forearms, and the legs sit mid-calf. Finding a costume on such short notice had to be hard.

"Hi, Birdo," I greet him with a grin. He smiles back with a roll of his eyes.

Kevin's here with his wife, who disguised her very pregnant stomach as Kirby. Kevin wears an "I heart Kirby" T-shirt, which is cheesy but adorable. Everyone and their plus ones are here, it seems. Or almost everyone.

I find myself upstairs a few minutes after arriving, opening the door to Lex's office. Of course, he's working while everyone is having fun downstairs. When he sees me, he does a surprised double-take, and I remember my mustache. Time to see if I'm sexy-creepy or just creepy-creepy.

"Hi, four-eyes."

"You look very … handy," he jokes when I'm by his side, pointing at my tool belt.

"That's exactly what I was going for. Thank you."

"Any time."

He, on the other hand, is wearing his usual clothes. "You look very boring."

"Thank you for the honesty. I appreciate it." His cheeky smile is endearing, and once more, I fight back the need to kiss him.

"You know what I mean. Where's your costume?"

"I don't wear costumes."

"What? Lex, you have to wear one. Everyone's on theme down there," I complain.

"Being the boss means I don't actually *have* to do anything. And I said I wasn't into costumes, not that I wasn't on theme."

Oh, does he have Donkey Kong boxer briefs on right now? My eyes drop to his crotch, and an amused smile stretches his lips.

"Alright, let's get downstairs then," he suggests, turning off his computer and getting up. "How's the party?" he asks as we walk to the stairs.

"So cool! It's like the '80s down there, so I love it."

"I thought you might."

"Did you choose the theme?"

"I know you really like the era, so—" I stop in my tracks, stunned by his attention, and it takes him a couple of seconds to notice. "Are you alright?"

Oh, I'm more than alright. I'm amazing. "God, I could kiss you," I blurt out.

His reaction tells me I'm not the only one feeling sex deprived. Especially since I'm wearing a mustache right now, and he still wants to kiss me. I guess Kate was right and I'm sexy-creepy.

"Soon," he mutters, for himself as much as for me.

We don't enter the party floor together, just to be safe, and don't share anything more than stolen glances once all my coworkers surround us. The music is very much to my taste, and although I'm not the best dancer, I spend a good part of the evening doing just that.

Probably thanks to Lex and Kevin, the bass is cranked to the maximum, and light installations allow people to see and feel the music. In that sense, the numerous deaf and hard of hearing guests also have fun and rock the dancefloor. Tamika is an incredible dancer, and we goof around a lot. I almost manage to forget that I can't do all that with the one person I want to, whose eyes are often on me as we exchange knowing smiles. He spends most of the party in a corner, observing the fun from afar, his arms crossed over his broad chest.

Eventually, the people, the music, and the lights become overwhelming, even though I didn't drink much.

In need of a quiet moment, I head to the Troll's Lair. The glass door has been covered by a graffiti panel, so it's dark in here. And the music is still fairly loud, but it's already much better. "I think the plumbing issue is upstairs," a familiar voice playfully notes.

Oliver is here, too, leaning on his desk in the dark. "Needed some quiet time?" I ask before I walk toward him. The upper part of his Birdo costume is tied around his hips, exposing his white tee.

"I had a phone call to take."

"Nothing too serious, I hope?"

"Just my sister."

I lean on the desk next to him, and we stay silent for a moment, the muffled sound of the music and the people filling the air.

"You looked like you were having fun out there," he says, pointing at the door.

"Yes, a lot. I haven't danced this much since college."

"I could tell you didn't have much practice," he teases. Amused as much as I am offended, I turn to him with my mouth open in a silent protest. "You dance like they do in *The Sims*."

"The first one or the last one?" I ask with squinted eyes, giving him one last chance to keep our friendship intact.

"Definitely the first one."

I softly punch his arm with a chuckle. "Take that back."

"Little lady, you should know only the truth hurts," he insists, massaging the spot I just hit.

"Seriously, Oli! Say I don't dance like a Sim, or I'll never be able to dance in public again."

"And it's a bad thing because …?"

Once more, I hit his arm, barely harder this time, stifling a giggle. We come up short of things to say, so there's nothing but the muffled sounds of "Maniac" by Michael Sembello for a moment.

"I miss how we used to be," Oli says out of the blue. "I miss *you*."

Confusion, pain, and shock strike me. I didn't expect us to have this conversation right now. But I know what he means because I feel the change, too. In the end, it's better this way, especially for him.

Oli is a friend, and I don't want it to change. I won't ever like him the way he wants.

I have Lex. I *want* Lex.

Misunderstanding my torn expression, Oli straightens up before me, and his hands reach for my hip. It feels so incredibly wrong for him to touch me like this. A cold shiver crawls up my spine, and my stomach churns when I understand he's about to kiss me. Sheer panic floods me. No!

A split second before I rip away from him, loud music invades the room as someone opens the door. Oli lets go of me, and I take a few steps back, giving him a reprimanding scowl, disappointed and disturbed by his attitude.

We both look toward the newcomer, and my blood freezes.

Fuck. No …

Lex is looking at both of us from the door's frame, doubt and confusion plastered on his face. Slowly, his features change and a mask of indifference tinted by a thin veil of anger replaces his turmoil.

"What the fuck is happening here?" he asks, his low voice dangerously calm.

Shit. This is bad.

"We were just talking," Oliver answers.

Lex doesn't buy it, an arrogantly inquisitive brow cocked up as he looks straight at me. My palms are sweaty, and even though I did nothing wrong, I feel guilty. "What he said."

Lex answers nothing, his attitude way too calm. Behind his stern facade, I worry there's a storm raging. Eventually, Oli mumbles with a shrug, "I should go back."

Once it's just Lex and me, the tension—which is already pretty high—climbs even higher. Especially when he steps closer to me. *Stop feeling guilty. You didn't do anything wrong.*

"What the fuck was that?" he angrily asks.

"I think he tried to kiss me," I explain, choosing to speak the truth. Lex saw something anyway. "He probably drank a little too much."

"And what's your excuse?" His unfair accusation is full of bitterness.

Appalled, I give him a scandalized glare. "*My* excuse?"

Oh, hell no. He better not be accusing me of cheating because it's not only untrue, but also insulting. Lex's eyes keep drifting to my fake mustache, so I rip it off with an annoyed move, worried he won't take me seriously otherwise. I manage not to grimace at the burn it causes, but my eyes fill up with tears, anyway.

"You were here, too. In the dark with him," he continues.

"Yeah, I needed a quiet moment because it got too much out there. I didn't know he was in here."

"But then you knew, and you stayed."

"What?! So I can't even be in the same room as Oli anymore?" I ask, confused and angry. He's being ridiculous. I get he's jealous, but this isn't rational.

"Not when you're drunk, and he is too."

"I'm not drunk, barely tipsy. And I mean it this time." I'm trying to remain calm but failing. Knowing that he doesn't trust me hurts. "I was thrilled to be with my friends and colleagues, so I was having a great time, and that's the extent of it." I wait for him to defend himself, but he says nothing. I can tell he still doesn't fully believe me.

"How can you imagine me capable of doing anything with anyone when you're the one constantly on my mind."

My words finally reach him, but it's too late. I'm beyond pissed. He offended me with his lack of trust.

"I was also excited about spending time with you later, you jerk! But I don't sleep with assholes who don't trust me, so I'll be spending my weekend with Idris instead," I blurt out, almost choking on my tongue when I realize what I just said. Okay, maybe I'm a little drunk.

Lex's eyes darken, his anger reborn at the mention of yet another man. Well, that'll teach him a lesson. Let the idiot worry over a stupid sex toy all weekend. That'll show him how ridiculous he is.

Eager to get out of here, I give him one last vexed glare and move for the door.

Lex grabs my arm as I pass by him, and before I can protest, argue, or even squeal, he slams me into his solid body and plasters his lips against mine. I shove his chest, still pissed, but I'm no match for his determination. Turns out I don't have much fight in me, anyway.

The intensity of his kiss melts me to the bones. He does it with anger, despair, and desire. A very explosive combination. I forget where we are, his accusations, being mad at him … I forget everything that isn't him.

His dominant temper, which he usually contains, is all out. He's imperious and commanding, his merciless tongue barely allowing mine to sample him, his greedy lips making it hard to breathe, his powerful hands holding me in place against him, preventing me from moving even an inch. The music out there is "You Spin Me Round", which is not only fitting but also turns out to be an excellent song for kissing.

Part of me swoons at his possessiveness, surprised by the novelty of him being like this. It isn't a kiss. It's a message. A lesson. He's marking me as his, showing me who I belong to.

As if I didn't already know.

Someone yells outside, and it's loud enough to break through the music, the door, and then through my lust-fogged mind.

"Lex …" I pant, ripping myself away from him.

His lips drag against my throat instead, devouring the soft skin, making me shiver. Fuck, I don't want this to end, but it has to. "Lex, we have to stop," I insist, pushing him away. He groans with disapproval but eventually releases me, standing straight and tall. He's flushed, and I have no doubt I am, too.

"Alright. Let's go," he orders. I first think he means to the party, but then he continues. "Where's your bag for the weekend?"

"Wait, I didn't plan on staying the whole weekend. All I have is a toothbrush and clean underwear."

"We'll stop by your place before going to mine."

I hesitate, the argument from just before slowly coming back. I want to spend the weekend with him, but I also can't indulge his behavior by rewarding it with sex. As much as I enjoy his techniques, it's unfair.

"You can't do that every time we argue," I say, gesturing between us back and forth.

"We'll see."

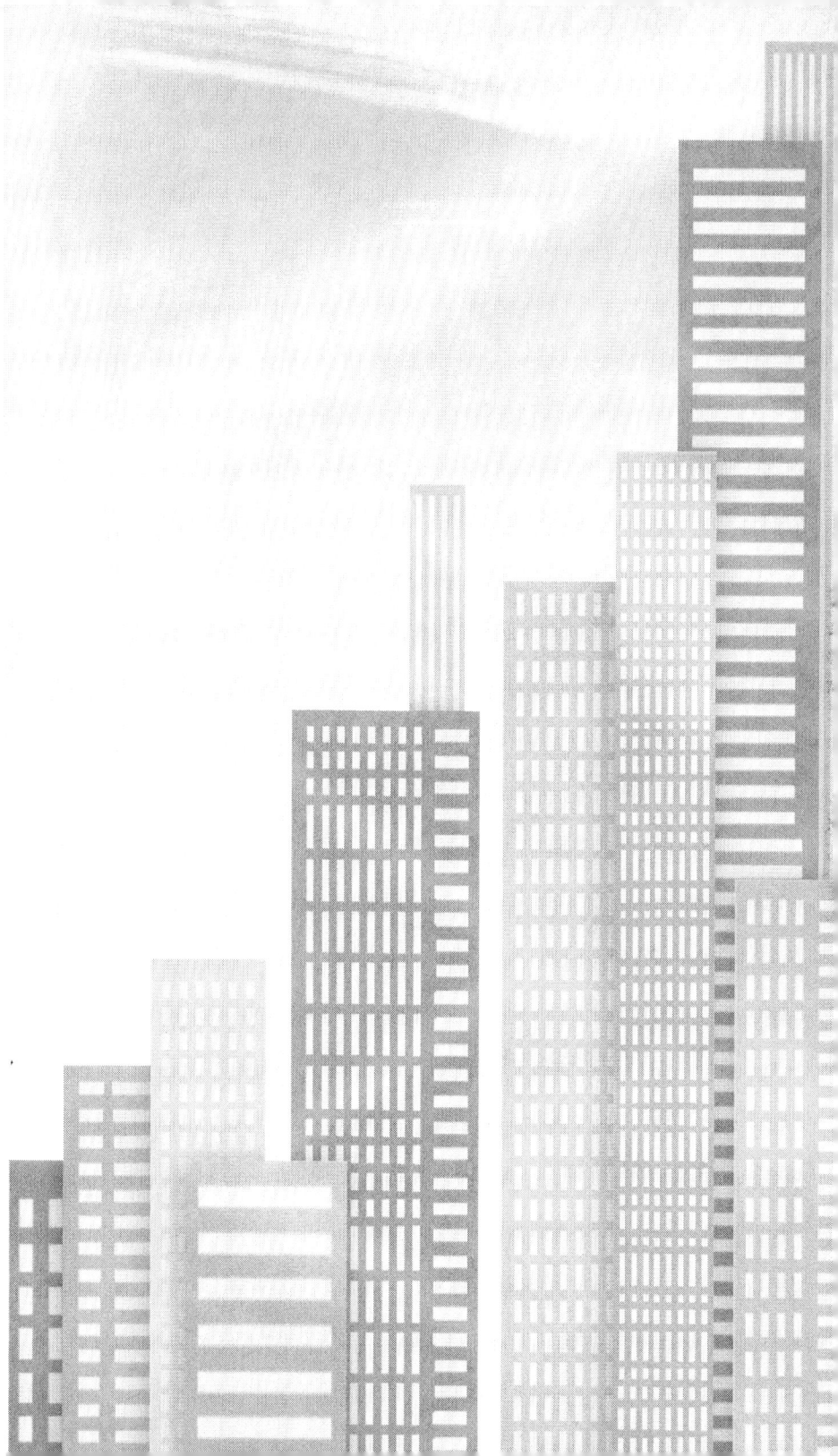

is_new_chapter = True

chapter_number = "29"

pov_name = "Alexander"

THE DRIVE TO ANDREA'S PLACE is eerily silent. Tension lingers in the air, and I use this time lost in my thoughts as I reflect on my actions. The novelty of her comes with ups and downs, and while the ups are exhilarating, I'm not good at handling the downs.

Expecting that she respects our agreement isn't ridiculous, is it? We agreed on exclusivity. I'm the only man she should be seeing, the only one she should welcome in her bed.

I park close to her building, and although I expect her to get out when I turn off the engine, she doesn't. "Do you want to come in rather than wait in the car?" she hesitantly offers.

I nod without a word, and we exit the car. Our ride up in the elevator is just as silent, and I can't bring myself to break it. I observe her nervousness when her hands tremble as she unlocks her door. We enter, and I discover the space with genuine interest. The main door opens to a short hallway, and then we step into the main space.

"So, living room, kitchen, and those doors are Tamika, bathroom, me," she explains. "Just give me five minutes, and we can go."

As she heads to her room, I venture into the apartment. My feet lead me to a shelf filled with trinkets, and I can easily guess which things are hers and which are Tamika's. Andrea's fondness for pop culture contrasts with her roommate's pastel aesthetic.

I distractedly listen to her shuffle in her room as I explore some more. When I notice that my nose, throat, and eyes seem slightly irritated by something, I ask with a clear voice, "Do you have a cat?"

"We kept one for a few days. Why?" she answers from her room.

"My allergy is acting up. I was wondering if it was normal."

"Oh … The cat never came into my room, if you want to—" She stops abruptly when she sees I'm already there, standing in the doorframe. There must be something on my face that triggers her apprehension because she asks, "What?"

Looking away, I nervously scratch my jaw to give myself time to think. I shouldn't say a fucking thing, but my stomach has been in knots since she mentioned him.

"Who is Idris?" I demand.

Surprise flashes on her pretty face. "Nothing. Ignore it."

"He's obviously not 'nothing' since you were about to spend the weekend with him."

She rolls her eyes, displeased by my insistence. Can she blame me for it, though? Doesn't she think I'm entitled to an answer?

"Isn't my word that I'm not sleeping around enough, Lex? Don't you trust me?" she asks.

The problem isn't trust. The problem is that as potent as this thing between us feels, it's flimsy at best. It won't take her long before she remembers we're not meant to get along and moves on to someone better than me. And the more men she allows near her, the faster it'll happen. And then what? I return to my boring, joyless life?

When I try to talk, my throat is tight with nervousness and anguish. "I'm not—It's not the—"

I pause, cursing my uncooperative tongue. Words rarely fail me, but I can't conjure one that could salvage this.

Something that resembles pity passes in her eyes. Without a word, she walks up to her nightstand and opens a drawer. She retrieves something small and pink from it and throws it toward me. I instinctively grab it as it lands on my chest. It's a sex toy—the kind that only focuses on the clitoris.

"This is Idris," she explains, her voice suddenly soft and compassionate. "Idris has been the only 'man' in my life, besides you, for almost a year."

For a moment, I feel like the dumbest piece of shit that ever lived. That's not something I'm used to.

But when I look at her and see the genuine care in her eyes and how hard she's trying to respect my feelings and appease my fears, another kind of emotion takes over. One that has my chest tightening so hard that I can barely breathe.

I'm falling in love with this woman.

How could I not?

She stands there in her overalls and red sweater, having just thrown her sex toy at me. There's not a doubt in my mind that she's the most authentic, true-to-herself person I've ever met. She's an open book, and I feel normal around her because she's so easy to read she might as well have subtitles.

From the moment I met her, she's always shown who she was, always been herself. And while some of it took a bit of time to grow on me, I now adore every single part she's shown me, from her impulsivity to her insecurities.

Oblivious to the havoc wreaking my mind, she comes closer, still adamant about clearing the air between us.

"You need to trust me, Lex. I believe you when you say you won't see anyone else, even though you probably have a swarm of willing women at your feet. The fact that you can't bring yourself to believe me is honestly hurtful, and it will drive me away."

"I believe you," I finally state.

I'm apparently not as convincing as I thought because she feels the need to step closer and say, "Lex, I've never been fucked as good as you do. I won't sleep around."

"There's more to life than sex. And you don't even like me as a person."

Despite the seriousness of the moment, she smiles. "I don't like you very much when you accuse me of doing things in the dark with Oli. But otherwise, you're growing on me."

"Hm … I suppose the exposure therapy is working."

"It really is. So much that even if I had men lining up at my door, I'd still choose you, *baby*," she concludes, hooking her arms around my neck. The endearment has the same effect as when she first used it. My entire chest goes warm at it, small fireworks going off in my head.

"Even if I'm a possessive jerk?" I ask.

"As long as you're *my* possessive jerk and you trust me, yes."

I lower enough to give her a tender kiss. "I trust you."

As if to seal the promise, she rises to her toes and kisses me harder. The following embrace is tender, sensual, and longing. We take our time, enjoying the moment and the closeness. Her proximity, warmth, and bed a few feet from us make me crave her.

I'm not the only one feeling that way since she pushes against me to make me sit on the mattress. She takes her sex toy from my distracted grip and throws it back into its drawer.

"Take your shirt off," she commands, turning around to get something from her closet. I comply, unbuttoning my shirt. When she returns with a pair of scarves, I immediately understand what she has in mind. Really? Now?

"My bed, my rules," she says, sensing my reluctance.

"I don't think watching a movie is the best idea right now."

"We're not watching a movie," she counters, her voice husky and sensual.

I'm about to refuse when something in her eyes stops me. This isn't just a sex thing. This is about showing her I'm willing to be vulnerable and trust she won't abuse it. About surrendering and letting go of the control I cherish. About letting her do to me something no one else has ever done.

"I promise you won't regret it," she tries.

"I highly doubt that."

Despite my words, I finish removing my shirt, let it fall to the floor, and center myself on the bed. The gratitude on her face already makes whatever's about to happen worth it.

I'm anxious the whole time she ties my wrists to the bedposts. She's meticulous, ensuring the restraints aren't too tight and making knots that can be removed easily.

"Is it alright?" she asks once it's done. I tug, writhe, and nod.

Satisfied with herself, she takes a couple of steps back and admires her work. The look of pure lust on her face is impossible to miss.

"Do you remember our safe word?" she asks as she slowly removes her overalls, pushing them down her legs and kicking them to the side.

I nod, mesmerized by her sensuality. I almost, *almost* wish she still had that ridiculous mustache on because it would have helped contain my arousal, which is already climbing dangerously high.

"Then say it for me," she demands.

My throat is dry as I mumble, "Pigasus."

To reward me for my cooperation, she then removes the red sweater, and what she reveals underneath has me cursing under my breath. She's wearing a lacy ensemble, the same red as her sweater, and it's the first time I see her in proper lingerie. I can see the dark circles of her nipples, as well as the triangle of curls between her thighs, and my hands tingle with the need to touch her.

"Fuck, you're gorgeous," I grunt, pulling on the restraints and sighing with displeasure. "I'm already regretting agreeing to this."

My suffering amuses her, and she crawls on the bed to straddle me.

"Hi," she murmurs, bending down to kiss me.

I barely get a graze of her lips before they follow an imaginary line down my upper body. She tortures me, kissing, biting, and licking an irregular pattern on my exposed skin. When she reaches a flat nipple, she lingers longer, licking and blowing cool air on it until it hardens. I'm sure she can feel my cock twitching underneath her, because it's so hard I can feel a pulse in it. After mirroring her ministrations to the other side, she resumes her exploration south. When her mouth gets to my belt, she gives me a sultry look as she unbuckles it.

Fuck, fuck, fuck, fuck.

I need to cool the fuck down, or I'll come as soon as I enter her.

She might be in charge, but I can't let that happen.

pov_name = "Andrea"

As I open Lex's slacks, all I can think of is how crazy it is that I never gave him a blowjob. I guess we're always busy doing other things. The suspense ends tonight, though, and I'll finally know how it feels to have Lex explode on my tongue. At least, I will if I can make him come with a blowjob. Which I'm not extraordinary at.

My lack of self-confidence hits me at once, and I hesitate, Lex's half-opened zipper between my fingers. He's incredible at oral sex, and I fear I'll disappoint him with my mediocre skills. The memory of the last time I went down on a guy returns to me. *At least you have a nice ass to compensate …*

Tears well up in my eyes before I can stop them, and Lex catches my sudden dismay.

"What's going on?"

"I-I lied when I joked that my head 'never had any complaints,'" I explain. He frowns, not sure what to answer. "I'm not good at it, but I can get better. You can teach me what you like, and I'll do my best." A frustrated tear runs down my cheek, and I angrily wipe it. "I promise I'll try, Lex."

Why didn't I practice more? Lex deserves someone who can match his experience. Someone who can blow his mind as much as he blows mine. Pun intended.

"To hell with these fucking scarves," he growls, trying to get free and making the bed rattle. "Andrea, there's no way your lips on me could ever feel wrong. But in any case, practice makes perfect, right? I'm a patient man."

"What if I never become good at it?"

"Then it doesn't matter. There are other things. I've never enjoyed sex as much as I do with you."

My eyes widen at the revelation. "Wait, how on earth am *I* your best lay?"

"I don't know how to explain it. I can't stop wanting you, and when I have you, I only want more. You're constantly on my mind."

"Are you lying to me to make me feel better?" I dubiously ask.

"That's really not my style." True, Lex isn't one to lie to preserve someone's feelings.

"Tell me gently if I'm doing something you don't like, okay?"

"I don't see what you could do that I wouldn't thoroughly enjoy. Except maybe bite me."

I giggle, truly reassured. I'm not bad to the point where I'd bite down on his dick.

With my confidence restored, I finish opening his zipper. Time to see if he has Nintendo-themed underwear.

To my great dissatisfaction, it's just black boxer briefs. The hard-as-fuck dick underneath doesn't disappoint, though. My discontented pout makes him smile broadly. God, he truly is the most gorgeous man I will ever see.

"This is the first time a woman has reacted so poorly to what she found in my pants," he jokes, a little cocky.

Then he taps his shoes together behind me with a mischievous smile. *Oh God, he didn't!* Because I can't miss an opportunity to tease the shit out of him, I straddle him the other way and bend in a way that surely gives him a glorious view of my ass.

He growls something, and the bed protests as he pulls on his restraints. This is so much fun. Once his shoes come off, it all makes sense. He's wearing Mario socks.

"Did you buy them just for me?" I ask, twisting around to meet his eyes.

"I thought you might like them, yes."

I move back to straddle him forward-facing and thank him with a passionate kiss. Is it stupid of me to find it so adorable? God, how I adore him.

"Look at us … I wear sexy lingerie for you, and you wear geeky socks for me. And we kind of had matching outfits."

The following kiss is somehow different from all the others we've ever shared. There's a profound longing, a lazy amorousness that makes our gestures languorous and patient. It's the intense clenching of my core that forces me to stop. My slim fingers slide under the waistband of his pants before tugging at it. He helps me, raising himself, as I pull them down, along with his boxers. His dick springs out to rest hard and long on his lower abdomen, pointing to his navel.

"I think I'll have you entirely naked, with only your socks on."

"Don't you dare."

"What if I *do* dare?"

"Walker, you don't want to know."

My pussy pulses at the threat, knowing perfectly well I'd love whatever punishment he'd cleverly come up with.

"How about this? I'll take your socks off, but you still do to me whatever you have in mind?"

His eyes become almost entirely black, and I quench my victorious grin. I'm becoming very good at getting to him. With avid movements, I remove his pants, socks, and boxers, throw the messy bunch on the floor next to us, and come back on top of him, low enough to level my head with his incredible erection. Trying to display confidence I'm not feeling, I circle his swollen girth with my fingers and gently massage it, locking my eyes on his.

"How are you always so hard for me, Alexander?" He groans and fists the restraints, his knuckles turning white.

Mischievously, I bend to bring my mouth closer to him. He waits, absolutely unmoving, and I find the moment strangely empowering. I'm still caressing him up and down with my hand when a clear stream of precum escapes the tip of his dick to roll down on it.

This is too tempting to miss, so I lick it up his rigid length, ending with a kiss underneath its round head, making him curse under his breath. The salty taste spreads on my tongue, and I hum appreciatively. Lex is about to become my favorite flavor.

Feeling amorous, I move along his impressive size, kissing and licking, following the veins with my tongue, giving special attention to the crease under the tip while I fondle his heavy sack with my hand.

I can hear the strained breaths he lets out, the wood of the bed protest when he pulls on the ties, and see his abs flex. I'm definitely doing something right.

"Since we agreed on honesty, I have to say I don't particularly enjoy being tormented like this."

As if to disprove what he just said, another clear drop seeps out of his tip. I dutifully lick it clean, enjoying his salty tang once more, and send him a dubious smile. "Betrayed by your own body. Must be tough for you, Coleman."

"Andrea, you will regret this when it's my turn to tie you up."

"You need to win a bet for that first."

"That, or I could just—Ah, fuck!"

I don't let him finish his threat, finally welcoming him in my mouth. It's only the tip at first, my tongue rolling around his swollen head while my hand pumps him from his base to my pursed lips. I try to recall everything I read in Cosmopolitan and on the internet. No teeth, suction, breathe through the nose, use spit, focus on the underside of the tip, eye contact … It's a lot to think of at once.

Hopefully my enthusiasm will make up for my lack of practice. I sheath my teeth with my lips and take more of him in. With a languid rhythm, I bob my head up and down, running my tongue across the veiny skin, as smooth as satin. My cheeks are hollowed out, my eyes fixed on his, and I'm greedy to feel his pleasure burst out in my mouth.

"Fuck, yes … Just like that," he groans. His face is red from my tormenting ministrations.

I must be quite the sight, with his thick length moving in and out of my mouth, because Lex moans, "I want to touch you. This is fucking torture."

With a pop, I let his dick out of my mouth to gaze up and say, "It's my moment, so deal with it, Coleman."

Enthusiastically, I take him in my mouth again and suck on his cock harder, enjoying every frustrated and desperate sound that escapes him. A little too ardent, I increase the pace, still pumping his base with my fist.

He jolts under me with a slight hiss. "Andrea, teeth."

Fuck. Moving up until he's out of my mouth, I offer him a confounded grimace. "Sorry …"

"It's okay. You're doing great so far."

When I take him in again, I force my jaw to open wider so I don't risk grazing his tender skin again. I swallow as much of him as I can, reveling in his unique taste and texture on my tongue.

It's frustrating to not have all of it, though. The part that doesn't reach past my lips is taunting me, defying me to do better. I've never tried to go further than what the inside of my mouth can hold. Before Lex, blowjobs were a necessary duty, something I never found appealing. Right now, though, it's as exhilarating as when I'm on the receiving end of his ministrations. I feel powerful instead of diminished.

He's obviously enjoying my efforts, and it gives me the courage to try to take it further. Settling more comfortably, I let Lex's dick glide as far as it can—about halfway in. When I open my throat and push further, the sensation of his cock in my esophagus is foreign. It isn't comfortable, but it's more than bearable.

Little by little, I take more of him, moving slightly up and lowering further every time. My eyes are closed to focus on my gag reflex and not puke all over him. To my great surprise, my nose reaches the trimmed hair of his lower abdomen. I'm less than an inch away from having it all in my mouth.

Because I've never had a reason to shove something down my throat, I'm only noticing now that I don't have an overwhelmingly sensitive gag reflex. Amazed to have realized that, I look up at Lex, moving back slowly, and then I swallow all of him again, forcing myself down until my lips reach the base of his length. He's positively helpless, his gorgeous face veiled with lust and desire.

"Andrea, I feel useless," he argues. "Untie me so I can at least return the favor."

Ignoring his pleas, I deepthroat him, feeling like a sex goddess. A little too enthusiastic, I trigger some gagging, which forces me to stop moving. Lex grunts, and given his rapturous expression, I understand my throat spasming around him must feel good. When it passes, I carefully resume my movements.

My jaw becomes sore, and I grow lightheaded, so I move on to his balls for a moment, pumping his cock with my hand as I do. I lick the thin skin and gently suck on them, taking as much as I can in the warmth of my mouth.

"Woman, you fucking lied."

"About what?" I ask, releasing his ball to move on to the other.

"You're incredible at this." Joy and pride have my head spinning with delight. "I don't want to come like this, but I can't hold back much longer. You have to stop."

As much as I want to feel his dick inside of me, I would rather make him come like this. I'm about to discover the taste of his cum, to feel it spurt out down my throat, to swallow it …

I adamantly take him in my mouth again, showing so much enthusiasm he can't ignore what I want.

"Fucking hell," he curses, making the headboard crack when he pulls on the scarves like a possessed man.

"If you break my bed, I'll bite you."

Following my sweet threat, I shove him down my throat again. Little by little, he loses his internal battle. His hips roll sinuously as he pushes himself further into my mouth.

"Andrea, I'm about to come." I suck harder, taking him further. "I'm serious. If you don't want it in your mouth, you have to stop now."

I move up to only keep the tip in my mouth, sweeping my tongue on the sensitive underside of it while I pump him with my hand. It slides easily on his skin, glistening with my spit as I jerk him off at a fast pace. He mumbles an endless chain of curses until a moan escapes his lips. Spurts of his pleasure shoot into my throat, warm and thick on my tongue.

My clit pulses with enthusiasm as his cum fills my mouth, his eyes looking at me intently the whole time. He tastes good, but then again, Lex never does anything poorly or average.

With hollowed cheeks and my busy hand, I push him as far as I can, taking all he has to offer. Once he gives me everything, I straighten up with my mouth full of his cum, and meet his unfocused gaze. Feeling wicked, I slowly swallow, wipe my mouth with my index in case any of it spilled, and then suck it clean.

I don't think I've ever felt prouder than when I slowly crawl my way up his perfect body on my hands and knees until I'm straddling him. Because I know it's a hang-up for some men, I won't force a kiss on him, despite how much I want one, so my mouth hovers near his lips, letting him decide what he wants. He surprises me when he takes what

I offer with unmasked hunger. We unabashedly share his taste, our tongues familiar and greedy. There isn't an ounce of toxic masculinity in this man.

After a moment, I move away, breathless. "I think I enjoyed that even more than you did."

"Impossible."

To prove my words, I press the dripping lace covering my pussy on the bare plane of his stomach.

An animalistic growl rolls in his chest, and he kisses my neck. "I'll return the favor if you untie me."

I long to comply, but I also enjoy having him tied up. It's great to see the almighty Lex not so domineering anymore. I'm in a conundrum until my inexperienced brain thinks of a perfect solution.

"Nice try, but you don't need your hands for that."

Very proud of myself, I slide my panties down my legs and move up, ready to get into a more suited position. When he understands what I have in mind, a naughty smile stretches his lips.

"You will be my doom," he says.

"And you will be mine."

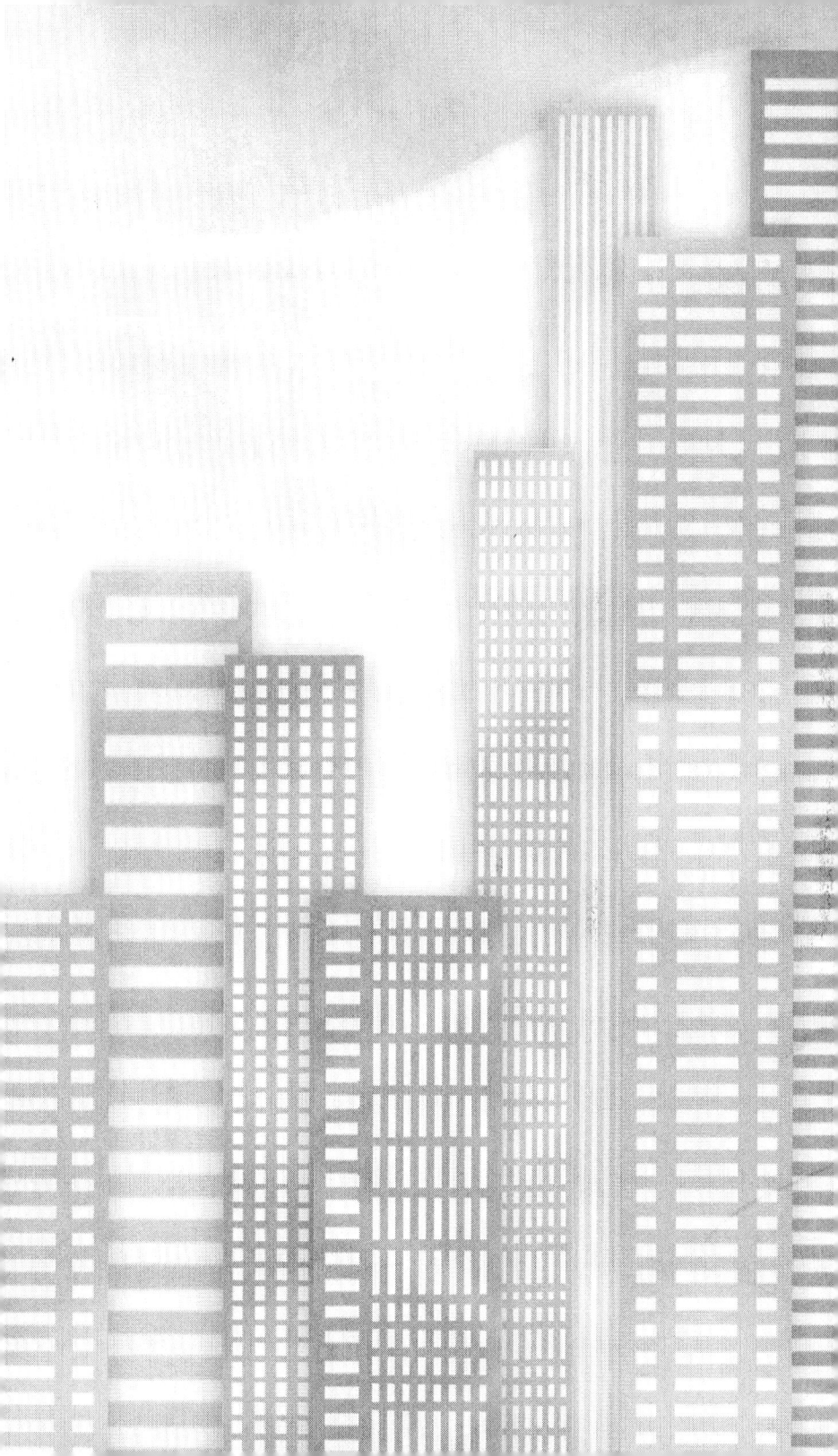

is_new_chapter = True

chapter_number =

"30"

pou_name =

"Alexander"

Andrea decided to test my stamina tonight. And how much her bed's headboard can take before it breaks.

But she looks so pleased with herself as she crawls up my body that I wouldn't change a thing. Being in charge has her shining with confidence, and I love seeing it.

And the fucking view I get when she sets her knees on each side of my head is spectacular. I groan at the sight, sensing my cock twitch.

"You weren't kidding. You're all swollen and open for me. And fucking dripping."

"I enjoyed it a lot, yes."

"You'll enjoy this even more." I have to lift my head to give her clit a small kiss, which makes her jolt and grip the headboard. "Now sit, Andrea, don't hover."

"I don't want to suffocate you."

"You won't."

"Lex, I'm not explaining 'death by vagina' to a coroner."

I chuckle and stretch again for a lick along her slit. Her taste is heaven … "If that happens, just know I died a happy man," I humor. "Now, smother me with that beautiful cunt of yours, Andrea."

She complies just a little. I reward her with long laps to clean off the excess wetness. Then my tongue curls around the needy bud of her clit, but since she isn't sitting on my face yet, I make it light enough to drive her mad. She gives up with a moany protest, and I finally allow myself to feast on her.

As I fuck her from below with my tongue and lips, she writhes and jolts, hands clasped around the edge of the headboard. I nearly lose it when she takes her bra off and fondles her small tits with her hands, pinching her nipples, rolling them between her fingers. That's my job, but my hands are still fucking tied.

Even in this situation, though, I manage to regain some control. I still get pleas out of her as she rides my face, keeping her balanced between pleasure and frustration. I withdraw, slow down, change the pressure … On more than one occasion, she begs me to let her come.

When she can't take the edging anymore, her fingers tightly clutch my hair as she fucks my face. She comes with a shaky cry, her legs trembling from the intense pleasure. When the sensation becomes too much and she pushes herself up, I bark, "Stay down."

She only hesitates for a second before following my command and lowering again. I stretch her orgasm to the borders of tolerable, and then I give her mercy, slowly lapping as she comes down.

I give one last kiss to her satiated pussy and let my head fall back with a satisfied sigh. Her limbs shake as she gets off my face to lie by my side. Using a corner of the sheets, she wipes away the wetness on my lower face and gives me a short but intense kiss.

"Can I be untied now?" I ask. I'm not begging, but almost.

The mischievous glimmer in her eyes tells me she isn't done with me yet. "Where's your wallet?" she asks.

When I understand why, my head falls back on the pillow. *Shit.* "It's in my jacket, in the car."

"Fuck … I don't know where Tamika keeps her condoms—if she has any."

"If you untie me, I'll go get one," I offer.

She scrunches her nose, disliking the idea. I lie there, useless, as her pretty little head thinks of her options while her fingers gently graze my erection. When she decides what she wants to do, she looks at me with a flirtatious smile and lifts herself to get on top of me. I'm still confused when she kisses me tenderly and grinds her wet folds onto my length.

Only when she aligns my round tip at her entrance do I understand what she has in mind. We're doing it raw, dismissing the use of a condom. Those were always a part of sex for me, first to prevent unwanted pregnancies, and then as a barrier for diseases and infections. Because I've never been in a committed relationship, I've never allowed myself to enter a woman without one.

So, I've been waiting for this for a while—not only with her but also my entire sexual life.

Which is why I refuse to do it helplessly bound like this, unable to fully enjoy it.

Just as she's about to lower herself onto me, I blurt out, "Wait! I'm not doing this tied up, Andrea."

There must be something in my voice or eyes that convinces her to untie me this time. She frees my right hand first, which I rest on her hip while she takes care of the left one. As soon as she's done, I pull her in for a long and thorough kiss, hands caressing and fondling her curves to make up for lost time.

She allows me to roll us around until I'm on top of her. I reach for my cock and press its tip on her wet cunt, making her moan and arch into me. It's as though the surrounding air turns electric, and the earth stops spinning. Something meaningful is about to happen, and time itself has gone still.

"Are you sure?" I ask, meeting her sparkly eyes. With a confident smile, she nods and gives me an encouraging peck on the lips.

Still somewhat anxious, I increase the pressure on her opening, and the heavenly sensation that follows has me clenching my teeth. Fuck, she feels even warmer like this, and the texture of her drenched walls is incredible around my cock. I take my time, slowly sinking in, savoring it. And there is so much to be savored …

The artificial sleekness of the latex is gone, so it's all her—all tight, and wet, and soft … It's so much more organic like this, so intimate.

"Fuck, this is amazing," I grunt roughly. "You feel so good."

"You too …"

I've waited fifteen years for this moment. And as I pull out and thrust back in, I know I'd wait fifteen more years just so I'd get to experience it first with her.

The woman I'm slowly but unavoidably falling in love with.

pov_name =

"Andrea"

MUFFLING A DESPERATE MOAN INTO the humid crook of Lex's neck, I spread my legs wider, demanding more. He lowers down, and the entirety of him sinks into me. Then he begins a sensual roll of his hips, filling and emptying me with a maddening fervor despite his slow pace. Already, pleasure grows within me, the promise of its heights making me fear I might lose myself tonight. Beneath him, I arch my hips in rhythm with his and lift my knees higher to his sides.

With my hands, I explore the firm shapes of his back, following its tense muscles, sometimes remaining on his round ass, inviting him to go deeper. I can feel the voluptuous movements of his body, and it makes me crazy. He has some sweet moves for a white boy.

It's insane how even missionary feels like an adventurous position with him. He does everything with skill and commitment. I'm all but drowning in his eyes, and what I see in them confuses me. He admires me with a mix of wonderment, adoration, and affection. It's too much. I can't help but have hope when he stares at me like this.

Intense waves of tenderness and conflicting feelings overwhelm me, and I don't know how to handle them. My chest swells, the ache of it painful yet delightful. It's like I can't hold everything I'm feeling, but I welcome all those emotions.

Tears gather in the corners of my eyes, which I fear he might misread. So, I kiss him, and he gladly falls for it, our tongues tangling passionately. My whimpering moans land in his mouth, echoing his heavy breaths and occasional grunts.

We've never had sex like this, with such intensity and care, or so many emotions passing between us … He's taking me with poignant devotion, his rhythm unhurried and intense, as if we have the entire night.

The truth of what's happening suddenly hits me. We aren't fucking or having sex.

We're making love.

Lex is making love to me.

The realization sends a plethora of conflicted feelings through me, and to my surprise, it triggers my orgasm. A cry passes from my lips to his, my body contracting from the pleasure. He slows down as I shatter, my hands desperately clinging onto his back, my short nails probably leaving red marks over his tanned skin.

Lex accompanies me, from the highest delights to the slow climb down, holding me tight against him. When my shivers regress, his lips come to rest on my temple as I press my forehead on his shoulder, my breathy moans now getting lost somewhere between us. The entire time, I'm aware that all my wetness is directly coating him, making it even better. It's all for him.

When my head falls back onto the pillow, Lex uses my relaxed state to drop pecks as light as feathers on my flushed face. He kisses every spot he can think of—between my eyebrows, my temples, the tip of my nose, my closed eyelids, the corners of my mouth … His tenderness adds to the swelling sensation in my chest to the point where it becomes almost unbearable.

It isn't right to be feeling all of this. We're still far from the end of our trial period. I can't fall for him so fast and so hard.

His kissing endeavor ends, so I slowly peel my eyes open to marvel at his perfect face. "Hi," he says with a charming smile.

"Hi."

My shy, exhausted reply earns me an indulging chuckle. "Ready for the next one?"

"Since when do you bother asking?"

"You just seem overwhelmed." With a delicate hand, he brushes away my sweaty bangs. "Are you alright?"

No, I'm not.

I'm falling in love with you.

"Yeah. I really enjoy having you in my bed, that's all," I lie.

"I really enjoy having you anywhere."

His amusement is contagious, and when our lips meet again, they're bent into grins. He attempts a few careful thrusts to ensure I'm good to keep going, and I spur him on by pulling him closer and writhing my hips under his. Following my encouragement, his momentum picks up.

"You can't fathom how badly I want to come inside of you," he grunts in my ear, giving me a deeper thrust. "I want to pump you full of my cum, so you'll keep some of me with you for days."

My insides clench around him, and I helplessly moan. On Monday, after this weekend of condomless sex, I'll be sitting in the office, where no one could ever guess what we did, but Lex and I will know. When we cross paths, we'll know some of his pleasure remains inside me.

"I want it too," I confess with a hoarse voice. "I want to walk around with your cum still in me and be constantly reminded that you came over and over inside my pussy, that you left it overflowing and overused."

My words affect him further than I intended, and he swears before hastening his pace. His tender lovemaking slowly shifts into something rougher. It's easier this way. I can handle fucking, but lovemaking is conflicting.

Seconds stretch into minutes as he plunges harshly in and out of me. His sweaty skin looks oiled like an actual Greek deity. My throat grows sore from all the cries and moans, my inner thighs aching from being spread open so widely. I know he's reaching his climax when he sends a hand between us to jumpstart my orgasm.

"Aah … baby, yes!" I'm about to come harder than ever.

It only takes a few rolls of his thumb over my clit for me to explode. I cry, arch, tremble … Shivers and jolts crawl through my body, my whole frame tense despite how light I feel at this very moment.

My insides quiver around him, bringing him to his climax. He moans in my damp hair and tenses on top of me, his hips buckling to go as deep as he can. I feel his pleasure spurt out inside me, filling me up with everything he has.

I hold him tightly, enjoying his increasing weight on my exhausted body. These moments are almost as enjoyable as the sex itself. I adore this vulnerability, these brief minutes where we're both at our weakest, supporting and holding onto each other.

We slowly regain our senses, and Lex pushes himself up enough to stare at me with another one of his confusingly intense gazes. Without a word, he kisses me tenderly before pulling out. He rolls away to lie by my side and pensively stares at the ceiling.

Because I'm not ready to let go yet, I roll against him and lay my head on his broad chest, hooking an arm and a leg over him. Lex moves to accommodate the new position and passes his arm around me, the tip of his finger drawing mindless swirls on my naked shoulder.

We stay like this for a while, in the aftermath of our mind-blowing sex, enjoying the silence. The whole evening was an emotional roller-coaster, from arguing about trust to proving how much we trust each other.

"Do you think I'm a bad dancer?" I ask out of the blue, remembering the moment in the Troll's Lair.

"I found you fascinating to look at. But then, I often think that when it comes to you, so I might not be the best judge."

His answer delights me beyond words, especially when I witness the genuineness in his gaze. Feeling amorous, I snuggle closer to him. *God, I wish we could stay like this forever.*

Alas, life has other plans.

"We should go before it gets late," Lex suggests. I frown and pout, reluctant to let go. "Come on. We'll be just as comfortable in my bed."

I groan and tighten my hold on him. "I still have to pack my things."

"Do it while I shower," he orders, ripping himself away from me after a quick kiss on my forehead. "We'll stop for some food on the way. I'm starving."

The mention of food stops me from complaining, and then he stands up and stretches, which incapacitates my ability to form thoughts. His ass is out of this world. And for some reason, I really like seeing the red marks I clawed all over his back, from his shoulders to low on his ribcage. He exits my room, so I force myself out of bed, trying to think about what I should take for this weekend. Clothes will be kind of optional.

I barely take one step before my door suddenly opens. Lex quickly returns in before slamming it shut, mumbling an endless series of "Fuck," and hiding his junk behind his cupped hand.

"What's going on?" I worriedly ask.

"Your roommate is home."

My eyes become wide, and my mouth drops open in shock.

Shit, Tamika told me she'd go clubbing after the party. But she's here. And she saw Lex coming out of my room.

Naked.

This isn't good at all.

With my heart pounding, I try to think rationally and decide what we should do. Lex is just as shocked, still hiding his junk.

"Are you sure she saw you?" I ask, fully hoping he noticed her before she could.

"I can assure you she did."

"Did she recognize you?"

"The level of shock in her eyes was from knowing you're fucking your boss rather than just having a man in your room," he frustratedly explains. "Fucking hell. I just exposed myself to one of my employees."

"Another one, you mean."

"Now's not the time for being clever, Andrea."

"I know … Fuck," I whimper, grabbing the first shirt I can find. I slip it on hastily while Lex gets his pants. When I check the clock on my nightstand, everything makes sense.

"We've been here for over two hours!?" Shit, we messed up big time. "What the hell are we going to tell her? I'm not ready for this. I thought we'd have more time before—"

My words die abruptly at the unmistakable sensation of semen dripping from me.

"What?" Lex asks, noticing my momentary distress.

"You're … leaking."

My cheeks burn at the admission while Lex frowns, needing a second to understand my meaning. When he does, his eyes drop to the apex of my thighs, and his pupils dilate. Oh, he really likes the image. In two steps, he's standing right before me, adamantly reaching down to run his hand up the inside of my thigh.

All notions of Tami are pushed far back into my mind as his fingers slowly slide up to gather the trail of cum there. Then, he shoves it back inside me with two thick knuckles. His gestures are experimental more than sexual, even when he thrusts his fingers inside me to feel how he's coating my walls, to experience the sensation of his semen filling me.

"Lex," I rasp. "I need to go handle Tami."

He releases me, gazing down at his glistening fingers, and then looks back up. "What will you tell her?"

"I don't know yet. But she's a good friend. She won't gossip if I ask her not to."

"I can leave you two alone and wait for you in the car," he offers, wiping his hand on the side of his pants before he gets his shirt.

With a wince, I offer him an apologetic look. "It's not a five-minute talk. And she just learned we're having an affair. She'll be shocked to see we're in this deep enough to spend the weekend together."

His gestures as he slips his shirt on are harsh but precise. When he's done buttoning it, I can see how much he dislikes this change of plans. I slip on a pair of jogging pants before going to him.

"I'm sorry," I say, hooking my arms around his neck. "I swear we'll find another time for it. But I can't take the risk of Tamika not understanding." He's still silent, which makes me realize how much he looked forward to this weekend together. "I'll make it up to you."

He finally reacts by wrapping his arms around me to hold me close. "Next weekend, you're mine." I fight the urge to tell him I'm his every day of the week. "And Wednesday, you come home with me."

I nod, agreeing to his terms, and we exchange a quick kiss.

Tamika is on the couch when we come out. She stares at us with confusion and shock, and I can't help but grimace. Lex gives her an awkward hand wave as I accompany him to the door. With a heavy heart, I open it for him. During a few silent seconds, he stands in the doorway, the regret in his eyes crushing my soul.

"I'll see you on Monday, then," he says, bending for a kiss.

I recoil out of habit, slightly distressed. Lex fails to hide his irritation. Shit, I'm not handling this well. "I'll call you tomorrow," I say, squeezing his arm.

Without another word, he's out. As I watch him walk away, a twinge of guilt twists my guts. Shit, I can't let him go like this. I impulsively rush after him, barefoot.

"Lex, wait!" I call. He stops and turns around, surprised.

Before he can anticipate it, I throw myself in his arms and bring him in for a long and intense goodbye kiss. He's going home alone because of me; I'm not denying him one last embrace.

I move away from him and give him an affectionate smile. "Talk to you tomorrow," I promise before returning to my door. He's still standing there when I'm back inside, so I shoo him with a hand gesture. A silent laugh, a shake of his head, and he walks away.

"I'll shower, and then we can talk," I sign to Tami once I return inside. There's no escaping it, so, following a long shower to rinse Lex off of me and a change of clothes, I dismiss my cowardice and sit cross-legged in the armchair opposite her.

She must have already thought of what she wants to ask first because she doesn't waste a second to raise her hands and sign, "Is he the man you've been seeing?" I nod. "When did it start?"

"We first kissed on the evening we celebrated the sale of my app. We started having sex the night I went MIA."

"So it's not been that long. Does anyone else know?"

"Only Kate, I think. Maybe Kevin," I admit.

"Are you going to tell people?"

"We're waiting to see how it goes first."

"And how has it been going?"

"It's been … ups and downs. It's complicated, with work and all. Lex is also a very complex person."

"I can imagine that," she signs with humor. She takes a short break, thinking of what to ask next. "Do you like him?"

The question surprises me, even though it's to be expected. "I really do. He can be very sweet and touching. I love spending time with him, outside of … you know."

"I would never have imagined you two being a thing, but now I kinda see it," she eventually signs. "I would ask how the sex is, but you're practically limping." She's mischievous when she signs the rest. "And I saw what he's working with, you lucky girl."

I blush profusely, embarrassed to have such details about my sex life out in the open. Tami isn't usually this bold, but I can tell she's still a little intoxicated from the Kelex party.

"Could you not tell anyone?" I sign with pleading eyes. "People will assume I'm doing this because he's my boss, or he's taking advantage of me … That sort of thing."

"But you'll have to tell people at some point, no?"

"Yes, but I want to make sure it's for something solid, not a passing fling. I can endure the judging looks if I have something worth fighting for."

"I get it," she signs with a sympathetic smile. "I'm so glad I ditched the club. This is so much better."

We talk for a while longer, and Tamika asks me a few more questions. I don't want to make it weird for her or Lex, so I keep the details to a minimum. Then it's time to sleep, and we go to our respective rooms.

Once I'm back in mine, I wince at the messy state of my bed. The scarves are still tied to the bedposts, the covers are rumpled and undone, and there's a patch of wetness in the middle of it. Shit, he made me soak the sheets.

Just so it's not only because I'm lazy, I tell myself I'll change the bedding in the morning so I can sleep with Lex's scent etched to my sheets. It's so potent that when I slip under the covers, I can almost imagine he's right there with me. And it makes me regret not going with him to his place, as intended.

Before I know what I'm doing, I'm calling him on my phone. It rings for a while, and I want to hang up more with each tone. I'm being clingy. Before the fourth tone is over, I cut the call. *Needy much?*

The phone vibrates several seconds later, startling me a little. I answer it with a smile. "Hi."

"Hi. Sorry, I was in the shower," he says.

"No problem, I just wanted to make sure you got home alright."

"You worry about me, Walker?"

"I'd hate to lose my amazing job because something happened to my boss," I tease. He chuckles low, and I swoon. "I wish I could have come with you."

"Yeah, me too. How did it go with Tamika?"

"Pretty well. She's delighted to have seen you in the nude and thinks it gives her leverage or something." Lex groans, and my smile grows wider. "I made her promise not to say anything to anyone, and I sweetened the deal with the promise of shopping tomorrow."

"That's good." There's a pause, followed by the electric buzzing of what I guess is his razor. When it stops, he says, "Turns out you'll be spending your weekend with Idris, after all."

"Oh, no … Idris stays in his drawer. I'm letting all this build up for Wednesday. My jaw is a little sore, but I think it'll be back to normal by then."

I efficiently make him lose his words. "Fuck, Andrea …"

"What? As you said, practice makes perfect, and I'm always looking to improve."

"I can't let you get any better at this. You'll have too much power over me if you do. Which now makes me realize I should have praised your skills more earlier, but I think my brain melted for a minute."

"Yeah, and then your mouth was too busy." Another moment of silence. God, I love teasing him like this.

"Fuck, that's it. Forget about Tamika and come here right now," he demands.

"Nuh-uh."

"So I'm supposed to go to bed like this?"

"Like what?" I ask, pretending I don't know what he means.

"I'd send you a picture, but I don't trust the internet."

Oh, wow … This is possibly the only dick pic I'll ever want to receive. "Fuck the internet. Make it impossible to identify."

"Nice try. What about building it up for Wednesday?"

"It's just for the eyes. I won't do anything with it."

"Hm …"

I'm jittery when the phone buzzes in my hand. I excitedly open the notification and let out a whimpering moan at the sight of Lex's massive hard-on. The shot isn't overly complex, taken from his venture point, looking down at his hard length. Shit, it truly is a gorgeous penis. And all of it was in my mouth, and then my pussy, mere hours ago. In the background, I recognize the marble floors of his bathroom.

"I never noticed how nice the floor of your bathroom is," I comment when I put the phone back to my ear.

He laughs openly, and I can envision him shaking his head. "You really have a gift for keeping me humble."

"At your service." I move the phone away, wanting to peek at the pic again. To my great dissatisfaction, the message box is now empty. "Where did it go!?"

"I told you I don't trust the internet."

"You could have at least warned me. I would have taken a screenshot."

"Which is exactly why I didn't warn you."

"I thought you trusted me."

"I do, but I don't trust whoever might get into your phone." He makes sense, but I still feel robbed. "If you want more of it, it's right here for the taking, waiting for you."

"But I can't come."

"Not until Wednesday, no," he cleverly replies to my whiny plaint. "Are you in bed?"

"Mhm …"

"What are you wearing?"

Holy Mother of Christ … The thought of phone sex is enough to make me press my knees together. It sounds so hot, taboo, and intimate … My pajamas aren't even near sexy, though. I consider lying, but then decide he knows me, anyway.

"I'm wearing an old Lilo and Stitch shirt with four holes in it the last time I counted. And with that, I have shorts that don't match with only two holes. But one's over my butt, so it makes up for it."

"Mmm, sexy," he mumbles, humor littered in his voice.

"You don't deserve to get any spank material after the way you robbed me of mine."

"I thought you weren't doing anything with it."

"I changed my mind."

"Then I guess I'm not doing anything until Wednesday, either."

I argue that we'll have to find time to start the movie lessons eventually, and the topic drifts to something else. We talk about cinema for a while, then general science fiction, comics, books, video games … When my arm is sore from holding my phone, I roll to the side and put the device on my cheek, letting gravity do the job. The minutes pass on my clock, but I can't bring myself to end the conversation.

Despite my best efforts to remain responsive, fatigue slowly gains on me, and we reach a point where I yawn every other minute.

"You should sleep," Lex proposes.

"I'm good, I swear."

"It's okay, Andrea. We can talk tomorrow, or I'll see you on Monday."

I nod distractedly before remembering he can't see me. "Alright, I'll talk to you tomorrow, Coleman."

"Good night, Walker. Or rather, good morning, given it's past five."

"Good morning to you, too."

Suddenly exhausted, I take the phone from the side of my face and cut the call, discarding it somewhere next to me. I hug the Lex-scented pillow, dipping my nose in it.

I really am falling in love with the man.

And I can't remember why that's a bad idea.

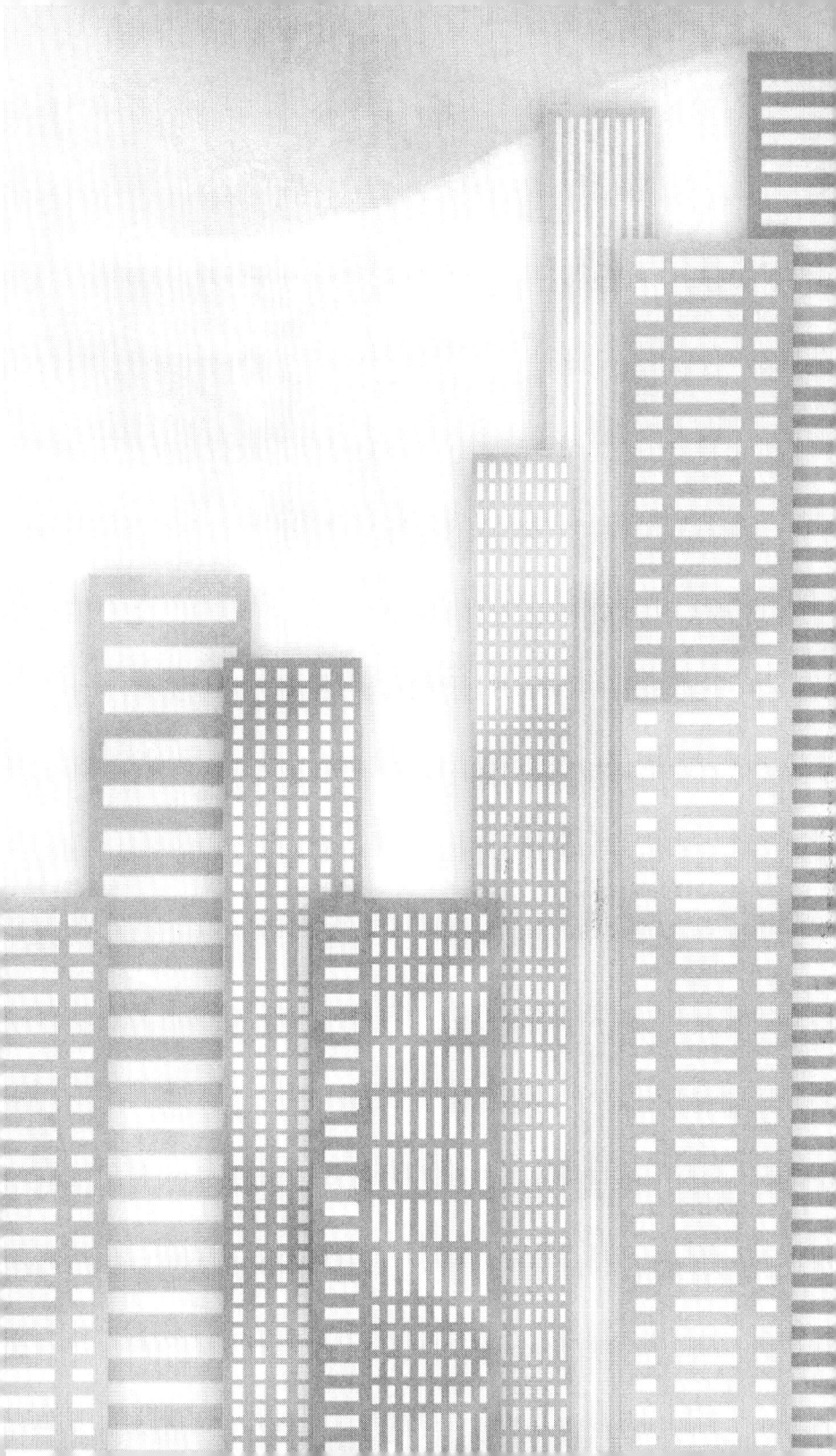

is_new_chapter = True

chapter_number =

"31"

pov_name =

"Andrea"

OUR LATE-NIGHT CALL TRIGGERS a need for more, and we now spend a lot of time texting each other. This odd situation, the relationship we don't want to label, is slowly shifting into something different. Clearly, it isn't just about the sex anymore. We genuinely enjoy each other's company and seek the meaningful, nerdy, or personal conversations we share.

I never had a lovey-dovey phase, so I never felt the need to keep in touch with someone as much as this. I feel like a teenager with a crush, jumping on my phone every time it makes a sound, giggling at Lex's texts, eagerly answering … At first, I try not to respond too fast so I won't seem too clingy, but since Lex is always quick to text back, I dismiss my worries.

I learn a lot about him from those texts. Not being physically together rids us of the insane sexual tension, which always ends with us naked and panting. So, for once, we're able to talk without being interrupted.

On Saturday, I accompany Tami to the mall, where she's getting her hair cut in the only salon she trusts to handle her hair type. After I help interpret everything to the hairdresser, I leave her at it and wander through the crowded mall. When I see the SALE signs in the Victoria's Secret windows, I casually step in. I have a good reason to invest in some finer underwear now.

I'm strolling through the pricey items when my phone vibrates in my back pocket. It's a text from Lex.

LEX

How are you surviving your imposed day of shopping?

ME

It's not as bad as I thought. Victoria's Secret is having a sale.

He calls seconds after I send it. I pick it up with a grin from ear to ear.

"I'm calling to see if you need a consultant," he says with amusement. I can't help but laugh.

"I think I've got this covered, thanks. But just to be sure, how do you feel about teddies?"

"What on earth is that?"

"It's like a sexy, one-piece swimsuit."

His voice is a little hoarse when he says, "I rather enjoy those."

"Noted. What about crotchless panties?" This time, he mumbles something inaudible.

"I find them practical."

"Last question. What's your favorite color?"

"At this point, I'd even find lime green appealing on you, so surprise me."

"Alright, surprised you shall be." My eyes catch something pretty and teal. "Oh, that's beautiful … But I'm not sure I can figure out all the strappy things."

"Andrea, if it takes more than five seconds to get you out of it, I'll end up ripping it off."

"Aren't you supposed to be an actual genius? It can't be that complicated. Maybe I should just try it on."

There's another moment of silence, and Lex clears his throat. "Sending a picture to your consultant would be wise."

"Sorry, I don't trust the internet," I humor. He chuckles, and my heart flutters with contentment.

"Then send one where you're not in it."

"Oh, smart! Give me a second." Looking around, I find a mannequin wearing it and send him a picture. "Done."

There's a moment of nothing, and Lex groans.

"What's the point of it going all the way to the shoulders if it doesn't even cover the chest?" he asks, confused and audibly turned on.

"Well, the only perk of having barely any boobs is I don't have to wear bras, so I can afford some creativity."

"I like your tits." His blunt honesty touches me, and my chest swells further.

"Thank you, but there isn't much to like."

"There's enough. And I'm discovering myself to be an ass man."

"Ah, then you got lucky."

"Several times already, yes." God, I love his quick and witty humor. "By the way, I like the pink one in the top left corner of the picture."

We talk for a little longer, and I'm the one who ends up cutting the call, arguing he can't know in advance everything I'm getting. He deserves to have a few surprises. Which he certainly will, as I nearly spend a thousand dollars there. But I'm kind of rich from selling my app, so I rationalize the spending by telling myself it's a rare treat and it'll make two people very, *very* happy.

Later that day, Tami and I are curled up on the couch, watching a romantic comedy, when I receive another text. I eagerly grab my phone, expecting it to be Lex, but my heart drops when I see Oli's ID.

Shit, with everything going on, I almost forgot that he tried to kiss me during the party. With a sense of dread clutching my throat, I open his text.

OLI

Hey, Hulkette. I wanted to apologize for the way I behaved yesterday. I've been feeling like an ass because I know you're not into me that way and should have respected it.

I'm not trying to make excuses for myself, but I was in a weird place because my sister had just told me our grandma passed away.

I don't even think twice before sending him a reply.

ME

Oh, my God. Oli, you should have let me know. I'm so sorry for your loss. Your grandma from Ireland or the one in Idaho?

OLI

Ireland. We weren't very close to her since we barely ever saw her. But it was still a shock.

ME

Yes, I imagine :(

OLI

Anyway, I'm so sorry that happened. I was looking for comfort, and it got the best of me.

ME

You really should have told me. We're friends. We talk about those things.

There's a pause there as he takes a couple of minutes to answer.

OLI

Thank you for being such a good friend, Andy.

Although I don't feel like a good friend at all, given everything I'm hiding from him, I reply with:

ME

Well, we get the friends we deserve, don't we?

We talk about it for a little longer, and by the time the movie ends, I feel as though our friendship is stronger. It seems he finally accepted we'll never be more than buddies now. No matter what some people think, men and women can be friends. I'll prove it with Oliver.

Satisfied with my discussion with Oli, I get ready for the night. When I return to my room, wearing my towel, I open my wardrobe to grab a T-shirt, and my eyes drop to the pink and black striped shopping bags. Tami, of course, recognized them, and the knowing smile she gave me had my cheeks burning with embarrassment.

After I lock my door, I take it all out. One by one, I admire the fine quality of my new things. Delighted with my investment, I lay it all on my bed. I can't wait to see Lex's face as he discovers each item.

I'm so eager for it that an idea blooms in my mind.

Maybe now would be a great time to thank him for the pic he so generously sent me. Trying not to overthink it, I impulsively grab the pink balconette bra and retro high-waisted panties he told me he liked. I hang my towel and slip the ensemble on. The bra's cut is so clever it almost looks like I'm a solid B-cup. I glimpse at myself in the full-length mirror of my wardrobe, hesitating.

The outfit is gorgeous, but I'm not confident enough with my body to take a picture and send it to Lex. I know all too well that he's used to nudes from women with Victoria's Secret bodies rather than just the lingerie. When we first met in the elevator, that woman in the pic looked flawless, blonde, slender, with fantastic boobs, a toned stomach, and a bomb body. And he was unfazed by that nude back then. How the fuck will he react to me in my underwear? I'm nowhere near that level of perfection.

But he really likes me, doesn't he? He won't mind my flat chest and wide hips.

To give myself some courage, I take the silk kimono I also bought and put it on, leaving it open and hanging on my shoulders. I do some touch-ups on my makeup and add ruby lipstick. Once I feel ready, I fluff my hair and take a pic, holding the phone in front of me. The result doesn't suit me, so I take another, and another …

I take well over thirty pictures, trying different poses, kimono off the shoulders, off only one, without it … I try different angles, from the front, slightly to the side, completely to the side … I try to hide my face with the phone, hold it up, at chest level …

It's my first attempt at sexy pictures, and I never realized how complicated the ordeal is. Nudes are *hard*, and I have all the respect in the world for the women who do it regularly. It's so much simpler for men. Lex removed his towel, snapped his junk, sent it, and it was enough to make me weak in the knees.

I keep the best pictures as I go and delete the ones I never want to see again. After maybe twenty minutes of this laborious photoshoot, I accept I won't do better. I have five shots to go by, one of which I like a lot more than the others. I'm angled slightly to the side, the kimono falling off one of my shoulders, with my hand on my hip. The pink ensemble is very much visible, and the phone partially hides my face.

ME

Do you have a moment?

I message him, my thumbs trembling a little. With my legs crossed in the middle of the bed with all my purchases, I wait, biting my nail. What am I doing? I've seen too many stories of revenge porn to be doing this. Even for Lex.

His answer is simple and efficient.

LEX

I do.

Alright, I can do this. A little quid pro quo.

ME

No screenshot.

Before he can ask what I mean, I select the picture. My heart is beating so fast that I wonder if I can die of a heart attack at twenty-six. The moment I hit the send button, a shiver runs up my arm to die in my chest. This goes against all of my beliefs, my education, and my comfort zone.

Everything stills as I wait, and when the seen checkmark appears, all my fears become too loud. *The fuck am I doing? He won't like it. I look ridiculous.* I count to ten internally and then delete the picture for both of us. Shortly after, he starts typing. With each second that passes, my anxiety grows more intense.

LEX

When I picked Wednesday to bring you home, I thought it would be a nice, reasonable day in the middle of the week. I should have gone with Monday. You're stunning in that.

Relief floods me, and I let out a heavy sigh, my shoulder collapsing as the tension leaves my body.

ME

I'm still trying to decide which one I should wear for Wednesday.

I half-expect it when he calls, so I pick up, acting innocent. "Yes?"

"Maybe you should send me more pictures so I can help you choose."

"Nice try, but no. That was a teaser. I bought about half the shop, and you'll get some sweet surprises in all that, as promised." I lie back on my bed on top of some panties and bras.

"Fuck, Andrea," he groans. "You have to stop making me hard like this when you're not here to take care of it."

"You're a big boy. Take care of it yourself."

"I have been. I don't think I've ever fucked my fist so much in my life. Maybe in my teen years, but I'm not even sure."

"Have you jerked off thinking of me?" I ask, almost honored by the thought.

"Is that weird?"

"Lord, I hope not. I've been putting Idris through overtime since I met you."

Lex lets out another groan, and I press my knees together, feeling like a temptress. I'm enjoying all this buildup immensely, this anticipation, this tension …

"And what were you thinking of as you made yourself come with me on your mind?" he asks, the low tone of his voice somehow finding its way straight to my clit.

I bite my lip, running my fingertips over the delicate lace of my panties, then up to graze an erect nipple. For the second time this weekend, I'm tempted to try phone sex with him. Given how *slex*-deprived I am, I'd come in no time, panting and trembling. However, I also want Wednesday to be mind-blowing.

"This isn't happening," I firmly declare. Anticipating his protest, I add, "But I appreciate the attempt. I'll see you tomorrow, Alexander."

"Andrea—" he starts with a warning tone.

I hang up and force myself to turn off the phone. If I allow him to insist, I'll cave in.

For a moment, I lie in a pile of lace and silk, my body tingling and demanding satisfaction.

Yes, Wednesday will be epic.

pov_name = "Alexander"

Andrea and I agree to arrive early on Monday so we can have time alone before work. The plan gets sidetracked, though, because Kevin is in my office before she is, to talk about our growing numbers and the board meeting coming soon.

We're in the midst of that when Andrea appears at the door—left open by Kev. When I see her, I can't hold back the smile that stretches my lips.

"Okay, I'll leave you two," my old friend decides. "We'll talk about the quarterly reports later." He gives me a knowing wink, and as he passes Andrea, he greets her with a nod and a smile.

Once he's gone and the door is closed, she turns to me, suspicious. "Does he … Did you—"

"He knows, yes. But I didn't tell him, he guessed. A while ago, actually."

"Oh … I see. Our Secret is slowly becoming common knowledge," she worriedly notes.

"Two people are manageable."

"Three. Kate knows, too."

"You told her?"

"She knew before *I* knew," she humorously explains as she walks up to me. "She basically engineered this whole thing."

"I knew I liked her for a reason." Slowly, I wrap my arms around her waist, hands caressing her through the thin material of her T-shirt.

"I can't see why. She helped me rip you off when I sold you my app."

"I helped you rip me off," I remind her, bending slowly.

She's still smiling when my lips unhurriedly meet hers. It feels like we haven't kissed in a month instead of a weekend. Little by little, our usual greed takes over, and things grow heated. She leans harder onto me, seeking support, and I grab handfuls of her ass to pull her closer.

The door flings open next to us, and we rip ourselves away from each other, flustered. Kevin stands there like a dickhead, seemingly very proud of himself.

"Just checking. You should lock the door," he says with a falsely reprimanding expression.

"Thanks for the lesson, Kev. Now, will you please get the fuck out?" I demand, irritated. Kevin laughs, not intimidated, and complies.

"Sorry about that." I pass a nervous hand through my hair. "I've wanted to kiss you all weekend. Especially after that photo. Which reminds me …"

Stepping closer, I slip two fingers into the collar of her shirt. I tug on it and try to peek at what's underneath. She squeals with a giggle and swats my hand away before resting hers flatly over her chest.

"How dare you!" Her unshakable grin negates the way she scolds me. "This is workplace harassment. HR will hear of this."

I don't even give her time to spin around before I pull her into my chest. "You drive me fucking mad, woman," I mutter, retaking her lips with domineering hunger. Someone knocks on the door, and I rip myself away with a curse. "I can't fucking wait for Wednesday."

Instead of Kevin, it's Tamika this time. Fuck … I briefly but surely exposed myself to her on Friday. She looks at me with a prying eyebrow cocked up. The twinkle of amusement in her dark eyes only heightens my embarrassment.

"I thought you'd want to have the numbers as soon as possible," she signs once I take the folder she extends.

"Thank you." I nervously scratch my jaw. "I apologize for—"

"It's all fine. It made my weekend," Tamika interrupts. She looks over at her roommate and gives her a wink before leaving.

"What exactly did you tell her?" I ask Andrea once we're alone, a little concerned.

"Well, she understandably had questions. But I remained as vague as I could."

When someone knocks on the door again, I roll my eyes with exasperation. "For fuck's sake."

"I should just go," she mumbles, following me to the door.

She stretches up for one last peck, which I gladly give her. Then she leaves, and Bertrand comes in instead. Swapping the delicate scent of jasmine for Axe body spray isn't the best way to start the week.

Wednesday can't come soon enough.

is_scene_break = True

IT TURNS OUT THE NUMEROUS IQ tests my parents forced me to take were fucking wrong. I'm a fucking idiot, not a genius. Why on earth would I think Wednesday was a good idea? I should have brought Andrea home as early as Monday.

The withdrawal is rough, and I crave so much more than the few stolen kisses and amorous gropes we exchange. Especially since she looks particularly stunning on Wednesday, wearing a pretty little dress and pink lipstick.

To minimize the risk of someone from Kelex seeing us leave together, we decide to wait half an hour after the end of the workday to meet at my car in the parking lot. I'm a little early, but she's even earlier, already leaning on my car when I arrive.

When I get to her, my hand slides over her hip, and I bend to give her the first kiss of the day. Showing some restraint for once, we keep it to a warm peck, and I gaze down at her with intensity.

"You look stunning," I say, clutching her hip. The blue shade of her sundress highlights her complexion, and the row of small white buttons that goes from her modest cleavage to her knees have my fingers itching to open them.

"Thank you. You don't look so bad yourself."

I've noticed she likes me in a button-up shirt, especially a black one, so I decided to wear one today. The sleeves are rolled on my forearms, and a few buttons are opened at my throat.

During the entire drive to my place, my hand is on her thigh, right where the hem of her dress has risen up, skin to skin. The contact heats my palm, and by the time I'm parking, the warmth has climbed to my chest.

The elevator ride up is silent but filled with anticipation. Once the bolted door of my apartment is open, I gallantly invite her to enter first.

"Iris, I'm home," I call out.

"Welcome home, Alexander," the AI answers as the lights turn on and the curtains open.

"Hi, Iris. I'm here too," Andrea says with self-deprecation.

Ah, turns out I won't even need to tell her what I did this weekend, instead of spending it with her.

"Welcome back, Andrea," Iris greets.

Shock has Andrea stopping where she stands, eyes bewildered, and her jaw drops as she turns to me.

"What the—"

"I added your voice to her system," I explain. "You're allowed some basic commands, but you still don't have access to the core ones. We'll see if you behave before those."

"You taught your AI about me?"

"I did. I thought you'd appreciate it."

"Appreciate it? Are you kidding! Iris, dim the lights," she asks. Sure enough, the lights' intensity diminishes slightly. "Holy shit, I feel like Tony Stark with Jarvis."

It took me a few hours to implement this change into Iris's code, since I never foresaw that someone other than me could have access to her commands. But it looks like the small attention delights Andrea beyond words.

Her bag drops to the floor, and she practically jumps me, pulling me down to give me a grateful kiss. She's a little too brutal in her elation, so I lose my footing for a second. I quickly regain our balance as she ravages me with gratitude, kissing, sampling, and devouring.

I reach for the back of her thighs and effortlessly lift her, pressing her soft shape onto me. Her legs wrap around my waist, her kiss deeper. My heart is in a frenzy, overwhelmed by her attention.

Since the moment doesn't seem to have an end in sight, I walk us to the couch and sit on it with her straddling my lap. With my hands free again, I explore that little body I adore, slipping under the hem of her dress to graze her thighs. She presses that spot between her legs harder onto me with a moan.

"Lex, I love—" Her words stop as abruptly as they started, and something in her eyes makes my heart clench painfully. She doubts herself for a moment, hesitant. Then she swallows hard and says, "I love it. Thank you for doing that, baby."

Was she about to say something else? It feels like she was.

Before I can think anything of it, she kisses me again. I welcome her, my chest tightening and expanding at the same time. She gets lost in our embrace, pulling, writhing, demanding … I maintain the kiss when she lifts herself just enough to access my belt. She unbuckles it, pops the button open, and slowly slides the zipper down. Taking her sweet, sweet time, her small hand grabs my thick length.

"Ah, fuck …" I moan with a short breath as she moves her hand along my erection. "I knew you'd like the gesture, but this is …" My words trail off with a hiss at the tightening of her hold.

"Imagine if you'd taught Iris how to put on music," she whispers in my ear before nibbling on the lobe.

"About that …"

She freezes and pulls away, her hand unmoving in my boxers, fingers still wrapped around me. My mischievous smirk makes her giggle with amazement.

"Iris, can you put on some Marvin Gaye?" she tries.

Within seconds, suave tunes fill the room. That, too, I knew she'd love.

Utterly stunned, she stares at me, looking overwhelmed. She doesn't say anything else as she opens the top button of her dress.

"You …" With every word that follows, another button gets undone. "… Are. In. For. The. Best. Night. Of. Your. Life."

Once she's out of buttons, she boldly pushes the blue fabric off her shoulders, revealing the scandalous lingerie she wore underneath all day, just for me.

Fuck, it's the strappy one that somehow reveals more than it hides, leaving her tits completely exposed. Alright, I understand the concept now. This isn't underwear. This is a lure, a maddening trick meant to bring me to my knees.

And fuck, I'll be damned if I don't do exactly that.

is_new_chapter = True

chapter_number =

"32"

pov_name =

"Andrea"

THERE'S AN UNFAMILIAR MELODY COMING from far away. It's pulling me out of my sweet and oblivious slumber. I slowly become aware of my surroundings, consciousness taking over my sleepy state. Lex's large, warm body is plastered on my back as I lie on my side. He has an arm around me, longingly keeping me against him, while the other is under the pillow beneath my head.

Finally, the sound seems to stir him up, and he mumbles something, his low voice getting lost in the curls on the back of my head. His arm releases me, and his body moves away from mine. When the music stops after fumbling for a few seconds, he returns against me, wrapping his arm back in its place and pulling me closer. With his front pressed to my back, I'm deliciously aware of his morning wood.

A soft pair of lips meet my shoulder, and an irrepressible smile stretches my lips. Pure joy radiates through my heart. The same kind I felt yesterday when I realized he allowed me into his AI's commands. It means so much more than the time he spent on it. It means he wants me here. It means he envisions a future for us.

That's why, high on that, on him, and on our kiss, I almost blurted out that I love him. Everything was so new and confusing, I didn't know how to express all of it, unsure I even should.

The one thing I know for sure is that I've never felt this way about anyone. Not even close. So this must be it, right? The big L. The one that's been missing from my life.

It's not like I ever stood a chance. He's too irresistible for me not to fall in love with him. He's rigid and disciplined, but he has a hidden sense of humor I adore, and he sometimes bends the rules for me. His intelligence is off the charts, and despite being very cerebral, he has a sensual side that goes beyond anything I've ever known. He cares about me enough to overcome his worries about the internet and send me a naughty pic, or to come on stage to help me out, or to add me to his AI …

All those things and so much more are why I'm falling for him so hard and so fast. Too hard and too fast.

"'Morning," Lex mumbles, his just-woke-up voice low and throaty.

"Morning, baby."

"You didn't sneak out of my bed."

I giggle. "I didn't have enough strength left."

"So, that's what I need to do to find you in my arms in the morning?"

At the memory of the night, every inch of my skin flushes. He was relentless, merciless, and amazingly skilled. He drew orgasm after orgasm, filling me with his thick pleasure, demanding much more than I ever thought I could give.

It started on the couch, then his bed, then his shower. And after a pit stop in the kitchen to refuel, one last time in his bed. Now, my body is aching, my pussy is tender, and I'm utterly exhausted. Building up his anticipation was stupid of me. I'm an absolute wreck.

But in all truth, I wouldn't change a thing.

Behind me, Lex is more awake, nuzzling my hair and kissing my exposed shoulder.

"Do we really have to go to work?" I whimper.

"One of us has to, or it'll look suspicious."

"I vote for you to go while I stay here all day."

There's a smile on his mouth when he kisses the slope of my throat. "And how am I supposed to get any work done, knowing you're spending your day naked in my bed?"

"Sounds like a *you* problem, Coleman."

His tender ministrations get more audacious, his tongue grazing the shell of my ear, his hand finding my breast and fondling it. Between my legs, the desire to have him is already growing. After the night we had, it's insane I have any need left at all.

"I can do either sex or work," I try, hopeful.

"Are you trying to bribe me?"

His hand slowly goes down my stomach, his fingers sending shivers that I can feel in my bones. I spread my legs slightly to give him the access he needs, eager for his touch. He toys with the curls of my mound for a few seconds, teasing me into begging. Weak and unwilling to fight it, I arch my back with a moan, pressing my ass onto his erection. He chuckles low and drops another open-mouth kiss on my shoulder, gently sucking on the skin.

Finally, he gets to the point and rolls a careful fingertip on my overly sensitive clit. I moan again, the sensations rousing my tired body. Morning *slex* sounds like the perfect way to start the day.

"Are you sure you can only do one or the other?" he insists.

"Positive."

"Hmm, a shame …" An unexpected slap on my ass makes me jump with surprise. "Get up. We need to get ready for work."

"Lex!"

"What?"

"Are you serious right now?"

"Very much. You wouldn't want to get fired, now, would you?"

"Alexander …" I warn.

"If I give you what you want, will you still come to work?"

"Yes!" I promise, exasperated by how astutely he manipulated me.

Within a second, he's back against me. "Okay, so it turns out you're not a morning person. I'll try to remember that."

With baffling ease, he rolls me on my stomach. Before I can protest, he straddles my thighs to lay random kisses on my skin. I'll forever love feeling his lips on me. After a few pecks, I understand he's kissing the dark freckles scattered there. Then, I get a more insistent kiss on the brownish mark on my left butt cheek.

"Did you know your birthmark is almost exactly the same shape as the Guangdong Province in China?" he asks, gently grazing the spot with his thumb.

It's so random that I twist my upper body to stare at him with amusement. "And how do you know that?"

"I was looking at some facts regarding Huawei for a potential partnership, and when I saw the outline of the province their HQ is in, I noticed the resemblance."

"You have my birthmark memorized in that clever brain of yours?"

"I have your entire person perfectly mapped in there," he corrects. I laugh, thinking that while it isn't exactly romantic, it's pretty damn close.

The birthmark gets one last kiss and then comes the sharp, unexpected bite of his teeth on my soft mound. He doesn't inflict any pain, or not much, at least. His hand slithers under me when he straightens up.

"Fuck, you're already soaked …" he grunts in my ear.

I arch with a sigh when he slips a finger inside me, giving him better access. "How sore are you?" he asks, sinking in a second one.

"Very."

"Lazy and tender morning sex it is, then."

Soon after, the round head of his dick replaces his hand. I push back against him, eager to have him, but he resists.

"Is this what you want?" He's in a teasing mood this morning.

"Yes."

"Say it."

"I want it."

"Say you want my thick cock in your tight cunt."

Fuck … That's enough to make my walls throb. I can't believe how much power he has over me.

Lex presses a little harder but doesn't penetrate me yet. "Say it, Andrea."

"I—I want your thick cock in my tight … cunt," I comply, lusty shivers making me pant.

"Good girl."

Inch by delicious inch, mindful of my soreness, he nudges inside of me. While he conquers my recalcitrant flesh, he kisses, bites, and licks my shoulders and neck, amorously distracting me.

"I could spend eternity inside you, and it still wouldn't be enough," he rasps. It sounds a lot like commitment, but I don't let it go to my head. I'm so starved for his affection that I might misinterpret.

This is lovemaking again, instead of fucking. It's slow, tender, almost lazy … Pressed against the mattress by his weight, I can't do anything other than push myself up on my elbows, keeping my hips tilted toward him.

"Lex … We're going to be late," I whimper, realizing he's in no rush to bring this to its apogee.

Instead of answering, he grabs my hips to lift them, and I'm suddenly on my knees and elbows before him. I foolishly think it means he'll pick up the pace and bring us to the finish line, but he keeps his slow and intense rhythm, reaching deeper now.

It's all very intimate and pleasurable, but as much as I enjoy it, we can't be late for work, so this has to be a quickie. Holding myself on one arm, I graze my clit to speed up the climb to my orgasm.

Lex grabs my wrist, rips it away, and pins it next to me, effectively immobilizing it. Because I can be strong-headed, too, I use my other hand. The tips of my fingers barely have time to roll on my swollen crease before he pins that wrist down as well.

"Behave, unruly woman, or I'll have to tie you up," he commands, giving me a deep thrust. My insides pulse around him.

"Aah, yes …" I'm discovering myself to have a submissive side with Alexander Coleman.

Still holding my wrists, keeping me helpless and complying, his maddening thrusts slowly speed up. This is animalistic, raw, and sensuous. It feels like we are sexual beings, existing solely for this moment in time, this purpose.

Lex's breathing becomes heavier behind me, answering my moans and whimpers, and his ramming grows faster, deeper, and longer. The fervor of his thrusts and the way his hips meet my ass resonates in the room, along with the bed lightly banging on the wall. Tension builds up between my legs, like an elastic stretching and stretching, the breaking point almost there.

I know he's close when he releases one of my wrists to shove his hand between my legs. He finds my clit instantly and rolls his fingertips over it, never halting his momentum. My own fingers tangle with his skilled ones, pressing him to go harder.

My orgasm is so fucking close.

Lex gets there first, biting my shoulder to muffle the carnal roar that rolls in his throat. His hips jerk as he comes, and the sensation of his pleasure filling me, coupled with his fingers flicking over my clit at a fast rate, push me into my own release.

He holds my hips with both hands as I tremor from the intensity of my orgasm. Completely lost in passion and wanting more, I push against the headboard to take him even deeper. Sobbing cries escape me, the experience so intense I wonder how I'm not passing out.

Fuck, morning slex is amazing …

When the trembling, quivering, and pleasure-consumed messes that we are finally come down, Lex allows me to collapse on the mattress before slumping next to me, as sweaty, disoriented, and overwhelmed as I am. He always looks puzzled after sex, as if something about it constantly surprises him.

As much as I want to linger in bed with him, we should get ready. "Iris, what time is it?" I ask, wondering how late we are.

"Good morning, Andrea. It is 7:03," the AI answers.

"What! Lex, how early is your alarm set up?"

"Six thirty. I like to get a workout done before I start the day."

"You mean I could have slept an extra hour?!"

He chuckles and presses a kiss on my lips. "But then we wouldn't have had the time for what just happened."

He gives me another peck, and I focus on keeping my mouth closed, not wanting to expose him to my morning breath. Especially since we forgot to brush our teeth after the quick stop at his fridge.

"When I come back you better not be asleep, Andrea," he warns. His tone makes my toes curl more than it scares me. I lie there in post-nut bliss while he heads to the bathroom to get ready. When he comes back, all dressed, he rips the duvet from my spent body and forces me to head there.

When I enter the marbled room, I grimace at my reflection. My curls are all over the place from getting wet during that middle of the night shower followed by hair-messing *slex*. My skin is flushed, what's left of my makeup is runny, and I have two giant bags under my eyes. It's a miracle he still wanted me this morning. Maybe it's why he took me from behind. That, or because of how he adores my ass.

Really, it's a fifty-fifty split in the probabilities.

Once I'm ready, I join him and prop myself up on the kitchen island, purposefully sitting on the very spot where we had sex for the first time. He notices and gazes at me with intensity, his eyes darkening. Apparently unable to resist, he comes to me and gives me a long, deep, and needy kiss. I took a moment to quickly brush my teeth, and his minty flavor proves he did the same.

"I think I preferred when you smelled like sex," he says, the tip of his nose grazing the column of my throat as he inhales.

"No one else in the office would have appreciated me reeking of sex."

The touch of his tongue between my collarbones startles me, and when he drags it up to my jaw, all sorts of shivers run under the heated skin. "That way, you aren't rid of all traces of me," he states, returning to his task.

After I recuperate from his surprising fit of possessiveness, I watch him prepare our first meal of the day. It's very entertaining to see him in his natural habitat. He already prepared two bowls of granola, two glasses of orange juice, and two plates with toast and lean ham. He's just done with a large portion of scrambled eggs, which he separates in equal amounts on the plates.

"Thank you," I say as we sit down, eager to dig in. "I usually don't take time to eat in the morning, but I definitely should."

"I can't start the day properly if I don't have my routine breakfast."

"You eat exactly this every morning?" I ask while buttering a piece of toast.

He nods and takes a bite of his eggs. "I'm a man of habit and like to stick to them."

It's pretty much in character since he is rather rigid and disciplined. His apartment is spotless, his desk is always organized and neat … Something I never realized before it suddenly dawns on me.

"Do you have OCD?" I impulsively ask.

He freezes with his fork halfway up to his mouth, taken aback. "I don't. If anything, I'm closer to OCPD."

"What's the difference?"

"Obsessive-compulsive disorder is unwanted and involuntary, while obsessive-compulsive *personality* disorder results from my own desires to keep things neat, organized, and repetitive."

"Oh, I see. So you're actually fine with following the same routines and all."

"I always preferred it that way. But I have been working on shaking my monotonous ways lately. It's going quite well, and you help a lot," he adds.

"How?"

"For the first time in my life, I had to put up with having a messy desk, which was surprisingly tolerable."

His explanation has me chortling with embarrassment, hiding the redness of my cheeks behind my hands. The sheepish look I offer apparently charms him, and he pulls my hands away to grant me an indulging peck.

"It's all good. I've realized I'm too rigid in my ways of life. So your unpredictable personality and messy habits are welcome." It's my turn to be charmed, and I pull him toward me for one more kiss.

We eat the rest of our breakfast, talking and learning more about each other. I'm feeling so comfortable around him, all this is so natural, I can't help but think I want this to happen daily. From the incredible wake up to the chatty and healthy breakfast and then the ride to work that will follow.

Yes, a girl could get used to this.

I could get used to him.

I want to.

is_scene_break = True

I'M MAKING MY WAY TO the dev office when Mason grabs my arm to pull me into an isolated spot. "Alright, sis, spill the tea," he demands with sparkling eyes. My heart launches itself into an insane rhythm. Fuck, what does he know?

"Hmm, what?"

"Oh, come on. You were all dolled up yesterday, and now you look like you barely slept. You had a hot date that went well, and I want to hear all about it."

Relief floods me, and my hectic heartbeat and thoughts settle down. Mason doesn't know about Lex and me. "It was … great," I admit, seeing no point in denying it all.

"Girl, give me some details. Was it your first time seeing the guy?"

"No, it started a few weeks ago."

"Okay, are you secretly seeing our resident ginger?" he bluntly asks.

My jaw drops. "Why would you think that?"

"We know you and Oli went on a date and then nothing," he says nonchalantly. "But you two are always cute and all together, so we thought you were secretly seeing each other."

"Who is 'we,' Mason?"

"Me. I'm 'we.' I have this matchmaker syndrome I got from my mom. I can't help it."

"Well, I'm not dating Oli," I state, hoping I'm firm enough. "We went out on one date, and then I realized I'd never like him like that. That's the extent of it."

"Oh, I see … And is it serious with that other guy?"

"It's slowly getting there."

"You go, girl! I can't believe you got a man and never told me."

"He isn't *my* man."

"Yeah, yeah … Answer me this, at least. Is he worth barely sleeping?"

I let out a surprised laugh, not expecting him to go so boldly into this line of questioning. Why is everyone so invested in my sex life? Surely, people are interested in sex in general, and the fact that it's me having it is irrelevant.

"Oh, come on," he insists. "I haven't found myself a good man in months. I need to know they still exist."

"I'm not sharing details, but I'll throw you a bone and say he very much knows what he's doing."

"Ugh, has he got a gay brother?" he presses. I give him a mysterious smile, wiggling my eyebrows. "Friends don't gatekeep, Dee."

"Well, I'm keeping this one all to myself, sorry, Mace."

He sighs and his shoulders sink with disappointment. "I see you, Dee. I see you …"

I'm on Cloud Nine all morning and feel like I'll never come down from it. Mason sometimes notices my elated mood and gives me a knowing look while shaking his head.

Later in the day, I'm seated with the guys for lunch when the free chair next to me is pulled back. My heart flutters before I even look up to see who it is, instantly recognizing Lex's hand. It's a struggle to contain my broad smile when our eyes meet as he casually settles his fried rice next to my lunchbox.

"Hi, boss," Brian greets him.

"Fancy seeing you here," Steven jokes. It is a rare occurrence indeed.

"Yes, I thought I'd come and check on everyone, see how you're all doing."

Honored he would sit with us, the guys don't waste a second chatting with him. A few of them are having some issues with scripts, and Lex offers to come and spend the afternoon with us to help out.

It's odd to sit next to him like this, pretending we're nothing more than work acquaintances. I long to touch him, graze his arm, steal a bite of his dish, laugh with him … But I have to keep up with appearances, to pretend we weren't having sex all night long and that I'm not entirely obsessed with him.

Whatever the future holds for us, I need to be patient. And if—*when*—the time comes to make it official, I hope it'll be far enough from the sale of my app to avoid having to deal with gossip. It would wreck me if people had the wrong assumptions about it just because I'm sleeping with my boss.

"Are you okay?" Lex asks, pulling me out of my thoughts. When I look up, everyone's looking at me, having noticed my lack of participation.

"Yeah, sorry. I'm just tired. I didn't get much sleep," I explain, even though Lex knows that.

"Did someone keep you up all night?" It's Brian trying to humor me.

Mason lets out a sassy "Mhmm," and I stare at him wide-eyed. "What? It's not my fault if he guessed!"

When I kick him in the shin to make him shut up, it's Brian who jumps and bends with a sobbing, "Ouch!"

"Sorry," I apologize with a grimace. "Mace, shut up!"

But it's too late. Next to me, Lex turned his stoic mask on, and I, for once, can't tell what's on his mind.

"Oh, I didn't know you had a boyfriend," Steven says.

Ah, shit, not that word. It's so official, so … final. "I'm—I don't want to talk about it," I stutter.

"But you have a boyfriend?" Brian insists, still bent over to massage the spot I accidentally kicked.

My skin is now crawling with embarrassment, and I don't dare to glimpse at Lex anymore. There's no way I'm telling them I have some sort of sex arrangement with someone until we figure out where to take it. Especially not with the someone right next to me.

"Drop it, man. Andy will tell us about it when she's ready," Oli says. I nod to reinforce his words, and Brian sighs.

Eventually, they start talking about some random world-famous gamer, dropping the matter of my short night. Lex isn't taking part anymore, and I can feel his discomfort. I push around the rest of the food in my lunchbox but don't eat anything.

The break ends, and we all move to the Trolls' Lair. "I'll get my laptop and handle a few things before coming back here to help," Lex tells us. Half a minute after he leaves, my phone buzzes with a message from him.

LEX

Come up.

Ah, shit …

Reluctantly, I turn my screen off and get up to follow him. He's waiting by the opened door. I feel like a lamb going to the slaughterhouse. He closes the door behind us, and I courageously face him, ready for whatever will come. After a few seconds of insufferable silence, he finally speaks.

"Boyfriend?" he questions with just enough humor for me to understand he isn't mad or annoyed—just intrigued.

A relieved sigh escapes me as I laugh a little, helpless. "I never used *that* word. Mason guessed I had a date yesterday because I look like I barely slept, so he drilled me with questions."

"Hmm, I see. I guess I shouldn't have asked so much of you."

"Oh no, please, keep asking."

"But you should always come into work well-rested," he points out with wit, reminding me of the exchange we had during my first week here.

It feels like ages ago. So many things have happened since. I can't believe how annoying I used to find him. The rage he could conjure in me is still vividly clear in my mind. All those explosive feelings evolved into something even more flammable but so much better.

"I have the feeling my boss likes me. He wouldn't fire me over this," I say with a crooked smirk.

"And what gives you that impression?" He feigns skepticism, and I bite back my smile.

"I'm not sure what's the biggest clue. The way he grunts when his cock is far down my throat, or how he hums in appreciation every time he's eating me out? Or maybe it's the intensity in his eyes when he rams into me with his huge cock." I witness the surprise on his face and guess he didn't expect I could talk dirty, too. "Now, if you'll excuse me, I have work to return to."

I don't even have time to turn around as he grabs and slams me against him. He holds me in his arms, lowering his head until his mouth is an inch from mine.

"You're such a fucking tease," he mumbles. "You'll drive me mad one of these days, Andrea Walker."

"I'll drive you mad tomorrow evening, Saturday, and Sunday."

"Is that a threat?"

"Oh no, Alexander … It's a promise," I whisper lasciviously.

He groans a curse before taking my lips, claiming what is already his. After a moment of heated embrace, he pushes me away gently, laying one last kiss on my lips.

"Tomorrow," he says.

Yes, tomorrow and then the whole weekend. And the one after that. And many other weekends, I hope.

I'll never get enough of him.

is_new_chapter = True

chapter_number =

"33"

pov_name =

"Alexander"

ANDREA AND I ARE A little more organized this time. We meet early in the parking lot so she can drop her weekend bag in my car. Then, we both work late again so the building is almost empty by the time we leave.

Once we're at my place, she enthusiastically greets Iris. She's so elated when the electronic voice answers that she gives me a generous but short kiss.

"I need to put my bag in your room and then stop by your bathroom," she pragmatically explains.

"Of course. I have a bottle of French wine for tonight. Unless you'd rather have a beer?"

"Wine sounds great. Be right back." After one last peck, she practically skips to my room.

While she does whatever she needs, I prepare our evening together. I notified the company in charge of restocking my fridge, so they added a couple of trays with an assortment of finger food. One goes in the oven while the other is served cold, so I handle that.

I'm done setting everything on the table when soft music fills the space. Andrea must have asked Iris to set the mood.

She appears when I'm filling a glass of wine, and my gaze immediately locks on her dress. It's the same one she wore during the evening with Kevin and his wife. The one that invaded my dreams for days.

"I hope this one's mine," she jokes, pointing at the now very well-filled glass. I abruptly straighten the bottle up, making a bit of a mess.

I take one of the napkins to wipe it. "Sorry, I was having the most intense déjà vu."

Smirking, she sits beside me, tucking a leg under her. She's barefoot, and I wonder if she's wearing the dress and nothing else. I already know she doesn't have a bra on, but has she also dismissed the bottoms?

I'm thinking of checking it out right now so the suspense doesn't eat me up from within, when she bends forward and grabs the glasses to even them out. She hands me one and licks the rim of hers, where a crimson drop is slowly rolling down.

The innocent lick has my cock awakening.

"To a productive week," she offers as a toast, tapping our glasses.

"And to an even more productive weekend."

An irresistible grin bends her mouth as she sips on her wine. "I didn't even ask you how your sister's visit went," she says, bending to take a pig in a blanket.

"It was alright. Lucy can be very bossy and hasn't realized yet that I'm a grown man."

"Rafa often forgets that as well. Lucy is the eldest, right? Why was she here?"

"She is, yes. And she was in Seattle for a seminar. She's the head of her pediatric department, and because she's excellent at her job, she gets invited as a speaker nationwide. She rarely goes, but since I live here, she accepted."

"Where does she live?"

"She moved back to Dallas when she finished her doctorate."

"Moved back? Are you Colemans originally from Texas?" she asks, genuinely surprised.

"I was born there, yes. But then we moved to Seattle when I was around five."

"Oh, so that's why you don't have an accent at all."

"Yes. I'm the only one still living here. Emilia moved to New York, and Julia followed Lucy to Dallas a couple of years after she left. My parents are always moving around, my father especially. Miriam is mostly in Dallas but comes to Seattle a few months per year."

"Miriam?"

"My mother."

"My mom would kill me if I called her by her name," she amusedly points out.

"Mine doesn't have a maternal bone in her body, so it's only fair."

Thankfully, she doesn't insist on that and switches the topic. "Why did you guys move here?"

"My father needed to get closer to Alaska for work, and my mother refused to live there. Seattle was the best compromise they found. It was that or a divorce. In hindsight, a divorce would have been preferable for everyone."

"They don't get along?"

"Worse. They ignore each other. For as long as I can remember, they've lived separate lives together without trying to keep up with appearances. My father has mistresses, and my mother has hobbies. The more he indulges in extramarital affairs, the more she spends on charities. The Colemans are renowned for their generosity, but it's only Miriam getting back at her husband by hitting him where it hurts the most—his wallet."

There's a moment of silence as I pensively sip on my wine. The example I grew up with convinced me that married life wasn't for me—among other reasons. I can't keep a woman happy for the rest of her life. And I was always confident no woman could ever make me happy for the rest of mine, but as I gaze down at the petite brunette by my side, I wonder if I wasn't wrong about that.

"Now, before my fucked-up family completely ruins the mood, let's switch to a much more interesting subject," I suggest, angling myself to face her better. "How did you become such a dorky nerd?"

An incredulous snort bursts out of her. "I'm not a dork!"

"I said dorky nerd. And I saw how you schooled Dakota when she thought Darth Vader and Kylo Ren were the same character."

"I'm just passionate."

"A passionate dork, then."

She accepts the teasing with a pout and brings her second leg under her to sit more comfortably. That brings her closer to me, especially since I extend my arm behind her on the backrest.

"Well, just like programming, it came from my dad," she explains. "He was an absolute geek before geeks even existed—hardcore *Star Trek* fan, had a computer as soon as he could afford one, loved video games … He's the one who passed it all to me. Rafa always preferred books over movies because he feels he's missing part of the experience. So, when my dad realized I was receptive to his passion, he bathed me in all that geek culture early on," she explains with an unwavering grin.

"He used to take me to this old-school arcade place whenever I came home with good grades—so nearly every week. He'd buy us twenty dollars' worth of tokens, and we'd stay there until we ran out of coins. I was crushed when they closed the place ten years ago. He also passed me his fondness for movies. Our tastes are very similar, except I love watching those terrible Hallmark Christmas movies with my mom and abuela. He also set me up with a state-of-the-art gaming computer when I was around nine and introduced me to the world of video games. When I was twelve, he opened the gates of online gaming. I got very good at *Call of Duty*."

There's melancholia in her voice as she tells me all this, her eyes lost on her glass of wine. She's beyond endearing. I want to grab and kiss her, but I love learning more about her, so I refuse to sidetrack the moment.

"You don't play much anymore. What happened?"

"It was taking up too much of my time; it left no room for anything else. And sometime in middle school, I began having other preoccupations. I was gradually becoming a woman, and all my interests were boy stuff, which became an insecurity. I drifted away from my dad a bit during that period and tried to deny my true nature. But then, I overcame my insecurities in my junior year of high school and embraced my affection for nerdy stuff."

As though she realizes she's rambling, she stops herself from continuing, looking up to meet my gaze.

"Your father seems like a great person," I genuinely say.

"He really is—always so loving and affectionate. I love my mom with everything I have, but I've always been closer to my dad. He made me into the person I am, and I can never thank him enough. I think you two will—"

The words die as soon as she realizes what she's about to say. I can't blame her. The moment is so perfect, I feel so close to her, that I'd let myself get carried away too.

"He must be proud of you," I say.

"He is. He originally hoped I'd work for a big firm like Avoss." I grimace at the idea of her working for Hugh. "But when he learned I was applying for Kelex, he was ecstatic. We all knew your company thanks to Rafael, who uses several of your apps."

We talk for a while, drinking over half the bottle and eating. We naturally move closer to one another, her knees over my thigh and my arm now on her shoulders, fingers drawing delicate patterns on her skin. This moment of casual chatter and comfortable proximity is everything.

I tell her about meeting Kevin in middle school and how we've been inseparable since. She tells me about her mom, who teaches Spanish in the same high school as her dad, and I tell her more about my sisters, Emilia and Julia, who work for the Coleman empire—the former in the New York branch, and the latter at the Dallas headquarters.

Somehow, the subject becomes geeky again, and she lets her passion take over. "I can't believe you tried to pretend you weren't a bit of a dork," I note with amusement.

"Well, I don't want you to see me that way."

"Why?"

"I don't know, because … I want to be sexy or cute in your eyes. Not a nerdy and geeky dork."

I put my glass on the table before reaching for her hip to rest a hand there. Bending forward, I kiss the softness of her neck. She shivers with delight, closing her eyes and angling her head to give me better access.

"I can assure you that I find you very sexy and cute," I promise. "But as attractive and gorgeous as I find you, the image wouldn't be complete if you weren't a nerdy and geeky dork."

I continue to lazily explore her exposed skin, ripping small sighs out of her every time my wet tongue darts out to taste her. My hand on her hip adamantly pulls her closer. She moans when I take the lobe of her ear between my lips and gently suck on it.

"I wouldn't have guessed you were into nerds," she breathes out.

"I didn't know it myself. As it turns out, I'm into everything you are. I'm an Andreaphile."

The shaky breath she lets out and the way her hand on my thigh tightens remind me that words of affirmation work well on her. As well as physical touch and quality time.

I take her glass from her distracted hold and put it on the table with mine before I return to my exploration.

With a precise tug, I loosen the tie on the back of her neck and pull the fabric down to reveal her bare chest. After a lustful glance at her hardened tips, I hungrily engulf one of them between my lips, gently nipping on the soft flesh around it, rolling a skilled tongue on the puckered surface.

My hand on her hip finds its way under the hem of her dress and tentatively traces a path up the smooth skin of her inner thigh. I smile around her nipple when my fingertips encounter the soft texture of lace. She did wear something under her dress …

She whispers my name when I press over her clit, and shivers when I circle it. As my fingers lower, I feel how wet she is for me. I let go of her brown tip with a groan to meet her enraptured expression.

"You drive me insane," I confess. Once her underwear is tugged to the side, I slide my fingers up her molten folds. "Sometimes when you're away, my mind drifts to you, and I often get hard at the thought of your wet and tight pussy." I slowly push two fingers inside of her, making her release a soft whimper. "I want you all the time. I want to be with you, around you, inside of you. I want to hear you laugh, talk, moan, and scream my name. I always long to see you, how you furrow your brows when you're confused, how you bite your lip when you're trying not to laugh, how you fidget when you're embarrassed …"

I hope she feels it, too, and this isn't just me. We have a connection, a strong bond tying us together. It goes beyond lust and desire.

"I feel the same," she whispers, spreading her legs more.

"I don't know what you're doing to me, Andrea. It's both hell and heaven when I'm with you. I finally get to touch you, to kiss you, to hold you, but I know I'll never get enough of you, and the thought of losing you is slowly killing me."

"Lex, I'm not going anywhere."

"Really?"

"Yes … I belong to you, baby."

An urge to be closer to her has me removing my hand and pulling her onto my lap until she's straddling me. The longing and the need in her eyes wreck me. She frames my face with tender hands, looking at me like I'm the eighth wonder.

"Say that again," I demand. My heart is seconds from exploding, but I need to hear it. "Say you're mine."

She looks torn, but not by doubt. It seems that whatever emotions are raging inside me are also overwhelming her.

"Say it, Andrea."

"I'm yours, Alexander," she whispers, claiming my lips tenderly.

Something warm blooms in my chest, so intense I can barely breathe. How? How did I ever get so fucking lucky that this woman, this stubborn, brilliant, funny, impulsive, beautiful woman is mine? She's perfection wrapped in a petite package, and she's all mine.

And I'm all hers for as long as she'll have me. My heart only beats for her anyway, my lungs breathe for her scent, and my body only craves hers. It was foolish of me to think I could be around her and not inevitably fall for her. But it's too late to do something about it now. Half of me will be ripped apart when she comes to her senses and this whole thing ends.

I love her like I never thought I could love anyone.

pov_name =
"Andrea"

IT'S A DANGEROUS THING TO belong to someone, but I don't care. I can't imagine anyone else making me feel the way he does. It's impossible. Lex is everything. He's become my entire world.

I'm undoubtedly, absolutely, and utterly his. My body, soul, and heart belong to this man. Regardless of how this may evolve, Alexander Coleman is part of my history now. A part of me.

While he carries me through his apartment, I cover his handsome face with ardent pecks, determined to show him how much I'm his. In this moment of abandoned passion, all my doubts are gone.

I'm in love with him.

I love Lex with everything I have, everything I am. I love his brain, his personality, his face, his spirit ... And I need him like I've never needed anyone or anything.

Given his own state of devoted fervor, it seems I'm not the only one prone to some meaningful revelation. Something's happening between us. I can feel it in the air, heavy and electric, almost as if a storm looms over us, about to wreck us with its intensity. Our relationship has reached a turning point. None of it is light and breezy anymore. It isn't even near casual.

I'm so engrossed in showing him how much I love him that I don't even notice when we enter his room. It's only when he bends to sit me on the edge of his bed that I do.

I sit up, bewitched, as he impatiently removes his shirt. At the sight of his muscular torso, a happy little pulse happens in my core. With two fingers into his waistband, I pull him closer to me, desperate to taste him. My lips press themselves on the hollow crest between his abs, just above his navel. I then lay a myriad of pecks on the skin I can access while I unbuckle his belt. When I finally open his slacks, I push them down just enough to reveal more of the deep V at his hips. Impatiently, I lick up one of the hollow paths, enjoying the smoothness of his skin under my tongue, pure lust and need coursing through my veins.

With a groan, he fists a handful of my hair at the back of my head to angle my face up. Our tongues meet and battle in a feverish attempt to get more. Then, he rips himself away from me to finish what I started. His pants come down quickly, exposing his impressive erection.

As eager as he is, I unzip the side of my dress. Lex observes me with a heated gaze while I remove it and expose the fine lace of my panties to his sight.

Ah, dammit ... He won't get to see how nice they look from behind. Because it would be a shame, I turn around and innocently crawl on all fours to the middle of the bed.

"Fucking hell," he mumbles.

Before I can rejoice in a well-accomplished mission, his hand catches my ankle and drags me back toward him. My protest turns into a giggling squeal as he impatiently flips me around. He graces me with a desperate kiss before feverishly pecking his way down my stomach and practically ripping my underwear off.

Like a starving man, he kneels before the bed and passes his muscular shoulders between my legs. My hips buck at the electric-like touch of his tongue on my clit. I let out a desperate whimper, tangling my fingers in his silky dark hair.

His mouth is merciless, flicking intensely, his lips sucking on the swollen bud. He doesn't want to make it last, nor is he aiming to drive me crazy. His goal is to make me come. He wants to be inside of me but still needs me to orgasm before that.

Desperate to hold on to him, I let go of his hair and seek his hands. While his skillful ministrations never stop, he releases my thighs, and we interlace our fingers together. It anchors me to reality, to him, and I bask in the bond we share.

Our hands locked together, I hold onto him, looking down to meet his eyes as he feasts on my throbbing pussy. My grip is tight, but he doesn't seem to mind. He grows more intense with each moan, cry, or jolt from me.

Utterly silent and unmoving for a few seconds, I plunge into ecstasy, the pleasure so great I can't do anything but endure it. Still keeping our hands intertwined, he secures my hips between his forearms to contain my jolts. He draws out my orgasm, and when I try to wriggle away or free my hands, he prevents it, tightening his hold on me. I'm as powerless as he's inflexible.

Then, when the last shiver has run its course, he frees me, wipes his lower face on the bedding, and helps me up the mattress. In seconds, he's taking his position over me, hooking one of my legs into his arm while I lift the other one high on his side. When he demands it, I kiss him back fervently, aroused by my taste on his tongue.

He's so hard that he doesn't need his hand to press his swollen head onto my sleek opening. One vigorous thrust later, he's planted into me, my walls stretched around the sudden intrusion.

"You're mine, Andrea," he grunts, adjusting his hips to reach even deeper.

"Yes … I'm yours."

He backs up until only the tip is in me and then rams in, wrecking me with how good it is. In this position, he reaches further than ever before, his head meeting my cervix. It's almost painful, but I don't mind. I want all of it, so I urge him closer with a hand while the other pulls him in for a needy kiss.

With our bodies angled like this, I could easily peek at the spot where we join. I suddenly crave to see him possessing me and the source of our lovemaking, so I rip my lips away from his and stare down. Lex does the same, and with our foreheads pressed together, we watch as he pumps in and out of me. The vision is mesmerizing. His thick and long cock is coated with my wetness as it appears and disappears between us.

I feel deliciously full whenever his trimmed hair meets my dampened curls.

Lex changes his movements and gifts me with very long, very slow thrusts, allowing me to peek at his full length before plunging it entirely into me again. Shit, how is it even possible for me to take all that? It almost looks like a magic trick.

"You feel so good, Andrea," he rasps, rolling his hips in a way that has my walls spasming around him. "I've never—It's never been—" He stumbles on the words, apparently not finding one strong enough to describe his feelings.

But I understand him because I feel exactly the same way.

Instead of expressing it with words, he decides to show it. He lets go of my leg and firmly holds my hips before straightening up to sit on the bed with me straddling him.

He adjusts his legs under me, spreading his knees to allow me to sink lower onto him, and I move mine to rest on each side of his hips. Our faces are almost aligned in this position, and I hook my arms over his neck to draw him in for a kiss. With his large hands clasping my ass, he encourages me to undulate.

I follow his guidance and use his support to rock my hips back and forth into him. This position is incredible. The whole front of my pussy rubs over the base of him when I take him whole, marvelously stimulating my sensitive bud. Like this, I can control the depth, angle, and intensity, which is insanely good. With each oscillation of my hips, my nipples graze the hair on his chest, adding to all the other stimulations.

Once I get the hang of it and can handle it alone, Lex caresses my back, igniting shivers of delight under my skin.

When I look at him again, he's staring at me with mixed emotions that shatter me. He seems almost lost, dismayed by what's happening. His eyebrows are slightly frowned, his eyes gliding over my features intensely. I can almost believe he loves me back when he looks at me like that, with so much longing and passion.

I keep my languid momentum up, our bodies meeting over and over, and lay tender kisses on his face, giving him every ounce of the love he deserves. He lets out a hoarse moan when I kiss the side of his throat, and his hold around me tightens.

Gradually, I swing my hips faster, and he helps me with the tiring effort, clasping my ass. I'm shamelessly grinding on his lap, impaling myself on his length, rubbing the sensitive front of my core on the stiff muscles of his lower abdomen, seeking my release with palpable yearning. Pleasure is quick to build up, our sweaty fronts gliding together, our lips meeting and separating, our arms clutching each other intently.

My soft cries meet each of his raspy moans, the tension between my legs so powerful my thighs tremble. With the intense way he stares back, I can see many things pass through his mind. His emotions are undergoing the same turmoil as mine, too strong to fight and too staggering to ignore.

Fuck, how I love him …

I have to tell him. He needs to know.

"Lex, I—"

But the words aren't coming. I'm lost too far into passion, too devastated by it to form that simple sentence. I whimper with annoyance, keeping up with the harsh cadence of my undulations.

"I know," he answers, seeking my lips for a second. "Me too."

Me too …

His declaration, whatever it means, breaks the dam. I cry out his name, holding onto him with all my strength. I shudder in his arms, ravaged by my orgasm, while he keeps lifting me up and down on his erection, chasing his own deliverance. It adds to my climax and makes my eyes water from the overwhelming sensations. Within seconds, he muffles a roar on the skin of my shoulder, keeping me down on him with a bruising hold as he comes deep inside me.

We remain like this for a long moment, holding onto each other with our intertwined limbs, our ragged breathing gradually calming down. I could stay in his embrace forever, his dick softening in me, his warm breath caressing my chest, the faint, masculine smell of his sweat filling my nostrils … But my legs eventually grow numb, so I have to move, dislodging his soft length from within me. Before withdrawing from him, I give him a light kiss, enjoying how bewildered he seems.

I move just enough to drop on the soft duvet of his bed, entirely spent. Lex joins me, lying against my side, seemingly as drained as I am.

"That was …" I start, not sure how to even voice it. The connection I felt to him was so intense, so perfect …

"Yes, it was."

His profile offers a lovely view as I admire the straight line of his nose, the grain of his stubble, and the thick arch of his eyebrows. He then twists his face toward me, giving me a genuine and cheerful smirk.

"You're a very gifted dork."

"A passionate one."

When the air on my sweaty skin makes me shiver, I crawl under the duvet. Lex joins me there and then rolls to get on top of me. *Oh, sweet baby Jesus, have mercy on me …*

But he grabs his phone on the nightstand instead, opens the drawer, and digs out a pair of glasses from it. "I'll need more than finger food if I want to keep up with you, Walker," he explains.

My jaw drops slightly when he puts his glasses on. These are very different from the ones he usually wears—rounder and thicker. He looks even nerdier. *Fuck … How can someone look so insanely hot and adorably cute at the same time?*

Lex notices my bewilderment. "What?"

"I like your glasses."

"They are old prescriptions that still work."

"I always wondered what you need them for."

"Hypermetropia. It's not too bad, but it can become straining, especially since I stare at screens all day. That's also why there's a blue-block filter on them."

"Ah, finally … A physical flaw," I tease, giving his broad chest a tender graze to compensate for the jab. "But you look very, *very* sexy with glasses on, so definitely not a loss."

He shakes his head with a grin and returns his attention to his phone. For the next ten minutes, we scroll through UberEATS to find what we'll order. I'm craving Thai, but he wants Greek, so we compromise and order Thai.

Once done, he rolls over me again to settle his phone back on the nightstand. His glasses remain on, though, and I know exactly why. *That cunning little …*

When he stays right there and doesn't lie back next to me, I understand what he plans on doing until the food gets here in twenty-five minutes.

"There isn't enough time," I argue with a charmed grin. He drops on the mattress with a groan, resigned.

There isn't time for sex, but we have other options. I'm suddenly too famished to wait, but thankfully, my first course is right here. A sensual sigh escapes him as I trail my tongue and lips down his half-raised cock, grabbing it gently. My mouth is already salivating, and I can't wait to make him come like this.

When he starts to remove his glasses, I shake my head. "Keep them on," I order right before I kiss the swollen head of his dick.

Can this weekend just last forever?

is_new_chapter = True

chapter_number = "34"

pov_name = "Andrea"

WAKING UP NEXT TO LEX will forever be the best thing ever. How is it even possible to be so happy before I even open my eyes? How can someone cause so much delight?

I'm awake first, so I can unabashedly ogle him for a moment. I take my time following the familiar lines of his beautiful face, memorizing them all. He's on his back, the duvet up to his midriff, his powerful upper body exposed to my adoring eyes. I'm lying on my side against him, my head resting on his shoulder, a leg bent over one of his.

The flutters in my chest and belly are unequivocal. I am in love with him—mind, body, and soul. He makes me complete, even though I never realized I was missing something. With him, I'm whole.

When he wakes up a few minutes after me, the satisfaction and delight in his gaze as it meets mine send my heart into a frenzy.

"Hi," I whisper, kissing his shoulder and resting my head there, our eyes still locked.

"Hi."

"I was thinking … I know you have your morning habits, but today feels like a pancake kind of day. Do you want me to make some for you?"

"Mmm, pancakes sound great."

He brings me against his warm body before seeking my lips again. We kiss for a moment, tenderly and lazily. I eventually push myself away from him to get on with my objective.

"Okay, just stay here, and I'll take care of breakfast."

He mumbles something that sounds like an agreement, and I sit on the side of the bed. Because I'm terrible at resisting my impulses when it comes to him, I twist, grab his face, and drop a series of quick but intense pecks on his lips.

He reaches out for me to get more, but I swiftly move away from his greedy hands and get out of bed. I snatch his discarded shirt and slip it on. Once at the door, I turn around and see him rolling on his stomach to hug the pillow under his head, ready to get back to sleep.

On my way to the kitchen, I stretch my arms and back, feeling less sore than I usually do after a night with him. Is my body getting used to him? I'm actually more flexible now.

I cook us a feast worthy of our nocturnal performance. We have pancakes, bacon, sausage, eggs, toast, smoothies I made from scratch, coffee is brewing, and there's also a fruit salad. In the household I grew up in, food is a significant way to express affection, a love language in itself. This succulent breakfast is my love letter to Lex, my way to repay him for the best night of my life. For *all* the best nights of my life, actually.

I'm just done putting everything on a gigantic tray when I see him come into the living area, only wearing a pair of light gray sweatpants. Damn, that very visible bulge in there is incredibly appealing. And the set of abs above is just as tantalizing, the deep V at his hips pointing straight to his tempting dick.

I'm so stunned by the vision he offers that it takes me a few seconds to realize my breakfast-in-bed plan is ruined.

"I told you to stay there," I remind him with a pout.

"I thought I shouldn't let you do all the work. I changed the sheets and tidied the bathroom." Oh, right … We got carried away before our shower, and the intense *slex* on the marbled counter left a mess. A smile bends the corners of his mouth upward when he sees the trays. "Were you going to bring me this in bed?"

I nod, not hiding my disappointment.

"Damn, I would have loved that. It's not too late. I can get back in there," he suggests with a witty smile. I giggle at his apparent excitement.

"No, it's alright. Especially if you changed the sheets. We can eat it here."

He pulls me into his embrace, his hands resting on my waist, his eyes radiating affection. "I'm sorry, Andrea. But the thought of you in my kitchen," he starts, one of his hands reaching for the hem, "wearing only my shirt—"

"Poor thing … That's why you didn't put one on?" I tease.

"Yes," he humors, his hand moving up along the smoothness of my hips. Soon, he gets to where my underwear would be if I were a good girl. "Give it back."

His attempt at getting me naked makes me scoff. "You need a better wardrobe if that's your only shirt."

"And you need to cover yourself better if you don't want me fantasizing about your bare pussy."

With that, he bends and takes my lips, hungry and demanding. I don't fight him, but when he pushes me toward the counter, I say, "Baby, the food will get cold." He ignores me and lifts the shirt to my waist before propping me on the counter. "Lex, it's better when it's hot."

"Don't I fucking know it," he replies, his agile fingers grazing up my intimate folds. Fuck … I'm already wet. He rubs gentle circles around my waking clit, and all notions of breakfast vanish.

The shirt is discarded on the floor next to him, and he gazes down at my breasts, his irises darkening with desire. My insecurities kick in despite everything we've shared, and I instinctively cover my exposed mounds. Lex grabs my wrist and easily pries my arm away.

"Don't hide from me, Andrea. There isn't one part of you I don't find thoroughly perfect, including your tits."

"You're the first person ever to like them."

I'm not fishing for compliments, only speaking the truth. While the general shape is rather round, they're so small that it doesn't even matter. And my areolas are too large for the overall size of my boobs and a little puffy. I know what I have to offer, and it was never enough for other men. Three bluntly pointed out I was too flat for their tastes, and two asked if I ever considered breast implants.

"I don't get people then," Lex argues. "I like how your nipples are smooth and a light shade of brown, but when I do this," he says, bending to take one in his mouth. My breath catches in my throat as he bites, sucks, and licks the sensitive tip. "When I do this, they get small, dark, and perky. I like how they move when you're riding me or when I'm taking you hard. I like how they fit so well in my palms," he continues, covering both of them with his hands and fondling them gently. "But I think what I like the most is that they are attached to you. I love them because they're yours."

"And a little yours, too."

The reminder that I'm his is enough to make him lose the little restraint he has left, and he kisses me like a starving man, desperate to own me. An elegant "ding" comes from the coffee machine, reminding me of everything I cooked.

"Lex, baby …" I whisper, framing his face to force him to meet my eyes. Not only am I starving, but I also want us to enjoy what I cooked to the fullest and not eat it cold. "Brunch first, please. Then you can have as much of me as you want," I offer.

He makes a sound halfway between a huff and a groan, then lowers to pick up the shirt. "Let's eat, then, so I can eat you after."

pov_name = "Alexander"

It might have been ambitious to think we'd be up for sex after the gargantuan brunch she cooked. Neither of us have the capacity to fuck, so we migrate to the couch instead.

When she suggests we use this time to start the movie lessons she's supposed to give me in exchange for all the sex, I tell Iris to set up the room.

Andrea watches in awe as the wide screen rolls down from the ceiling and a 4k projector comes out of it as well. The curtains close, and we're left in near darkness. Once she's fetched her hard drive with her movies, I help her plug it in and we get settled on the couch.

Her choice for this first lesson is *The Lord of the Rings*, a trilogy I've heard many things about but never seen. I've always preferred science fiction and the projected future they depict to fantasy. I say nothing, though, and tell myself I'll at least enjoy the three hours and twenty-eight minutes together. Fucking hell, who makes movies that long?

To my surprise, I find myself quickly engrossed by the story and its characters. Andrea is lying down with her head on the couch's armrest, and her legs are over my lap. Every now and then, she reaches for a candy in the bag on the low table—leftovers from Lucy's visit. She looks good in her booty shorts and my hoodie, but Frodo and his friends have most of my attention.

Despite the compelling plot, I realize we've never felt like a couple as much as we do right now. This is the kind of intimacy I never expected to have with anyone, but I now crave to share more of this comfortable easiness with her.

Out of nowhere, she sits up, grabs my face, and gives me an intense peck on the lips before lying back down.

"What was that for?" I ask, slightly disoriented.

"You looked too adorable, all focused and intense."

I shake my head with a light laugh and return my attention to the screen. After a few minutes, when Frodo and Sam leave the Shire for their quest, my hands begin to gently massage and graze the softness of her legs. Yes, I definitely want more of these moments. In fact, I think I want them for the rest of my life.

Whenever I get too engrossed in the movie and stop, she wriggles her legs, silently demanding that I resume. I give her an amused glance every time and return to the task.

I don't miss the way she slightly presses her knees together whenever my hands venture too far up her thighs, even more so when I graze the inner part of them. What started as a platonic endeavor soon turns into a game I'm the only one playing, and I make it my goal to make her discreetly writhe and twist on the couch.

Right after the chaotic Council of Elrond, she gives up and grabs the remote on the table. "We're taking a break," she decides.

"Everything okay?" I ask, feigning innocence.

"Don't act like you're not perfectly aware of what you're doing to me, Coleman."

I'm not good at hiding a smirk. "You can't even watch a movie without having me?"

"Can you?" she retorts, pressing her calf harder onto my crotch, where my dick has been hard for a while.

A broad smile stretches my lips as I yank one of her legs on the other side of me and lean in to cover her body with mine.

"You taste like candy," I say after an urgent kiss. I've never liked sugary treats, but I love it on her tongue, so I try again. Needy, she slips a slender hand under the elastic of my sweatpants, wrapping her fingers around my hardened length.

"Fuck, your hand is cold."

"And you're so hard already," she whispers, licking my upper lip. I groan and thrust into her palm.

Clearly, we're still far from having satiated all our wants and needs for one another, and although we're actively working on it, we still have some way to go.

I'm pulling down the zipper of the hoodie when her phone vibrates next to us. Whoever's calling will have to try again later. Andrea tenses under me as I lay passionate kisses over her exposed breasts.

"Lex, wait," she worriedly says. "Kate knows I'm spending the weekend with you. She wouldn't call unless it's life or death," she explains.

I move away from her as she straightens up and takes the call. "Hi, babe. What's going on?" she asks. I'm close enough to hear her friend's response, but it's incomprehensible gibberish. "Wow, slow down, Kate. Tell me what's happening."

Andrea sits straight on the couch, visibly anxious, and I rest a comforting hand on her thigh. I stay right there as she talks to her friend, understanding that whatever is going on is very serious.

"I'm going to kill that fucking Italian prick," she mutters into the phone at some point. "You stay home, I'll be there in a few hours."

What? Is our weekend together coming to an abrupt end?

After a few more reassuring words, Andrea hangs up.

"What happened?" I ask.

"Her ex has a sex tape of them, and he's threatening to leak it," she explains, fidgeting with her phone. "I'm sorry, I can't leave her alone in this situation."

As much as I dislike what that means, I can't put my needs and desires before hers and her friend's. "I understand. I'll drive you to your place."

She gives me a sheepish smile and hugs me tightly. "My God, you're so perfect," she mumbles as my arms envelop her, half her face plastered against my chest. "I swear I'll make it up to you."

"I'm sure you will. I was rather enjoying the moment."

"You mean the movie?"

"I don't. But I enjoyed the movie too," I playfully retort before giving her a quick peck. "Now go get ready. You have a friend to rescue."

After one last look full of apologies, she disappears into the corridor. I tell myself that her friend needs her more than I do. And I know Andrea wouldn't be able to enjoy the rest of the weekend if I didn't let her go.

We'll have more time together. Plenty of it.

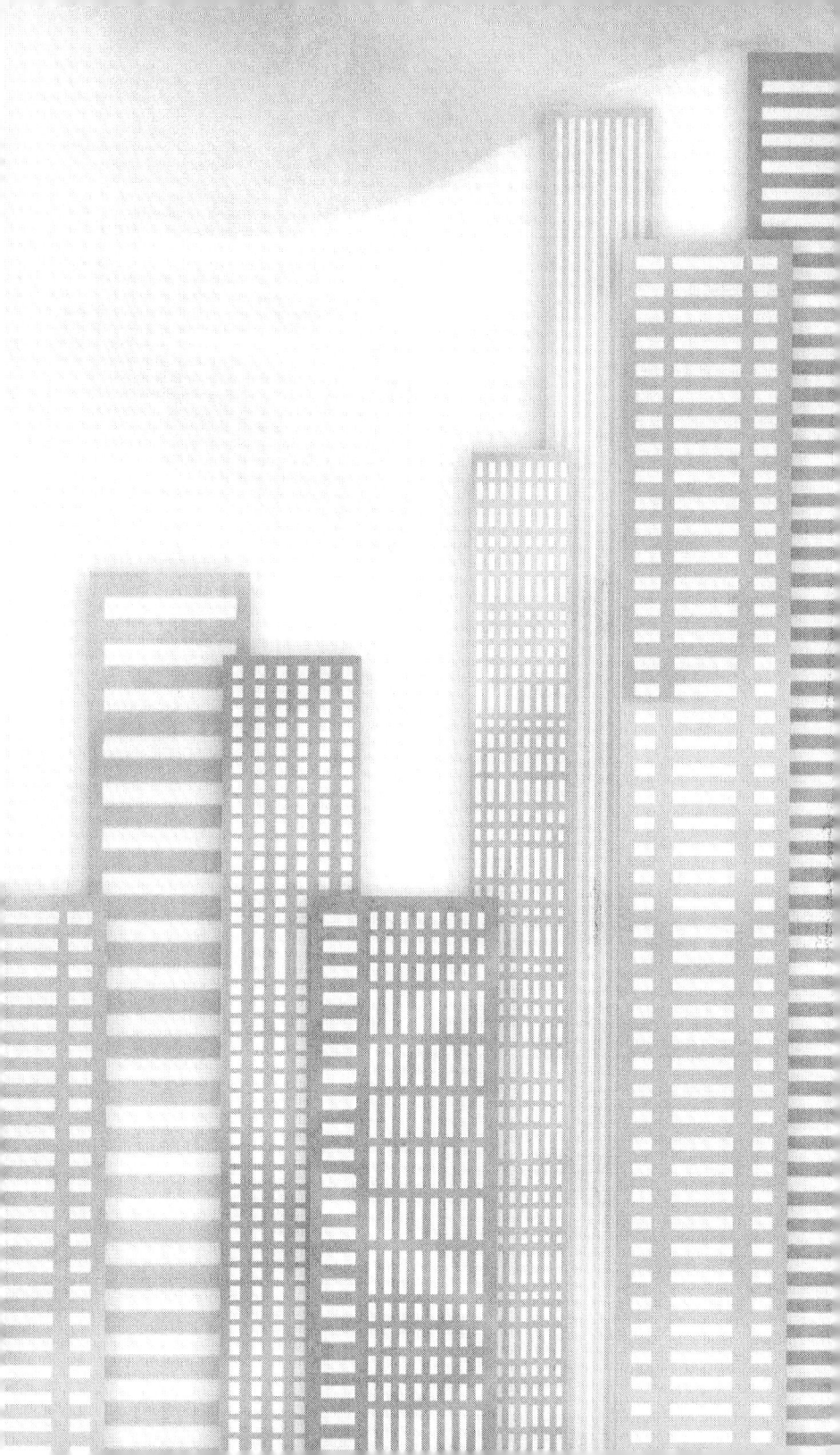

is_new_chapter = True

chapter_number = "35"

pov_name = "Andrea"

KATE LIVES IN A SMALL suburban house in the neighborhood we grew up in. As I drive through the familiar streets, I realize how much I missed it. In a little over two months since my move to Seattle, I haven't been back here. I talk a lot with my parents, abuela, and Kate, but it's not the same.

I park in her lane, behind her powder blue Mini Cooper, and quickly exit my old Ford before taking my bag from the trunk and locking the car. The few steps to the patio are quickly ascended, and the door swings open as I'm about to knock.

Kate stands behind it in pink pajama shorts and a flimsy white top, with red and puffy eyes. We instantly fall into each other's arms. A series of sobs overwhelm her as I hold her tightly in my comforting embrace. We stay like this for a while as I whisper reassuring words in her ear.

"I'm so sorry this is happening to you, babe. I swear, he won't get away with this. I'll take care of it."

Little by little, her breathing returns to normal. When I sense she's well enough, I let go of her after one last squeeze. We move inside, and she locks the door behind us.

As always, her house is all tidied up and nicely decorated. Kate has a whole Scandinavian aesthetic going on, with soft and elegant pastel tones. Although it isn't for me, I always found it cozy and girly, and it suits her very well.

"I'm so sorry I ruined your weekend," she says with a shameful pout.

"It's okay. Lex was fine with it. He practically wanted to drive me here," I reassure her. Upon remembering the pile of rust that is my car, he offered that option. Several times.

"I didn't know who else to turn to. Nobody can know about this."

"It's okay. I'll always be here for you, blondie," I insist.

I'm just settling on her light teal sofa when Mr. Fluffybutt comes from his hiding spot to greet me. The old, overweight, and lazy Persian has been with Kate for over eighteen years. He's her loyal companion, the one male in her life who would never leave her. He and I have a love-hate relationship since he never forgave me for waking him up from a nap with a garden hose when I was eleven. But over the years, his old rancor slowly shifted into indifferent acceptance.

So when the white fur ball jumps directly on my lap, I'm genuinely shocked. Unsure of what to do about this unusual display of affection, I turn to Kate, stunned.

"Yeah, I told you he wasn't doing great lately," she says with a mirthless smile.

"No, it just took him fifteen years to forgive me," I counter, petting his soft fur. Mr. Fluffybutt lies down on my thighs and starts purring. "What does Stefano want exactly?"

"He wants to get back together. That woman apparently meant nothing to him, and I'm overreacting."

"Yeah, you can't do that."

"Oh, trust me, I know. I'm so done with his bullshit."

"I swear, babe, I don't know how you keep picking the worst possible guys."

"They aren't like that at first. They're perfect, kind, considerate, and charming. But then it shifts so slowly that you barely realize it. And when you do, it's too late. You're dating a possessive jerk. Stefano was great until he wasn't. He was so good with me at first, treating me like a princess, and I still can't believe it's the same man doing this to me now."

"You need to find a decent guy."

"I'm trying, you bitch," she retorts, a faint trace of humor in her voice. "We can't all be as lucky as you and end up working for Mr. Perfect."

I blush slightly. "He isn't Mr. Perfect. He's just perfect for me. And we were talking about you. That's more important right now."

"Please, I just need a distraction for a few minutes. I've been thinking about Stefano all day and need to clear my mind a little. We'll get back to it after you're done telling me about Alexander."

"Your advice to sleep with him to get him out of my system backfired monumentally."

"Of course it did, you moron."

Her smug expression tells me she always knew things would spiral out of control with Lex. "But—you-you said it would work," I stutter, half-amused and half-scandalized.

"First of all, I said it *might* work. Second, I said whatever you needed to hear to take that leap. I saw you two together and knew there had to be more to this."

"You manipulated me?"

"I know how blind and stubborn you can be, you cretin."

"So you made me sleep with him?"

She snorts, unimpressed. "I didn't make you do anything. I suggested it, and you very much went for it on your own. And why are you even arguing about this? Are you pissed that I pushed you to try, you ungrateful brat?"

I shake my head, struggling to hide my contented grin.

"Now, thanks to me, you finally have a good boyfriend."

"He's not my boyfriend."

"Oh, did you two elope already?" she teases.

"Will you just shut up," I protest, hiding my flushed face.

"Andy and Lex, sitting in a tree," she starts to sing with a shit-eating grin. "K-I-S-S-I—Oof."

The pillow I throw right in her face stops her, but it's quickly returned with the same strength, but I whack it mid-air to protect the cat. It's ridiculous how our personalities regress to our dumb teenage selves when we're together.

Kate stays silent for a moment, studying my face carefully. Before I can figure out what she's onto, her face lights up. "Oh, my God … You're in love with him!"

It isn't a question, so I don't answer. "Have you told him yet?"

I shake my head, wondering if I should mention I was very close to doing it a few times. But I didn't in case he doesn't love me back, or if it scares him, or if he'll remind me he isn't the relationship type …

"Are you planning on telling him at some point?" Kate carefully tries. I nod, and she smiles. "When?"

"When I'm sure."

"Of what?"

"That he feels the same way."

"Aw, Deedee … If I were him, I'd be on the verge of proposing by now."

"But you love me for sure, so you don't count. Can we get back on track, though? We need to handle your problem, K."

At the mention of the Stefano debacle, we both fall silent for a moment. Only the regular purring of Mr. Fluffybutt on my lap continues as I distractedly pet him.

"I still can't believe that fucking prick filmed you."

"Me neither. It looks like he taped us from the bookshelf in his room. I feel so violated, Deedee. The worst part is, if he had asked, I might have agreed to do it. Can you imagine? At least I can't hate myself for allowing him to film us. All I can do is hate myself for dating him in the first place."

"We should have seen it coming. Only someone mentally imbalanced would wear that much gel in their hair," I say. She always knew I hated him since I was pretty vocal about it in the past. But this isn't an I-told-you-so moment, so I don't remind her.

She turns herself into a tight ball as she always does when stressed, with her knees against her chest and arms around her folded legs. "He did wear too much gel, didn't he?"

"Absolutely. The first time I saw him, I remember thinking you could put a dictionary on his head, and nothing would move."

"One of those big ones, with thick pages and hardcovers." We laugh together softly, and silence slowly settles in the room again. She lays her temple on her knee. "Andy, what am I going to do?" she asks, despair making her voice crack.

"We'll find a way. We'll brainstorm together and get the video back, all the versions of it, and also make him pay for what he did to you."

"He knows the law in and out, Dee. I don't want you to be in danger because of me."

"I won't. You know the law, too. And we're smart as fuck. We can figure something out. You already thought about going to the cops, I imagine?"

"I've seen how they treat women who come in with a broken arm and a black eye. I don't even want to imagine how little they will care about my case. And Stefano said he'd leak it if I do."

Even a few minutes of it on the internet could damage Kate's reputation and social life. It's unfair how women get so hurt by leaked sex tapes, but the fucking pigs who spread them in the first place usually come out of it unscathed.

"My biggest worry is that he saved it somewhere, and even if he deletes something in front of us, he can still have it elsewhere and use it at some point," I explain. I have no way of knowing how many copies of it exist. For all we know, he can even have burned it on a DVD and hidden it in a book.

"Maybe we could—" Kate starts as my phone rings in my pocket.

"Sorry," I grimace, struggling to reach for it because of the obese cat on my lap.

Mr. Fluffybutt jumps down anyway, and my eyebrows come together when I see my mom's face on the screen. I take the call and put the phone to my ear.

"*Hola, mamá*, what's up?"

"Andrea Grace Walker! *¿Qué hice para merecer una hija como tú?*" she yells in my ear. *What did I do to deserve a daughter like you?*

"*¿Qué?*" I ask, confused. Why is she pissed at me right now?

"Susan just passed by Kate's house, and she told me she saw your car there."

Mrs. Temple, that gossipy snitch …

"Mom, I'm sorry. Kate has an emergency. I'll come tomorrow."

"Tomorrow? *¡Por Dios!* We haven't seen you for six months, and when you're finally back, you can't even come to the house?!"

I roll my eyes so hard I'm pretty sure I see my brain. "Mom, it's barely been two months, and Kate needs me."

She finally catches something's wrong, and her attitude changes entirely. "Oh, no … Is she okay?"

"She will be," I say, looking at my best friend with hope.

"You two are coming home tonight. You'll get a nice, warm meal, and you girls can have a sleepover in your bedroom like you used to."

"Mom, I don't think she's up for a sleepover right now." Kate understands what's happening, so she nods enthusiastically, urging me to accept my mom's offer. "Oh, actually, she … wants to … come?" I carefully reply. I set the phone on my chest, ignoring my mom's exclamations of joy, and turn to Kate. "Are you sure?"

"Yes, my God. Anything to get out of my head right now. And I miss your mom's cuisine."

I put the phone back to my ear, ready to negotiate the modalities of our detention. "Okay, Mom, I just arrived from a long drive, so we'll stay here a bit and then come to you."

"You will be just as good here. Oh, Rafa is thrilled to know you're coming. Your dad, too. And your abuela just pretended she doesn't remember who you are since you haven't called her in two weeks."

I look at Kate, who still needs to get ready, and myself, still wearing Lex's hoodie. Or *my* hoodie now—it's one of the unwritten laws of dating.

"Mom, we'll be there in thirty minutes. I can't do better than that," I offer.

"Okay. I'll prepare your bedroom while *mamá* works on dinner."

"Oh, MC is cooking," I enthusiastically whisper to Kate.

"Ugh, even better!"

Alright, we can do this. We'll head to my parents' place, feast on my abuela's food, and then figure out how to kill and bury Stefano without getting caught.

is_scene_break = True

As Kate and I walk to my parents' porch, I'm reminded of the hours we spent playing in the front yard, often with Rafael. Various toys used to be scattered over the lawn, but those times are long gone. In the backyard, there's a small pool where we spent entire summers, living off PB&Js and lemonade.

I knock using the dragon door knocker my dad installed against my mom's will three years ago. It's always strange to be a guest in what feels like my own house. Some activity happens inside, and soon enough, the door opens wide, revealing my mom's familiar silhouette.

Isabella Walker, born Ibanez, isn't precisely a coquettish woman, but she takes care of herself, trying not to let the years passing become too obvious. She's a little chubby despite counting calories and race-walking with her friends three times a week. And she dyes her hair to hide the growing number of white strands in it. Sometimes, like now, she doesn't have time to take care of her roots, so she wears a headband to maintain the illusion.

As unfeminist as it may sound, she was put on this earth to care for kids—always warm, compassionate, and sensible. That's why she's so good at teaching, and it explains why, at the end of every year, her students pitch in to offer her a thank-you gift. She can be strict at times but she's always fair, and I couldn't have asked for a better mother. And I'm a bad daughter for not coming back sooner.

But she doesn't mind, engulfing us both in a tight and motherly hug.

"I'm so happy you're here, my girls," she says, kissing each of us. The affectionate reunion lingers for a few seconds, and she eventually releases us before inviting us inside.

We follow her to the dining room, where Rafa and Dad have just finished setting the table.

Thanks to our video calls, I know my brother has been growing a little scruff, almost a beard by now, so the sight doesn't shock me too much. Still, it's odd to see him with so much facial hair. He's tall, has our father's green eyes, and our mother's brown complexion. But we share curly dark hair, a straight nose, and plump lips. People often tell us that we look a lot alike. It was a terrible insult during childhood, but now, we're both glad whenever someone points it out.

It's hard to be objective since his ugly mug has graced my life from the very beginning, but it's my understanding that he's a handsome devil. The fact that he's an artist on top of being deaf apparently makes for an irresistible combination. All he has to do is snap his fingers for ten women to rush in, ready to fulfill his every need. Somehow, people expect him to be a sweet and sensible guy. But it doesn't work like that. Rafael was destined to be a man-whore, deaf artist or not.

My father lets Rafa continue alone and comes to me.

"Hi, peanut," he greets me, giving me a tight hug and a quick kiss on top of my head.

"Hi, Dad."

As Kate gets the same treatment, I lovingly look at my dad.

Michael Walker is tall and—to my mother's great envy—lean without even trying. For as long as I can remember, my dad has worn the same model of rimless glasses and variations of blueish short-sleeved button-ups and beige pants. While his fast metabolism might help him age well, his receding hairline doesn't. For years, my mom has been trying to get him to buzz cut it all, insisting he would look like Bruce Willis, but he hangs on to what he has left with tenacity. Rafa and I don't want to get involved in this debate because we both know there's no way he'd ever look like the *Die Hard* actor.

I let my dad and Kate discuss, moving on with the salutations. Rafa and I fist-bump as I pass by him, and then I follow the mouth-watering smells to the kitchen.

The delicious-looking food surrounding my abuela almost makes me drool. She went overboard and prepared way too much. I'm not complaining, though. There are corn cobs, Pozole, homemade tortillas, fried rice, sautéed veggies, and I can see some meat roasting in the oven.

"*¡Hola, MC! ¿Cómo estás?*" I ask her, using the street name Rafael and I teasingly picked for her. It was initially a joke, but it stuck around.

Maria Carmen Ibanez was busy her entire life, working hard to raise three children while earning a salary as a maid in a luxurious hotel. She's remained active since retiring, and one could never guess she's seventy-six. To her great pride, she can still do pretty much everything with impressive efficiency. Her quick wits also remain untouched by the years, and her repartee is legendary. I don't look much like my mother or father, but from what I've heard and the old, damaged pictures I've seen, I'm MC's spitting image. I certainly inherited her short height since both my parents are taller than average.

She barely pays me any attention, busy tasting the stew before her. "*Estoy bien.* Hand me the salt, *mija*," she asks, without even turning toward me. Knowing how she gets when she cooks, I smile and obey swiftly.

When I reach her, she takes the salt from my hands and extends her cheek for me to kiss it. Once more, I comply, enjoying the familiar scent of her face moisturizer, and offer my cheek in return. She gives me a peck and returns to her cooking.

"Do you need any help?" I propose in Spanish.

"No, I'm almost done. Go make sure the boys set the table correctly, and you can tell everyone we're eating in five minutes."

When I'm back in the dining room, Rafa, Mom, and Kate are talking while Dad sets the wine glasses on the table, as well as two beers—for him and me.

Dinner unfolds nicely. It's delightful to be here, surrounded by my loved ones. The food is fantastic, and catching up with them is great. But I can't help it as my mind regularly drifts to another loved one, spending his evening alone instead of with me, as intended.

Fuck! I was supposed to text him when I arrived! I take my phone out swiftly and open my messages.

ME

Sorry, I forgot to text you!

Right after, typing bubbles appear.

LEX

It's alright. I figured you were busy and didn't want to bother you.

ME

You could never bother me.

For the duration of the dinner, my mind is divided between the conversation I'm having on my phone with Lex and the one with my family. Although I love my folks, I'm much more interested in whatever Lex texts me.

LEX

The suspense has been killing me. I think I might keep watching the movie without you.

ME

Don't you dare. This is our first movie together. You can't do that.

LEX

Fine. But next time you cut short one of our weekends together, I'll have to discipline you.

The temperature goes up at once as a delicious warmth spreads through my body. Images of Lex sexually chastising me flood my mind.

ME

How would you do it?

There's a moment of nothing before the bubbles on his side appear again. Jesus Christ, I love when he takes charge. I'm not submissive in any other aspects of my life, but during sex, I turn into an absolute simp for him.

"Andy, have you been exercising?" my mom asks from the other side of the table.

I'm abruptly reminded of my surroundings, and my cheeks burn with shame. Dammit. My eyes fly to Kate's, who's biting back a smile.

"Oh, yes, she has," she answers for me. "She found an amazing coach in Seattle. She's very devoted to working out. You exercise what, at least three times a week now? Or is it three times a ni—"

Her attempt at exposing my illicit affair is cut short when I slam my hand on the table.

"Yes! I've been working out with Tamika a little. She's into Pilates. I swear, she's one good action away from becoming my main girl," I pretend, squinting my eyes at Kate. She doesn't take my threat seriously and holds back a grin.

When the topic changes and Kate isn't at risk of exposing my sex life to my entire family, I pick up my phone to see if Lex answered.

He did.

And holy *fuck*.

LEX

I need to win a bet first because you'll have to be tied up for this. Then, I think I'll work on a question I've had for a while now: how many times can I make you come with just my tongue in an hour? By the time I'm done answering it, you'll already be begging for mercy, spent, and feeling like you can't take more.

But you're being taught a lesson, so I say when we're done. I'll fuck you hard, pushing you further than what you think is possible. I'll make you come repeatedly until you are so raw you feel like your heart has relocated between your legs. It will only stop when I know you have actually reached your limit, and I'll come with you, filling your tight, overworked cunt with my cum.

Holy Mother of God …

That's so ridiculously hot, I'm forced to squeeze my legs together, my clit palpitating at the naughty promises. Under my very proper clothes, I grow impossibly wet as my mind conjures images of what he described. Shit, the fantasy is so intense that I can almost feel Lex powerfully thrusting into my willing flesh. Goddamnit, Stefano will get so much shit—not just for what he did to Kate, but also for keeping me away from Lex.

I type my answer, holding back a conflicted chuckle.

ME

Alexander! My abuela is two chairs away from me!

LEX

Sorry, was it too much?

ME

No, but how dare you make me this wet during family dinner?!

LEX

Well, have a glass of water to stay hydrated.

I giggle, which attracts my mom's interest. I hide my phone better as I type:

ME

Screw the bet, baby. You can tie me up whenever you want.

LEX

You're not helping with my hard-on.

ME

I'm afraid you'll have to handle this one alone. Think of me while you do it?

LEX

Always.

Deciding it's enough *slexting* over family dinner, I wish him good night and settle my phone face down, ready to keep my attention focused on the people around me.

About twenty minutes later, my mom and I are in the kitchen, finishing the dishes while the others are in the living room.

"So, who is he?" she asks out of the blue.

"What? Who?"

"That boy you're seeing."

"I'm—I'm not—"

"Oh, please. You've been blushing and giggling at your phone all evening long. I see teenagers do this every day. I know what it means."

Shit, busted …

"Uh … his name is Lex. Alexander. And he isn't a 'boy.'"

"Don't get sassy on me. For how long have you been seeing him?"

"Almost a month."

"It's a good start. Is he husband material?"

I laugh, both shocked and amused by her boldness. "Mom, slow down. I'm still trying to figure out if he's boyfriend material."

"Hmm … Is he handsome? Will my grandkids be gorgeous?"

"*¡Por Dios, mamá!*" I protest.

"Alright, alright. I'll stop."

The silence stretches, with only the sounds of the dishes distracting us. She probably has dozens of questions, but she holds back. "Could you not tell Dad?" I ask, not wanting the news to spread too fast. She nods, handing me a pan to dry.

Once we're done, I head upstairs to my room and fish my phone out of my pocket. There's only one person I know who has the potential to help Kate, and I hope he'll be able to do it.

"What's up, Hulkette?" Oli greets when he picks up.

"Hi, son of Jared. I need a favor. It's a bit tricky, so I'm just gonna go ahead and ask."

"Yeah, sure. I hope everything's fine," he says with slight worry.

"For me, yes. It's my best friend, Kate."

"What's going on?"

"Well, her ex is a fucking prick, is what's going on. He's got footage of her he's taken without her consent, and he's now threatening to leak it unless she gets back with him."

"Ouch, okay. That's fucked up."

"Yeah, I know. And I'm so worried he'll actually do it, Oli," I explain, sitting on my bed and grabbing my plush armadillo to hug it tightly.

"Do you want me to … take care of it?"

"You think you could get everything?"

"Yeah, that's what I do—among other things. Kate wouldn't be the first one I'm helping like this. I've done it dozens of times."

"Are you saying you're some sort of cyber knight in shining armor?"

He chuckles at the idea, and his assurance when he speaks again comforts me. "I guess you could say that, yes. It started with my sister when some asshole began harassing her on Instagram. I found him and scared the shit out of him. I made this super creepy threat video and essentially ruined the guy's computer by unleashing an army of viruses on it."

"Wow, that sounds extreme."

"Yeah, well, I wasn't letting anyone make death threats to my baby sister. Anyhow, I'm known in the hacking community as the savior of ladies. Especially since I stopped doing anything else a while back."

I hesitate for the longest time, refusing to let him put himself in danger. But clearly, this wouldn't be his first rodeo.

"You're pretty good at this hacking thing, aren't you?" I ask.

"Let's say I can help your friend without breaking a sweat, Hulkette."

"If you do this, I'll owe you a huge one," I say, rolling onto my stomach.

"Nah, you really won't. You're actually giving me something to occupy the boring Sunday incoming." His insane kindness has me laughing with relief. God, this man is truly a gem, and whichever girl snatches him up will be very lucky.

Knocks on my door make us cut the call, and Rafael's tall frame enters my room. "Hi, dickhead," I sign.

"'Sup ass wipe?"

I bite the inside of my cheek, holding back my amusement. Old habits die hard. We didn't get along so well as kids, like most siblings, really. He was the big one, but I could be cruel. Like when I would close my eyes during an argument to rob him of his ability to communicate. I stopped doing that as soon as I realized how fucked up and unfair it was.

His charisma has been there for a while, and many of my girlfriends during our teenage years were infatuated with him. And sometimes, he indulged in their interest, only to crush their heart later on. The process usually left me with one less friend. So, after multiple debacles like this, we agreed I had the right to call dibs on certain girls, and he couldn't, under any circumstances, get into their panties. Kate was the very first one I claimed, even though there wasn't any risk there. Rafa always considered her a childish little sister as much as he does me.

Since I'm sprawled on the bed on my stomach, he pretends to sit on me, adding enough pressure to make me groan in protest. He moves up when I wriggle, allowing me to switch positions. As I'm bringing myself up, he harshly whacks the outer side of my ass.

"Ah, you dick!" I shout.

Swiftly turning around, I kick his side to shove him away in retaliation and send a soothing hand there to appease the burn from the violent blow. Damn, the whole area stings with pain.

"Be faster next time. Even abuela is in better shape than you," he signs as he sits down.

"What do you want?"

He suddenly looks serious before he signs. "Is Kate okay?"

"I'm working on it."

"Do you need help?"

I vaguely explain that her ex is causing trouble, keeping out the part about the sex tape since she doesn't want others to know. Rafa is glad to hear I already have a plan but still offers to beat the shit out of that Italian prick. As tempting as his offer is, I'm confident Oli can pull it off.

Stefano has no idea what's coming for him. I don't either, but I know it'll hurt.

is_new_chapter = True

chapter_number =

"36"

pov_name =

"Andrea"

"What could I do to thank Oli?" Kate asks, sitting cross-legged on the floor by her cat's basket. It's Sunday, and we're back at her place. Today, Oli will handle the Stefano problem, and we only have to wait patiently for him to finish.

"What do you mean? Like a blowjob?"

"No! I meant something like cookies or cupcakes or something."

"He has a sweet tooth, so he might actually appreciate that a lot," I say after giving it a quick thought.

"Okay, great. I think I have everything I need. Will you help me? It'll be like old times."

With her irresistible blue eyes, she begs me to agree. Honestly, I can't refuse her anything when she looks at me like that. And anyhow, it'll be a great way to keep ourselves distracted. I give in with a nod, and Kate gives Mr. Fluffybutt a quick kiss before standing up as if mounted on springs.

I follow her to her kitchen, amused by how excited she is. "Oh God, I hope I remember how to do this," she says, heading to the sink to wash her hands.

"What do you mean? You're like, the queen of baking."

Back in high school, Kate always baked for her cheerleading squad to support charities, raise awareness, or do fundraisings … I was always there to help, even though I mostly ended up licking the bowls or trying whatever she needed me to taste.

Kate grimaces and avoids my gaze, taking out some of the necessary ingredients. "I haven't baked in at least six months," she confesses.

"Oh, wow. Has work been that intense?"

"Actually, it is because of—No, you'll get mad at me."

"I promise I won't. Tell me, K."

"It was … Stefano. I gained a few pounds earlier this year because I was stress-baking. And he noticed, so he told me I was getting fat and should be careful."

I think she's joking at first, but then I notice the shame in her eyes. "Wait, are you for real right now?" I ask, incredulous.

"You promised you wouldn't be mad at me."

"I'm not mad at you. I'm mad at him! What the actual fuck? You gained two pounds, so he told you you were getting fat? When you have the body of a fucking model?!"

"It was over six pounds, actually."

"Babe, no! Don't try to justify his assholeness. Oh my God. I'm two seconds away from calling Oli off to hire a hitman instead. That fucking prick, I can't believe it. Please, at least tell me he was good in bed."

"He was acceptable. I mean, most times, it was good. But yeah, I had to finish myself off in the shower now and then," she confesses.

"Okay, you know what? That's it. You're grounded from dating. The next guy you want to date must go through me first. I'll set up a thorough interview and a quiz to make sure he deserves you before you're allowed to do *anything* with him."

The idea has her giggling, even though I'm dead serious, and she shakes her head. "Something tells me not a single one will pass the test."

"Yeah, probably not. Anyhow, let's get on with these cupcakes. Actually, you know what? I think Oli deserves more than cupcakes. We're making your peanut butter cookies, the red velvet cupcakes, and the Snickers brownies. And we're making batches of those for my parents, you, me, and Lex—or else he'll eat *my* stuff."

"Deedee, that's a lot."

"You bet your sweet ass it is. We'll be baking the entire day." She's too clever not to understand why I'm doing this, so she gives me a teary smile full of appreciation and affection.

"I love you so much, you incredible bitch," she tells me, coming my way to give me an intense hug.

"And I love you right back, you magnificent skank," I reply, wrapping my arms around her slender frame.

"I'm almost out of baking powder, though, so I'm not sure we can cook all that."

"I'll text Rafa. He can't resist your baking, so he'll get some if it means he can get his own share of cookies."

For over three hours, we're thrown back a decade into the past, having fun baking like we used to do in high school. For the occasion, we even put on a playlist from back then, missing those years when everything was so much simpler. Kate is still impressive at all this, and I'm still excellent at assisting her and tasting things. It's honestly the best distraction we could ever have come up with since we're too busy to even give Stefano a thought. From time to time, though, I check my phone to see if I have any news from Oli.

A little after 2 p.m., it finally comes. We stop what we're doing, and after wiping my flour-covered hands on my apron, I read the message out loud for Kate. "Hey, Hulkette. It's done. Everything went smoothly. I removed the copy on his cloud, computer, and a hard drive that was luckily plugged in. I also let him know that a few of us would be watching him, so he better not do anything like this in the future. Tell me if he bothers Kate again, and I'll see what else can be done. Oh, I also turned his computer into an overpriced brick."

"Hulkette?" Kate asks, amused.

"It's because of the T-shirt I wore on my first day."

"Still can't believe you thought that was a good idea … It's a cute nickname, though. I like it."

"Me too."

We both reread the message, and the tension fades. It's done. It's really done.

"I can't believe it's finally over," she says, an incredulous smile stretching her pink lips. "Stefano's been harassing me for months, and now it's finally over."

"You should have come to me sooner, babe. I could have helped and supported you."

"I didn't want to bother you. You had so much going on with your job, and new life, and Lex. I didn't—"

"You're more important than any job, K. You're my ride or die. I need to know these things."

She laughs softly, returning to her piping bag. "Okay, I promise. Next time some asshole breaks my heart, I'll tell you immediately."

"There won't be any more assholes. I'm the one approving the next ones, remember?" I humor. She snorts, refusing the statement with a shake of her head.

About an hour later, we're nearly done with everything. The last batch of Snickers brownies is cooking in the oven, and the dishes are almost finished. We're a mess, with flour and traces of chocolate on our aprons, exhausted by our impressive accomplishment. Never in the past had we baked that many things. Not even for my *quinceañera* or her sweet sixteen.

I'm still washing the dishes when the doorbell rings, so Kate handles it. I hear voices but can't make out what's being said. However, when the tone rises, I perceive the distress in Kate's voice.

Fuck … Letting go of everything, I rush out of the kitchen to join her by the entrance. When I see the man she's talking with, I stop as abruptly as if I'd bumped into a wall. Stefano is trying to come in, pushing against Kate, who's doing her best to keep him outside.

Pure rage courses through my veins, and I charge at him like a bull. With our combined efforts, we make him stumble back to the porch.

"You stupid as fuck waste of air," I snarl at him.

"I should have known you were a part of this, you fucking bitch," he yells at me. Kate seems to be in a state of shock, unable to react, and I make sure to be between them. "Do you have any idea what you two stupid whores did? I had work on that computer!"

"Go rot in fucking hell, *hijo de la chingada*."

"I'll get you for this, you immigrant fuck. And you—"

He turns to Kate again, but I don't let him, reclaiming his attention with, "If you touch a single hair on her head, I'm going to fucking kill you!"

"I'd like to see you try, you dumb bitch," he says, intimidatingly approaching me. Fuck, I didn't think this through.

"If you come near us, I'll call the fucking cops, *pinche puto.*"

"Really? Here, call them," he snickers, extending his phone. "Call them and tell them how you crazy whores hacked into my stuff and destroyed my computer."

"You dense fuck, we didn't do shit," I defend us, whacking his hand out of the way, slamming his phone to the ground. "Now get the fuck away before—"

"Before what?" He looks at his phone and then glares at me, even angrier than before. "You're like a Chihuahua. What the fuck do you think you can do to me?"

To prove his words, he backs his hand away, ready to violently slap me. A sharp wave of panic hits me, and I mentally prepare myself for the blow. The rest unfolds in a rapid blur as his hand comes down hard across my face, just as Kate pulls me back. The impact makes me stumble into her, the painful heat of it radiating from my cheek to the entire side of my face.

But before I can process any of it, Stefano is brutally tackled to the ground by an unexpected newcomer. Completely stunned, Kate and I stare at Stefano on his back and the feral man administering painful blows to his face. Why is Rafael here? But also, thank God he is.

Still disoriented, I watch as Rafael beats the shit out of him, my ear still ringing and pain searing across my cheek. Kate's the first one to react, trying to pull my brother away from Stefano's whimpering form. Since I don't want Rafa to get charged with assault and battery, I go to assist her, but we're not strong enough. Out of nowhere, two big, muscular Latinos come to help us. Eventually, we tear Rafael away from Stefano, pulling him to his feet.

I've rarely witnessed it in the past, but I can see how much my brother wishes he could utter all the thoughts and insults he wants to throw. In his eyes, I can read the hateful things he wants to shout at Stefano but can't.

The two men holding him back seem to know him, so I guess they arrived with him. Because of their muscular builds, tattoos, and baggy clothes, they're particularly intimidating.

Stunned and shaky, Stefano rises to his feet, his moves slow and imprecise. Now that we have three big guys on our side, his attitude has changed entirely—from pompous jerk to scared little boy. My confidence grows as if fueled by his deflating assurance, even though my cheek is still burning.

"You do not talk to Kate, you do not look at her, contact her, or even think of her," I tell him. "She is off-limits. *¡Tu pinche madre!* If I hear you've been trying anything with her, I will fucking rip your balls off myself and feed them to you. Is that clear?"

He hesitates, his eyes going from me to the three guys behind me to Kate. "I can't believe you planned all this. You're a crazy fucking bitch," he bellows at Kate.

Unable to hold back, I use all my weight and strength to sucker punch him. The sensation of my knuckles colliding with his nose is uniquely strange and empowering for some reason. Although all this is new, I distinctly feel something crack under my fist.

I'm not expecting the pain radiating through my hand, but the look of pure shock on Stefano's face is worth everything when he grabs his nose with a cry.

"Did you not hear me just now?!" I yell at him, shaking my hand to diffuse the pain. "You do not even look in her direction, you daft fuck. Is that clear?"

He nods, still holding his nose. "I think you broke it," he whimpers, moving his hands away to check on them.

Oh, wow. That's a lot of blood.

His lower face is covered in thick red liquid, seeping from his nostrils and the cut on the bridge of his nose. Whimpering like a wounded animal, Stefano walks down the few steps and enters his car, double-parked in front of the house.

Kate and Rafa swiftly come to me. "Are you alright?" she asks, examining the side of my face.

"Yeah, don't worry about me." It still hurts a lot, but now so does my hand, so I feel it less.

"You should have let me beat him to a pulp," Rafael signs with angry gestures.

"I broke his nose. I think I'm avenged. Why are you here?"

"You texted me about baking powder." Oh, right … We ended up having enough, so I completely forgot about that. Rafa points to the front yard before he signs, "I think I threw the can in Kate's hydrangeas when I saw him slap you."

The heavily tattooed guys come our way to introduce themselves, and I do the same with Kate and me. We thank them profusely for their intervention. "I don't know how we can repay you for everything," I say.

The biggest one, Antonio, looks down at me with an amused expression. "It's all good, *chica*. You've got some *cojones* on you. I like it."

"Well, still. Thank you for your help."

"Oh!" Kate suddenly lets out. "Wait right here! I've got pastries. I'll give you some."

As she's about to go in, Rafa stops her, grabbing her arm. "Leave some for me, yeah?"

"There's more than enough for everyone," she laughs. With that, she disappears into her house, leaving us on her porch.

Five minutes later, Rafa's friends are gone, and I'm back inside with Kate and my brother. As I hold a bag of frozen peas on my cheek while a bag of frozen strawberries rests on my hand, I look at everything we baked. Yeah, we got a bit carried away.

I can't wait to tell Lex I broke some asshole's nose. I'm confident he'll be proud. I know I am.

When we get back home, Mom and Abuela are playing a game of Spanish Scrabble—which means MC is wiping the floor with her. Rafael is off to the kitchen with boxes filled with pastries, and I stand behind my mom to see her letters. When I find a word worth a lot of points, I bend to her ear to whisper the solution, not even trying to be discreet.

"No cheating! *¡Condenada chamaca!"* MC protests.

"Oh, come on. We need the combined power of two brains to stand a chance."

My abuela smiles with pride, my flattery sweetening the offense. Inconspicuously, I go around the table, and as soon as my mom looks up, I quickly sign the letters to form the word I have in mind. MC catches it, so she sends me a colorful collection of threats while she bends to grab her *chancla* under the table. I expertly avoid it when it flies my way and grin when my mom winks at me and plays my word. Because it's this household's rule, I fetch my abuela's slipper and return it to her.

"Your dad is out back, finally repairing the fence," Mom explains. "We all know how it ends when he gives home improvement a try, so maybe you could check and see if he needs help?"

"On it!" I agree without hesitation, looking forward to quality time with him.

"Before you go. What happened to your face, *mija*?"

Fuck, is my cheek that red? "I, uh, walked into a lamppost."

"Again?!"

"Yep."

As I enter the kitchen on my way to the back door, I grab a few homemade cookies from a jar my mom always keeps filled. It'll be a reward for my dad's hard work and mine for potentially helping him.

I'm just passing the door when my phone buzzes in my pocket. With my mouth filled with oatmeal and chocolate chip deliciousness, I check the notification. My heart beats a little faster upon seeing it's Lex.

LEX

How's your Sunday going?

We barely talked today, and as pathetic as it may sound, I miss him.

I glance at my dad, busy sawing a wooden plank, and decide he can wait a little for his cookies and my help. Instead of texting Lex back, I call to hear his voice.

"Hi there, vigilante," he greets me. I chuckle, delighted by his teasing. "How's helping your friend going?"

"Everything's good now. Her ex won't bother her any longer, and the videos are gone."

"How did you manage that?"

"I scared him to death with my big muscles."

It's his turn to laugh softly. We talk for a while as I aimlessly stroll around the backyard, circling the swimming pool, and end up sitting on an old swing. Unable to resist, I take bites of cookies as we exchange. Turns out my dad might not get any sugary reward after all. At some point, I'm unable to answer for a few seconds, busy swallowing a mouthful.

"Sorry, I was eating a cookie. I should be on time tomorrow morning if the traffic allows it."

"Is it good?"

"We're north of Portland, so it should be fine."

"I meant the cookie, not the traffic," he corrects, clear amusement in his voice.

"Oh! Yes. It's one of my mom's best recipes. They are why my ass got this big," I bitterly explain.

"I'll have to thank her for baking those, then."

An incredulous laugh flows past my lips, stunned that he so boldly affirms his appreciation for my backside. He really, *really* likes my ass, doesn't he?

Once the initial shock passes, I realize what he just said. Was it just a harmless joke, or is he considering the possibility of meeting my parents? It may have just been a quick retort, as it often occurs during our playful banters, but the thought of him coming here with me one day, meeting my dad and mom, sends all sorts of feelings through my chest. I want him to know them, and I want them to know the man I love.

"What are your plans for tonight?" I ask, hoping the mundane conversation will divert the subject.

"Well, for the lack of a better idea, I might end up working."

"I know you're a workaholic, but don't you do anything for fun?"

"I do, but she's currently in Portland, visiting her parents."

My cheeks heat up at his playful teasing, and then the entirety of my skin. An irrepressible laugh bubbles in my chest. God, I love him …

"We need to find you fun things to do other than me."

"It would pale in comparison. Although … There is this movie I'd like to watch, but I'm forbidden to do so."

"Yes, you are. And I swear if you—" I'm interrupted by a series of curses my father lets out. Crap, he just hit himself with the hammer.

"I'm sorry, I have to go. I'm supposed to help my dad with some chores, and now he hurt himself, and I'm the worst daughter ever."

"Ah, sorry for distracting you."

"It's okay. I'll talk to you later, Coleman," I promise.

"Go save your father, Walker."

I hang up, a broad smile stretching my lips from ear to ear. On my way to my father, I shake my head, wondering why my mom even allowed him near a power tool. She usually handles most of the handiwork since my dad is terrible at it. However, she hates circular saws and has a nasty scar on her left thigh to justify it. So, my dad has to take one for the team now and then.

By the time I reach him, I still have a stupid grin plastered on my face.

"What's up, MacGyver?" I ask him.

He grumbles something not very optimistic. "Can you hand me the screwdriver?" I obey and watch as he takes care of a loose screw.

"Were you on the phone with … Alexander, is that it?" he asks, taking me by surprise. I hold back the urge to roll my eyes. *Seriously, Mom?*

"She wasn't supposed to tell you about him."

"We've been together for over thirty years. There's nothing we don't tell each other. That's the secret to a functioning marriage."

"Well, I wasn't ready to talk about him to either of you."

"It's okay. We don't have to if you don't want to," he says, giving me an understanding smile.

I remember the cookies, so I hand him one of the remaining two, and we eat silently. In all truth, I terribly want to tell him about Lex, since he's my favorite topic of conversation.

"We work together," I tell my dad, not ready to admit I actually work *for* Lex. "He's a programmer too. Incredibly smart. You should see him do his thing—it's impressive."

"Better than you?"

"Much better. But I'll get there, eventually. And he has a dry sense of humor, which I like a lot. And because he has zero knowledge of popular culture, I took it upon myself to teach him—and he's cooperating. We were supposed to watch *The Lord of the Rings* trilogy this weekend."

"The extended cuts?"

"Of course."

"I taught you well, my young Padawan." We finish eating, and instead of returning to his task, my dad ponders, obviously wanting to ask me something else. "I think I already guessed, but you really, *really* like him, don't you?"

I gnaw the inside of my cheek and look down at my feet, wondering if I should be honest. I usually tell my dad these things, but this is different. This time, it's real.

"I'm sorry, peanut," he says after a few seconds of silence. "You said you didn't want to talk about him, and I'm pressing you with big questions."

"It's fine, Dad. As a matter of fact, I'm in love with him, yes. And I realized I was never in love before him because nothing ever felt like this."

He gives me a tender smile, his eyes slightly glassy with emotions. "When you know, you know, Dee. Does he love you too?"

My heart twists in my chest at the innocent question. I don't know what to answer. I hope Lex does, but I can't say for sure.

"I-I don't know," I answer sheepishly. "Neither of us took that leap yet."

"Oh, I see … Well, love can be expressed in many ways. Saying the words is one thing, but there are many other ways to know. Sometimes, you have to read between the lines to get what's not being said but is being shown."

My father's sensible words throw me into a spiral of thoughts as I try to think of clues I may have missed.

Lex might have expressed his feelings in various ways, like when he added me to his AI, cooked me breakfast, or agreed to watch a nearly four-hour-long movie for me. He also displays his care in the small things, like taking a detour to take me home, ordering Thai instead of Greek, or forgetting his stage fright to save me from embarrassment. Even that time he let me win at *Counter-Strike* during a lunch break might have been a display of his love. And maybe he expresses his feelings through his sweet, romantic words, by making love to me with tenderness and passion, or even just by welcoming me into his personal space. His gaze always speaks volumes, betraying that he finds me beautiful and precious. His stunning eyes always look at me like they'll never tire of me.

Holy shit …

Lex is in love with me.

He's shown it again and again, but I was too blind to see it.

He's in love.

With *me*.

The nerdy genius, the sex god, the ridiculously handsome Alexander Coleman, is in love with me, Andrea Walker.

My skin tingles, my heart races, and my breathing speeds up. Happiness, joy, and exhilarating feelings ravage me, taking over any other senses. I long to be with Lex right now, to grab his face and kiss him with all the adrenaline, love, and passion I hold.

The urge to voice my epiphany becomes unquenchable as if saying the words out loud will make them true.

"He's in love with me."

"What was that?" my dad asks. He's back to work and stops to look at me with a drill in his hand.

"Lex is in love with me."

"Then why are you still here?" he asks bluntly, an amused smile on his face.

"I—What do you mean? I'm here to spend some time with you and mom."

"Seriously, Deedee. We've had you at home for twenty-three years and some. He can have you tonight."

"Are you throwing me out?" I ask, slightly appalled.

"I will if I have to. Go! We can take care of ourselves."

"Mom will be disappointed if I leave," I argue, grimacing.

"I'll handle your mom, don't worry about it."

My heart fills with love for this incredible man, and I thank him with a tight hug. He wraps his arms around me, and I feel his pointy chin rest on top of my head.

"I love you, Dad."

"I love you, peanut. And you better tell this Alexander I'll make him regret it if he ever breaks your heart." I roll my eyes, my sigh muffled by his shirt.

"I'm not a little girl anymore. You don't have to protect me like this."

"You'll always be my little girl," he counters, releasing me. "Now, shoo! Go say bye to everyone and pack your things. I'll be back inside in a few minutes."

I comply with a military salute and trot to the house, excited to return to Seattle earlier than expected. To go back to Lex. Who is in love with me.

Holy fuck, that's amazing. We're the real deal. This isn't just a passing fling. We're in love.

Damn, I sound like a bad Telenovela …

is_new_chapter = True

chapter_number = "37"

pov_name = "Alexander"

WHOEVER THOUGHT DROPPING BY UNANNOUNCED would be a good idea is wrong. I'm never in the mood for impromptu calls, but even less so at this hour and on a Sunday.

I'm wondering who it could be as I walk up to the interphone that just rang. "What?" I ask when I pick it up.

"Mr. Coleman. I have someone here who wishes to come up."

"Who is it?"

The concierge hesitates, clears his throat, and answers, "Well, she insists I only say, 'the fun has arrived,' sir."

The instant I understand Andrea is the one in the hall waiting to come up, a throaty laugh rips out of me. *That greedy little …*

"Let her up," I instruct the concierge. "Actually, add her to my list. She can come up whenever she wants."

"Alright, sir, she will be added to the system."

I pace the length of the entryway as I wait for her to come up. She was supposed to return tomorrow and go straight to work, not here. Whatever changed her mind, I'm thankful for it.

The elegant doorbell doesn't even have time to finish before I open the door. My smile upon seeing her with her bag, a pack of beers, and a pizza fades in an instant. Even with the uneven light of the hallway, I notice the redness on the side of her face. Wordless, I pull her in, take her things to set them on the console, and gently grab her face to angle it with the overhead lights.

Fury replaces all other emotions when I recognize the pattern of a hand, right on the delicately freckled skin.

"Who the fuck did this to you?" I demand, my rage barely contained.

"It was … Stefano. He came by Kate's place and tried to start shit."

She's dismissive, but it isn't enough to contain my wrath. As softly as I can, I trace the length of her cheekbone with the pad of my thumb, hating seeing her like this. That cunt deserves so much worse than whatever is coming his way.

"Lex, I'm okay," she says, laying a soothing hand over my chest.

"You're not. I'm going to fucking—"

"I broke his nose," she cuts me off. "And my brother beat the shit out of him. Stefano had it ten times worse, so it's all good, baby."

For once, it's my turn to gape as I try to process her words. "You broke his nose?"

"There was so much blood."

I don't know what to answer. I'm proud of her for defending herself and doing that. But I still wish I could have that asshole right here to finish what she and her brother started.

"I've never punched someone before. And I didn't expect it to hurt like that," she continues, stretching the hand she must have used to punch him.

I take her hand before she can lower it and gently press my lips on her knuckles.

"Is that better?" I ask, gently grazing the spot with my thumb.

She nods and swallows, her eyes harboring nothing but affection and gratitude.

Unhurriedly, I hold her face and bend to her height so I can lay the softest, most caring kisses on the reddened skin where the cunt slapped her. "Better?" I softly murmur.

She looks mesmerized, and I smile at her transfixed expression. "Yes …" she breathes out. "But for some reason, my lips are a little sore too."

My low chuckle fans between us, and I don't resist her adorable demand. Ever so tender, I hold her chin with my index finger and sweetly bring my mouth to hers. When I move back, I caress the plumpness of her bottom lip with my thumb.

"Is that better?" I ask again, my voice so soft I barely recognize it. I can't believe I'm this relaxed when I was mad enough to kill someone moments ago. Her influence on me is almost worrying.

She shakes her head with a slight frown.

I'm still grinning when I kiss her again, harder this time. Before I can move back, she grabs my face to pull me closer. In a few seconds, the tenderness I initiated is gone. She gives everything, and I return it all. My hands go rogue and course over her body with hunger. We both move toward the couch, peeling away each other's clothes on our way there.

One day, we'll behave and not jump each other like this. Today isn't that day. We need to finish what we started yesterday.

pou_name = "Andrea"

PANTING, SWEATING, AND EXHAUSTED, I'M sprawled over Lex, trying to get down from the immeasurable high I just experienced. When I look down at him, he's in the same state of bewilderment as I am, his cheekbones adorably red, his body covered with a thin veil of sweat, his breathing short.

After one last kiss, I move up to dislodge him from within me before wriggling closer to him with my cheek on his firm chest.

"I take it you didn't want to help your dad out with his chore?" he says, his voice a little hoarse.

"He was doing fine by himself. And I couldn't stop thinking of you, spending your Sunday working. I thought a movie and pizza would make for a better evening. Unless you already finished it."

He lets out an amused chuckle that has me jiggling over him. "I didn't. I wouldn't risk angering you."

"I knew you were a smart man." With a satisfied sigh, I push myself off of him. "I need a moment in the bathroom. Can you get everything ready?"

He nods, we exchange one last kiss, and I'm off to clean myself up. When I'm back, Lex took out the fluffy blanket and put all the food I came in with on the coffee table. The screen is rolled down with a paused frame of Rivendell projected on it.

We're both sparsely dressed now, and I only notice the tube of arnica cream on the table when I sit down. "Come here," he says as he picks it up.

My mom already smeared my face with an anti-bruising cream earlier, but I'm never one to refuse his touch. I get closer, offering him my cheek, and watch as he squeezes some of it on his fingertip. Then I sit there, fighting against my endeared smile as he applies it with the utmost care and gentleness. The way his face is focused, with so much warmth in his eyes while he works, makes my chest ache with too many emotions.

I'm so stupid for not seeing it earlier. It's right there, in the concern in his steel grays, in the delicate touch of his finger, and merely in the fact that he's doing this. At this very moment, I don't think I've ever been happier in my life. Lex is everything.

We both realize I'm tearing up when a drop rolls underneath his cautious caress. The worry on his face deepens the crease between his brows. "You should have told me I was hurting you, Andrea."

Yes, he's hurting me. In the sweetest, most fantastic way. *I love you, Alexander Coleman.*

"You're not. I'm just tired."

Not convinced, he finishes his tender treatment with even more meticulousness and then gives me a kiss on the lips as a reward for cooperating. Soon after, we resume our viewing of Peter Jackson's masterpiece.

Usually, I observe religious silence during movies, but I'm feeling particularly chatty tonight, and I can't help but talk to him during quiet moments. He doesn't seem to mind, though, asking follow-up questions and taking part.

"Why does it feel like I was gone longer than a day?" I ask, feeling like we were separated for an entire week.

"Maybe it's because the hours felt so long. Five more, and I would have forgotten your face."

I let out an incredulous laugh, turning to him with an offended expression. "Am I that forgettable?"

Instead of answering, he turns his gaze to me, and I silently wait as he examines my face, frowning slightly at the redness on the side. "Every time I see you, I'm reminded of how bewitching you are, so I must keep forgetting."

My jaw drops half an inch, my heart hastens in my chest, my skin flushes, and my mind races with too many feelings to think clearly. For someone who pretends to be bad at romance, he's fucking incredible at it, isn't he? How could I be so blind? Even though it isn't the three words I'm dying to hear, it's basically the same.

After a few seconds of stupor, I take my phone from the coffee table and open the front camera. Before Lex can say anything, I position myself for a selfie with him, resting my head on his shoulder, subtly hiding Stefano's blow.

"What's happening?" he asks, taken aback.

"I'm giving you something to remember my face by."

The first pic is a failure, and I giggle at Lex's expression in it. "We're taking another one. Try not to look like a deer caught in the headlights."

We do a lot better for the next two. Delighted by my enterprise, I sit up, looking at the three shots alternatively, a broad grin on my face. "We look adorable," I say before sending him the photos. His phone buzzes on the table, and I give him a proud smile. "There, now you won't ever forget what I look like."

His chuckle is contagious, and we share a brief peck. Ready to get back to the movie, I grab a box of cookies from the table and snuggle against him. Now that my mouth is busy with pastries, I'm much quieter.

The only interruption comes when my phone vibrates. It's Oli, answering the thank-you message I sent before leaving Portland.

OLI

No problem. I'm happy I could help. Just know I'll always be there if you need me, Hulkette.

I grin slightly at the nickname and type my response.

ME

Thank you, you're the best. I don't know what I would have done without you. I'll see you tomorrow.

I add a kiss emoji and send it. Getting into Kelex has to be the best thing that ever happened to me. Not only did I find an incredibly fulfilling job with fantastic opportunities and the sense that I'm doing something to improve the world, but I also made great friends and discovered love.

Had I missed their recruitment post on Instagram, none of this would have happened. But as chance would have it, everything lined up just right, and I'm now the happiest I'll ever be.

I squirm closer to Lex, who's absorbed by the movie. Being in the crook of his arm, safely tucked in the blanket with him, feels like home.

My phone buzzes in my hand again, and I mindlessly pull it up, already knowing it's another one from Oli.

OLI

Maybe it's unfair for me to say this, but I'm in love with you, Andy—

Instantly, I freeze and stop reading.

My heart drops low in my chest, and my breath catches in my throat. My dismay is so great that I can't do anything but stare at Oliver's declaration for a few seconds. *I'm in love with you, Andy* … What the hell? He can't be in love with me. We went out on *one* date.

And yet, I'm perfectly aware of how easy it can be to fall in love with someone. Lex used to be the last person I wanted to be with, but now I wouldn't want to be anywhere else.

This isn't happening.

With my hand slightly trembling, I stare at the screen, confused, troubled, and ashamed. Ashamed for not noticing, for leading Oliver on for too long, for not preserving him, for letting him fall for me … His feelings can't and won't ever be returned.

Remembering Lex right here, I finally move the phone away, face down. For a few minutes of pure confusion, I stare emptily at the movie unfolding before us. My mind is frozen, and I can't think of what I should do or say—to both Lex and Oli.

Lex has always been jealous of Oli, and if he knows this … Things might change at work. His attitude toward Oli and me might cause problems at Kelex. I can't lose Lex or Oli, and I can't let these relationships make things messy at work. My mind is filled with questions and insecurities, and the guilt never fades. I need to read the rest of the text. There's more to it, and I need to know what it says before I decide anything.

I subtly shift away from Lex, moving out of his embrace, and twist just enough so I can hold my phone in a way that won't be suspicious.

My heart beats insanely fast in my chest as I unlock my phone and read on, struggling to keep my hand steady.

OLI

Maybe it's unfair for me to say this, but I'm in love with you, Andy. I think I fell for you the moment you first came into the Lair with your Hulk T-shirt and inappropriate jokes. My feelings have only been growing since, and while I know you're seeing someone, I need to say it, or I'll regret it.

I'm not expecting you to drop him and choose me instead. I just need you to know I'm here. I'm an option. I can make you happy, and you'd always come first.

I'm sorry for doing it like this. I tried to tell you so many times, but I always hold back. I'm only now finding the courage to say it after thinking about it all day.

Don't answer right now. Just think it over, and then we can talk about it. Whatever you choose, I'll accept it. I just needed you to know the truth.

By the time I'm done reading, I contend with all sorts of conflicting emotions. Mostly, I'm sad for him because he's a fantastic person who deserves to be loved and cherished by someone. But that someone isn't me. I'm not the woman for him.

There's only one outcome to this, and the sadness of it overwhelms me. His heart will break. Sweet Oli … The kind, gentle, and amazing knight in shining armor who always had my back. I'm going to hurt him because I've been a fucking idiot.

During the rest of the movie, I remain pensive, trying to come to terms with everything that's happening and think of the best way to handle it. When the credits finally roll in, I'm anxious to leave. Lex's presence near me puts me on edge, which isn't helping my troubled mind.

I push the blanket away to get up and grab the rest of my clothes. Lex sends me a questioning look, and I offer him a sheepish frown, sorry to cut things short again.

"I have to get back home. This weekend was a fucking mess, and I need to get some sleep before starting the week," I explain, hoping my excuse isn't too weak—my brain isn't very efficient at the moment.

"And you can't do that here because …?"

"You'll wake me up three times for sex, and I'll end up more tired than I am right now."

"I can also do sexless, you know. Unless that's all I'm good for," he argues, with no traces of humor in his voice.

"I'm sorry, baby," I say, purposefully using the endearment. I don't have the mental capacity to handle this right now. "I have nothing to wear for tomorrow. The past two days have been intense, and I need proper rest."

He doesn't argue, but I can see the matter isn't entirely solved. He rearranges the couch's cushions as I put my clothes on. While he puts the leftovers away, I fold the blanket and lay it on the couch. By the time I'm done, I grab my hard drive, do a final sweep to ensure I'm not forgetting anything, and turn to Lex, forcing a smile on my face.

"I'm sorry for abandoning you for the second time this weekend," I say apologetically. "We'll do better next time."

After a dry nod, he accompanies me to the door.

"I'll see you tomorrow, Coleman," I say, feigning a lightness I'm not feeling.

"Stay safe, Andrea."

With a heavy heart, I give him one last forced smile and make my way into the deserted hallway of his building, eager to be home. Tomorrow, I'm breaking the heart of a wonderful guy. But it's for the best.

It's the right thing to do for all of us.

is_new_chapter = True

chapter_number =

"38"

pov_name =

"Andrea"

DESPITE MY ATTEMPT AT GETTING a proper night's sleep, I don't. My thoughts are still all over the place, and I'm no closer to figuring out the best way to handle all this.

My main concern is the Oli situation, but I also realized how poorly I handled things with Lex. Back at his place, confusion and dismay made it hard, if not impossible, to think. We had a great time cuddling on his couch, and I was distant and absent-minded in a blink.

So, today, I have two missions. One is to have a serious talk with Oli and make him understand that there will never be anything more than friendship between us. The other is to make it up to Lex and explain my weird mood last night.

When Oli arrives ten minutes late, I understand he also got very little sleep. Visibly tense and uncomfortable, he sits in his chair without a glance at me, and my heart clutches. This is it. After today, we won't remain friends.

On his desk, I dropped the box of pastries Kate gave me for him. He takes the note taped on it and reads the few words written in Kate's lovely handwriting. Curious, he tries a cookie, turns around to finally look at me, and offers a small, embarrassed smile as he shakes the bitten cookie. I return one just as awkward.

We all work for a while, and after about two hours of me barely managing to do anything, I send him a message with the company's internal software.

ANDREA WALKER: Hey, can we talk sometime today?

Anxiously waiting for his answer, I lean forward in my chair.

OLIVER PAULSON: Yes, of course. Could we not do this at work?

I let out a small sigh of relief and bring my hands to my keyboard.

ANDREA WALKER: Absolutely. Maybe we could grab a beer after work?

OLIVER PAULSON: A beer sounds perfect. Charlie's?

Charlie's is an Irish pub about ten minutes from here. It's always crowded enough to never feel intimate, yet the rich wooden interior and very loaded decor make it cozy and warm enough to not be too impersonal. I agree with one last message, and we both refocus on work.

Some time later, I get an overly excited text from Kate.

KATE

OMG! YOU'LL NEVER GUESS WHAT HAPPENED!!!!!!

I wait a few seconds, thinking she will send the rest, but it never comes.

ME

Elaborate!

KATE

You know Monica, that friend who works with Stefano? The one who introduced me to him?

ME

Considering she put him in your life, do you still consider her a friend?

KATE

Don't be jealous. You know you're my ride or die. Anyway. She just called me, and it's fucking insane.

The bubbles bounce for a while, confirming that Kate is typing. As the seconds stretch, my guts twist and turn in my stomach, wild scenarios flooding my mind. Kate is worth everything, but I can't bear the idea that I may have endangered others. My brother, his friends, Oliver …

KATE

Okay, so apparently, two cops came to their firm this morning to bring Stefano in for questioning. She doesn't have all the details, but from what she heard, they received an anonymous tip, and he embezzled and did all sorts of shady things. And when the cops were reading him the charges, she also heard them mention distribution of nonconsensual pornography.

Utterly shocked, I stare at my screen. What the actual fuck? How can Stefano be an even bigger asshole than I thought? Kate sends more.

KATE

He'll probably do some jail time and be registered as a sex offender for the rest of his life! Isn't this crazy?! And that timing ... It has to be Oli, right?

The timing is indeed too perfect to be coincidental. I look at Oli, who's busy debugging an app on one of the testing phones. Did he do that? From what I know, he has the skills and the spine to pull it off.

ME

It was probably him, yes.

KATE

Shit, the pastries weren't enough. Tell him I'll have his babies.

I chuckle low and put the phone down before sending another look at the back of Oliver's messy red hair. Feeling grateful and indebted, I reopen our conversation on the messaging app.

ANDREA WALKER: Thank you again for this weekend. Thanks for everything.

OLIVER PAULSON: You're welcome. I'm glad I could help your friend out.

It's a shame that Kate and Oli live three hours apart because I'm convinced they'd get along well. Oli is basically my male counterpart, and Kate loves the shit out of me. Really, it would be a phenomenal match, and it would literally solve everyone's problems.

ANDREA WALKER: Well, just know she's eternally grateful for all you did. She just told me she wants your babies.

Oliver's chuckle is loud enough for me to hear it.

OLIVER PAULSON: You can tell her I'm touched by the thought, lmao. But the pastries are enough. They're delicious.

Knowing she'd be pissed that I overshared but still amused, I grab my phone to tell her. It buzzes in my hand the moment I do. I expect it to be Kate, but Lex's name is on the screen instead. The sudden lightness I feel vanishes, and concern takes its place.

Right, I still have to make up for my tactless exit—escape—yesterday. I read his message and stare at it for a while, confused.

ALEXANDER COLEMAN: Did you know there are two definitions of what a month is? It can be the lapse between the same dates in successive calendar months, from September 2nd to October 2nd, for instance. It can also be a period of four weeks, from one Monday to four Mondays after that.

It takes me an embarrassing amount of time to get it.

A month.

According to the second definition, our thing started in his kitchen a month ago. Today could mark the end of our trial period.

This is our make-or-break point. The moment of truth. This is when we decide what we are and what we will become.

I know exactly what I want, but what does *he* want?

Until yesterday, things were so smooth that this probation period slipped my mind. I've known for a while now that I want to take whatever we have to the next level. And I suspect that Lex wants a lot more of me, too. But my stupid insecurities kick in. What if he doesn't? What if he remembers he doesn't do relationships?

I see him type, and I wait, impatient and apprehensive.

ALEXANDER COLEMAN: So, I was wondering, Walker, what definition do you think is more accurate?

Although the tone is usually hard to guess in a text, it doesn't feel like he's sour or annoyed. He sounds … playful. Feeling more confident, I send him my answer, nibbling on my bottom lip.

ANDREA WALKER: I like four weeks better. It's simpler, more precise, and you don't get random intervals of days between each month.

Around me, the guys stand up to head out to lunch, but I don't budge, waiting for Lex's answer. Brian stops by me, pointing a finger toward the door. "Aren't you coming?"

"I'll join you guys later."

When Lex's answer is finally here, I'm alone.

ALEXANDER COLEMAN: I like it better, too. It's more precise, rounder, and it means I can ask you out on a proper date earlier than I thought.

The breath I'm holding leaves my lungs with a surprised exhale. A dumbfounded smile slowly grows on my lips, my eyes reading his text over and over. He's asking me out on a date. An official date. A real thing, like real couples do.

After everything we've already shared, it's ridiculous for a date to mean so much. First the sex, then the genuine appreciation for one another, and now, the dating. Everything is backward.

I *so* want to go out on dates with him. Maybe it'll be awkward, but I long to go see a movie, go to dinner, or spend a day somewhere together. Everything has been behind closed doors, and I want us to escape the secrecy.

Not even taking the time to turn anything off, I jump out of my chair and swiftly walk out of the office. As I walk upstairs, I cross the paths of several people on their way to the lunchroom, including Tami, with whom I exchange a smile.

No one's left in the hallway when I reach Lex's door, so I confidently knock on it. His rough, oh-so-familiar voice invites me in, so I obey, my heart hammering a hectic beat against my ribs.

All the way from the door, I notice his sharp gaze behind his glasses, focused on his screen. He lifts his eyes after a few seconds to look up. I witness his surprise when he sees it's me.

Lex follows my movements as I close the door and walk further in, like a hawk locked on its prey, and I fight back a smile, trying to look displeased instead.

"Did you just ask me out on a date via text?" I ask, raising a falsely condemning eyebrow at him.

A slow, knowing smile bends his lips as he cocks his head to the side, amused. He stands up with his natural elegance and comes toward me. "I was merely making an observation regarding what a month means."

By the end of his sentence, he's a foot away from me. With him towering over me like this, I should feel small and intimidated. Instead, I feel feminine, powerful, and strong. Because he's mine.

My eyes move down to his tempting mouth, its corners barely bent upward in a failed attempt to conceal his amusement. Bewitched, I lick my lips, fighting the temptation. A languorous tension settles around us like static electricity charging the air.

God, how I love him.

Remembering we're in the middle of a meaningful conversation, I gather my few brain cells still active and shrug my shoulders. "Oh well, I guess you won't need an answer, then," I tease, forcing myself to turn around.

Before I even take a step, he grabs my arm and tugs me into him. My mouth opens in a silent gasp, a flash of arousal warming me up from the inside out.

"Always a fucking tease," he mumbles, his voice so low it flows like warm sand over my skin, making the tiny hairs on the back of my neck rise. "Of course, I need your answer, you impossible dork."

"You have to ask first." My voice is weak, like my legs, but I hold firm.

His crooked grin proves he enjoys this as much as I do. "Andrea Walker, will you go out on a date with me?"

My heart seems to explode like a firework, pure happiness coursing through my veins. Still, I say, "I'll have to think about it."

I see him flinch before he understands I'm kidding. He groans, tightening his hold on me. "You drive me mad."

"The feeling's mutual."

Rising on the tip of my toes, I move up to claim his lips, but he fights it, keeping himself out of my reach.

"Say it."

My insides melt into a wet pool of need and desire. *Hi there, dominant Lex.*

"Yes, I'll go on a date with you, Alexander."

I barely have time to finish his name before he hungrily takes possession of my mouth. In an instant, our tongues meet with greed, wet silk grazing and pressing, our hands grasping and pulling.

This isn't forbidden anymore, but right, real, and strong. In our hunger to feel more, we stumble around until we end near one of the armchairs. Things are getting slightly out of hand, but I don't care. I love this man with all I have; this is all I can think of. He, however, has more restraint than me, delicately pushing me away and framing my face with his warm hands. His loving gaze glides over my probably flushed face.

"We'll work out the details later, but we'll have to disclose it to HR soon," he explains, his thumb caressing the apple of my cheek where I'm still a little red. Two weeks ago, signing those papers sounded so scary and overbearing. Now, I look forward to it.

I take him by surprise and shove his chest hard. He stumbles back onto the armchair, as I intended, and before he can react, I straddle his lap, grabbing his face with determination. His strong hands find their way to my hips, and I sense he's trying to push me away.

"I thought you said we wouldn't have sex in my office again?"

"We aren't having sex; we're just making out. *Heavily* making out."

I resume my amorous enterprise, but he isn't having it, remarkably reasonable for once. "Andrea, it's the middle of the day," he manages to say despite the enthusiastic perseverance of my lips.

"They're all downstairs, eating their lunch."

"Anyone could come in."

"They'll knock, and you'll tell them to go to hell," I propose, nibbling at his earlobe.

"I thought you wanted to be discreet."

Lex's gestures grow soothing as he tries to quench the lustful hunger I have fallen victim to. My feverishness slowly fades away, and I give him one last, thorough kiss before moving back to look at him.

His fingers graze down my neck and my chest, brushing my hardened nipple as they pass it. His large palm then settles against my ribs, just under my breast, where he can surely feel the steadfast beats of my heart.

It's his. Entirely. The heart under his hand, my soul, my body, my mind, my thoughts … I'm his. All of me.

Now's the right time to tell him. Finally. He must know my heart belongs to him, so he'll be sure not to break it.

"Lex, I—"

Two quick knocks on the door interrupt me. Before I can react, it opens.

"Sorry, I just saw your—"

Oliver stops dead in his tracks as I rip myself away from Lex, struggling to get on my feet. Pure dread invades me as I stare at Oli's shocked expression.

My eyes move from Lex, still sprawled on the armchair, to Oli, stiffly standing in the doorway. Helpless, I witness how my friend's face sinks into a wounded and troubled expression, and my heart drops low into my stomach.

Fuck, no! Not like this.

is_new_chapter = True

chapter_number = "39"

pov_name = "Andrea"

OLIVER TRIES TO PROCESS WHAT he just witnessed, his mouth parted in a silent accusation.

I remain unmoving as Lex slowly rises from the armchair. He stands next to me, ready to face whatever is coming. The traces of the intense kiss we exchanged are still on his flushed face and messy hair, and I'm sure they are also on me.

In Oliver's eyes, I can perceive heartbreak and betrayal. Fuck, why did this have to happen like this? When I was so close to telling him?

"Oli, I—" I start, but a rush of humiliation clogs my throat, in the back of which I can almost taste bile. I never wanted to hurt him.

I need to explain, to make sense of this situation, but guilt paralyzes me. Before I can come up with something to say, Oli steps back into the hallway and closes the door behind him, leaving me with Lex.

When I look up at Lex to find some comfort, all I see is remorse. Why does he look so guilty? It doesn't make any sense. Without him being so reasonable, Oli would have found us in an even more compromising position.

"Andrea, I'm sorry. I didn't want this to—" He hesitates, struggling to find the words.

Regret. There's undeniable regret in his voice.

An insidious, unwelcome thought claws its way into my head. But it's too manipulative and cunning, and Lex isn't like that. We discussed this; he knows how scared I am about my colleagues knowing the truth. He knows I wanted to preserve Oli's feelings.

Lex wouldn't do this to me.

Right?

"Tell me you didn't know he was coming," I beg.

But he doesn't answer, doesn't try to deny it, to reassure me, to lie … Instead of innocence, his eyes only display more and more guilt. My heart pounds as wild, terrifying thoughts swell into my mind.

No … No, no, no … This can't be happening.

"Why?" I can barely contain the outrage in my voice.

Lex hesitates, his eyes locked on mine, trying to gauge the words that could appease me. "He needed to know. It was the right thing to do."

"He didn't need to learn about it like this!"

"You've been leading him on for weeks. It was the merciful thing to do." My jaw drops with outrage. Is he being serious right now? His accusation is so unfair, wrong, unjustified …

My voice is too loud when I speak again, but I can't contain it. "This was cruel, Lex. Not only for Oliver but for me too. And I haven't sent him any mixed signals for *weeks*."

"Really? Then why is he so certain he still has a chance with you?" His tone is rising, too, which doesn't help my irritation.

"He doesn't! He never even had a chance."

"You expect me to believe that? He tells you he's in love with you, and you immediately distance yourself from me," he argues, his finger angrily pointing at the door.

Shit, he saw the text … Of course, he saw the fucking text. Now I'm angry at him, but also at myself. I should have been more careful.

"So, what is it, Andrea? Are you, or are you not leading him on? Because kissing emojis and grabbing beers after work aren't helping your case."

How does he know about Charlie's tonight?

"You're reading our messages?" I struggle to ask. Fuck. It's too much, too fast. I can't believe any of this.

"It's a company tool, not social networking. I have access to the conversations."

"That doesn't mean you should read them!"

Everything hurts. I'm distressed and confused, completely lost in the absurdity of what's happening. Lex saw the texts yesterday, and this morning, he monitored my conversation with Oliver out of resentment or jealousy. And then—Oh, God …

"Is this-is this the reason you asked me out two days in advance?" My question is met with silence. "Was it because you were jealous, or was it because you were impatient to go on a date with me?" I insist.

"Can't it be both?"

"Fuck!" I flatten my hand over my forehead, a headache threatening to take over. Tears are coming, and my whole nasal cavity and throat ache from holding them back. "I can't believe this. You're so wrong about Oli and me."

"Really? I think you're keeping him as a backup plan if things don't work out between us."

His words are like a punch to the chest. Is this really what he thinks of me? That I'm the kind of woman who would do that? Does he not know me at all?

An overwhelming sadness spreads through my mind, my combativeness slowly leaving me. Despite his promise, he doesn't trust me. He doesn't have faith in me.

My whole body is numb, my soul bruised, and my mind aching with conflicting thoughts. I have to get away from him, his judging glare, and insulting words, but I can't. My pride won't let me. I'm not going anywhere until he understands how deeply he hurt me.

I stare at him, at how handsome he is, with his hair still tousled from my amorous enthusiasm, his shirt sitting wrong on his shoulders. He's still the most gorgeous man I've ever set my eyes on, but all I see is the humiliation.

"I had to leave yesterday because I *knew* I'd break his heart. It wasn't about you, but about losing one of my best friends," I explain, my voice cracking despite trying to maintain my composure. "Tonight, I was going to tell Oli I can't ever return his feelings." I pause, the rest of my confession sitting heavy on my tongue. "I can't because I'm in love with someone else."

Lex's fierce and furious expression crumbles as my words make their way into his brain. Numerous emotions pass in his eyes, including regret, confusion, and uncertainty.

He tries to reach for my arm, but I swiftly avoid it, leaping away. If he touches me, it's game over.

"Andrea, I—"

"No," I cut him off. "It's too easy. You're going to apologize, to tell me you didn't mean to hurt me, that you're sorry … And it will work because life without you doesn't have meaning anymore. But this goes beyond a forgivable fit of jealousy."

I look at the door where Oli stood moments ago, tears suddenly gathering in my eyes, blurring my vision. "You *knew* how scared I was about this. When the others hear about us, what do you think will happen? They'll question every opportunity I have had since starting this job. Selling my app to Kelex became the casualty of us having sex. Becoming the project leader, being in charge of the convention's presentation … Everything I ever did is now irrelevant because you've been inside me. And you knew how I felt about that.

But you didn't think of me! You didn't even care. You let your absurd concerns about Oliver take over."

My voice is ragged as tears roll down my cheeks one by one.

"Andrea, please," he begs. "I didn't plan for things to unfold like that. I lost control. I didn't think."

The weight of his words dawns on me. "You asked him to come up because you were going to tell him without my consent," I state, understanding it was his plan. That's why Oli barged in like this. Lex doesn't answer, but the guilt on his face is all I need. "Lex, do you not see how wrong it would have been?"

He takes a step forward, and I take one back, keeping a safe distance between us. Everything in me wants to forgive him and pretend it never happened. But I'm not like that. I'm not a pushover that runs away from my issues.

"I couldn't risk losing you," he explains as if it can justify everything.

"I told you I wasn't going anywhere! I begged you to trust me. You knew this was exactly what would chase me away," I remind him, the resentment in my tone obvious even to me.

"Andrea, can you just listen to me?" he insists, reaching out to grab me.

"Don't you dare touch me." I raise a warning finger between us, quickly putting it back down when I see how much it trembles. "I can't be near you right now," I say, moving for the door.

"Andrea, please."

"I need some time to think. Can you at least give me that, Alexander?"

The name is what stops him. He isn't "Lex" or "baby" anymore. He's back to being Alexander, and that brings sadness to his beautiful eyes.

Once I'm out of his office, I walk through the hallway as fast as I can. The pressure on my chest is so intense it makes breathing painful. Swiftly, I step into the restroom as I pass it and then push a door to enter one of the stalls.

An inevitable sob shakes my shoulders as I lock the door behind me. My sight blurs with tears, and my throat clenches so tightly I can't breathe.

How could Lex do this to me? To us?

All I can think of are Kate's words.

They're perfect, kind, considerate, and charming. But then it shifts so slowly that you barely realize it.

Is this Lex shifting? Is he revealing his true nature? The ruthless, dominant, and imperious control freak I fell in love with is indeed all that. I ignored the signs because he was never like that with me, but what if he was destined to become this all along?

The same kind of assholes Kate dates. The ones who are so perfect early on, only to turn into a controlling nightmare. I want Lex with everything I have, but not like this. Becoming the willing victim of an overbearing partner is out of the question. I can't let my parents and friends watch me deteriorate into an empty shell of myself.

But as fucked up as what he did was, it's not enough to counterbalance the happiness he brings into my life. I tasted bliss and love, and I can't go through life without them. Without *him.*

So, he gets one more chance at this. One *last* chance, I promise myself.

We need to communicate, fix this, and move on with a healthier mindset. Lex has his insecurities—God knows I have mine—and I threw them back in his face, unwilling to listen to him. Yes, what he did was wrong, and his assumptions were incorrect. But I can only sympathize because I'd probably do some batshit crazy things to keep him.

Everything in me wants to go home, but leaving things like this with Lex might cause irreparable damage. Before the day ends, we'll have a level-headed talk where feelings aren't running high, and we aren't shouting at one another—blood runs hot in Ibanez women.

The rest of the day is a hazy blur, my mind elsewhere. I skip lunch for lack of appetite, and when the guys notice my somber state, I tell them I have a nasty migraine. That isn't entirely a lie since my head is pounding. In the Lair, Oli doesn't look at me a single time, just as tense as I am. How long until the others know? How long until everyone thinks of me the same way Hugh did? *Someone who sleeps around to succeed …*

Lex respects my demand to have some time, so he doesn't come down here, he doesn't text, doesn't call … I'm not sure if I like that or not. Part of me values that he's mindful of my wishes, but another would appreciate it if he apologized and did whatever he could to fix his mess.

When five-thirty arrives, Oli's the first to go, mumbling a vague "Goodbye," and the rest soon follow. Once the guys are gone, I wait a little longer, mostly out of cowardice. My heart weighs a ton as I make my way upstairs. Nearly everyone's gone by now, and I hope Lex remains true to himself and is working late. The ray of light under his door tells me he is.

I stare at the door for a while, trying to conjure the strength to knock on it. It's ridiculous. I've been in Lex's office on dozens of occasions and passed it countless times. I shouldn't be scared by it, but I can't help it.

I need to get in there and trigger the conversation that will fix us.

The first knock is weak, but the next two are firmer. His command to enter comes quickly, and I take a deep breath. Surely, we'll have more work ahead of us, but this is the first step. The hardest one.

As soon as I push the door open, my eyes find him in the room, focused on whatever is on his screen. His gaze lifts from his task, and his concentration fades when he sees me. Instead, a slightly concerned look takes over for a split second before he conjures his stern, neutral expression. It's been a while since he last used this one on me, and it stings.

I will my feet to take me inside and close the door behind me. "Hi," I let out, my voice uneven.

My heart clutches when he doesn't answer. He's supposed to say "Hi" back. It's our thing. *Come on, Andy. Fix the mess.*

"We need to talk," I bravely say.

"I have to leave in ten minutes for a dinner meeting." His icy tone is hard to bear, but I can work with this. He'll forgive me for how I reacted, just like I'm forgiving him.

"It's a longer talk, but we can start it now and get back to it whenever you're ready?" I propose. He hesitates, his impregnable expression cracking for an instant to reveal doubt.

"I have things I need to prepare for it."

Fuck … He doesn't want me here. Lex being so reluctant isn't something I expected. What am I supposed to do? Force it on him? Tie him up and make him listen to me?

Finally moving away from the door, I take a few steps toward him. "Lex, I just … I'm sorry. I overreacted a little, and I think we should talk because I can't—"

He interrupts me with a raised hand and stands from his chair. "I'm going to stop you right here. We both got carried away, and I am as much to blame if not more." A faint, distant glimmer of hope makes its way into my mind. "I told you from the start I wasn't cut out for relationships, and I somehow forgot that fact along the way."

What? No. This isn't what I want. He can't be putting the entire thing in the balance.

"You knew as much as I did that I would eventually hurt you. The unavoidable happened, and I think we should leave it at that, Andrea," he says, his face as neutral as ever.

Leave it at that? Is he breaking up with me? Shit, how can words hurt so much? Whatever's left of my confidence crumbles into tiny shards.

"Lex, no … We both got hurt, but we can grow past it and keep what we have," I insist, my voice trembling slightly. I'm slowly losing it, already about to tear up.

"And then what? What happens the next time I hurt you? When we're even further down the path?"

"You don't have to hurt me. We don't have to hurt each other."

"I don't know how to do that. I can't be the man you want me to be."

"But I don't want you to be another man. I want you as you are."

He lets out a small sigh as if irritated by my insistence. What the fuck is happening? Why doesn't he want to fix things?

"I'm not built for this. I can't do the whole romance, and dates, and flowers …"

"What we have is different from your other relationships," I protest.

"Why?"

Because we're in love.

"You know *why*, Lex."

He tenses all over, his brows knitted together. "I should have ended this sooner, but I warned you it would end this way, Andrea—with you hurt."

"The fuck kind of answer is that?!"

"What do you want me to say?"

He sounds annoyed, almost angry at me. "I don't fucking know, Lex! Say you want to be with me. Say you love me."

Instead of answering, he clenches his jaw, looking down at me with determination. The obstinate asshole won't say it. Anger rises from inside of me as I want to curse his stubbornness. He's holding his ground, refusing to open up and admit I'm right.

"I'm sorry you got so involved in this," he says coldly.

I'm about to protest again, but then an unwelcome thought claws its way into my mind. What if I'm wrong? What if he never loved me?

The things he said after Oli found us, how I was leading my colleague on to keep him as a backup plan, should have opened my eyes. How could Lex believe it and still love me? Our relationship was never equal in trust, so how could it be equal in heart? Obviously, he likes me. But he was never in love with me. Otherwise, how can it be so easy for him to dismiss everything we shared? My heart drops low in my stomach at the thought, and my guts twist. I'm about to be sick.

That's why he didn't do anything to try to get me back this afternoon. Not a single text, not a single attempt to bargain, to talk, to fix us … His radio silence wasn't because I needed space. It was because he didn't care enough. And he's so aloof now because I was just a fling. Not the great love of his life.

I'm so fucking stupid. A month. Of course, Lex couldn't have fallen in love with me so fast. He swept me off my feet, but the other way around isn't true.

As the world falls apart, I look up at him with tears blurring my vision. His expression twitches slightly when a drop rolls down my cheek, sorriness veiling his handsome face. He cares about me, but not enough.

"You never loved me," I whisper. Voicing it is even worse, and another surge of tears overwhelms me. With shaky hands, I get rid of them as they come.

He doesn't deny it, his brows stuck in a perpetual apologetic frown. "I'm sorry, Andrea. I tried to warn you."

I ruined it. Maybe with more time, he could have loved me. But I destroyed my chances because of my reaction, involuntarily shaking some sense into him.

"I'm sorry," he says again, his voice softer.

I don't want his pity. I don't want him to see me so pathetic and puerile like this. I want him to love me with the same maddening intensity as I love him. But I see now how foolish it was of me to believe he could.

The great love of my life only goes one way.

"I'll let you work," I say, straightening my shoulders and gathering the little dignity I have left.

Before I can turn around, he grasps my arm, and I send him a confused look after glancing at his strong hand on me. "I *really* am sorry, Andrea."

His free hand reaches for my face and settles so his palm embraces the curve of my cheek. With the pad of his thumb, he wipes a stranded tear away. When he leans forward as if to kiss me, I don't stop him. I can't. I'm fucking weak, and I want his lips on mine one last time.

At the last moment, he hesitates, and instead of my lips, he kisses my forehead, crushing my heart one last time. It's such a platonic, patronizing gesture that I want to hate him for it. But I can't. Not when he's so close to me, his familiar scent filling my nostrils, his large hands on me …

His mouth lingers for longer than it should before he slowly moves away. "It's for the best," he insists. I can't tell if he's saying it for himself or me.

I force myself to nod, and I exit his office as fast as I can. It takes everything I have not to look back at him, but I do it.

It's over.

We're over before we ever began.

My feet bring me to the stall where I cried this morning. Given how my eyes fill with more tears, I'm on for a do-over. *Fuck* …

Images of my time with Lex, *my* Lex, the one I thought I knew, flood my mind, adding to the agonizing pain in my chest. I'll never wake up in his arms again. I'll never experience his adoration, taste his lips, experience his playful teasing … All of it is gone.

How did we end up here? We were so fucking happy together, not even twenty-four hours ago. I can still feel the gentleness with which he cared for my bruised cheek, hear the devoted words he whispered into my ears, sense the affection that seeped through his touch as we made love …

The excruciating pain grips every inch of my being as endless flows of salty tears pour down my cheeks, gathering at my chin. Desperate sobs shatter the stillness, echoing against the white tiles of the restroom.

I slump against the door, powerless, as my limbs give way. My numb body slides down until it reaches the floor, my hectic breathing impossible to control.

It was so stupid of me to fall so desperately, irrevocably, and utterly in love with him. Now, I'm shattered and broken beyond repair.

I am lost in a sea of despair, waves of agony crashing down on me. I can barely register the toilet bowl a couple of feet away or the probably filthy tiles under me that add to my humiliation. As torment wrecks me, I know nothing could be worse than this.

The heartbreak I desperately wanted to avoid inevitably caught up with me. From the start, I knew Lex would hurt me, but I chose to ignore my intuition, blinded by stupid love.

I should have trusted my instinct. All of this was a giant error from the start.

And now, he corrected my mistake, leaving me with nothing but the bitter taste of regret.

He was right—he should have put an end to it sooner.

Put an end to us.

pov_name =

"Alexander"

THE CITY LOOKS COLD AND bitter veiled in darkness like this. I never realized how unwelcoming and gloomy this neighborhood gets this late at night. Those lifeless buildings of glass and concrete look even emptier than I feel.

Raising the glass, I take another sip of whiskey. It stopped burning my throat two glasses ago, and I'm not sure it's a good thing. I stare at the amber liquor as I make it twirl. I stole it from Kev's office, along with the glass. It's the expensive shit he keeps for celebrations. He'll give me an earful in the morning for finishing the bottle, but I'm celebrating, am I not?

I did a good thing today. Something selfless that cost me so much more than anyone will ever know. It was the hardest thing I've ever done, but it was necessary.

She will hate me for it. She'll hate me because she doesn't realize I did it for her. I've freed her of the burden of loving someone like me. Someone who can't make her happy. Not like she deserves.

Somewhere along the way, I fooled myself into thinking I could give her everything. Selfishly, I told myself that I could return every ounce of the happiness she brings me. I convinced myself that maybe I could be the kind of person she needs me to be.

But today reminded me that I can't. I barely lasted a month before I hurt her.

She asked me to trust her in the past—begged me to, even. And I couldn't even do that.

In reality, I do trust her. Andrea is too open-hearted and honest for me not to. But I don't trust myself. I know who I am better than she does, and I know that, with time, I would have made her miserable. I'm not built for what she needs.

That's why I intended to tell Oliver about us. I can't compete with him, so I didn't want him around her any longer. Because I'm a selfish asshole.

I can't even blame him for pining after her the way he does. Hell, I never expected to fall for someone, but here I am. It isn't our fault, though. She's too lovable, clever, talented, funny … And so fucking pretty it hurts. I'm an imbecile for even thinking I might deserve her.

Andrea's sadness, her teary eyes, are seared into my retinas. I can't chase the image away, which is what prompted me to go get Kevin's whiskey. But it's not working, and I don't know what else I can do.

I can't go home. Or rather I don't want to. She's everywhere there, the memory of her lingering in every corner of the rooms she's been in. I'll see her when I look at my kitchen counter, the couch, my bedroom … And then I'll see the tears and the look on her face when she believed I didn't utterly and hopelessly fall in love with her.

That was the moment I almost broke, almost let her pain convince me that she was better with me than without me. I wanted to shake her for even doubting my love for her. But it's better if she thinks that. It will be easier for her to move on.

When the pain in my chest returns at the thought, I finish my drink with two gulps and reach for the bottle to pour what's left in the glass.

Yes, she will move on to someone more deserving than me. Someone who can give her all the things I can't give her. And I will watch in silent agony as she does.

My secrets and lies forever hidden from her.

To be continued …

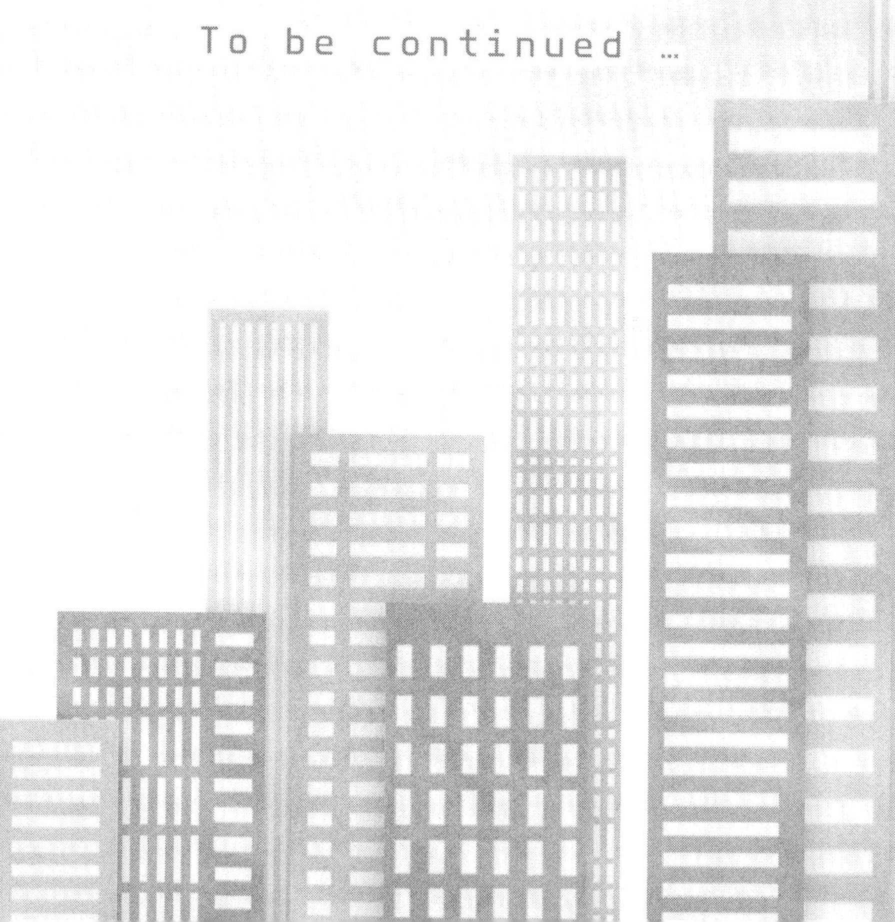

Acknowledgments

What a journey this has been! It took us a while, but we made it, didn't we, guys? (Iykyk.)

First and foremost, thank you, dear reader, for picking up *The Desire Variable* and diving into Andy and Lex's story. As my first contemporary romance, this book holds a special place in my heart, and I hope these characters have found a little corner in yours, too. If they have, I'd love for you to join me in the next chapter of the *Binary Hearts Trilogy*, where we'll unravel more of Lex's mysterious past and watch as Andy tumbles even further into the whirlwind of **passion** and **love**.

When I first started writing *The Desire Variable* back in 2019, I had no idea where it would take me. Over the years, both the story and I have grown in ways I could never have imagined. It's been an incredible experience to develop these characters and watch them come to life on the page.

But this journey wasn't one I took alone. Along the way, I've met so many amazing people who've supported me, inspired me, and become dear friends. To everyone who's been with me from the very beginning, and to those who joined somewhere along the way—thank you from the bottom of my heart. Your encouragement has meant everything to me, and I'm forever grateful for the love and support you've shown.

Mads, Trini, Gülşah, Nic, Dai … thank you for being so patient with my 536 daily questions and doubts. To the OGs, my incredible street team, my darling Claire (who first inspired me to write this story through her amazing writing), and my wonderful parents—Maman and Papa—thank you for your unwavering support.

Katie, my brilliant editor ... thank you for always working so hard to polish my work while respecting my voice. I'll forever feel blessed to have stumbled upon you, and I hope the future holds many more collaborations between us. Your the best ;)

Also, thank you, Marta, for creating this amazing cover! You did Andy and Lex justice and brought them to life better than I could have ever imagined.

And to everyone who helped make this release a reality on Kickstarter—you blew my goal through the roof, and I'm so, so thankful for your backing. A very special thanks to Iris, Xenia, and Tessa—you girlies are amazing!

This book is as much yours as it is mine, and I'm beyond excited to finally share it with you. Here's to many more stories ahead!

With all my gratitude,

Ana

About the Author

Ana D'Arcy writes romances packed with heart, humor, and plenty of steam. Her stories often feature a hero who falls first, but rest assured—they both fall hard. Most days, you'll catch her at her desk with a cozy cup of tea, while her three cats snooze nearby. When she's not lost in her fictional worlds, Ana enjoys kicking back with a great TV show or movie to refuel her creativity.

If you liked *The Desire Variable*, Ana would love to hear from you! You can find her on Instagram, TikTok, and Facebook under the handle @authoranadarcy, where she shares updates on upcoming books, along with fun, behind-the-scenes glimpses of her writing life.

As an indie author, your feedback means the world to Ana. If you have a spare moment, she would be incredibly thankful if you left a review of *The Desire Variable* on your favorite retailer or platforms like Goodreads and Storygraph. Your reviews not only help other readers discover Andy and Lex's story, but they also play a huge role in supporting her work.

Thank you for joining Ana on this journey. She can't wait for you to dive into the next book in the *Binary Hearts Trilogy*, where you'll follow Andy and Lex as their passionate and tumultuous love story unfolds. Expect all the heart, humor, and steam you've come to love—there's so much more to come!

More by the Author

Up the Ladder

Genevieve has it all-great job, stunning apartment, perfect boyfriend... When the latter dumps her for being terrible in bed, she sets out to prove him wrong. With the help of a silly online quiz and her best friend, she compiles a list of things that'll make her a better lover, determined to go through them one by one. Because she's too focused on climbing the corporate ladder for anything serious, she creates one simple rule: never see the same man twice.

The first item on her list leads her to Jake, a dashing Aussie with surgical steel in unexpected places. As charming as he is sinful, Jake is like nothing she's ever known before, with his perfect body covered in tattoos and penchant for teasing. Before long, the silver-tongued devil comes in the way of her resolve, making it hard to stick to her rule.

Can she resist the temptation, or will she give in to her desires? Or better yet, for how long can she resist him?

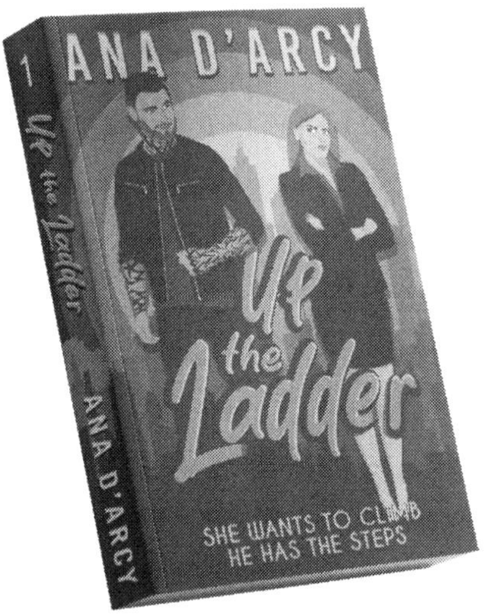

Find it here

Made in the USA
Columbia, SC
09 May 2025